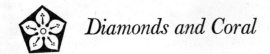

Diamonds and Coral

DIAMONDS AND CORAL

Anglo-Dutch Jews and Eighteenth-Century Trade

GEDALIA YOGEV

Leicester University Press 1978

Holmes & Meier Publishers, Inc.

First published in 1978 by Leicester University Press
Published in North America by Holmes & Meier Publishers, Inc., New York

Copyright © Leicester University Press 1978

Designed by Douglas Martin
Set in Linotype Caledonia
Printed in Great Britain by
Western Printing Services Ltd, Bristol
Bound by Redwood Burn Ltd, Esher

British Library Cataloguing in Publication Data
Yogev, Gedalia
Diamonds and Coral
1. Jews – Commerce 2. Great Britain –
Commerce – History – 18th century
I. Title
382'.0941 HF3506
ISBN 0 7185 1157 3

Library of Congress Cataloging in Publication Data
Yogev, Gedalia
Diamonds and Coral. Anglo-Dutch
Jews and 18th century trade.
Bibliography P includes index.
1. Jews in Great Britain –
economic conditions
2. Diamonds, industrial and trade –
Great Britain
3. Israel Levin Salomons (firm)
4. Great Britain – economic conditions –
1750–1860
I. Title DS 135. E5 Y6 1978
330.9' 41' 07
78 – 301
ISBN 0–8419–0369–7

To the memory of my parents Dr Otto and Gretel Feldmann

Contents

Acknowledgments	page	9
Foreword		11
Introduction		15

PART ONE: GENERAL SURVEY

Chapter 1	The Spanish and Portuguese Atlantic Empires	25
Chapter 2	The trade in precious metals and bills of exchange	50
Chapter 3	Trade to the West Indies and North America	60
Chapter 4	The India trade	67

PART TWO: THE DIAMOND AND CORAL TRADE 1660–1800

Chapter 5	The beginnings	81
Chapter 6	Stabilization and development	94
	a. East India Company policy towards the diamond trade	94
	b. The coral trade	102
Chapter 7	Competition from Brazilian diamonds 1730–1740	110
Chapter 8	The diamond and coral trade at its zenith 1700–1770	124
Chapter 9	The collapse of the Anglo-Indian diamond trade 1765–1793	169

PART THREE: THE HOUSE OF THE PRAGER BROTHERS (LEVIN SALOMONS) AND THE ANGLO-DUTCH TRADE 1760–1796

Chapter 10	The firm and its business	183

8   *Contents*

Chapter 11   The firm in the Anglo-Dutch trade   209

Chapter 12   The Jewish framework   253

              Abbreviations   275
              Notes   276
              Appendices A–K   331
              Bibliography   341
              Index   349

Acknowledgments

The present book is based on a Ph.D. thesis originally suggested by the late Sir Lewis Namier. I was privileged to have his guidance, especially during the initial and most difficult stages of the research, and it is largely due to his sound advice that I was able to find my way in the maze of archival material.

I am deeply indebted to Professor J. L. Talmon, my teacher and tutor at the Hebrew University of Jerusalem, for his constant encouragement and invaluable help and advice.

I should also like to extend sincere thanks to Dame Lucy S. Sutherland and to Professor A. H. John of the London School of Economics for their guidance and advice; to Dr Richard D. Barnett of the Jewish Historical Society of England for his continuous interest and help; to Dr H. E. S. Fisher for numerous references to Jewish merchants in documents relating to the Portugal trade; and also to the Directors and staff of the Public Record Office, the British Library, the India Office Library, the Bank of England, Hoare's Bank, the firm of Mocatta and Goldsmid, and the Central Archives for the History of the Jewish People in Jerusalem.

Special thanks are due to my friend Edgar R. Samuel for his unfailing assistance, encouragement, and catching enthusiasm.

I am much indebted to the British Council and to the Friends of the Hebrew University in England whose generous grants made this research possible, to the Jewish Historical Society of England for its help towards the publication of this book, and to the Marc Fitch Fund for a grant towards editorial expenses in its preparation.

Profoundest thanks are due to Dr Aubrey Newman of Leicester University, who edited this book for publication, for his selfless and invaluable help. He devoted much of his precious time to the task and successfully accomplished that most difficult of assignments – the turning of a Ph.D. thesis into a book. Although his name does not appear on the title page, he has a very prominent share in this book.

G.Y.

Foreword

The study of Jewish economic history in modern times involves a number of unique problems which the economic historian does not usually have to tackle. Although in the eighteenth century Jews were still subject to various disabilities, even in tolerant countries like England and Holland, they did not constitute a clear-cut juridicial entity, as they had done in the Middle Ages. There is therefore very little documentation referring specifically to the economic activities of Jews, and the facts have to be gathered laboriously from a very great number of documents belonging to a variety of archival series and collections of papers of a general character, which can be assumed, *a priori*, to contain, among much else, information relating to Jewish economic activities.

This, however, is not the main problem confronting the student of Jewish economic history. A meticulous and systematic search is liable to uncover a large amount of relevant information; but even at this stage we still have to face the question: what does it all amount to? Does it really enable us to reconstruct a coherent and reliable picture and to draw reasonably safe conclusions? After all, a mere collection of anecdotes is hardly worth the trouble involved in collecting them. In view of the inevitable paucity of statistical data, this is a very dangerous pitfall which students of Jewish economic history have not always been able to avoid.

In the present book an attempt is made to tackle the problem in a somewhat unconventional manner by getting to grips with the subject at three different levels, represented by the three sections into which the book is divided.

The first part is a general survey, based to a large degree on information gathered from a considerable number of Chancery and, to a lesser extent, Exchequer cases, relating to disputes involving commercial activities of English Jews. A great amount of information can be gleaned, not only from the arguments advanced by the litigants; often the attached appendices, including copies of correspondence, contracts and balance-sheets, are

even more important. To give only one example, the statement
detailing Moses da Costa's overseas investments (see p. 331),
though it cannot compensate for the lack of general statistical
data, is an extremely enlightening document because the conclusions which can be based on it tally with information derived
from other sources. Although the facts which this type of document can supply may at first sight seem fragmentary, they do,
taken together and collated with other sources, enable us to draw
a fairly reliable outline, though many details may still be missing.

The second part of the book is devoted to a single branch of
trade in which English Jews played an outstanding and often
predominant part – the trade in uncut or rough diamonds, as they
were called at the time. This section represents an attempt at a
systematic reconstruction of the history of this trade from the
second half of the seventeenth century, when, following the
Resettlement of the Jews in England, London became its chief
European centre, up to the end of the eighteenth century.*

Thanks to the preservation of a major part of the archives of
the East India Company there is abundant source material on the
history of the Anglo-Indian diamond trade – i.e., the importation
of uncut diamonds from India – during the whole period. This
includes detailed statistical data, both general and relating to the
Jews' share in the trade. The East India Company's General Cash
Journals, by listing the duties paid by each merchant, have supplied the information embodied in Appendices H and I of this
book, thus making possible the construction of a solid numerical
framework. This framework is filled in by a great variety of other
sources, e.g., the minutes of the Company's Board of Directors
(Court Books), the Company's and other correspondence, and
minutes of the Company's 'factories' in the East.

The third and last part of the book deals with the subject from
yet another angle: the description of the business of a single
Jewish firm. This was made possible by the unexpected discovery
of a major part of the papers of the firm of Israel Levin Salomons,
owned by the brothers Prager of London and Amsterdam, covering the period 1762–95. This unique collection of papers has not

---

* The book deals mainly with the eighteenth century, though a general
 survey of the earlier period is included. The latter is based mainly on
 published sources. Mr Edgar R. Samuel is presently engaged in a detailed
 study of the English diamond trade in the seventeenth century, and his
 research will undoubtedly throw much additional light on the subject.

only enabled me to make a detailed study of one of the more important Jewish commercial houses in the City, but has also contributed a wealth of information on the last stage of the Anglo-Indian diamond trade, which was incorporated in the second part of the book.

The references to the Prager Correspondence require a short explanation. The Israel Levin Salomons (Prager) papers are preserved among the Chancery Master's Exhibits in the Public Record Office. The PRO references are given for all documents with one exception: the numerous references in Part Three to letters sent by the Amsterdam branch of the firm to the London branch give only the date of the letter. The list of sources at the end of the book includes a table of references for this correspondence (see p. 342) which enables the reader to look up the PRO reference for all letters belonging to this group.

All quotations from the firm's internal correspondence have been translated from the original Yiddish.

Introduction

These studies attempt to answer a number of basic questions concerning the nature of the business activity of the Anglo-Jewish 'patriciate' and the economic foundations on which it stood. It is impossible to measure the Jews' role in statistical terms. Only in regard to the Anglo-Indian diamond trade do we have sufficient numerical data to enable us to draw accurate conclusions about the Jews' part in that branch of commerce. For all other fields of business activity we must be content with evidence of a different kind, but although the latter will never have the same degree of accuracy inherent in comprehensive and reliable statistical information, it may still carry much weight.

The most striking aspect of Jewish business activity is the degree of its specialization. At first sight this specialization may seem to bear a geographical character – Jews traded mainly to the Iberian peninsula and its colonies, to India, Holland and Leghorn. But a close examination will show that Jews, on the whole, tended to concentrate in certain branches which determined the geographical limits of their activities, and not vice-versa. They were most prominent in the precious metals, diamonds and exchange trades – all very much in accord with Jewish commercial tradition, though they also played a significant part in other fields: in the supply of manufactured goods to the Spanish colonies in America, in the trade in the agricultural products of the Spanish and Portuguese colonies – mainly dye-stuffs, but also coffee, sugar etc. – and in the distribution of Indian goods in Europe.

A distinction must be made between Jewish activities in the Latin-American and in the Indian trades. The difference concerns not only the sort of goods dealt in, but also the merchants themselves: the Jewish businessmen who invested in Latin-American trade mostly belonged to the Portuguese community, while Indian goods were distributed mainly by Ashkenazim, resident in England, Holland and Germany.

The specialization in 'Jewish' branches of trade was less marked in the case of Portuguese Jews. It can, of course, be maintained that the export of consumer goods to Latin America was but the complement of the import of precious metals from there, the latter being a 'Jewish' business *par excellence*. But imports from Latin America also included agricultural products and we have no way of determining, at least on the basis of the information at present available, the relative importance of precious metals in Jewish commerce with the Spanish and Portuguese colonies. We are unable to say whether Jews tended to concentrate more than their Christian colleagues on precious metals and less on agricultural products like cochineal, indigo and cocoa. Food products and dye-stuffs were sold to private buyers in London and Amsterdam and no trace of these transactions has remained, while much of the gold and silver was bought by the Bank of England and the East India Company – the ledgers of which are extant. It does, however, emerge from the Prager letters that colonial products were prominent in the trade of Portuguese houses like Mendes da Costa, D'Aguilar, Franco and Lindo, and even an Ashkenazi firm like that of the Pragers, which served as an intermediary between the English importer and the Continental merchant, specialized in this kind of goods.

The commercial activity of Portuguese Jews was thus confined to certain geographical areas and limited, on the whole, to certain categories of goods. Despite all difficulties and the necessity of having recourse to the services and cover names of Christian firms, English Jews of Iberian origin stuck stubbornly to the commerce of their 'old country'. Though, in view of the lack of statistical data, it is impossible to accept as an indisputable fact the statement of the British Ambassador to Lisbon that the Jews of London were the chief exporters of English woollens to Portugal, or Philo-patriae's assertion that the greater part of the English capital invested in the Spanish trade belonged to Jews, there can be no doubt that the Jews of the City played a very prominent part in this commerce. It must not be forgotten, however, that precious metals, and later also diamonds, were among the chief items in the Iberian and Ibero-American trade and that the Jewish activity in this field must be seen in the wider context of the commerce in precious metals and diamonds. The import of gold and silver into Europe was part of a complex commercial network, comprising the activity of precious metal brokers in London and Amsterdam and closely bound up with the exchange trade between the two cities.

The distribution of Indian goods belongs to another category of mercantile activity. English and Continental Jews had some standing as buyers at the public sales of the East India Company, although there is no evidence that they enjoyed a dominant position, except as buyers of damaged cloth. It is, however, clear that in this case, too, the Jewish merchants specialized in a category of goods in which Jews were wont to deal, although the tradition of the textile trade as a 'Jewish' branch was less ancient than that of the commerce in precious metals, money and precious stones.

The activity of Jewish merchants, and especially that of Ashkenazi Jews, in Anglo-Dutch trade reflects their tendency to specialize in a number of well-defined branches. Although the trade was already on the decline, it was still very diversified, Amsterdam serving as a distribution centre for goods produced in England and her colonies. Jews were very prominent in this trade and most Jewish businessmen in the City, both Sephardim and Ashkenazim, had relations on the other side of the Channel. But they concentrated in a few branches: diamonds, precious metals, bills of exchange, Indian goods (mainly textiles), and stocks. The merchants belonging to the Portuguese-Jewish community also dealt in products of colonial agriculture, but it seems that their transactions were usually small compared with those of the big Christian houses operating within the framework of Anglo-Dutch trade. Jews did not apparently figure at all as exporters of English industrial products to Holland or as importers of Dutch products to England.

In some branches of England's overseas trade Jews were very inconspicuous. There were apparently no Jews among the great importers of sugar, tobacco and other products of the West Indies and North America, and no evidence has come to light which would point to Jewish participation in Anglo-Russian trade or in the trade to the Levant, despite the prominence of Jewish brokers in the market of Smyrna.

Jewish specialization went even further. The Jews not only concentrated on a few branches of trade, but seem to have been completely absent from spheres of economic activity not directly connected with international trade or with stock transactions, but which were no less typical for the development of capitalism in England. There is no trace of Jewish investments in industry, banking, and transportation, nor do Jews seem to have been at all prominent in the country's internal trade, except at the lowest level, as pedlars.

The economic basis of the Jewish business class was not only narrow, it was also shaky. In almost all branches in which Jews tended to invest the risks were unusually high. The trade with Spain and her colonies was subject to the constant fluctuations which characterized the relations between England and Spain. In both the Spanish and Portuguese colonial trade transactions took a long time to complete and Jews were obliged to rely on non-Jewish agents and to trade under assumed names. The diamond trade was subject to great fluctuations of supply and demand and suffered from the instability which marks all trade in luxuries. Although the Jewish diamond merchants benefitted from the strengthening of the English East India Company, they were dependent on it and had to adapt themselves to its rules and to the limitations which the company put on private trade, without being able to take part in the Company's management or to influence its policy directly. In this branch, too, a considerable period of time was required before profits on investments could be realized.

What were the causes which brought about this confinement to a very limited range of economic activities? There is no wholly satisfactory answer to this question, but it is possible to suggest some hypothetical explanations, based on the yet incomplete information at our disposal. There were various external restrictions which hampered the free activity of Jewish businessmen in the City of London. They were not yet quite equal before the law to their Christian colleagues. All those who were not British-born – and these still made up a considerable part of the Jewish community in England – were unable to attain full naturalization and had to be content with 'denization', which did not exempt them from the obligation to pay alien duties. A Jew could not vote in parliamentary elections or be elected to Parliament and, though not legally barred from being elected to the Court of Directors of the East India Company, Jews, in fact, never sat on that body and were therefore deprived of an important means of 'influence' in the Company. The anti-Jewish attitude of Christian merchants prevented Jews from taking part in the Russian and Levant trades[1] and it is quite conceivable that similar causes restricted their activities in the trade with the West Indies and North America. It must also be borne in mind that many fields of professional and economic activity were still closed to Jews, and this put a heavy strain on the resources of Jewish firms which had to care for and support a host of children and relations.

All this cannot explain the strange phenomenon that for a long period of time the Jews failed to make use of the unprecedented economic opportunities which England offered them after the Resettlement. Though not enjoying all the rights of Christian subjects, they laboured under no heavy disabilities and, unlike their brethren in most European countries, they were not dependent on the arbitrary attitude and whims of an autocratic ruler. In fact, the road to a full and many-sided participation in the economic life of the country was wide open, but the Jews continued for over a century to restrict their business activities to a few branches and by no means to the most advantageous.

The effect of restrictions which had been imposed on Jews for centuries could evidently not be shaken off overnight and for a considerable period of time after their settlement in England it continued to be reflected in the limited scope of their commerce. There was a world of difference between the Jewish City merchant and the German court-Jew. The Hanover merchant Meyer Michael-David once told David Prager of Amsterdam that the difference between London and Amsterdam, on the one hand, and the German states, on the other, was comparable to that between Heaven and Hell,[2] but the English Jew too was still bound to the old mercantile tradition: precious metals, precious stones, bills and stocks still figured most prominently in his business.

It would seem that this represented the combined effect of a number of causes. The weight of a tradition which had moulded Jewish economic life for generations, the limited capital resources at the disposal of the majority of Jewish merchants, their dissociation from the land, their still inferior legal status and the jealousy of Christian merchants, all prevented the Jews from making full use of the new economic opportunities which England offered. At first they tended to exploit these opportunities only in a way consistent with their old pursuits. England's economic development, its rise to the rank of a major commercial entrepôt and the position of dominance it enjoyed in Lisbon enabled the Jewish-Portuguese merchant to keep up his trade with the Iberian peninsula and its American colonies from London. The increase in the power of the English East India Company at the expense of foreign rivals was put to good use by the Anglo-Jewish diamond merchants, who established a virtual monopoly of European diamond imports from India and made London the chief centre of the trade. The close mercantile and financial ties between London and Amsterdam and the growing demand for international exchange services encouraged the intensive activity of Jewish exchange merchants. On the face of it, it is surprising that we do not find Jews in banking, which was then undergoing a process of rapid expansion in both London and the provinces, but their absence from this field is really a striking example of the deep-rooted conservatism of the Jewish businessman. The new kind of banking, the most prominent feature of which was the profitable investment of deposits, was not familiar to Jews and at first they showed no eagerness to take it up, despite their familiarity with monetary affairs.

Were the Jews then, during the period under review, never in the vanguard of English economic development? Did they have no importance as pioneers and openers of new paths? The answer to this question can be affirmative only in a very limited sense. Jewish merchants of the Portuguese community had a stimulating effect on Britain's Iberian trade and may have played a decisive part in the attainment of Britain's dominant position in that trade, thus helping London to become an international market for precious metals – a development of great significance for England's standing as a major commercial power. The Jewish merchants of the City of London made it into the foremost European centre of the trade in uncut diamonds, a position which it has maintained to this day. The importance of this contribution to the British economy must therefore be regarded not solely in the context of eighteenth-century trade, but in the light of the enormous expansion of the diamond trade in the following two centuries.

These fields of commercial activity cannot, however, be regarded as typical of the processes which revolutionized economic life, first in Britain and then in other parts of the world. There were only two kinds of business in which Jewish merchants were not prevented by their inherent conservativism from playing a pioneering role: the stock market and the exchange trade. As to stocks, it would seem that it was largely due to Jewish enterprise that men and women of limited means and people who did not want to be personally involved in business were enabled to make investments in the City and to share in the profits of commerce.

The Jewish stockbrokers and merchants at the same time helped to create new methods of financing both business and Government activities.

It has already been shown that the Jews occupied a central position in the Anglo-Dutch exchange trade. Although it must be borne in mind that in the second half of the eighteenth century the biggest dealers on the London and Amsterdam exchange markets were non-Jewish firms, there can be no doubt that this essential branch of commerce would have collapsed without the Jewish exchange merchants and brokers who kept it going and were all too often among its first victims. Joseph Addison wrote: 'they [the Jews] are like the pegs and nails in a great building, which, though they are but little valued in themselves, are absolutely necessary to keep the whole frame together.'[3] This comparison can only be understood in the light of their intensive activity and central role in this field where the Jews formed a most important link in the structure of international commerce.

On the whole, however, Jews played only a small part as pioneers of modern capitalistic development, and they did so only in branches which were in any case closely related to their economic traditions. When the first Jews arrived in England during the late 1650s England was already well on the way to becoming a major commercial power, and in the eighteenth century English Jews took almost no part in developments which were to revolutionize the economic life of Britain. Only in the next century did they evolve that many-sided economic activity with which we are familiar today.

PART ONE

General Survey

Chapter 1
The Spanish and Portuguese Atlantic Empires

Most of the major Jewish merchants of London before the middle of the eighteenth century belonged to the Portuguese Community. They or their fathers had come from Holland or Leghorn, but some came directly from Portugal, and as late as the first part of the century a thin but steady stream of fugitives from the Portuguese Inquisition was still arriving in London. This last stage of Jewish immigration is reflected in the list of ketubot (marriage-contracts) of the Bevis Marks congregation. Married couples arriving from Portugal would undergo a second marriage ceremony according to the Jewish rites, because this had been impossible in their native country. The number of these couples, who were registered in the congregation's records as *vindos de Portugal*, increased rapidly after 1727, and for certain periods between 1724 and 1733 're-marriages' amounted to more than half the total number of marriages registered in the Bevis Marks records. The year 1733 marks the end of this last wave of Marrano immigration.[1] Many of these continued to trade with Portugal under false names, or at least kept up the trade with which they had been familiar in Portugal. This commercial tradition, moreover, was kept alive not only for one generation; it was handed on to sons and grandsons, even though they may have passed through more than one country before reaching England. One of the foremost Jewish merchants of London in the middle of the eighteenth century, for example, Benjamin Mendes da Costa,[2] was born in Bayonne in 1697, emigrated with his parents to Amsterdam, and in 1724 settled in London. He traded, *inter alia*, to Brazil and Portugal.

The role which had been played in Spanish-American and Portuguese-American commerce by the Jews of those countries and their colonies still awaits thorough investigation, but what is known indicates that the Jews were for a long period of time an important, and perhaps dominant, element in the trade of Latin

America. Spain had tried to prevent the settlement of 'New Christians' in the colonies, but after the Inquisition was set up in Portugal in the first half of the sixteenth century many of its Jews emigrated to Brazil and from there to Spanish colonies. Concentrations of Jewish merchants appeared in the large commercial centres of Lima and Cartagena, Mexico and Vera Cruz, and these 'Portuguese' are said to have captured the commerce of Latin America, distributing the imported goods throughout the continent by means of 'Portuguese' agents.[3]

Nonetheless, by the time when the first Jews settled in Cromwellian London the prosperity of the Jewish merchants of South and Central America was already a thing of the past, having vanished as a result of an unrelenting persecution by the Inquisition of Lima and Mexico. During the first half of the eighteenth century the persecution of the remnants of the Marranos was intensified and resulted in the final disappearance of Portuguese and Brazilian Jewry.[4]

Some of those who were liquidating their Brazilian holdings in the 1720s may well have invested the proceeds in English securities, like the plantation-owner Moses Marcus Monforte. The Jewish merchants who settled in England after 1660 could not therefore make use of family connections in order to maintain their trade to the Iberian peninsula and to the colonies in America. That they succeeded nevertheless in playing an important role in England's trade with Spain, Portugal and their colonies demonstrates the strength of the commercial traditions which they brought with them.

It is true that conditions were favourable, particularly for trade with Portugal and Brazil. Since the second half of the seventeenth century England had enjoyed a special standing in Portugal. A strange situation developed; just at the time when the Jewish newcomers in London were beginning to penetrate England's Portugal trade, English merchants and agents were replacing the Jewish merchants of Lisbon who had been eliminated or driven out of the country by the Inquisition.[5] The Methuen Treaty of 1703 abolished the restrictions on the importation of English cloth into Portugal and gave the English a marked commercial preference. By 1715 Portugal occupied third place among buyers of English cloth, and English capital soon came to dominate Portugal's economy. English merchants took a growing share of the Brazil trade, the legal part of which passed through Lisbon.[6]

Anglo-Portuguese trade not only grew rapidly but also changed its character. In the seventeenth century England had bought Brazilian sugar and tobacco from Portugal, but with the development of its own sugar and tobacco plantations in the West Indies and North America England ceased to be a market for these Brazilian products.[7] It is indeed very doubtful whether England's Portugal trade would have been capable of the rapid development which it experienced as a result of the Methuen Treaty, had not gold been discovered in Brazil a few years earlier. Widespread prospecting took place between 1699 and 1711 and gold began to be exported in increasing quantities. For a time Brazil was the foremost supplier of gold to Europe. The discovery of gold determined both the growth and the character of Anglo-Portuguese trade during much of the eighteenth century. England's exports to Portugal, and through it to Brazil, were consumer goods – particularly woollen cloth and fish – while imports consisted mainly of Portuguese wine and Brazilian gold, the latter representing a considerable portion of the total output of the mines.[8] To these after 1730 were added uncut diamonds from the newly discovered Brazilian deposits. The growing economic resources of Brazil and the intensified emigration of Portuguese to their American colony – which resulted from the discovery of gold – naturally increased Brazil's importance as a market for European goods.[9]

From the point of view of the English merchant there was a close resemblance between the Portuguese and the Spanish trades, and they were sometimes regarded as a single branch. Spain's colonial trade was also largely in the hands of foreigners who traded under the cover of Spanish agents at Cadiz,[10] and like Portugal Spain imported consumer goods for herself and her colonies, which were paid for in a number of raw materials – cochineal, indigo, hides and the like, but chiefly in silver.[11] England, however, did not dominate Spain's trade as it did Portugal's and had to face strong competition from the French who had greatly strengthened their position in the Spanish trade during the War of the Spanish Succession.[12] England's share was nevertheless considerable, and Daniel Defoe, while regretting France's growing penetration, remarked on the 'vast quantity' of English woollen goods which Spain bought yearly.[13] English houses were established at Cadiz and at a number of commercial centres in Spain's American colonies.

The English were not content to trade with the Spanish and Portuguese colonies indirectly, through the mother countries. By the Treaty of Utrecht they acquired the right to send an annual ship to Spanish America, but older and more stable than this privilege was the contraband trade between Jamaica and the Spanish Main. This trade constituted the third channel through which the silver and gold of South and Central America reached London. The contraband trade had some advantages over the legal or semi-legal trade transacted through Cadiz. The Spanish fleet system was inefficient, and neither the European nor the American merchant could rely on a regular supply of goods.[14] Moreover, the contraband trade was free from the duties which encumbered the legal commerce and it avoided the 'unstable pyramids of credit with their base in Manchester or London, their intermediate layers in Cadiz and Vera Cruz or Lisbon and Rio, and their peak in some remote Indian village' which were prevalent in Spanish-American commerce.[15] The contraband trade, which was mainly carried on by the English, constituted a vital complement to the legal Cadiz trade.[16] The structure of the West Indian contraband trade was, in all essentials, similar to the legal trade, the colonies paying in raw materials and precious metals for English consumer goods. One author estimated the English imports by the way of Portobello-Jamaica and Cartagena-Jamaica at 6 million pesos per annum,[17] while according to Macpherson the value of gold and silver imported was between 10 and 20 times greater than the value of goods.[18]

The coins and the bars of silver and gold which reached London through Lisbon, Cadiz and Jamaica, were not solely payments for English goods. The eighteenth century saw the rapid development of the London money market, and the British capital became an international clearing centre, a development which was greatly encouraged by the Portugal trade.[19] The predominance of English houses in the Portuguese commerce, their privileged status – which gave them a partial immunity from the intervention of the Portuguese authorities in their illegal gold transactions – and the excellent communication kept up by English packet-boats between Lisbon and Falmouth, all helped to direct the flow of Brazilian gold to England. Indeed, these packet-boats were very convenient for the illegal export of gold and diamonds from Portugal and for the smuggling of Jews out of the country.[20]

Even Portuguese payments to Spain were made through

England, and Spanish merchants used to remit specie home by the same way in order to avoid duties. Spain and Portugal paid the balances of their trade with Germany through London, so that a great part of the precious metals which reached London from the West was immediately sent on to the East. Magens described the complicated system of payments:

> Of the many English authors on the subject of the balance of trade, I do not recollect to have met with any one who has observed that a great part of the gold and silver remitted to England from Spain and Portugal, is the return of goods from Germany, where against bills of exchange payable at London, go to Germany. And the Germans cannot take all the returns in goods from England, so part of the bullion must be transmitted to them, without any relation to the balance of trade between England and Germany, and whereout the English can only have the profit of freight etc.
>
> The next remittance is to Holland, and what is not requisite to remain there passes on to the proprietors in Germany.[21]

But, as the Jewish merchant Joseph Salvador remarked, 'Gold in handling will stick to the fingers like meal.'[22] The part that 'stuck' was used for financing England's trade with India, the Levant and the Baltic countries. The situation can be summed up by quoting Defoe:

> Not a fleet of Portuguese ships, not the galleons or flota from New Spain, but the gold of the first and the silver of the last, or at least a great share of it, is the product of English stocks and belongs to London merchants, whose goods, sold upon credit at Lisbon and Cadiz, went first out to America to purchase that gold and silver.[23]

It has already been mentioned that the Jewish merchants of London kept up their old connections with the Portugal and Spanish trades. This was not at all as obvious as it would seem, because the Jewish merchant laboured under several disadvantages as compared with Christian merchants of London. If he was of Portuguese origin, he had to trade under a false name in order to hide his identity. Paradoxically, it was the English merchant who had members of his family stationed in Lisbon, while the Jew was deprived of all family connections with the old country. In Cadiz there were probably no Jews at all, and no Marrano

living in Lisbon would endanger himself and his family by maintaining commercial connections with relatives in Northern
Europe. This inability to maintain or establish family connections
was a serious disadvantage in the Iberian trade which was difficult to handle from afar, and the use of false names in order to
get round this difficulty was very common among English Jews of
Portuguese extraction. The British Consul at Lisbon reported to
London in May 1731:

> It may be proper to acquaint Your Grace that some of those
> Jews run out of this country and are considerable in debt to
> His Portuguese Majesty, that upon going to England they
> either changed their names or traded hither in borrowed ones,
> to cover their effects.[24]

These words need not be taken literally, however. From the
point of view of the Portuguese authorities every Jew escaping
abroad was in debt to the Crown; his property in Portugal was
confiscated, and any property which he may have transferred
abroad was considered as in law belonging to the Crown. The
property of these merchants was in danger of confiscation whenever the Portuguese authorities had reason to suspect that they
were Portuguese-born. In 1727 a consignment of gold sent from
Brazil to Lisbon for Benjamin Mendes da Costa of London was
impounded on the grounds that da Costa had left Portugal without permission, while in fact he had been born in France.[25] Most
probably the Portuguese mistook him for Joseph and Emmanuel
da Costa Villa Real who had fled from Portugal to England in
1726.[26]

The danger of discovery was exceptionally great during the
1720s and early 1730s, when the Inquisition started a new cam-
paign against the remnants of Portugal's Jewry. The vulnerability
of Anglo-Jewish merchants who traded to Portugal posed a difficult problem for the British Ambassador at Lisbon, and during
the spring of 1731 and the summer of 1732 the question was
raised in the Ambassador's and the Consul's correspondence with
the Secretary of State in London. Directly concerned were two
Jewish merchants of London, both of Portuguese origin. One was
Gabriel Lopes Pinheiro, of whom the Ambassador wrote: 'Gabriel
Lopes Pinheiro, when he was got safe with his effects into England,
began to trade largely to Portugal, for the house of Messrs. Buller.
But in his whole correspondence never makes use of the name he

went by in Portugal, but calls himself Pedro Forte, and is not to be found by any other name in any of his letters of Mr. Buller, or in any books or accompts between them.'

'Pedro Forte' was not Pinheiro's only cover name. When he first came to England he called himself Joseph or Daniel Vianna, but when this identity was discovered by the Portuguese authorities, he changed his name again, this time calling himself 'Pedro Forte'.[27] During the 1730s he maintained commercial connections with Vienna and consigned diamonds to his son, Abraham Lopes Dias, who lived there. In another document Pinheiro describes himself as 'agent for his Imperial and Catholic Majesty at the Court of Great Britain'.[28] Pinheiro may have been connected with Moses Lopes Pereira, Baron d'Aguilar, who then resided at Vienna, but already had a big firm in the City of London, under the name of Pereira and Lima.

Pinheiro's first fictitious name brought about the entanglement of another Jewish merchant named Fernando Fernandes, alias Abraham Dias, or – as he called himself after his escape from Portugal – Miguel Vianna.[29] Vianna fled Portugal in 1706, after his wife had been burned at the stake by the Inquisition. After a short stay in Spain, he went to England:

I resolved to move to the cold climate and mild Government of Great Britain, where by my industry and the help of God I acqu'd a fortune sufficient to trade to several parts and, among the rest, to Portugal, as well as for the sale there as to be consigned on my account to the Brazills.[30]

In the spring of 1731 there seems to have been some anxiety among Jewish merchants of London caused by the bankruptcy of the English house of Woodward at Lisbon, and the possibility that it would result in the discovery of the names of the firm's Jewish correspondents. It appears that, at the request of Newcastle, the Ambassador at Lisbon approached the English merchants, who replied that 'they were under no apprehensions in this affair, that their correspondents, though Jews, were not Portuguese, had never had any dealings with the King of Portugal, and consequently they did not conceive any goods in their hands were liable to enquiry into from any persons here'.[31] The English merchant Buller admitted that his correspondent Gabriel Lopes Pinheiro did not share this immunity, but declared that, if required, he would be ready to declare on oath that he had no connection with the latter. His Majesty's Ambassador naturally expressed disapproval of this kind of tactics.

The person who finally got involved was not Pinheiro but Vianna. In the spring of 1732 the Portuguese authorities impounded all the mail which had arrived with the fleet from Rio de Janeiro, after some gold smuggling had been discovered. The seized mail included bills drawn on Vianna for diamonds consigned to him from Brazil,[32] and his name being identical with the old cover-name of Pinheiro – which was known to the Portuguese authorities – the diamonds were confiscated on the assumption that they were Pinheiro's property.

Vianna submitted two petitions in April and June 1732.[33] He did not at first mention that he had formerly lived in Portugal, stating only that he had had 'the happiness of living in London for about these thirty years'. The petition was sent to the Ambassador at Lisbon with instructions to approach the Portuguese authorities. When the Ambassador discovered that Vianna had had trouble with the Inquisition, the latter confessed to his Portuguese past, but maintained that he had been born in Toledo, Spain. The subject figured prominently in the correspondence between Newcastle and Tyrawley at Lisbon. It is clear that despite England's privileged status in Portugal and London's desire to protect the interests of its Jewish subjects little could be done on their behalf. The case was more difficult than that of Benjamin da Costa had been in 1728 because, although there was a similar confusion of names by the Portuguese, this time both merchants concerned were refugees from Portugal, Vianna having had a sentence of death passed on him by the Inquisition.

Tyrawley admitted that in view of the importance of the English Jews in the Portugal trade, the problem was serious, but he was very reluctant to intervene:

> I think the present case very unfit for the King's minister to meddle in, for when once people come to carry on business under different names and under ambiguities, not to say prevarications of this sort, I can't think it for the King my master's honour for his minister to concern himself in these duplicities.

He thought that the only chance of success lay in making strong representations for restitution of the goods which had been seized from an English merchant, while ignoring the Jewish aspect of the case, 'for to mention even the name of Jew condemned by

Inquisition, is to these people something so odious, that they won't hear of it.' In a later letter Tyrawley argued similarly:

> The cry at present runs grieviously against the Jews, and an Auto de Fe that we are expecting every day, will be the fifth that has been in four years and a half that I have been at Lisbon, at which they have burnt ten or twelve Jews at each Auto. Therefore, tho' the time is always improper here to make representations in favour of Jews, yet it happens to be more so just at present.[34]

The non-Jewish English firms were better able than the Jewish houses to maintain family ties with Lisbon. It is true that at the time of the Jew Bill dispute of 1753 the English Consul in Portugal maintained that the British Portugal merchants feared that the Jews, if granted naturalization, might completely monopolize the Lisbon trade 'by the connection many of them must have with friends and relations of their own persuasion scattered up and down the Portuguese dominions'. The fear, however, seems to have had no foundation in reality. We know the names of the Lisbon correspondents of several Anglo-Jewish firms: they were all Christians, mostly English.[35] The connection with these houses was sometimes established even before the Jewish merchant left Portugal. Joseph da Costa Villa Real had business ties with Arthur Sturt, an English merchant who had resided in Lisbon from 1702 to 1721, and again, after an interval in England, after 1726, and appealed to him for help when arrested by the Inquisition. Villa Real's business affairs in Portugal show that ramified activities could still be carried on by Jews in that country during the early eighteenth century. Arthur Sturt wrote about Villa Real's business (about 1720):

> Joseph da Costa Villa Real, at that time merchant at Lisbon, did then, and for several years had dealt considerably as a merchant, by buying and selling several sorts of goods and by large remittances of money and by contracting and dealing with the Government of Portugal for supplying the Army with several sorts of provisions.[36]

When Sturt left Portugal in 1721, he entrusted his Government bonds to Villa Real's care. We also know the arrangements made by Duarte (Isaac) Rebello de Mendoca, a Jewish merchant who escaped from Portugal some time before 1749. While still living

in Portugal, Mendoca did business with the English house of
Mayne and Burn who later described how he had, before leaving
for England, ensured the continuation of his commercial connections with Portugal:

> The said [de Mendoca] did formerly live and reside in Lisbon
> ... and ... was a native thereof and professed the Roman
> Catholic religion. .... But he being suspected there to be a Jew,
> and hath openly professed himself to be a Jew, was obliged to
> quit that Country to prevent his person from being seized by
> the Inquisition there. And the said [de Mendoca] hath since
> that time and for many years past resided in England and there
> carried on the business of a merchant. And ... as the effects of
> the said [de Mendoca], in case they should be discovered or
> found out at Lisbon, would be liable to be seized by the
> Inquisition, he, the said [de Mendoca] did therefore ... request
> [John Mayne] and the said William Mayne his partner to cover
> his property under their names and to permit him to make
> consignment in their names to the house ... at Lisbon. And the
> said [de Mendoca] proposing to correspond with them under
> the name of Edward Anthony ... he the said [John Mayne]
> and William Mayne did consent and agree that the said [de
> Mendoca] might make use of their names in such consignments,
> for the purpose of enabling him to carry on such trade ... with
> the greater security to him in the respect to the preventing his
> property in such goods being discovered.

Under this cover Mendoca traded to Portugal in corn, wax,
rice, and fruit.[37]

Despite the difficulties which confronted Jewish merchants in
the Portugal trade, especially if they were Portuguese born, the
Jews of London were prominent in Anglo-Portuguese commerce.
In fact, despite the lack of statistical data, there can be no doubt
that, apart from the diamond trade, this was the most important
branch in the business activity of the Jewish-Portuguese community.

There are many legal documents relating to Jewish participation
in the Portugal trade, and its importance is explicitly confirmed
by two sources. One is a letter by the British Ambassador to
Portugal which is part of the correspondence between him and
Newcastle mentioned already. The Ambassador was none too
friendly towards the Jewish merchants and thought that Portu-

guese-born Jews should keep out of the trade with their old country, but he could not deny the pre-eminent position occupied by English Jews in the trade and regarded the 'Jewish problem' as a danger to its future:

> This affair, my Lord, tho' I think without remedy in its present circumstances, is a very unfortunate one, and will deserve Your Grace's very serious consideration, in respect to our trade to Portugal. For if it is true, as I believe it is without contradiction, that the greatest dealers to Portugal in our woollen goods are the Jews in London, we may be often liable to things of this nature, whenever such Jews are of those that have fled from Portugal themselves or are in partnership or correspondence with such as lye under lash of the laws of this Country.[38]

The second source does not mention the role of the Jews generally, but concerns the house of Salvador, one of the leading families of the Portuguese-Jewish community, and pre-eminent in diamond and the precious metal trades. Joseph Salvador was the author of, or at least supplied the information for, a most illuminating booklet published as part of the Jew Bill dispute of 1753.[39] The booklet, entitled *Further Considerations on the Act to permit persons professing the Jewish Religion to be naturalized by Parliament in a second letter from a merchant in town to his friend in the Country*, contains a description of the role which the English Jews played in the overseas trade of the country. It evoked a response to Salvador from a well-known merchant and author, Jonas Hanway, who opposed the granting of naturalization to the Jews. Hanway did not, however, try to dispute the Jews' importance in the Portugal and Spanish trades; on the contrary, 'I remember the time when I was an apprentice, and afterwards a factor in Lisbon, that your name, as a great trader, carried with it more weight and importance than those of fifty German barons. Happy did we think those factors who had such a principal – and yet your father was but plain Mr. S–r, merchant.'[40]

The Jews of London did not only maintain ordinary commercial ties with Portugal; sometimes they represented Portuguese official and even religious institutions. Most merchants of Portuguese origin resident in London were Jews, and the Portuguese chose to ignore their agents' religion as long as they needed their services. An interesting instance of this kind of connection concerns Andrew Lopes (Abraham Lopes de Britto), one of the early leaders of the Portuguese-Jewish community. In 1696 the Spanish Government granted the Assiento (the right to supply slaves to the Spanish colonies in America) to the Portuguese Royal Guinea Company, stipulating that it must supply 30,000 'piezas de Indias' between June 1696 and March 1703.[41]

The Portuguese Company was unable to accomplish this task without help, and had to employ foreign ships. It commissioned Andrew Lopes as its agent in London, and he assumed the name of Andreas Alvares Noguera for this purpose. Lopes had been active in the trade to Portugal and to Madeira[42] as well as in the African slave trade, and it was probably due to the connections he had thus formed that he was able to get the Portuguese agency. He also took an active part in the slave trade between Africa and Mexico.

Lopes introduced other Jews into the business. There is a contract signed by him on 30 November 1697, as agent of the Portuguese Company, with two Jewish ship-owners of London – Isaac Rodrigues and Isaac da Costa Alvarenga – and with the English captain of their ship. Rodrigues and Alvarenga undertook to send their ship with goods to the Guinea coast, there to be exchanged for slaves, who were to be carried to Vera Cruz. There they were to be graded, in agreement with the local agent of the Assiento, who was to pay 120 pieces-of-eight – about £24 – for each 'pieza de Indias'. The contract allowed the captain to take back to London the silver and gold which he was to receive for the slaves.[43]

The voyage of this ship seems to have been typical for two reasons. Firstly there was the private business which the captain transacted in violation of his contract and to the detriment of the Company. Lopes maintained that the captain, in violation of the contract's provisions, took many slaves on his own account, thus causing serious overcrowding on board ship which resulted in a high death rate among the slaves. He also accused him of selling the best slaves for his own account at various ports, before reaching Vera Cruz. Lopes said he had known that such practices were common, and therefore included in the contract explicit provisions forbidding them. Secondly there was the predominance of Jews in the undertaking. It was just this sort of illegal private trade, as well as the important role which Jews played in the Company's affairs, that prevented the renewal of the Assiento contract by the Spaniards, when it expired in 1701.

Another example of connections which did not fit into the regular pattern of commercial relations were those maintained by the Salvador family. Francis (Daniel) Salvador was acquainted with the Portuguese Ambassador in London, Sebastian Carvalho, later Marquis de Pombal, who was consistent in his attitude towards the Jews. He did not share the prevalent hostility and during his premiership the persecutions were stopped.[44] There can be little doubt that Philo-patriae's booklet, *Considerations on the Bill*, endeavouring to refute the argument that the passing of the Jew Bill would antagonize the ruling circles of Portugal, refers to Francis' son, Joseph:[45] 'It was soon made clear, that there was not the least probability of disgust from the Court of Portugal, since a Jew has the transactions here of their chief mercantile affairs and those of some of their chief convents.'

There is another example of connections between a Jewish merchant and a Portuguese official in an appeal submitted in 1739 to the East India Company by Gabriel Lopes Pinheiro, on behalf of a certain da Fonseca Rabello, 'his Portuguese Majesty's Commisary'. Pinheiro, who, as will be recalled, had escaped to London from the Portuguese Inquisition, asked the Company to permit da Fonseca Rabello to send on to Lisbon goods which he had brought with him from Goa.[46]

The lack of statistical data rules out any attempt to ascertain the Jews' share in the Portuguese and Spanish trade and in their various branches. It is only possible to gain a general impression from the relevant documents, mainly Chancery and Exchequer bills and answers. Only in a few cases is there a little more exact information enabling cautious conclusions. At the beginning of the eighteenth century, there were a number of Jewish merchants exporting corn to Lisbon. During the War of the Spanish Succession, Portugal imported large quantities of corn, in part from England, and Jews like Fernando da Silva, Andrew Lopes, Simon Francia, and Moses de Paiba were among the exporters. They bought the corn at Portsmouth or Falmouth through an agent who directly consigned it to Lisbon.[47] Andrew Lopes also did business of another kind which was occasioned by the war, supplying uniforms for the Portuguese army. He bought the materials in London, had uniforms produced there, and then sent them to Lisbon. It seems, however, that the Jewish merchants who traded with Spain and Portugal were mainly exporters of woollen goods and importers of precious metals. Although wine was Portugal's staple export commodity, there is no evidence to show that Jews imported wine, except Madeira wine, and that only during the early period.[48] The Court Books of the East India Company contain lists of merchants who imported Portuguese wine to East India around the year 1745; there is no Jew among them. In view of the intensive participation of Jews in other branches of the Portugal trade, their absence from the wine trade seems rather astonishing. Perhaps the reason was that Jews were usually not acquainted with this trade. Furthermore, the wine trade was centred in Oporto and so lay outside the main stream of the Anglo-Portuguese commerce which went through Lisbon and was closely connected with Portugal's colonial trade. Be that as it may, the combination of exports of woollens and imports of precious metals fitted well into the general pattern of Jewish business. There is an illuminating petition,[49] submitted by Jewish merchants when it was proposed to levy a special tax on Jews after the Glorious Revolution. Two passages in this petition deal with the activity of London Jews in international trade. One speaks of the diamond trade, the other says:

> That not withstanding the smallness of the number of merchants, and their estates being so moderate, (they being employed as factors by their friends and relations abroad) do drive a considerable trade, exporting great quantities of woollen manufactures of this nation and importing vast quantities of gold and silver and other foreign staple merchandise.

Some 60 years later, a petition issued in favour of granting naturalization to Jews spoke of 'encouraging the exportation of woollen and other manufactures of this kingdom, of which the persons who profess the Jewish religion have for many years last past exported great quantities'.[50]

There can be no doubt that many Jewish firms imported gold. We have three lists of Jewish merchants who imported gold from Portugal. The earliest, dating from 1718, has a special interest because it shows that close links existed between the Jewish precious metal merchants of London and Amsterdam – a not altogether surprising revelation in view of the fact that both cities were central markets for precious metals and that their Jewish communities were closely linked by family and business ties. This particular case concerns the joint placing of orders for gold by several merchants of London and Amsterdam: Francis

Salvador Sen., Jacob Mendes da Costa, Francis Salvador Jr,[51] John Mendes da Costa Jr, Moses de Medina, Abraham da Costa, and Samuel Ximenes of London; and Joseph Salvador,[52] Lewis Mendes da Costa, John Mendes da Costa, Joseph de Medina, Isaac de Medina, Solomon de Medina, and Aaron and Moses Brandaos of Amsterdam. These merchants were described as 'having for several years imported ingots and bars of gold of very great value from Portugal', and our documents show a number of family partnerships between importers from both sides of the Channel; thus the Salvadors of London, in partnership with their Mendes da Costa relatives,[53] ordered gold which was to be consigned to Joseph Salvador of Amsterdam. Moses de Medina of London together with his Amsterdam relations[54] and with Aaron and Moses Brandaos of the same place ordered six bars of gold, while Samuel Ximenes of London had two bars of gold and two parcels of Portuguese gold coin ordered on his own account to Amsterdam.[55]

The second list, preserved in the State Papers – Portugal, is dated February 1723.[56] It consists of the signatures of 56 London merchants on a document empowering captains bringing gold for their several accounts from abroad to deliver it to John Godall, 'Portugal merchant' of Fowey in Cornwall, the home port of the packet-boats sailing to Lisbon. Of the 56 merchants 13 were Jews. The names of the Jewish merchants on the list are: Pereira and Lima, Fernandes da Costa and Son, Jacob da Costa, Anthony Mendes, Jacob Mendes da Costa, Miguel Vianna, Francis Salvador Jr, Isaac Salvador, M [oses] de Medina, Abraham and Jacob Franco, Jo [seph] and Daniel Vianna, Solomon de Medina, Moses Son and Co., Jo [seph] Mendes da Costa Jr. Many of their names are identical with those on the list of 1718 – Salvador, Mendes da Costa, da Costa and Medina. There are, however, some additional firms. We have the signature of Abraham and Jacob Franco – who had emigrated a few years before from Leghorn and were rapidly rising to the first rank of Jewish City merchants as importers of precious metals and of diamonds.

There is also the signature of the firm of Pereira and Lima, one of whose proprietors was Moses Lopes Pereira, Baron d'Aguilar. The firm of Pereira and Lima was a partnership between Moses Lopes Pereira (Baron d'Aguilar) and Jacob Alvares Pereira, alias Gabriel de Lima, who came to England as a refugee from Portugal some time before 1720. De Lima was his cover name for the Portuguese trade. It is quite possible that Moses Lopes Pereira, too, fled Portugal to England before he settled in Vienna in 1721. Be that as it may, the firm of Pereira and Lima was established about the time Lopes Pereira went to Vienna, and the London branch was headed by Jacob Alvares Pereira. In 1756 Moses Lopes Pereira, Baron d'Aguilar, settled in England, apparently in order to take care of the London house, Alvares Pereira having died in 1754. His sons were known as d'Aguilar. The list also includes the signatures of our acquaintances, the two refugees from Portugal Miguel Vianna (alias Fernando Fernandes or Abraham Dias) and Gabriel Lopes Pinheiro. The latter's cover name – 'Joseph and Daniel Vianna' – had not yet been discovered by the Portuguese, and was still being used by him.

Although almost a quarter of the gold importers who signed the said document were Jews, we must beware of hasty conclusions. A later list gives a somewhat different picture. This is a list of merchants who received gold from Portugal by packet-boats during the months January–June 1741. Nine of the merchants were Jews and they received gold worth £12,304, out of a total of £133,562 imported, that is to say only a little over 9 per cent.

The quantities of gold which arrived for Jewish merchants were:[57]

> Francis Salvador, £8,550
> Moses Lamego, £1,209
> Jacob Espinoza, £479
> Benjamin Mendes da Costa, £337
> Jacob da Costa and Benjamin Mendes da Costa, £337
> Abraham and Jacob Franco, £337
> Lewis Mendes, £270
> Isaac Lindo Jr, £243
> Anthony da Costa, £135

The list shows that of the gold destined for Jews almost 70 per cent was the property of Francis Salvador. It seems as if, while Salvador personally was obviously an important gold merchant, the share of other Jews was quite negligible.

This makes the figures somewhat suspect, and in fact, it would seem that the list was incomplete. There is a second list, covering the period between 15 March 1740 and 25 March 1741, thus being partially concurrent with the former. This document, which yields another four Jewish names, Pereira and Lima, John Mendes da Costa, Diego and Moses Mendes, and Joseph da Silva Jr, gives a total of £414,000 worth of gold imported from Portugal during the year it covers, or an average of £34,500 a month, as compared with an average of £5,500 for the first list. It would therefore seem that the first list was by no means comprehensive.

If Jews were indeed prominent in the export of woollen goods to Portugal, it would be difficult to explain why they had only an insignificant part in the import of gold, especially if we remember their apparent absence from the wine trade. At least a partial solution to this riddle suggests itself on examining the list of non-Jewish importers of gold. Many of them were English houses of Lisbon which served London merchants, including Jews. It is quite possible therefore that a considerable part of the gold consigned by these houses to England under their own names was the property of their correspondents in London, and if that was so, the share of Jewish firms may well have been much larger than is indicated by the lists.

It is also possible that after the discovery of diamonds in Brazil (1728), the Jewish Portugal merchants to some extent switched from gold to diamond exports. We shall later deal at some length with the entry of Brazil into the diamond market. Here it will suffice to state that after 1730 uncut diamonds began to arrive at Lisbon in increasing quantities, and from there were brought to England, together with gold coins and gold bars, on board the packet-boat plying between Lisbon and Falmouth. The export of diamonds from Lisbon to Falmouth was, like that of gold, illegal, and we know little about it, except that it attained a considerable volume.[58] We cannot determine the Jewish share in these diamond imports, but if we may judge from the Anglo-Indian diamond trade, Jews must have been prominent, if not indeed dominant in it. A petition submitted in 1732 by London's Portugal merchants on the subject of the Lisbon diamond trade,[59] was signed by 25 merchants, of whom 10 were Jews – a striking percentage in view of the fact that the Christian Portugal merchants usually let no Jew sign their petitions.[60] Miguel Vianna, already seen importing gold from Portugal in 1723, imported only diamonds in 1732. To a certain degree, Jewish merchants may have switched from gold to diamond imports after 1730 or 1740, and there were probably times when it was more profitable to import diamonds rather than gold.

It must therefore be assumed that the lists of 1741 do not reflect the true importance of the Jews as importers of Portuguese gold, let alone the role they played in the Portugal trade as a whole. It is rather a frustrating business – here we have two documents with some statistical data relating to Jewish activity in the Portugal trade, but instead of being able to use them we must try to explain them away.

The Sephardi Jews of England and Holland had by tradition closer connections with Portugal than with Spain. Most of them were of Portuguese extraction and spoke Portuguese. Their commerce with Cadiz seems, nevertheless, to have been as intensive as their Lisbon trade. Spanish America was a greater consumer of European goods and more important supplier of raw materials and of precious metals than Brazil. Cochineal, indigo, and other goods were imported through Cadiz, and Spain's colonies supplied Europe with silver long before gold was discovered in Brazil. Furthermore, the two branches of trade were closely interconnected. A considerable part of British manufactured goods imported to Brazil through Portugal ultimately found their way to the Spanish colonies as contraband.[61]

Chancery bills and answers show that many of the more important Jewish firms of the city were active in the Spanish and Spanish-American trades. We find Abraham and Jacob Franco, who also traded to Portugal, Italy, and India, sending corn and barley to Cadiz in 1750.[62] The same firm, now under the name of Jacob, Moses and Raphael Franco, imported silver from Vera Cruz on board the ships of the Spanish Flota.[63] The case concerned the insurance of a cargo of silver by the Francos, on a journey from Vera Cruz to Cadiz. The first of the two documents cited contains a detailed explanation by the Francos of the Spanish Flota system and the methods employed for insuring cargoes belonging to English merchants. They point out that the law explicitly permitted English subjects to insure their goods on Spanish ships sailing between America and Spain 'interest or no interest' (i.e. in case of damage or loss, they were not required to prove a real interest in the cargo):

> They have been informed and believe that such intention of the legislature arise from an understanding that many English subjects were covertly concerned in adventures in British

woollen manufactures carried in Spanish register ships, as the sole property of Spanish subjects, from Old Spain to the Spanish Dominions in America, and on other goods carried betweixt Old Spain and Spanish America as the sole property of Spanish subjects, and that discovery of such covert concerns would subject the Spanish subjects lending their names to cover such concerns of English subjects to incur very severe penalties.

The Francos also sent slaves from West Africa to Porto Rico.[64] In 1767 the Francos chartered a ship to carry a cargo to Africa, barter it there for slaves, and bring the latter to Porto Rico, where they were to be delivered to the agents of the Francos. The document gives a precis of the contract between the Francos and the owner of the ship. It was agreed, *inter alia*, that the Francos would provide the captain with four 6-pounder guns.

Alvaro da Fonseca, whom we shall meet again as one of the pioneers of the Anglo-Indian diamond trade, had at the time of his death in 1742 profits due to him from 'a cargo of sundry goods sent to Cartagena and Porto Bello'.[65] Anthony da Costa sent in 1737 a consignment of gold and silver lace to his agents at Cadiz, with orders to sell it there or to consign it to America.[66] Moses de Medina had at the time of his death in 1731 an interest of £3,560 in loans given in Cadiz and Spanish America.[67] Alvaro Lopes Suasso had close connections with both Cadiz and Lima, the capital of Spanish America, and received regular information from those places.[68] Aaron Capadose had connections with Cadiz.[69] David and Isaac Ximenes acted as agents in London for a (French?) firm of Alicante.[70] Isaac and Jacob Lopes Dias were the London agents of the firm of Raphael and Daniel Pilkington – an English house established at Cadiz – and sold silver which the latter consigned to them from Spain.[71]

The Salvadors played an important role in the Spanish, as well as the Portuguese and Indian trades. Details concerning their Spanish business are, however, scarce. We know that Francis (Daniel) Salvador acted as London agent for the Anglo-Spanish house of William and John Turry of Cadiz[72] and insured on their behalf goods which they imported from Spanish America. It is quite possible that at least part of these goods belonged to Salvador himself, as an English firm could take part in the trade between Spain and its colonies only under the cover of a Spanish agent, and Salvador may have preferred to have the insurance run under the name of his Cadiz agent.[73]

Joseph Salvador himself put great stress on the importance of England's Jews in the Spanish trade, and especially of one Jewish house – obviously, his own. In the second pamphlet which appeared in 1753 under the name of 'Philo-patriae', the following passage occurs, immediately after the description of the Jew's activity in the coral-diamond trade:

> The Spanish West India trade is of that nature and duration, that none but such as have great capitals can deal largely in it with success, and has this circumstance peculiar to it that, to carry it on, it is necessary to have goods from most parts of Europe, and by consequence, it is not material where the person lives, who carries it on. However, partiality generally engages the merchant to augment the assortment of the manufactures of his own country, beyond those of others. By much the greatest part of this trade, so far as British Capitals are concerned in it, is carried on by Jews. The value of this trade will be better understood when we reflect that the getting a licence for one ship yearly, was reckoned an equivalent for many faults in the Treaty of Utrecht, and was on all hands acknowledged for a great national benefit. Now, great as it is, there is one Jew in this city, who constantly has a licence for a larger ship than the South Sea Company ever had, and, giving many people shares under him, employs her constantly in this trade. Neither is he the only one, there being several Jews who carry on this trade as extensively. This surely is a national advantage, as, were the Jews absent, there is not a set of merchants in this country that either could or would undertake it.[74]

This statement must not be discounted merely because the pamphlet was written for propaganda purposes, in order to justify the demand for granting naturalization to Jews. Not only are the facts, as represented by Philo-patriae, borne out by other evidence, it is also most unlikely that he would have maintained that most of the English capital invested in the Spanish trade was Jewish, if they did not in fact have a very significant share in it. The authenticity of Philo-patriae's statement is further strengthened by the reply made by Jonas Hanway, his opponent in the Jew Bill dispute. Hanway made no attempt to contradict Philo-patriae's statement, but only argued that the system of the registered ships was well known and he did not doubt that Salvador's agent procured for him the right to send a shipload on more than one occasion – there were sometimes up to 20 such ships. Hanway said nothing about the share which the Jews in general had in these ships.[75]

Evidence similar to that supplied by Philo-patriae's pamphlet is given in a document, apparently dating from the 1760s, which includes answers to questions concerning the trade in precious metals, attributed to Joseph Salvador. These answers were apparently written by Salvador when the causes for the decline of the contraband trade between Jamaica and the Spanish colonies after the Seven Years' War were being inquired into in London.[76] On the Spanish trade it says: 'This branch of Trade by Old Spain seems to be in the hand of those who cannot be clamorous – that is to say in the hands of Jews and Catholics.'[77] The Catholics here mentioned are obviously Anglo-Catholic firms which were numerous in England's commerce with Spain. Salvador thought that the British authorities neglected the interests of the Spanish trade, because the Spain merchants did not constitute what we should call strong pressure groups – Jews and Catholics were both minorities without representation in Parliament. These statements cannot be corroborated by statistical data, but there is a document showing the importance of the Spanish trade in the business affairs of the house of Moses Mendes da Costa, one of the most prominent Jewish firms in the city at the middle of the eighteenth century. Mendes da Costa belonged to a very respected Jewish-Portuguese family. His father Jacob had been a well-known merchant, and Moses himself became active in the affairs of the community at an early age: he was a member of the Beth Holim (hospital) committee of the Bevis Marks Congregation in 1749, at the age of 30. In 1741 he had married Rebecca – the sister of Joseph Salvador – and there can be no better proof for the standing of Jacob Mendes da Costa than this alliance with the great Salvadors. Moses died in 1756, aged 37, and shortly after, his daughter Sarah married Ephraim d'Aguilar (Lopes Pereira), the eldest son of the Baron Diego d'Aguilar. According to the *Gentleman's Magazine*, she brought with her a dowry of £30,000.

Jacob Mendes da Costa, Moses' father, had also been active in the Spanish trade. In 1737 he 'was concerned in several goods loaded at Cadiz on board the galoons which sailed from thence to Cartagena in New Spain'.[78] But we are much better informed about the business of his son, thanks to an extant balance of his investments at the time of his death.[79] We know the interest which Moses Mendes da Costa had in several ships in the Spanish and Indian trades, the profits he made on sailings for which the accounts had already been made up, the names of the agents at Cadiz which handled da Costa's business, and even the names of the ships by which the goods were consigned. Da Costa's investments were concentrated in two branches, the Spanish-American and the Indian, and were of two kinds: investments in goods and bottomry loans. To India he sent coral and also made some bottomry business. His main interest, however, lay in the Spanish and Spanish-American trade, £25,639 out of a total of £31,852 being invested in it (just over 80 per cent). Of his Spanish investments, £20,792, or 81 per cent, were in goods, the rest being in bottomry loans.

The consignments made by da Costa were destined chiefly, if not exclusively, for Spanish America. It is true that some consignments are grouped under the heading 'Adventures to Cadiz', and one was sent to Seville, but it is stated that some of the goods sent to Cadiz were sent on to Vera Cruz in Mexico, and the same may have been true about at least part of the other goods in this group as well. It is furthermore mentioned explicitly that goods to the value of £12,898 were consigned to Vera Cruz. We must not conclude, of course, that the distribution of da Costa's investments represented a pattern common to all Jewish firms which were active in international trade. Other Jewish houses were much more interested in the coral-diamond trade with India than was this branch of the da Costa family, or were interested in Portuguese rather than in Spanish trade. But there can be little doubt that the concentration on Spanish (or Portuguese) and Indian business was characteristic of Anglo-Jewish merchants. It accords very well with the description given in Philo-patriae's pamphlet, which, as has been explained, was either written by Joseph Salvador himself or was composed on the basis of facts supplied by him. There can be little doubt that the major concentrations of Jewish capital were to be found in these branches of international trade.

We must now examine whether English Jews also took part in the contraband trade between Jamaica and the Spanish colonies. Jamaica contraband trade was part of the great complex of Iberian-American commerce and served as one of the channels through which the precious metals of South America reached Europe. In this branch of South American trade the Jews did not labour under the same disadvantages which hampered their activity in the semi-legal trade through Spain and Portugal. Jamaica was British territory since 1655 and many Jewish firms were established on the island, making it possible for Anglo-Jewish houses to exploit ties of family and religion. We have knowledge of several such firms which maintained branch houses in Jamaica. Various sources testify to the importance of Jamaica and English Jews in the contraband trade. In 1696 three Jewish merchants of London submitted a petition, in the name of the Jewish community, protesting against a bill which would have forbidden foreign subjects to act as merchants or mercantile agents in English colonies. The petition points to the activity of Jews in the English West India trade, and particularly in the trade with the Spanish colonies:

> That their trade is in goods sent them from England, for which they make returns in product of their respective plantations ... and they keep up and transact that very beneficial trade, which is between the Island of Jamaica and the Spanish West Indies, that produces the great quantities of silver daily brought from Jamaica.[80]

Significantly, while the petition speaks in a general way about the activity of Jews in the trade between Jamaica and England, it puts the main stress on their importance in the contraband trade with the Spanish colonies, which they are said to 'keep up and transact'.

Other sources tell a similar story. A sworn declaration made in 1728 by John Burnett, who had been for some years an agent of the English South Sea Company at Porto-Bello and Cartagena, declared 'that there was not a mariner in the [slave-carrying] packet-boats who did not carry a commission to the value of two thousand or three thousand pesos from some Jamaican Jew on every one of the four or five trips made annually, by such boats'.[81]

Edward Long, in his *History of Jamaica* published in 1774, also described the dominant position which Jamaica's Jews enjoyed in the contraband trade: 'Their knowledge of foreign languages, and intercourse with their breathren dispersed over the Spanish and other West India Colonies, have contributed greatly to extend the trade and increase the wealth of the Island, for they have always been the chief importers of bullion'.[82]

Some modern historians have pointed to the Jewish connections with the contraband trade. London Jews were almost the only merchants who sent goods to Jamaica on their own account, part of these goods being sold locally, the rest shipped on to Spanish America.[83] If it is true that Jamaica's Jews were the chief importers of contraband bullion from the Spanish colonies, while London's Jews were the main suppliers of manufactured goods which reached the colonies through Jamaica, then we can safely infer that the Jamaican contraband trade was dominated by Jews. Manufactured goods were also ordered by planters through their English agents, but these goods were destined to supply their own needs and not for use in trade. It is of some interest that a petition concerning the trade with the Spanish colonies, which was submitted by 42 Jamaica merchants in 1712, does not bear a single Jewish signature! If we had only this document to go by, it would certainly be concluded that the Jews had no share in the contraband trade. The exclusion of Jews from collective actions, already witnessed in the Portugal trade, undoubtedly reflected an anti-semitic attitude rooted in economic jealousy.[84]

Detailed information on this Jewish activity in the contraband is scarce, and I have been able to trace only one relevant document. It concerns the importation, in 1752, of gold and silver from Jamaica by three London merchants – Abraham and Jacob Franco and Benjamin Mendes da Costa – who, as we have seen, were active in the Spanish and Portuguese trade. They state in a Chancery bill:

> One of His Majesty's ships of war called the Assurance being at Jamaica, and being some short time afterwards to return to England, several correspondents of your orators [i.e. Abraham and Jacob Franco and Benjamin Mendes da Costa] at Jamaica and other parts in the West Indies shipt on board the said ship ... sundry bags of gold and silver and several large quantities of wrought plate upon the several accounts of your orators in order to have the same be brought to England there to be delivered ... in the Port of London.[85]

After receiving this load, the ship proceeded to Lisbon, where it received a consignment of Portuguese silver coins, also destined for London. In addition to the three merchants already mentioned other London Jews also had an interest in the cargo of precious metals, although it is not clear whether it was in that part of it which was imported from Jamaica, or in the coins loaded in Lisbon, or in both. They were Jacob Gonzales and Co., Francis and Joseph Salvador, and Raphael Vas da Silva. Of the 31 firms which had a share in the cargo, five were Jewish, but it may be of some interest that of eight members of the committee which was elected by the owners, after the ship had run aground, for the purpose of receiving the salvaged cargo, three were Jews, namely Joseph Salvador, Abraham Franco, and Benjamin Mendes da Costa. Their inclusion in the committee was certainly no matter of chance; they were perhaps the most prominent Jewish merchants of the day, and the fact that they made up almost half the committee shows that they must have owned a considerable part of the ship's cargo of precious metals.

The document is also interesting in that it shows the interconnection which existed between the various branches of the trade with South and Central America. The same merchants were active in all three branches – trading through Lisbon, Cadiz, and Jamaica – and in the particular case just considered one visited Jamaica and Lisbon on the same voyage. Another document indicates that English Jews had a considerable interest in the trade between Jamaica and the Spanish Main. This is a petition submitted by dozens of merchants, Jews as well as Christians,[86] protesting against the imposition of special taxation on the Jews of Jamaica. The list of Jewish merchants who signed the petition[87] includes all important names in the Jewish business community of that time, and, although the petition does not explicitly mention the Jamaica contraband trade, it is almost certain that, in view of the Jews' insignificance in the regular West Indies trade,[88] the Spanish colonies were the main object of the commercial activity reflected in the petition.

Chapter 2
The trade in precious metals and bills of exchange

The Jews were active in the London market for precious metals as importers and sellers, as buyers and exporters, and as brokers. It is difficult to form any conclusions about their activities as importers, because of the unreliability of statistical material, but if the Jews are considered as sellers rather than as importers – for they usually sold the gold and silver they had imported on the London market – there is some information from the account books of the Bank of England and the East India Company. From the books of the Bank it is clear that the Bank's purchases from Jewish firms or individuals during the second and third decades of the eighteenth century were only a small fraction of the Bank's total purchases of either gold or silver. Much more significant were the loans given by the Bank on the security of gold and silver deposits. There are very accurate figures relating to this branch of the Bank's business.[1] In the period 1713–25, a large proportion of the total lent by the Bank on such security was to Jewish firms, and even if the loans made to the broker Abraham Mocatta be omitted, on the grounds that much of the silver he deposited belonged to unnamed clients, there remains a total of £362,000 lent to individuals on the security of silver, of which £157,000 – 43 per cent was to Jews.

Prominent among both sellers and depositors of gold was the house of Medina,[2] followed by that of Salvador. After 1720, however, the Medinas ceased to sell gold, while the Salvadors too disappear after 1724. There were numerous other Jewish firms, such as the houses of Mendes, Mendes da Costa, Nunes, Rodrigues, and d'Adranda, but their total sales were often less than that of the Medinas alone.[3]

There is a different situation with loans given against silver deposits. The Medinas were prominent in this field too, though not to such an extent as in the gold business, but we find also some merchants who do not appear at all in the gold transactions but who deposited considerable quantities of silver at the Bank, notably the brothers Abraham and Jacob Franco and the Ashkenazi merchant Isaac Franks. At the time both houses were rapidly becoming major importers of Indian diamonds[4] and needed large quantities of silver for their purchases, which they may have temporarily deposited with the Bank.

The figures from the East India Company[5] are less clear, for the account books do not often specify names of sellers. Even the information for the period when the Company's books do give the names of the sellers of silver, 1744–56, does not enable any clear-cut conclusions to be drawn. Jewish brokers are very prominent, and we do not of course know on whose behalf they sold silver to the company. They were Isaac Lindo, Abraham Mocatta, Sampson Gideon, Moses Machado, Alexander I. Keyser, and Joseph Salomons. One can, however, distinguish between several classes of Jewish sellers. In the first place there are merchants who are known to have been active in the Iberian trade and as importers of precious metals. To this group belonged Francis Salvador and his sons, Benjamin Mendes da Costa, Isaac and Moses Lamego, Moses Mendes da Costa, the brothers Franco, and the firm of Pereira and Lima. The most conspicuous was the house of Salvador which in 1751 sold the East India Company £168,222 of silver – some 35 per cent of the total quantity purchased by it during that year. A second group consisted of Ashkenazi merchants active in the Anglo-Dutch trade, who undoubtedly played a role in the exchange and precious metals trade between London and Amsterdam. The most prominent merchant in this group was Joseph Salomons who frequently sold large amounts of silver to the Company: £140,000 worth of it in 1753 (20 per cent of the total quantity purchased), nearly £80,000 in 1754 (again about 20 per cent of the total), and £26,000 in 1756. The brokers constituted a class by themselves, and it would seem that Jews dominated in this group. The Bank of England as well as the East India Company employed Jewish brokers, chiefly members of the families of Mocatta and Lindo. Elias Lindo and, after his death, his son Isaac supplied the Company with silver and with bills of exchange for the purchase of silver, but a permanent connection between Mocatta and the East India Company was only established after he had been acting for some time as broker to the Bank of England. Once it came into existence it was a very close one, and much more is known about it than about Mocatta's relations with the Bank. It seems that in 1735 Mocatta obtained a permanent status as broker to the Company. In February 1736 the Court of Directors of the East India Company decided to grant him a gratuity of 20 guineas 'for his extraordinary trouble in procuring of silver for the Company for this year',[6] and as from November he received a monthly salary of £100. For a certain period, in the 1740s, Mocatta was the biggest Jewish seller of silver to the Company. In 1747 he received £313 for his commission, representing about £250,000 in silver transactions.[7] In 1746 payment orders amounting to £134 were made out to his name and to that of his son-in-law Moses de Mattos, and in 1748 they received £200,[8] both sums probably being commissions for extensive silver purchases. The East India Company bought large amounts of silver from the Bank of England during that time, and it is quite possible that Mocatta acted as broker in these transactions. After 1747 his connection with the Bank was discontinued and he died in 1751.

Mocatta's place was taken, for a short time, by the famous Jewish financier Sampson Gideon.[9] The Company had already had occasion to make use of Gideon's services as broker in 1745, when it purchased a large amount of silver from Admiral Anson. In March of that year the Court of Directors resolved to grant Gideon £200 'for being instrumental in facilitating the agreement between the Company and Mr Anson'.[10] In 1749 Gideon concluded an enormous silver deal on behalf of the Company. Three merchants – John Bristow, Francis Salvador, and David Pratviel (not a Jew) – undertook to supply the Company with three million ounces of pieces-of-eight, at a price of 63¼ pence the ounce (totalling approximately £790,000). The contract, which was signed in July, obliged the merchants to supply the whole quantity by Christmas. A copy of this contract as well as a copy of Gideon's letter relating to the transaction have been preserved in the Company's books,[11] and in its account-books were entered the sums paid for the silver through Sampson Gideon.[12] The contract was kept secret for a time at the request of the suppliers. When the deal became known, it aroused opposition among the Directors and a resolution was moved which would have forbidden the grant of silver contracts without public tender. The Court of Directors rejected the resolution, and instead expressed its gratitude to those who had concluded the deal.

But Gideon did not serve the Company for long and the office soon returned to the Mocatta family. When Abraham Mocatta died in 1751 his grandson Abraham Lumbroso de Mattos was a youngster of 18, but despite his youth he succeeded in regaining his grandfather's place within 10 years, after having added the latter's family name to his own.[13] The young Mocatta entered a partnership with the Ashkenazi Alexander Isaac Keyser[14] around 1760, and between that time and 1765 the Company bought most of its silver through the firm of Mocatta and Keyser, paying £459,000 between February 1762 and May 1765.[15] Later it becomes more difficult to trace the activities of the firm, but there can be no doubt that it continued to serve the Company on a large scale. After Keyser's death in 1779, Mocatta took another Ashkenazi, Asher Goldsmid, into partnership, and around 1790 they yearly sold silver to the Company to the value of several hundred thousands of pounds. The firm, under its new name of Mocatta and Goldsmid, has continued to act as silver brokers from that time to the present.

The precious metals brokers of London were not mere mediators between sellers and buyers. They formed the connecting link between the various branches of England's precious metals trade, with the Iberian peninsula, with the Spanish and Portuguese colonies in America, with the Amsterdam market for precious metals, and with the countries to which England exported silver and gold, notably India, the Levant and the Baltic area. Within the framework of Jewish trade, the brokers stood between the importers of precious metals from the Western hemisphere (most of whom belonged to the Portuguese community) and the Ashkenazi exchange merchants, who kept up a lively trade in bills of exchange and precious metals between London and Amsterdam. The brokers themselves were a mixed lot: there were Sephardim (Mocatta, Lindo, Gideon, and Machado) and Ashkenazim (Salomons, Keyser, and Goldsmid). The firm of Mocatta and Goldsmid united the two elements and it was perhaps not a matter of pure chance that this firm, with its close connections with the Sephardi importers of precious metals on the one hand and the Ashkenazi exchange merchants of London and Amsterdam on the other, proved the most stable and lasting of all Jewish City firms of the eighteenth century.

What conclusions can be drawn from the available data, statistical and other, about the part played by the Jews in the London market for precious metals? Information is still too meagre for a definite statement, but there is a good basis for trying to formulate a hypothesis, especially about the importance of the Jews as importers of precious metals. The lists of merchants who sold gold to the Bank of England during the 1720s and 1730s are 'disappointing' for the student of Anglo-Jewish economic history. Between 1711 and 1717 the Jews sold less than 9 per cent of the gold bought by the Bank; between 1718 and 1724 their share amounted to a little over 3 per cent; and in the following six years it sank almost to zero. But the figures relating to deposits of gold at the Bank give reason to think that the sellers' lists do not reflect the Jews' true importance. It is difficult to understand on what Clapham based his statement that the Bank, at this time, bought most of its gold from Sephardi Jews[16] – the figures prove the opposite. But the fact that Jews were much more prominent as depositors than as sellers of gold can be construed to show that the Jewish merchants, as a group, tended less than others to sell their gold to the Bank. This is not really surprising. The non-Jewish importers of gold generally had no close connections with the other branches of the precious metals trade. The houses which were active in the Portugal trade did not figure in the Anglo-Dutch trade. The Jewish firms, on the other hand, usually maintained strong family and business connections with Amsterdam, and were probably less dependent than others on the Bank's services in their gold and silver business. As has already been pointed out, this is not more than a hypothesis, but it is certainly not an unreasonable one, and it would explain what at first sight seems to be contradictory evidence.

We must not overlook the fact that the gold transactions of two Jewish firms by far surpassed those of any other Jewish merchant. Of the total amount of gold which the Bank purchased from Jews between 1710 and 1724, exactly three-quarters was sold by the firms of Medina and Salvador, and their share in gold deposits was even larger, amounting to more than 80 per cent of all gold deposited by Jews. The two firms were clearly in a different category from other Jewish houses, and we may well ask whether we can speak of the significance of Jews, as a group, in the Bank's gold business, when conclusions must be based chiefly on the volume of business done by two single firms. It is not easy to answer this question. There cannot be much doubt that the houses of Medina and Salvador were by far the most important Jewish firms on the precious metals business. On the other hand, it is most improbable that houses like those of Mendes da Costa, Franco, Lamego, Pereira and Lima, and the like were so utterly insignificant, in comparison with Medina and Salvador, as would seem to be the case on the evidence of the Bank's ledgers. Perhaps smaller importers tended less than the major ones to sell their gold to the Bank? This conjecture seems to be supported by the fact that the number of Jews who sold gold to the Bank underwent considerable fluctuations. In the years 1713–14 there were over 20 Jewish sellers, but their number decreased during the following years, and it is rather improbable that all the merchants who ceased to sell gold to the Bank after 1714 stopped business alto-gether. One must, however, remember that the Bank's ledgers tell us more about the share of the Medinas and Salvadors in the Bank's gold business than about the general significance of the Jews in the gold trade.

What about the Jews' importance in the silver trade? The ledgers of the Bank of England and of the East India Company show that they played a significant part, although they certainly did not dominate or monopolize the trade. Here too, we cannot discount the possibility that the extant records, which touch only a limited, though important, section of the trade, may be mislead-ing, and that perhaps the Jewish merchants were more prominent in the precious metals market than would seem from the ledgers of Bank and Company. The central position occupied by Jewish brokers in that market testifies in itself to the importance of Jews as dealers in precious metals. It surely cannot have been a matter of chance that many of the outstanding brokers were Jews, and their position would seem to indicate that the extant records do not reveal the full importance of the Jews in the precious metals trade.

Addison's comparison of the role of the Jews in trade to that of 'pegs and nails'[17] may not have been applicable to England's international commerce as a whole, but it was certainly true as far as the exchange trade between London and Amsterdam was concerned. The only field in which London's Jews played a truly essential part was the exchange trade. The most spectacular advance made by international trade during the seventeenth and eighteenth centuries was in evolving efficient methods for the settlement of international payments. First Amsterdam and then London became centres of discount. Payments were now usually made by drawing, and it was essential for the smooth working of the system that a merchant receiving a bill drawn at another place need not see personally to its being honoured, and that a person wanting to make a payment at a distant place should be able to get the necessary bills. It was also important that international payments be made according to a generally accepted rate of exchange and not be subject to arbitrary fixing of the relative values of different currencies. All this required an advanced system of mediation by exchange brokers and exchange merchants,[18] and it is in this field of commercial activity that Jews excelled. The exchange business fitted well the traditional economic pursuits of Jews. It was closely connected with the trade in precious metals with which Jews had for long been familiar. Their widespread connections, reaching to most parts of Europe, and their common languages – Hebrew, Yiddish, Portuguese, and Spanish – were an enormous advantage in the exchange business. Big banks were few and connections between them still irregular. The Bank of England and the Amsterdam bank did an extensive discount business, but they, too, needed mediators for the settlement of international payments. The intensive activity of Jewish exchange merchants in the trade between London and Amsterdam testifies to the vital role which they played in this field.

The importance of this activity for the smooth working of international trade was explained by Philo-patriae in 1753. After describing the usefulness of the Jews in various branches of commerce, he says:

They are so likewise in another branch of commerce, which has some analogy to banking, I mean the negotiating of foreign bills of exchange. The increase of late years in this branch is very considerable and useful to the traders in our manufactures particularly, and to all trade in general, as formerly the difference of the foreign exchanges between this city and Amsterdam was very considerable, and on the least surplus of bills here a great profit was expected by the negotiators of them. The Dutch Jews take such bills for a trifling profit, being by their correspondence more expert in this branch than any other people. And when bills are wanting they bring them from abroad with the greatest ease. That this is a great advantage to all importers and exporters is undoubted, as it steadies our exchanges and hinders the extra-ordinary profits that the dealers in exchanges would otherwise expect.[19]

The trade in bills of exchange was closely connected with the precious metals trade between London and Amsterdam; the two in fact constituted a single branch of commerce and the same people dealt in both.[20] It was not an ordinary field of commercial activity, but rather served all other branches by settling and adjusting payments between the two great financial centres and, through them, between other cities. It therefore belonged to quite a different category of business than the importation of precious metals from overseas which was part and parcel of an ordinary branch of trade. While the gold and silver imported through Lisbon, Cadiz, and Jamaica was usually sent in return for goods, the precious metals which were sent to and fro between London and Amsterdam constituted an integral part of the exchange business between the two cities. Philo-patriae pointed out the Jews' importance in this branch:

> The Dutch Jews are particularly useful in the bullion trade. They export the surplus treasure brought here, with that ease and small profits to themselves that the merchant, considering the longer time it takes him and the danger of the voyage to Holland, finds his account in importing and vending his treasure here, for them to export, and by these means the freights and other profits accrue to the nation, which formerly the Dutch, by means of the Bank of Amsterdam, enjoyed. They likewise import specie with the same ease.[21]

This activity was vitally important for the very existence of a central market for precious metals in London:

> That our enjoying this valuable trade to the present extent is owing to our frequent conveyances is undeniable and that, had we not the ease of exportation, when requisite for our own surplus, our conveyances would not be so frequent, is likewise undeniable. What demonstrates it to be owing to the Dutch Jews' dexterity is that the Dutch merchants never follow this trade, but on extraordinary occasions – when the profit is by some casualty augmented, yet are always ready then. Were the profit or differences of price considerable, it would invite all people to send bullion from foreign parts directly to Holland, and we would have nothing pass through this kingdom but our own balance of trade, especially as by its passing directly through Holland some small charges be saved. It is therefore

very beneficial for this nation to have a continental market for bullion, for otherwise all our trade would suffer, by our returns not yielding equal to what they do now.[22]

What does Philo-patriae mean when he speaks of 'Dutch Jews'? It is improbable that he is referring only to residents of the Netherlands. When the pamphlet was written there were already Jewish firms in London taking a lively part in exchange business with Amsterdam (e.g. the houses of Joseph Salomons, Ruben and Levy Salomons-Norden, and Aaron Goldsmid).[23] It is true that all these merchants were of Dutch origin, had settled in London fairly recently, and were perhaps still regarded as 'Dutch'. Philo-patriae undoubtedly included these people in his definition of 'Dutch Jews', and perhaps he was referring to Ashkenazi Jews in general, as most of the leading Ashkenazi families at that time were of Dutch origin, and were frequently referred to as 'Dutch Jews'.

Indeed, there was in the second quarter of the eighteenth century a considerable immigration of Dutch Jews into England, and branch houses of Jewish-Dutch firms were being established in London. This development was undoubtedly connected with, if not directly caused by, the rapid expansion of the Anglo-Dutch exchange trade. London Jews, including many members of the Portuguese community, had been prominent in this sort of business for a long time. When, after the Glorious Revolution, England was seized by one of the frequent mercantilistic panics, a parliamentary commission found that vast amounts of silver were being taken out of the country by Jews. The Mahamad of the Portuguese-Jewish community reacted by forbidding members of the community to export silver, and imposing further restrictions in the 1690s.[24] The early discount books of the Bank of England are full of Jewish-Portuguese names and several outstanding merchants of that community were in the exchange and discount business: Joseph Pereira, Francis de Caseris, Moses de Medina, and Anthony da Costa.[25] Almost a century later Sephardim like Franco d'Aguilar and Mendes da Costa are mentioned in the Prager Papers among the more prominent Anglo-Dutch exchange merchants.[26] It would seem, however, that for all these Jewish-Portuguese houses the exchange trade constituted only one among many fields of mercantile activity. In their case there is not that intensive, and in many cases probably exclusive, activity in the exchange trade which was typical for many Ashkenazi merchants. Profits in the exchange trade were small, and business had to be carried on continuously and rapidly. The Hanoverian banker Meyer Michael-David once wrote to his London agent, Yehiel Prager: 'If we want to carry on this trade, we must absolutely send to and fro with every post, otherwise it is not worth the trouble in this trade.'[27] It is this sort of feverish activity which characterized the Ashkenazi exchange merchant of those days.

The Prager letters clearly show that in the second half of the eighteenth century the Ashkenazi exchange merchants played an essential part in the exchange of trade between London and Amsterdam. We shall later examine various aspects of their activity;[28] here it will suffice to point out that the Prager brothers frequently used the word 'Jews' in the sense of 'exchange merchants'. These 'Jews' sent and received bills of exchange, coins and bars of gold and silver, thus fulfilling a vital function in a highly developed international system of payments. One aspect of their activities was the smuggling of English gold coins to Holland. Jewish merchants, especially the house of Cantor at Amsterdam, were very active in this field. The Prager letters give many details about this trade and about the exchange trade in general.[29] But the Prager letters also show that the leading houses in the exchange trade were not Jewish. There were, of course, Jewish houses of good standing, like those of Salomons, Norden, and Goldsmid, enjoying a prominent and influential position on the exchange market, but they could not compare with the non-Jewish firms which carried on an intensive exchange business. Only the firms of Hope and Muilman were able to determine the rate of exchange and they could always draw on better terms than their smaller competitors.[30] Before the end of the century no Jewish house attained the status of a *real* banking firm, and it appears that Jews were not active even in a field so closely related to the exchange trade as the discount of bills. Perhaps most Ashkenazi merchants at that time still lacked the substantial amount of capital needed for this type of business.

Chapter 3
Trade to the West Indies and North America

If city merchants had been asked, between 1650 and 1670 at the time of the Jewish Resettlement, in what branch of commerce the new immigrants could be expected to distinguish themselves, they would probably have pointed to the West India trade as the most likely field of Jewish commercial activity. There is indeed some evidence indicating that this is what they expected (or feared). When a discussion arose in the early 1660s about the advisability of permitting Jews to settle in the colonies (meaning chiefly the West Indies), both supporters and opponents assumed that the Jews would play an important part in the West India trade, if given the opportunity. The supporters – mostly plantation owners – thought that Jewish competition would lessen their dependance on English merchants and enable them to do better business. The merchants, fearing what the plantation owners hoped for, maintained that if Jews were given liberty to trade with the colonies, they themselves would be driven out of the trade.[1] These opinions were only natural in view of the intensive activity of Dutch Jews in the West India trade. Much of the trade with Barbados, which had been English since the beginning of the seventeenth century, was still in the hands of Dutch Jews during the second half of the century.[2] Many of the Jews who had escaped from Brazil, after its re-conquest by Portugal, settled in the West Indies. When the English took Jamaica in 1655 they found a Jewish community there, and at the time of the Jewish Resettlement in England Jews also began to settle in the English West Indian islands.[3]

In other ways, too, conditions seemed favourable to a rapid penetration of the English West India trade by Jews. Unlike the trade to the East Indies, it was not a monopoly of any company, and every English subject was free to trade with the western plantations and to keep agents there. The Spanish and Portuguese Jews were familiar with the products of colonial agriculture, and could trade through Jamaica directly with the Spanish Main.[4] Jewish-Portuguese communities were spread over the English islands and they naturally maintained close connections with their brethren in London. Despite these expectations and apprehensions, however, London's Jews were never to play a very conspicuous part in the West Indies trade proper. A superficial examination may, nevertheless, give a misleading impression. Lively commercial relations did develop between the Jewish communities of the Caribbean area and the Jewish City merchants, and a considerable number of Jewish firms traded to the West Indies, especially to Jamaica and Barbados, but nonetheless there can be no doubt that the West India trade was comparatively of little importance as a field of Jewish commercial activity, and as such ranked much below the coral-diamond trade, the Portuguese and Spanish trades, and the exchange trade.

What is the basis for this conclusion and how can it be explained? None of the major Jewish City firms is known to have traded to the West Indies, excepting always those who imported precious metals through Jamaica. This business did not, however, from its very nature, truly belong to the West India trade and was not regarded as part of it, but was rather classed as a branch of the Iberian-American trade. Major houses, like those of the Francos and of Benjamin Mendes da Costa, though using Jamaica as a basis for their contraband trade with Spanish America, did not, apparently, import West Indian products like sugar or cotton.

Documents intended to point out the value of Jewish business activity for England's international trade are a very good source for estimating the comparative importance of the Jews in its various branches, since nothing was omitted which might strengthen the author's argument. There are three documents of this kind, petitions submitted by the Jews of London, two of the seventeenth century, and the third dated 1738. To these can be added Philo-patriae's pamphlet of 1753, which is the most detailed contemporary exposition of the Jews' role in England's commerce. Two of the petitions are on behalf of the Jews of the West Indies. The first petition, of 1689, did not concern the West India trade in particular, but was designed to prevent the imposition of a special tax on English Jews. The author pointed out the importance of the Jews as exporters of woollen goods and as importers of precious metals and diamonds. Significantly, it makes no mention of West India trade or of West Indian products.[5] The second petition, submitted in February 1696 by Isaac Corea, Isaac Pereira, and Joseph Henriques, argued against a proposal that only English-born people should be allowed to act as merchants and agents in the colonies and was submitted in the name of 'those of the Hebrew nation residing in London . . . on behalf of their brethren, merchants and factors in His Majesty's Plantations'. The petition stated that the trade of the West Indian Jews was 'in goods sent them from England, for which they make return in product of their respective plantations'. It also stressed the importance of the West Indian Jews in the trade with the Spanish colonies.[6] This petition dates from a period in which Jews seem to have been more prominent in West India trade than they were later, and yet it really says very little. It does not argue that Jews played a significant part in the trade, but only that they were active in it. On the other hand, it does say that they are prominent in trade with the Spanish colonies. The distinction, obviously, was not accidental. The petition of 1738 was submitted on behalf of the Jews of Jamaica by many Jewish and Christian City merchants, who stated that they 'are either greatly interested in trade to the said island or greatly concerned in interest for the preservation and encouragement of the commerce to it'.[7] This statement cannot, however, be considered as proof for intensive Jewish activity in the Jamaica trade proper. The statement is somewhat ambiguous, and it should also be remembered that many of the signatories were not Jews; many of the Jews who signed the petition no doubt had a stake in the Jamaica contraband trade with the Spanish colonies and could therefore say truthfully that they had a considerable interest in the Jamaica trade. This does not mean that they consigned goods for use in Jamaica itself or imported the island's products.

It is quite clear that Joseph Salvador ('Philo-patriae') regarded the West India trade as being of secondary importance from the Jewish point of view. He stresses the importance of Jews in the coral-diamond trade, in the trade to Spain, Portugal, and their colonies, in the importation of precious metals to England and their re-export to Holland, as well as in the exchange business. The Jamaica trade is also mentioned, but only as part of a list of branches of commerce in which Jews were active, but obviously not prominent, and again with stress on the contraband trade: 'There are among the Jews many useful men in other branches, especially among our silk, cotton and Jamaica trades, and in the trade from the last place to the Spanish Main they are of great utility; this is a trade which yields large sums of bullion to the nation'.[8]

The conclusion that the West India trade was not an important Jewish branch is illustrated by the balances of the firm of Joseph and Menasseh Mendes of Speightstown, Barbados, covering the period 1681–1709. Although the house of the Mendes brothers was one of the foremost Jewish firms of Barbados, its average annual turnover was less than £3,000. Furthermore, a considerable part of the proceeds received from the sale of goods imported by the firm from England had to be returned there in bills of exchange instead of being invested in West Indian goods destined for England. The foothold which Jewish firms succeeded in maintaining in England's trade with the West Indies was apparently extremely restricted and precarious (see Appendix B).

The reasons for the Jews' weakness in the West India trade are not difficult to discover – they were closely connected with the special character which that trade assumed in the eighteenth century. Sugar became the major export item of the British islands, while the importance of other products declined. The cultivation of sugar cane was profitable only on large plantations which became the characteristic form of land ownership on these islands. The plantation owners showed a growing tendency to dispense with the services of the local merchant and to consign their products directly to agents at London or Bristol, who also saw to it that their West Indian principals received the European goods which they required. The plantation owners were usually in debt to their English agents and dependent on their goodwill.[9] The West India merchants were a small and closed group, and it seems that there was no Jew among them.[10] The Jews trading to the West Indies stood outside this small circle, and they apparently were the only ones who consigned goods to the Islands on their own account.[11] However, the scope for independent business activity was shrinking rapidly and what survived was mainly due to the Jamaica contraband trade in which Jews, as we have seen, were very active.

An unidentified author, writing at the beginning of the nineteenth century, thought that the decline of the Jews of Barbados was due to the rise of the English out-ports at London's expense:

They are as a people very much reduced in numbers and wealth, and are little more than retailers. The causes of this declension appear to be chiefly those mentioned below, growing out of the wonderful rise of Liverpool, and commerce taking an entire new direction from thence. The canal system and the machinery in that part of England have raised the commerce of Liverpool beyond any competition, either in prices or expedition, and the Jews having been supplied from London in big measure, they have lost in succession the linen trade, the cotton goods trade, the hardware and pottery trades and the bullion trade.[12]

The passage is interesting in that it shows that by the early nineteenth century the Jews of Barbados had ceased to be of any importance in the island's overseas trade, but it seems that the author had either exaggerated the part which they had played in earlier times or was thinking of a very early period of colonial commerce. It is also extremely doubtful whether the Jewish decline can be ascribed to the rise of Liverpool. All evidence seems to show that the Jews were being pushed out of the West India trade long before Liverpool began seriously to rival London, and had the Jews had a strong hold on the trade, they would in all probability not have been dislodged by a mere change in the relative importance of English ports. A much more plausible explanation was suggested by the late Professor Richard Pares, when describing the decline of the Nevis merchant class as a result of the development of direct relations between plantation owners and English merchants:

This stagnation of commercial activity in Nevis is illustrated by the decline of the Jews. As late as 1724 they were still estimated to be a quarter of the population of Charlestown, and doing more than their fair share of the trade, but there was little trace of them a century later.[13]

At a time when the Jewish merchants of the British West Indies were already undergoing a process of economic eclipse, the Jewry of North America was still at the very beginning of its development. Small communities were spread over various ports – Boston, New York, Philadelphia, Charleston, and Savannah. But the economic importance of these groups was negligible, and although commercial relations existed between the Jewish merchants of

North America and of England, they evidently did not amount to much.[14]

Basically, the situation was not unlike that which we have seen in the West India trade. Here, too, there was one principal product – tobacco – which throughout the eighteenth century was the most important export item of the 13 colonies and, as far as exports to England were concerned, overshadowed all other products.[15] Like sugar, tobacco required large plantations, and the North American plantation owners, like their counterparts in the West Indies, maintained direct connections with agents in England or sold their tobacco through American agents in Virginia and Maryland. Most of the latter were Scots,[16] while Jewish merchants in the two tobacco colonies were few in number.[17] To judge from the lack of positive evidence to the contrary, neither the Jews of England nor those of the colonies were prominent in the Anglo-American tobacco trade. The fact that Philo-patriae did not mention tobacco or North America in his review of the economic activity of England's Jews, can be taken as conclusive proof that this impression is correct.

It is also supported by what is known about a number of Jewish houses who enjoyed a good standing in Anglo-American trade, such as that of the Franks family. The Franks belonged to the uppermost strata of Jewish business in both England and North America. Abraham Franks had been one of the earliest Jewish brokers in London. His sons Isaac and Aaron were very successful in business and established one of the best-known Jewish commercial houses in the City. A third brother, Jacob, emigrated to America and established a house in Philadelphia. His sons, Naphtali and Moses, married their English cousins, the daughters of Isaac and Aaron. Naphtali moved back to London and maintained from there business connections with his brother Moses in Philadelphia. After a time Moses, too, returned to England and became an important City merchant.[18] There is nothing to show that the Franks were active in the tobacco trade. What is known about their business, outside the coral-diamond trade in which they were one of the leading firms, mostly concerns contracts for the supply of goods to the British Army in the Western hemisphere. In 1740 Naphtali Franks had a hand in the transactions of Sampson Levy, who had undertaken to supply the British forces in Jamaica. It was agreed that supplies should be sent from New York, and the handling of the affairs at that place was entrusted to Jacob and Moses Franks.[19] During the Seven Years' War, Moses Franks, who had in the meantime moved to London, had a part in a big contract for supplying British forces in Jamaica and was one of the two partners empowered by the rest to supervise the execution of the contract.[20] Franks continued to do business with the Government and held a permanent contract from the Treasury up to 1776.[21] The Franks' intensive business activity in this field stands in sharp contrast to their apparent lack of participation in the regular branches of Anglo-American Commerce.

The Jews of London evidently did not play an important part in the trade with the British colonies in the Western hemisphere and had a very small share in the importation of their agricultural products. No doubt they exported considerable quantities of 'dry goods', but a large part of these were not destined for the British colonies at all, being sent to Spanish America. The balance was returned to England either in precious metals or in bills of exchange.

Chapter 4
The India trade

There is good reason to suppose that the India trade was the most important field of Jewish business activity in the eighteenth century – not, however, the regular India trade, which was a monopoly of the East India Company, but one special branch of it, namely the coral-diamond trade. London achieved its position in the diamond trade 300 years ago as the result of the immigration of Jewish diamond merchants from Holland and Portugal, and later also from Leghorn and Germany. The growth of the English diamond trade is already mentioned in a resolution of the Court of Directors of the East India Company passed in 1684,[1] and 11 years later the centralization of the trade in English hands was regarded as an accomplished fact by the diamond merchants of London. They stated in a petition to the East India Company:

> That the petitioners have for near forty years past, been permitted without interruption to trade to the East Indies in diamonds and all sorts of jewells and precious stones, which they have managed so much to the advantage of the nation, that the diamond trade, formerly driven by the way of Italy and Portugall, is become allmost a sole English trade.[2]

Private business letters dating from the beginning of the eighteenth century show that London was supplying uncut diamonds to France and Germany, that the quantity of Indian diamonds available in London strongly influenced the state of the market in these countries, and that fluctuations in the demand for stones there had immediate repercussions in London. In 1707 for example one London merchant wrote to Madras about the unstable situation in Germany after a Swedish raid into Saxony: 'this effect it has, that at present there is no demand for diamonds from thence which there used to be'.[3]

The advantages which England enjoyed from its dominant position in the trade were pointed out by the diamond merchants whenever they tried to gain concessions from the East India

Company or from the State. They usually added a warning that if the desired concessions were withheld England might lose the diamond trade. In the petition of 1713 the merchants stated: 'That the diamond trade for Europe hath centered here at least seventy years [sic] by which the nation upon a modest computation gained heretofore at least twenty thousand pounds per annum.'[4] Twenty years later the diamond merchants, who claimed to be exporters of diamonds and jewels 'into France, Spain, Portugal, Germany, Flanders, and other foreign countrys', protested to the Lords of the Treasury against the publication of figures relating to the import and export of diamonds, 'which is not practiced in any other parts of Europe and if not disused in this Kingdom there is great reason to fear the intire loss of this valuable trade which England now possesses in a much greater degree than any other nation.'[5] The evidence of the diamond merchants may perhaps be regarded as biased, but the facts were similarly stated by others who had a less direct interest in the trade. In 1715 the Court of Directors recommended the General Court of the East India Company to allow the export of silver for the purchase of diamonds. The recommendation opened as follows:

> That it be represented to the Generall Court as the unanimous opinion of this Court that the licensing of the trade of diamonds, on the Company's ships, is of advantage to the nation in Generall, by making it the centre of the diamond trade, which other nations would be glad of.[6]

The Act of Parliament of 1732 which abolished customs duties on diamonds and other precious stones opened with a description of England's paramount position in the trade: 'Whereas this Kingdom is now become the great mart for diamonds and other precious stones and jewels, from whence most foreign countries are supplied'.[7]

Though London became the great centre of the diamond trade, with a virtual monopoly in the importation of uncut diamonds from India,[8] most of the diamond industry stayed in Amsterdam. This industry too was largely in the hands of Jews.[9] The diamond business thus became one of the major components of Anglo-Dutch commerce. The uncut diamonds which reached London from the East, and later also from Brazil, were usually sent to Amsterdam for cutting and polishing. But London not only imported uncut diamonds, it had a further function as a distribution centre for polished stones. Jeffries maintained in the middle of the eighteenth century that three-quarters of the products of the foreign diamond industry were sold through London's diamond merchants.[10]

While London was rapidly becoming Europe's central market for diamonds, a similar process took place in India. English Madras took the place of Portuguese Goa as the chief purchaser of diamonds from the mines. For a period of about 25 years after the Resettlement, the Jewish merchants of London continued to maintain their old connections with Goa, directly or through Surat. But with the passing of the first generation of immigrants, the old ties began to loosen and the merchants directed their business to the English settlement which was best situated geographically: Madras or, as it was usually then known among Europeans, Fort St George. Surat, which during the second half of the seventeenth century had served as a link between London and Goa, now lost its importance as a diamond market. In the resolutions passed by the Court of Directors of the East India Company in the 1680s, Surat and Fort St George were both mentioned as centres of the diamond trade, but the rules adopted by the Company in 1713 speak only of Fort St George.[11] Goa gradually lost her importance as a diamond market after the turn of the century. Henceforth it was not a serious competitor for Madras, though apparently it still had some importance as a market for low grade stones. In 1703–04 Sir Stephen Evance was still sending silver to Goa for the purchase of diamonds, and in 1734 there were large quantities of second-rate diamonds to be had there.[12]

Between 1680 and 1690 the first Jewish merchants of London settled in Madras. In December 1684 James de Paiva was permitted to proceed to India with wife and servants[13] after the Company had consented in principle to the settlement of Jews at Madras. The Directors were apparently not quite happy about this decision: they still hoped for the success of the Company's own diamond trade, and were jealous of the Jewish merchants. In February 1684 they wrote to the Council at Fort St George:

We writt you last Year to permitt the Jews to reside at the ffort . . . but nothing of any value shall go consigned by our ships to any of them or any other free merchant, but to our agent or some of our councill, which we hope may prevent their spoiling our diamond trade, our resolution being to continue our endeavours to make your place the mart for that commodity.[14]

This ambition was soon to be realized, but it was the private merchants, and not the Company, who brought it about.

In 1687 we already find six Anglo-Jewish merchants at Madras; besides James de Paiva there were Isaac de Porto and Francis Marques, as well as three who had been mentioned in 1683 as 'interloping Jews at Covelon':[15] Bartolomeo Rodrigues, Domingo de Porto and Alvaro da Fonseca.[16] In the century which elapsed between the arrival of the first Jewish merchant – James de Paiva – at Madras in 1686, and the departure of the last one – Moses de Castro – in 1786, there were only very short periods without at least one Anglo-Jewish diamond merchant at Madras.

Within a few years after the settlement of Jewish merchants at Madras, Indian diamonds were being exported mainly through that port. In a petition to Parliament the Jews of London stated:

That the market for diamonds in the East Indies was formerly at Goa (belonging to the Portuguese) and by the means and industry of the Jews the market hath been brought to the English factories, and by that means England has in a manner the sole management of that precious commodity, and all foreigners bring their monies into this Kingdom to purchase the said diamonds.[17]

Madras' position in the diamond trade was threatened for several years by the activity of the New East India Company from its base at Masulipatam.[18] This threat was removed, however, by the unification of the two companies, and the Secretary of the Company wrote to Thomas Pitt at Madras: 'Since ye rivalship of Metchlepatam, backed with the New Company's trade, their President there and ye appendages thereto belonging are now removed, Ffort St. George must be ye centre of all the diamond trade, the China etc. country trade.'[19] And indeed, Madras enjoyed for the next 70 years a position similar to that which London had gained in Europe as the centre of the diamond trade. There can be no doubt that during this period the greater part of India's diamond exports passed through these two centres. As late as 1766 Joseph Salvador maintained that the proceeds from coral sales could be invested in diamonds only at Madras, and that this was not possible in Bengal and on the Malabar Coast.[20] But, while London maintained its central position in the diamond trade, Madras lost its paramouncy to Benares after 1765.

Outside this coral-diamond trade, the private merchant had only limited possibilities for participation in the East India trade. The interloping days of the seventeenth century were over; the East India Company reigned supreme and no extensive private trade was possible without its permission. Except for a limited list of goods in which the Company permitted private merchants to trade, there remained only one breach in its monopoly: the 'privileges' of the ships' officers employed in its service. The officers were allowed to take a certain quantity of goods on each voyage, the value depending on the officer's rank. They were, however, often unable to finance this trade from their own resources and had to resort to merchants for assistance, thus giving them a limited opportunity for participation in Indian trade. It could be done in two ways: by buying the 'privilege' outright or by advancing the officer a bottomry or respondentia loan. These loans always included maritime insurance, the borrower being obliged to return the amount lent him only if the journey had been successfully completed. Damage or loss at sea, of the kind usually covered by insurance policies, were at the risk of the lender. The money was returned on completion of the journey, plus a certain percentage which represented interest as well as the insurance premium. We know of a number of Jewish merchants who indirectly invested in Indian trade by advancing bottomry loans. Sampson Gideon, Aaron Franks, Anthony Lopes Suasso, Francis Salvador, Moses Mendes da Costa, Benjamin Mendes da Costa, and Moses Lamego made bottomry contracts with officers of East India ships,[21] and we shall see that during the 1750s the related respondentia loans came to form an integral part of the Anglo-Indian diamond trade (see pp. 126–9 below).

The 'privileges' did not, however, offer the private merchant opportunities for large-scale investment in Eastern trade. He could of course acquire an interest in the Company's business by buying its shares, and if he had large holdings, he had a chance of being elected a Director and taking part in the conduct of the Company's affairs. To Jews even this road was closed, as they were never elected to the Court of Directors. Theoretically a Jew could be elected a Director, but in fact this never happened during this century. The only Jews who succeeded in acquiring an influential position in the Company were Joseph Salvador and, to a smaller degree, Aaron Franks. Even they were only able to do so because of violent internal rivalries within the Company.[22]

The only part of the East India trade which was left entirely to private enterprise was that concerned with the distribution of goods imported from the East. It was an important function because a considerable portion of Europe's trade with India and China passed through London. Already in the seventeenth century the English East India Company became the major European importer of Indian cloth and large quantities of cloth were re-exported from England to the Continent.[23] In the eighteenth century the English Company also gained the upper hand in its competition with the Dutch East India Company for the Chinese tea trade, and after 1740 London became the chief centre of distribution for Chinese tea, which was rapidly becoming a popular beverage.[24] Like other colonial goods re-exported by England, the East India wares were distributed with the help of the secondary centre at Amsterdam, from where they were sent to Germany and other areas. At the time of the public sales held by the East India Company, many Continental merchants flocked to London, and among them there was always a considerable number of Jews who were very active in certain branches of Anglo-Dutch trade. What do we know about the Jew's role as purchasers and distributors of East India goods? Unfortunately only a few lists of buyers have been preserved in the Company's archives and we must try to extract information from other sources.

An interesting kind of evidence for the importance of Jewish buyers at the sales of the East India Company are the instructions issued for the postponement of such sales in order that they should not coincide with Jewish holydays. An early example is the adjournment of a sale till after the Tabernacles holiday of 1679: 'The East India Company having several ships come home, began their sale as usual last week. But because the Jews were engaged in their feast of Tabernacles it was adjourned, but is now begun again.'[25] For many years after 1720 a Jew named Henry Eleazar used to supply the East India Company with lists giving the dates of impending Jewish holidays, and in 1774 he offered to prepare a calendar of holidays up to the year 1867 'to be a guide in appointing the days for selling the Company's goods'. In 1779 his widow offered to sell the Company a list of Jewish Holydays up to 1804.[26] The advance information which the Company received from Eleazar did not prevent hitches occurring from time to time. There are several recorded requests by Jewish buyers for postponement of sales on account of Jewish holidays, to which the East India Company seems usually to have acceded.[27]

The same problem, seen from the Jewish side, is mentioned in the Prager letters. On the eve of the feast of Tabernacles of 1776 Jacob Prager of Amsterdam approached his brother Yehiel with the following request:

> The cloth merchants have been informed that the sale of damaged cloth has been fixed exactly on the holiday of Succoth [Tabernacles]. They request you to arrange with the Directors [of the East India Company] there that the sale be postponed for 14 days. They have asked Blauw's firm to write about it and have asked us too. They think that Simon Tanhum has done this so that Jews from here [i.e. Amsterdam] would not be able to attend and he alone has the choice; or Jews would have to leave here immediately after Rosh Hashona [the Jewish New Year] and that does not suit many people here. So, if you can arrange this, it would be a good thing and another good deed on behalf of all Israel.[28]

Jews were indeed numerous among buyers at sales of damaged cloth. We do not know for certain why Jews 'specialized' in this particular field, but the fact itself is not in doubt. The documents show clearly that Ashkenazi merchants of London and Amsterdam dominated the market for this sort of goods. A solitary surviving list of buyers dating from 1721/22, already points to this. The list does not indicate the value of the goods bought by each merchant, but Jewish names, mostly of Ashkenazim, are prominent among the buyers of cloth. The Ashkenazi names are: Levy, Moses, Salomons, and Gompertz. The Sephardi buyers were Supino and Franco.[29]

The Prager Papers show that Jewish merchants from Amsterdam attended all sales of Indian cloth held by the East India Company in London. In May 1779 Jacob Prager wrote that his brother-in-law Levy had gone to London 'in a fishing boat filled to capacity with Jews',[30] and in January 1784 he told his brother about an acquaintance, the merchant Jacob ben Moshe: 'Little Jacob goes over with this mail, together with a dozen other Jews, for the sale of damaged cloth',[31] and a few days later: 'again there is half a congregation of Jews there for the sale'.[32] On 13 February he reported: 'here comes another load of Jews going over with this mail'.[33] A year later Jacob Prager wrote again 'with this mail-boat several Jews, of the lower sort, are going over for the sale of cloth',[34] and eight years later Jacob's nephew, Isaac, wrote in a similar vein: 'Many Jews have gone over with this packet-boat for the sale of cloth.'[35]

A document concerning a public sale of damaged cloth held by the East India Company in 1778 sheds light upon the part which Jews played in these sales.[36] We learn from it that during the 1770s combinations of buyers were formed before each sale by the Jewish merchant Simon Daniels, who was known among Jews as Simon Tanhum. Having formed his combination, Daniels used to appear as the only buyer at the public sales of damaged cloth.

Daniels himself described how the combinations were organized:

> [Daniels] has been for fifteen years or thereabouts concerned in buying, and for the greatest part of that time has been the principal buyer of damaged piece goods at the said East India Company sales. And as such goods at such sales, if the buyers and bidders are few in number, are to be bought cheaper than they would otherwise be, it has been customary for the persons, or the principal part of the persons, dealing in such goods to permit this defendant ... Simon Daniels to purchase the same by his broker, and afterwards the goods to be valued and resold to or among the persons in the said trade, at sums valued at. And if the same are valued at more than the original price – the difference to be considered as the profits, and such profits, after the deduction of forty-six pounds, ten shillings per cent to the second buyers, to be divided among the said persons. But it has been on such occasion customary for this defendant Simon Daniels to have the management and distribution of such profits in such shares and proportions as he should think the several parties interested therein were or ought to have, on considering the nature and extent of their dealings in such trade or in such articles of trade.[37]

Daniels goes on to explain that from the point of view of the Company there is only one buyer, he himself, and he alone is responsible for payments and has to bear all losses. On the other hand, Daniels' partners shared any profits he was able to make,

this being the price they received for staying away from the sale
and letting Daniels have a free field.

The big textile merchants were not the only ones whom
Daniels had to bribe in order to eliminate competition at the
public sale, as he himself explained in the following passage:

> at the India Company's said sale several hundred of the poorer
> sort of people attended, of whom the greatest part were Jews,
> with a view, as they pretended, of becoming bidders and
> purchasers. And it has been usual for such sort of persons to
> attend at former sales made by the said India Company, and –
> to prevent such sort of persons from becoming bidders – it has
> been usual for this defendant Simon Daniels to give them his
> promise that a certain number of shares of the profits which
> should arise on the goods in the manner aforesaid, should be
> divided among them by him. And it has been usual for such
> persons, on such promise being made them, to depart without
> bidding. And the shares so promised to such people by this
> defendant Simon Daniels were always distributed among them
> by him in such manner as he judged proper, they always leav-
> ing it to him to make the distribution thereof.[38]

After Daniels had bought the goods from the Company a
second sale was held, in which the purchased goods were re-sold
to various merchants. There is a full list of the buyers at such a
secondary sale, held in 1778, including the quantity bought by
each person and the price paid. The list shows that the total value
of goods sold was a little over £24,000. Of 25 buyers 12 were
Jews, but they bought much more than their proportional share.
The biggest buyers were the organizers of the combination,
Daniels and Levy Barent Cohen. Daniels bought goods worth
about £10,000, approximately 40 per cent of the total, while
Cohen bought cloth for about £3,500, and the combined share of
Jewish merchants amounted to £18,258, or a little over 75 per
cent of the value of goods sold.[39]

The Prager Papers show that similar combinations, designed
to produce conditions of a buyers' market at the Company's sales,
were also prevalent during the 1780s, but they also indicate that
agreements resulting in such 'corners' were sometimes difficult to
reach. Before the sale of 1778 Jacob Prager wrote to his brother:
'If the Jews could agree among themselves, it would be possible
to earn a lot of money in damaged cloth. But who can hold such

people together? Only the devil could keep order here. In our
opinion there will be murder there, seeing the sort of people who
are there now.'[40]

We have seen that on that occasion Simon Daniels nevertheless
succeeded in forming the combination, but in 1784 Yehiel Prager
reported from London that the efforts to reach an agreement
among the buyers had almost failed 'because the Jews have made
the Gentiles too clever' and had also quarrelled among themselves. 'This is an old fashion among Jews', wrote his brother
Jacob in reply.[41] Even so, a combination was again formed, and
three years later David Prager wrote from Amsterdam that they
had heard 'that there was a general combination there [in London]
and that they have bought very cheaply, and have even received
a quantity of goods gratis, receiving money in addition – the
drawback being more than what they gave for the goods'.[42]

We must not, however, conclude that the distribution of Indian
cloth was dominated by Jews. In the first place, what we have
learned about their activity in this field concerned solely damaged
cloth. Moreover, all the merchants who participated in their trade
were relatively small people. The organizer of the buyers' combinations, Simon Daniels (Tanhum), is often mentioned in the
letters of the Prager brothers, who sometimes acted as his agents
and took care of his cloth consignments. It is clear from their
attitude towards him that he was not a substantial merchant. In
January 1782 Jacob Prager warned his brother in London not to
get too involved with Daniels because he engaged in smuggling,[43]
and in February he wrote that they did not consider Daniels to
be entirely reliable as all his goods at Amsterdam were pawned.[44]
Some months later Jacob Prager reported about Daniels-Tanhum:
'All his goods are Jews' small wares, and not fit for a proper
merchant, but for people who travel with them to markets and
fairs'.[45]

In October 1782 Yehiel Prager wrote that Daniels was unable
to draw in London[46] and in March 1783 his brother Jacob told
him that 'this Tanhum [Daniels] ... is trying by all means to trade
without money'.[47] Daniels' partner, Levy Barent Cohen, was also
only a minor merchant, and the attitude of the Pragers towards
him was one of haughty contempt. Another merchant often
mentioned in the Prager letters was Jacob ben Moshe, who, as
Jacob Moses, took part in the sale of 1778, and was a regular
visitor to the damaged cloth sales of the East India Company.

We have Jacob Prager's description of Moses' business methods: 'He has got Gentiles here. When he has goods and cannot sell by the time he must pay for them,[48] he pawns them and then sells everything without giving credit, because he is unable to do such extensive business with his own capital.'[49] The letter also throws some light on the method employed by Moses in the sale of the goods he bought in London: 'Jacob ben Moshe has good children who travel to all markets and fairs and sell many goods.'

These persons could scarcely have ranked as major distributors of Indian cloth. Indeed, two extant petitions by London merchants and exporters of Indian cloth bear only a single Jewish signature each: Benjamin Mendes da Costa signed such a petition in 1740[50] and the brothers Modigliani in 1779.[51] Both were well-known Jewish firms. It would seem that lesser houses usually had to content themselves with damaged goods with which the big houses would not bother. Here again, as in the exchange business, the Jews did not rank among the foremost houses, even though these were branches in which they played a special part. The only business in which they were truly dominant was the coral-diamond trade.

PART TWO

The Diamond and Coral
Trade 1660–1800

Chapter 5
The beginnings

Up to the second quarter of the eighteenth century the only known sources of uncut diamonds were India and, to a lesser extent, Borneo. Indian diamonds had been earlier known in the Mediterranean world[1] but a regular export trade had begun only as a result of the intensification of trade between India and Europe in the sixteenth century.[2] Although transport by sea was not, for the diamond trade, such an overwhelming advantage as it was for heavier goods, it gave an important stimulus to the trade by reducing the risk of the voyages. At the same time the diamond industry developed in Europe. It was first centred in Antwerp, but shifted to Amsterdam in the seventeenth century. New methods of cutting and polishing were evolved, and it was not long before Indian diamonds were being sent back to their country of origin after having been cut and polished in Europe.[3] Italy and Portugal were also early centres[4] and in both Jews apparently played an important role as lapidaries and jewel merchants. The Portuguese, as the pioneers of the European trade with India, were the first to import diamonds by the new sea route. The French traveller Tavenier, who was something of an expert on diamonds, stated in the 1660s that Goa had formerly been the great centre of the diamond trade.[5] This seems to show that others had already become dominant in the trade during the first half of the seventeenth century, a trend which is also reflected in the papers of the English East India Company.

The East India Company endeavoured from the very first to gain a foothold in the diamond trade with the East. The English had some success, despite sharp competition from the Dutch both in Borneo and in India, and in the years 1615–21 there was a regular trade in Borneo stones which were sold in public sales held by the East India Company in London.[6] The Company also encouraged its agents at Masulipatam to buy stones, but they were hampered by lack of means and by the monopolization of the trade by the Dutch. In April 1632 the English agents reported to London that the Dutch had established themselves near the diamond mine 'so that nowe the trade of diamonds is mainely and principallest followed by them'.[7] The English did not even know the prices of diamonds at the mines! Notwithstanding this discouraging report, the Directors of the Company in London persisted in their demand for diamonds. In March 1624 the Council at Batavia, on orders from London, instructed the Masulipatam agents not to miss any opportunity of purchasing diamonds. In June the agents were asked to invest 10–20,000 Rials: 'If diamonds be at the same rates as in the time of Mr. Methwold, we preferr your imploiements in diamonds before all other investments.'[8] But the Company's enthusiasm for the diamond business did not last. After 1625 the Company permitted its servants in the East and officers of the East India ships to carry on a trade in diamonds. The rule of 1609 which prohibited private trade in diamonds[9] fell into abeyance, and in the period between 1630 and 1660 uncut diamonds figured as an important item in the estates of many Company servants who had died in the East.

It is only possible to guess at the reasons why the Company relinquished the diamond trade to private persons. Possibly the entrenched position of the Dutch in the trade discouraged the Company, but it may well be that a more basic factor was involved: experience had shown that the diamond trade did not fit into the monopolistic, joint-stock framework of the East India trade. The Company had to learn the same lesson again in the 1680s, when it made another attempt to exclude private persons from the diamond trade with the East. In 1650 the Company gave official recognition to a state of affairs which had existed *de facto* for 20 years. Permission was granted to ship-owners – the Company had no ships of its own – and to ships' officers to import diamonds, pearls and other precious stones from India.[10] It is not quite clear whether this rule applied also to the Company's servants in the East, but there can be no doubt that they too used to send diamonds to Europe. In 1659 Henry Revington complained to the Directors in London about some of the Company's servants: 'neyther doe they understand more (some of them) but to buy amber-greece, pearls, cuff and diamonds'.[11] The English therefore did not play an important role during the first half of the seventeenth century in the importation of uncut diamonds to Europe, though on the whole they were steadily gaining ground in their competition with the Dutch and Portuguese for the trade to the East. The Company people imported stones on their private account, but there is no evidence whatsoever for the existence of a regular and organized importation of diamonds into England during this period. There is no trace in the papers of the East India Company of names of English merchants who imported diamonds before 1660. Thereafter the situation changed completely.

In the early 1660s the East India Company discovered that unauthorized persons were carrying on a trade in precious stones with India, under the cover of the privileges which had been granted in 1650 to owners and officers of East India ships.[12] The Court of Directors discussed the problem at the beginning of 1664 and decided not to oppose the new trend. The trade was thrown open to anyone who wished to participate in it, provided he paid certain duties to the Company. Permission was given for the export to and import from India of precious stones and other goods of high value. Exporters had to pay 2 per cent of the value to the Company, and importers had to pay 2 per cent if they were stockholders of the Company, 4 per cent if they were not.[13] We do not know for certain what considerations moved the Directors to take this wise decision. It was probably brought about by a number of factors – past experience, expected profits to be derived from the duties levied by the Company, and perhaps also the personal influence of interested merchants. In the same year diamond exports were declared duty free. The decision provided the basis on which the Anglo-Indian diamond trade was to be carried on for the next 150 years. It made possible the rapid development of England's trade in uncut diamonds, in consequence of which London became the foremost international centre of the diamond trade before the century was out.[14]

Who were the people who became active in the English diamond trade around 1660 and for whose benefit new rules concerning the trade were adopted by the East India Company? It was not by chance that these developments coincided with the settlement of the first Jewish-Portuguese merchants in London. Precious stones were one of the main items in the business affairs of these people, who came at the time chiefly from Holland, with its thriving diamond industry. They, or their fathers, had already been prominent in this branch in Portugal.[15]

In 1662, for example, Matthew Andrews, the President of the Company's factory in Surat, sent diamonds to London 'for the account of several Portuguese'.[16] The same ship brought a parcel of pearls for a certain Mr Dormedo, who is without doubt Manuel Martinez Dormido. He was one of the earliest leaders of the Jewish community in London, who had settled in England in 1654 and became a denizen in 1661.[17] We know the names of several merchants who were active in the trade of precious stones between England and India at that time, as well as something about the character of their connections with India. Among the papers of Sir George Oxenden, who was in charge of the factory in Surat between 1662 and 1669, are a number of letters which he received from Jewish merchants in London during the years 1666–8. These letters show that the merchants employed Oxenden as an agent in India for their business in precious stones. They sent him consignments of silver coins, precious stones (mainly emeralds), and coral, and received uncut diamonds in return. Of special interest is the connection which the Jewish diamond merchants maintained with Portuguese Goa. Fernando Mendes and Alvaro da Costa asked Oxenden to send their emeralds and coral as quickly as possible to their agents at Goa, while he was to sell their silver coins at Surat and make them returns in diamonds.[18] It is impossible to say whether the agents at Goa were Jewish too, but, to judge by their names – Simon Ribero, Simon De Almeida, and Diego da Fonseca-y-Silva – this is not at all improbable.[19]

Two questions arise in connection with this correspondence: whether from the list of Oxenden's correspondents any conclusions can be drawn about the importance of the trade with India in precious stones to the commercial activities of the early Jewish settlers in England, and whether these correspondents are identical with the new element which appeared in the English diamond trade at that time and for whose benefit the East India Company liberalized its rules.

There can be no doubt that Oxenden's London correspondents represented the upper stratum of the Jewish-Portuguese immigration at the time of the Resettlement. Except for Salvador d'Andrade of Venice, who had previously lived in Amsterdam, they were all leading members of the Jewish community in London. It is instructive to compare the names of the Jewish merchants who figure in the Oxenden Papers as importers of diamonds from Goa[20] with the names of Jews who had large current accounts with the London banker Backwell at that time.

Lucien Wolf gave the names of nine people with large accounts (out of 38 Jews who had accounts with Backwell in 1663).[21] Of these nine, one is known to have died before 1666,[22] and of the remaining eight seven were correspondents of Oxenden. This comparison demonstrates in a striking fashion the important place which the precious stones trade with India occupied in the affairs of the Jewish merchants who settled in London. There is also interesting evidence in the Oxenden Papers which shows that these Jewish diamond merchants were none other than the anonymous people who began to import diamonds from India around 1660, at first illegally, later with the Company's blessing. The liberalization of the diamond trade which was introduced in 1664 by the Company met with some resistance in Company circles. Sir Samuel Barnardiston, a member of the Court of Directors,[23] wrote to Oxenden in March 1666: 'I note what are and may be the inconveniences by the Company giveing leave to the Jewes to trade in dyamonds etc., and I believe in time they will grow weary of it, and during this interruption by the warr will hardly be persuaded to make any new orders'.[24] Barnardiston evidently regarded the Jews as the chief beneficiaries of the liberalization of the diamond trade. The new rules were obviously adopted in order to enable them to carry on the trade in a legal fashion. Evidence connected with alien duties confirms these conclusions. In 1667 a customs official at the port of London, by the name of Dawson, demanded that the East India Company pay scavage – a sort of alien duty – on diamonds imported from India. It seems that Dawson was satisfied for a time with the doubling of the gratuity paid to him by the Company,[25] but when he raised the problem again in 1671 the Company agreed to pay scavage for diamonds imported by aliens.[26] There can be little doubt that these aliens were mostly, if not exclusively, Jews.

As we have seen, the Company demanded higher dues from diamond importers who were not stockholders. This meant that Jews, on the whole, were at a disadvantage compared with non-Jewish competition, as most of them were still aliens and as such could not be stockholders in the Company. It was not until the appearance of a real stock exchange that the Company ceased to be a closed association. Nor is it even certain that denization enabled the Jews to join the Company; the Jewish merchant Alvaro da Costa was accepted as member only after being naturalized by Act of Parliament.[27] This discrimination against aliens resulted in attempts to import diamonds belonging to aliens under the names of people who were stockholders. In 1676 the Court of Directors decreed that all freedmen of the Company who received diamonds from India must declare that they were the true owners, 'that the Company may not be defrauded of the four percent due from foreigners, as freight for the same'. It appears that among those who allowed their names to be used by 'aliens' in order to enable them to pay the lower rate of 2 per cent was Alvaro da Costa, who by now was a freeman. The Court of Directors ordered in 1675 that no permission be granted to da Costa to export precious metals without its sanction. In December the Directors allowed him to export gold, but he had to declare that the consignment was his own property. A little time later he was caught red-handed 'having exported a considerable sum of money for the purchase of diamonds without paying freight'. The Court eventually agreed to deliver to him the diamonds which had been consigned to him from India on payment of 6 per cent instead of 2 per cent to the Company and an additional £10 to the poor box. Only in 1680 were foreigners put on an equal footing with Englishmen.

Jews are also mentioned as being involved in smuggling, from which the diamond trade was never free. In March 1677 the Company informed the Captain of an East Indiaman about to sail for India that 'they had particular information that some Jews and others have gone to the Downs and intend to put a considerable quantity of bullion on board the ships bound for Surat, without permission or payment of freight'.[28]

The Jewish merchants maintained their former business connections, with Holland on the one hand and with Goa on the other, after they had settled in London. Thus began the process which was to make London the foremost international centre of the trade in uncut diamonds. Francis de Lis (Jacob Berakhel), who had been a correspondent of Oxenden's in the 1660s, received in January 1675 a certificate from the East India Company 'touching their practice of delivering diamonds and other fine goods returned in their ships from India in 1672 and 1673, for account of any Hollanders dwelling in Amsterdam or elsewhere, to their attorney in their absence, notwithstanding the late war [The Third Anglo-Dutch War]'.[29] There is clear evidence here that already at that time Amsterdam received part of the uncut stones needed for its diamond industry through agents in London.

At least a portion of the stones sent to London through the English factory at Surat were still ordered from Portuguese Goa. In January 1675 the President of the Surat factory complained about the hostile attitude of the Portuguese. This hostility manifested itself, *inter alia*, in a prohibition of diamond exports to England and the seizure of money sent from England for the purchase of diamonds at Goa.[30] It was probably in connection with these difficulties that Gomes Rodrigues (*alias* Abraham Israel de Sequeira) and Diego Rodrigues (*alias* Abraham Hesquiah Marques) asked the Company's permission in 1674 to send out three people to India to recover their effects impounded at Goa. The request was rejected by the Directors. This refusal may have been caused by opposition to the settlement of English Jews emanating from the Company's officials there, for whom diamonds constituted a profitable field for private investment. The opposition weakened only after 1685.

There is some interesting information relating to the connections of Diego Rodrigues-Marques with Goa and with several commercial centres in Europe. Marques, who was born in Lisbon, settled in London and maintained his ties with Portugal to the end of his life.[31] In 1673 diamonds were sent from Goa to Portugal through Marques in London,[32] and his will (1675) supplies details about his widespread diamond trading.[33] Marques owed £400 to John Machado of Goa for diamonds sent to him.[34] The will mentions diamonds – the property of Abraham de Soto – which Marques sent to Antonio and Simon Mendes de Achanda in Venice and emeralds to the value of £4,000 consigned to Gabriel de Medina at Leghorn. Isaac Alvares of London consigned diamonds belonging to Marques to his brother Lewis Alvares at Paris. Lewis de Morais owed him money for precious stones and diamonds. The will also mentions two parcels of diamonds sold to Moses Mocatta, other parcels sold to Emanuel Dias Vas, and three parcels sold to the widow of Melchior Dias and heirs at Amsterdam. Francis de Lis too was at the time of his death in debt to a correspondent at Goa. The East India Company rejected a petition by his widow and the widow of Diego Marques for permission to send the sum due by a ship sailing in the service of the Company.[35]

In spite of the attempt made by the governor of Goa to obstruct the diamond trade with the English the connections were maintained. In 1679 English ships reached London with parcels of diamonds 'brought from Goa and consigned to several merchants strangers and others in Europe'.[36] In 1684 diamond imports from Goa were still so common that a certain Mr Rodrigues (obviously Alfonso Rodrigues *alias* Isaac Israel de Sequeira, son of Gomes Rodrigues who died in 1678) asked the East India Company, in his own name and on behalf of other merchants, to settle once and for all what dues were to be paid for diamonds and so on imported from Goa.[37] The ruling was that importers of diamonds must pay 5 per cent on value, if they had not already paid duty on silver or goods sent out for purchase of the diamonds.

The establishment of Marranos as importers of uncut diamonds in London gave a new character to the trade. It no longer consisted exclusively of chance transactions by Directors of the East India Company, its servants or ships' officers, or of transfers of private fortunes and estates from India. Though this form of diamond imports never disappeared completely, there now existed by its side a regular trade by professional merchants. These merchants consigned to India precious metals (chiefly Spanish pieces-of-eight and gold), precious stones (mainly emeralds), and coral beads, and received uncut diamonds in return. Diamonds were ordered from Holland through London, and probably most diamonds reaching London at that time were sent on to Amsterdam for cutting and polishing.[38] At the same time, the Dutch East India Company found that its diamond trade was becoming less profitable because of the activities of the English private traders, and it was ultimately forced to reduce it to small proportions.[39] There is evidence that diamond imports were on the increase. Sir Samuel Barnardiston complained in 1666 about the small profit derived from the latest diamond consignment, which he partly attributed to 'the greate quantity of dyamonds now come'.[40] It is also reasonable to assume that the rise in the prices of diamonds which took place in India in 1678 was occasioned by an increase in demand.[41] By 1680 relations between the East India Company and the private merchants had been regularized. The trade in precious stones was thrown open to individuals by the rules adopted in 1664. Later, a system of controls was developed by the Company; sea-captains were obliged to report on diamonds and precious stones imported in their ships,[42] and registers of silver exports were compared with those of diamond imports as a check on illegal transactions.[43]

In conclusion it should be noted that this period, during which a group of Jewish diamond merchants established itself in London, marked a turning point in the history of the diamond trade. There is first-hand evidence for this in the memoirs of Glueckel of Hameln, the Jewish business woman of Hamburg. Chaim of Hameln and his wife Glueckel opened a jewellery business at Hamburg after their marriage (between 1660 and 1665). Glueckel, who wrote after 1690, tells that 'at that time [during the early days of the business] the trade in gems was not as flourishing as it is now, and burghers and young engaged couples among the gentiles seldom or never wore jewels. Instead, it was the fashion to wear solid gold chains, and gifts, if the occasion demanded, were all of gold.'[44] Only in later years did diamonds become an important item in the trade of Chaim and Glueckel, with Amsterdam as their chief source of supply. Their son-in-law and their grandchildren appear as diamond merchants in England and India. It is not easy to say whether it was the intensified importation of diamonds, and the subsequent fall in prices, which enabled more people to afford the expensive stones, or whether it was the increased economic prosperity of Europe, the recovery of central Europe from the ravages of the Thirty Years War, and the emergence of a prosperous middle class which brought about an increase in the demand for items of luxury in general and for diamonds in particular. It probably worked both ways. One thing is beyond doubt: the establishment of the Jewish importers of rough diamonds in London was bound up with a rapid development of the European market for polished stones.

The development and prosperity of the diamond trade in the 20 years that had passed since the Jewish Resettlement was reflected in a striking manner in the altered attitude of the East India Company to the trade. Half a century had passed since the Company had given up its own diamond trade. During this period the Company had regarded the trade as a branch of secondary importance, from which their servants and ships' officers were allowed to derive any profit they could get, a privilege which was later extended to all persons interested in the trade. But it seems that the success of the Jewish diamond merchants evoked the envy of the East India Company, and there is evidence showing that in the later seventies the Company again purchased diamonds in India. In 1679 the Court of Directors discussed a proposal to reimpose its monopoly on the diamond trade. The proposal was rejected, 'the Court being satisfied that it would be both difficult and impracticable'.[45] Perhaps they were still under the effect of recent fraudulent activities of the English diamond agent at Madras, Nathaniel Cholmley. In 1678 he had been permitted by the Company to deal in diamonds at Golconda. The Committee of Private Trade was informed in December 1678 'about damage caused by rise of price in diamonds': 'It was found that Nathaniel Cholmley was employed in making the investment returned this year, who for his own, and the advantage and gain of others, has not performed the trust reposed in him.'[46] A year later the same proposal was raised again, and this time an affirmative resolution was passed: 'The Court taking into consideration how the trade for diamonds may for the future be managed . . . upon serious debate had of the said affair, have thought fit and resolved that the sole trade of dyamonds be henceforth appropriated unto the Company and to be prohibited to all other persons whatsoever.'[47] The Company was entitled to deprive private persons of the right to trade in diamonds because it had a general monopoly of trade with India and no private trade could be carried out without its permission.

The Directors were not blind to the difficulties involved in the implementation of this radical change, and in preventing the private merchants from competing with the Company. The Court passed a series of rules with the object of preventing a private trade in diamonds and of compensating the Company's servants in India for their loss of diamond business. This they hoped to achieve by a system of reward and punishment; ships' captains were promised $1\frac{1}{2}$ per cent of the purchase price of all diamonds imported in their ships 'as a gratuity for their care and faithfulness in preventing private trade and traders in diamonds etc. and for their encouragement in the punctual performance of the other covenants of their charter-parties'. Another $1\frac{1}{2}$ per cent was promised to ship-owners, $2\frac{1}{2}$ per cent of the purchase price to be paid to Presidents or Chief Agents of factories where the diamonds were bought for the Company, and $2\frac{1}{2}$ per cent to all other members of the Council. The Directors also decided to let the Presidents or Chief Agents have 25 per cent of all profits exceeding 60 per cent, to be made by the Company in its diamond trade, and another 25 per cent went to the other Council members. A price was offered for any information leading to the discovery of illegal diamond trading. The Directors evidently expected a considerable profit from this newly acquired branch, if they could promise in advance 8 per cent of the purchase price to the various parties whose goodwill was essential for the success of the venture. Side by side with these inducements for good behaviour are threats of dire punishment for offenders. Ship-owners and captains were to pay the Company fines equivalent to the full value of any silver exported or diamonds imported illegally. Captains and other persons serving on East Indiamen were liable to dismissal on a first offence contravening the new rules concerning the diamond trade and the same applied to the Company servants.[48] The Directors also provided new facilities for the transfer of private fortunes to England by the Company's people in India, for which diamonds had served as a convenient means. Bills of exchange drawn on the Company were to be provided for this purpose.[49]

The Company hoped for business on a large scale. Out of a total amount of £380,000 to be invested in the year 1681, £60,000 was earmarked for the purchase of diamonds at Fort St George – over one-third of the sum to be invested at that place.[50] The Company announced its intention to make Fort St George 'the mart of India' for diamonds within a few years.[51] The Company thus adopted every conceivable measure in order to ensure the success of their plan. Yet the monopolization of the diamond trade proved a complete failure. The Court of Directors decided in the summer of 1682 to reverse the decision of 1680 and to reopen the trade to private persons.

What were the reasons which brought about this new turn? The election of Sir Josiah Child in 1681 as Chairman of the Court of Directors, which inaugurated the era of his nearly absolute rule in the Company, may not have been without significance in this connection. Child was well disposed towards the Jewish element in the City and appreciated its commercial importance,[52] and his economic views bore a liberal character. Perhaps it was more than a mere coincidence that Sir Samuel Barnardiston, who had objected in 1666 to the opening of the diamond trade to the Jews, was among the chief opponents of Child in the Court of Directors. Though there is no direct evidence connecting Child's rise to power with the reopening of the diamond trade, it is a reasonable hypothesis.[53] It was perhaps also due to the influence of Child's opinions that the Directors' letters to their Council at Fort St George reflect a change in the attitude towards the private merchants after 1685. They urged a policy of religious toleration as a means for achieving economic prosperity, and explicitly mentioned the Jewish merchants in this connection. This attitude accorded well with Child's views. The new policy was opposed by a number of City merchants who made the complaint against the Company 'that they have permitted the Jews to establish themselves in India, and made them a part of their Government there, which has in a manner given them the entire possession of the diamond trade to the great discouragement and loss of the English subjects.'[54]

There were however substantive reasons which induced the Company to give up the attempt to monopolize the diamond trade. It was frustrated by lack of co-operation on the part of its own officials in India and by the illegal trade to which the diamond merchants resorted as a measure of despair. The President of the Company's factory at Surat left the Directors in no doubt about his negative attitude to the expropriation of the diamond trade, though he expressed appreciation for the measures taken by the Company to compensate its officials in India for the loss of what he described as 'the cheife and only benefitt' they had hitherto enjoyed in the Company's service.[55] One must assume that the Company's people in India pursued the Company's diamond business with something less than their usual vigour, and only part of the money sent out for the purchase of diamonds at Surat was used for that purpose.

The diamond merchants could not comply with the new rules if they were not prepared to acquiesce in the ruin of their business. At least some of them decided to ignore the Company's monopoly. In March 1682 the Court of Directors informed the Portuguese Ambassador:[56]

> That there is an English ship called [   ][57] of London, whereof one Capt. Edward Says comander, is contrary to his Majesty's proclamacon and his royal charter granted unto this Compa[ny], gone forth on a voyage to Goa and thence to Surat in ye East Indies, to the manifest wrong as well of ye crown of Portugal, as of this Compa[ny], many Portuguese Jews being concerned in ye said ship's lading.

The Directors asked the Ambassador that instructions be sent to Goa for the arrest of Captain Says, whose voyage was evidently connected with an illegal trade in diamonds. But only three months later they decided to give up and to allow private merchants to resume their diamond imports from India. The Court passed this resolution 'finding that an open violacon is like to be made on that commerce by interloping ships now gone to India and otherwise'.[58]

Chapter 6
Stabilization and development

A. EAST INDIA COMPANY POLICY TOWARDS THE DIAMOND TRADE

The lesson learned from the failure of the short-lived attempt at monopolization of the diamond trade was not lost upon the Directors of the East India Company and they showed great consistency in framing the new liberal policy. Merchants of precious stones were allowed once more to trade with India, and during the next five years the Council passed a number of further measures calculated to facilitate the private diamond trade and encourage its growth.

The resolution of 1682 described the purpose of rules as 'the encouragement of the adventurers [i.e. shareholders] and all other merchants both English and others'.[1] The rules permitted the merchants to export and import silver, gold, diamonds and other kinds of precious stones, as well as other goods in which the Company was not particularly interested. It is true that the duties imposed were rather high and discriminated against part, at least, of the Jewish merchants; Englishmen had to pay 4 per cent on the value of diamonds etc., and aliens 8 per cent.[2] But only a fortnight after these duties had been fixed the Court decided to lower the rates to 3 per cent and 6 per cent respectively, to abolish the distinction between Englishmen and aliens, and to reintroduce the old one between stockholders and merchants who had no stake in the Company.[3] A duty of 2 per cent was imposed on the export of silver and gold for the purchase of diamonds. It may well be that the former rules constituted an attempt to make things easier for Christian competitors of the Jewish diamond merchants, and that pressure was brought to bear upon the Company in order to prevent it from carrying out this policy. The fact that the Court decided to change the rules reflects its sincere intention to encourage the private trade in diamonds.

In 1683 the Court decided to impose strict limitations on private trade with India, because of the alleged harm which it was causing to the Company's trade. It was, however, explicitly stated that these rules did not impair the right of stockholders to send out silver and gold for the purchase of diamonds etc., though the consignments allowed to each stockholder were limited to 25 per cent of the value of his stock.[4] In the long run this limitation would have resulted in the strangulation of the diamond trade, all the more so because it was implied that only stockholders were allowed to take part in the trade. But the interests of the merchants were again victorious. In the following year the Court of Directors, 'taking into consideracon the enlargeing of ye trade of diamonds etc.', decided to raise the limit to the equivalent of 100 per cent of the value of stock and of Company bonds in possession of the merchants who wanted to import diamonds. Diamond importers were allowed even to go beyond this limit if they were prepared to pay 3 per cent instead of 2 per cent on exports of silver and gold. Non-stockholders were explicitly allowed to take part in the trade, and the additional duty which they had formerly been forced to pay on diamond imports was abolished.[5]

In 1687 a further concession was made to non-stockholders, and the last distinction between them and members of the Company was removed. They too were to pay only 2 per cent on consignments of silver and gold for the purchase of diamonds. The introduction to the resolution of the Court reflects the goodwill which now prevailed towards the private diamond trade:[6]

> The Court taking into Consideracon an order of the Court of 27th August 1684 made concerning the permissive trade for exportacon of bullion and other goods to be invested in diamonds, pearl and other precious stones in India to be brought for England, and being willing to give further and equall encouragement for ye enlargement of that trade, to merchants of all nacons, as well as aliens as English, have thought fit & accordingly doe order.

Some of the rules adopted in the 1680s for the regulation of the private diamond trade and its control by the Company remained in force till the nineteenth century. The merchant was obliged to make a declaration concerning the value of bullion exported and of diamonds imported by him. The Company's Committee of the Treasury was empowered to open any parcel of diamonds if there was ground for suspicion that the declared value was not true. It was made obligatory for the merchants to employ the President

of the Company's Council at Surat or Fort St George, or some
other member of the Council, as one of his agents in India.[7]

In 1687 it looked as if the Anglo-Indian diamond trade had
been put on a stable and permanent basis and the relations between the Company and the private merchants regulated to the
mutual satisfaction of both sides. The diamond merchants had
gained freedom of action in return for comparatively low payments which the trade could bear without much difficulty. Yet
this promise was not to be fulfilled until some 30 years later. The
Revolution of 1688 and the period of internal tension and international instability which followed it, seriously affected the diamond trade. Relations between the East India Company and the
Government, which had been excellent during the 1680s, became
strained after the Revolution. The Company had to fight for its
monopoly, and the diamond merchants for their right to trade
with India. Paradoxically the legal position of the diamond
merchants was shaken just when the interlopers in the East India
trade were gaining in influence, finally receiving permission to
establish a rival company, in 1698. In 1694 Parliament declared
that any English subject might trade with India if there were no
law specifically against it. The deterioration in the position of the
diamond merchants can perhaps be explained by the hostility of
many Whigs to the Jews and by the close connections of the latter
with the East India Company, which was on bad terms with the
new rulers. An outcry was also raised against the Jews because
they were allegedly causing silver to flow out of the kingdom.
The Indian diamond trade was then largely dependent on silver
export. In 1693 the Company managed to get a new charter with
the aid of bribes. This charter forbade the import of diamonds
from India by private merchants – this was one aspect of the
tightening of terms of the Company's charter – and in the following year the prohibition was put into effect by the Company.[8]
Merchants were even forbidden to send out foodstuffs and clothing to their agents in India.

The diamond merchants petitioned the Crown in January 1695
for permission to carry on the trade. They pointed out that the
trade in precious stones, which they described as 'so important to
the merchants of England', was in danger of being lost to the
country. They also approached the Company's General Court –
the Assembly of Stockholders – through the intermediacy of Sir
Joseph Herne.[9] Herne belonged to a group of goldsmith-bankers

who during the 1690s helped to finance the war against France, and who were all connected with the diamond trade.[10] Perhaps it was due to their influence that the demands of the diamond merchants were partly accepted. The General Court agreed with Herne that 'in regard the said trade would be very beneficial to the Compa[ny]', it would be more appropriate if the petition were to be submitted by the Court itself instead of by private merchants, and the Directors were asked to formulate one.[11] Yet despite this success the matter was not treated as urgent. Some months later the problem was discussed again by the General Court and a special committee appointed to deal with the affair. But only in 1697 was the committee convened by the Directors 'to consider what is fit to be represented to his Majestie for preserving to this kingdom the trade in diamonds, jewels, and other fine goods from India, which otherwise is in danger to be lost'.[12] Only towards the end of the year was a petition formulated, while two of the Directors were asked to explain the matter to the Lords of the Council of Trade. It was not before the spring of 1698 – five years after the trouble started – that the private diamond trade with India was again made lawful.[13]

It is evident that the Court of Directors was by now favourably inclined towards the private diamond trade and that its advantage to the nation and to the Company was recognized.[14] But the achievement of 1698 did not end the period of instability. Twenty more years were to pass before the trade was put on a permanent and stable basis. The freedom of action which had been granted in 1687 and lost soon after was regained only several years after the termination of the War of the Spanish Succession. Two main obstacles prevented an undisturbed development of the trade at the beginning of the eighteenth century: restrictions on the exportation of silver, and a prohibition against stockholders carrying on any private trade with the East. The diamond trade also suffered from the violent competition between the two East India Companies which ended only with their merger in 1702. In 1700 the Custom authorities, by request of the New Company, impounded diamonds and goods from the ship *Neptune*. The Old Company agreed to compensate the owners of the diamonds after the latter had hinted that they might reach agreement with the New Company if their demands were not satisfied. In November 1701 the Jesuit George Ongarety of Goa wrote to Sir Stephen Evance in London: 'The buying shall be bought in diamonds for them to go in this monsoone, for still in diamonds there is much difficulty by cause of the Companyes of England, Old and New, for they being quarilsome one with the other they doe themselves much damage and to others two [sic].'[15]

The prohibition against stockholders trading privately to India was fixed by Act of Parliament in 1698.[16] We can only guess at the reason; it was perhaps an attempt to prevent too strong an influence of the private merchants on the Court of Directors and to deny them the means of applying pressure. There can be no doubt that the prohibition was a severe blow to the diamond merchants. Presumably the Jewish merchants were particularly vulnerable in this respect because dealings in securities were becoming a typical Jewish activity at that time. By preventing diamond importers from holding East India stock this rule also limited their opportunity for safe investments, at a time when the stock exchange was still in its infancy. Bank of England stock, however, already represented a good alternative. The prohibition remained in force for many years, and in 1709 a special committee recommended 'that any person except members of the Company be permitted to trade in diamonds'.[17] Four years later the diamond merchants tried to induce the General Court to give a different interpretation to the Act of 1698 and to allow stockholders to take part in the trade. In this they failed; the prohibition remained in force[18] and it is not clear when, if at all, it was revoked. It was probably allowed to lapse, as later stockholders are found trading to the East without hindrance.

The restrictions on the exportation of silver for the purchase of diamonds constituted an even more difficult problem. English trade to India had for long been under criticism based on mercantilist or bullionist theories; it was argued that the negative balance of trade between England and India was the cause of a continuous flow of bullion to the East. The struggle against Louis XIV put a heavy burden on the economic resources of England and it naturally intensified protests against the consignment of silver to India. As was to be expected, the East India Company's first reaction to the intensified pressure was to curtail the export of silver by private merchants. When Thomas Pitt went out to India in 1699 to take over his post as Governor at Fort St George he hoped for a considerable income from the payments due to him as Governor for all diamonds purchased at Madras (2½ per cent on the purchase price). He later maintained that before his departure

Sir Josiah Child had promised him that his income from this source would amount to £3,000 per annum. But already in 1701 Pitt was complaining bitterly, in his letters to London, about the restrictions imposed by the Company on the export of silver for the purchase of diamonds, which would reduce his annual income from this source to 500 pagodas, a Madras gold coin then equivalent to about nine shillings.[19] In a letter to his friend – the Jewish diamond merchant Alvaro da Fonseca – Pitt warned that 'unless our Company finds some way to give permission for money, that trade [in diamonds] will be carried to Metchulaptam'.[20] Masulipatam was the seat of the New Company's headquarters in India. With typical irony Pitt wrote to Sir Stephen Evance, his chief London agent, about the possibility that the Company would appoint someone else to supersede him as Governor of Fort St George:

> I hope he will give 'em better satisfaction than I have done and then I am sure he will have better encouragement from them, and whereas they hinder'd dureing my time money comeing out for diamonds, I doubt not but in his time they will encourage it.[2]

The situation was not made easier by the renewal of the war in 1702. In January 1704 Sir Stephen Evance wrote to Pitt:

> Last year we consigned to you and Mr. Plymer [a Christian diamond merchant at Madras] a parcell of money amounting to eighteen hundred pounds to be invested in diamonds, and the persons concerned would have sent a larger sum this year but that there is a great complaint in Parliament against the Company for their carrying out soe much silver in warr time; upon which the Company have made an order that noe money shall be sent out this year in private trade, and we doe believe here, they will permit noe more money goeing out dureing the warr.[22]

Events justified this pessimistic forecast. The prohibition continued in force during the nine remaining years of the war and beyond. It is true that the Court Books contain only one resolution, passed in December 1705, which explicitly prohibited the issue of licences for the export of silver intended for the purchase of diamonds in India;[23] but the diamond merchants stated in 1713 that the Company had prevented them from sending out silver to India since the beginning of the war.

The restrictions are also reflected in the official figures relating to diamond imports.[24] In 1698 £92,000 worth of diamonds were imported, whereas in the first decade of the new century the annual value of diamond imports never exceeded £12,000, and generally was much smaller.[25] Child's promise to Pitt about his expected income from the diamond commission was also based on the assumption that diamond imports would amount to more than £100,000 per annum. Child evidently had in mind the volume of trade in 1698, and mistakenly assumed that imports would continue on a similar scale during the following years.

The difficulties caused by the war had one beneficial result from the point of view of the diamond trade: they induced the East India Company finally to give up the coral trade in favour of the private merchants. In the autumn of 1709 the diamond merchants approached the Court of Directors with a proposal 'relating to the carrying on of the diamond trade'.[26] The Court appointed a special committee to deal with the matter and, acting on its report, decided to allow the merchants to export to India and Borneo 'all sorts of corall, corall beads, amber, amber beads, pearl, emeralds, or any other sort of precious stones' for the purchase of diamonds and so on.[27] The export of coral to India was to become an integral part of the diamond trade in the eighteenth century; this new measure of liberalization, which was designed to compensate the diamond merchants for the provisional prohibition of silver exports and to enable them to carry on their business during the war, had a lasting effect on the whole character of the Anglo-Indian diamond trade.

Despite these concessions the trade could not flourish while the restrictions were in force. The diamond merchants, who even in normal times were under constant temptation to indulge in smuggling, resorted to unlawful means in order to save their business from ruin. There is reliable evidence that silver was smuggled to India on a large scale, and it seems that most diamond merchants were involved in these illegal affairs.[28] This was discovered in 1717, when Sir Joseph Hales, Sir Stephen Evance's late partner, accused the diamond importer Roger Bradyll of having smuggled £2,000 worth of silver to India. He alleged that 'while Sir Stephen Evans kept his shop, severall persons, at least twenty in the whole, were used to drive the like sort of clandestine trade, during the time of shipping out goods to the East Indies ... great sums of money were sent from their shop on board the

East-India ships, without licence of the Company.' Hales also described how Bradyll had instructed him in December 1711 to supply 40 bars of silver, which were then smuggled on board East Indiamen in wheat sacks. According to Hales some twenty people were involved in this clandestine business. It is virtually certain that the silver was destined for the purchase of diamonds: heavy goods could not be imported in return on a large scale, and both Bradyll and Evance were important diamond merchants. This assumption is further strengthened by the fact that in 1709 Bradyll and his partner Alvaro da Fonseca were fined for smuggling diamonds into England.

With the end of the war in sight, the merchants made another attempt to remove the restrictions which had impeded the trade for some 15 years past. Eleven diamond merchants, of whom seven were Jews, presented a petition to the Court of Directors,[29] pointing out the benefits which the nation derived from the trade and the advantages it brought to Fort St George 'thorough [sic] the concourse of natives it brought thither'. They maintained that the sale of coral and so on to India 'will in no wise answer the sum of money that trade requires'. They also complained about the high duties levied on the trade and warned that the restrictions and impositions 'will drive the trade from this nation'.[30] The Court of Directors asked three of its members to investigate the matter, including its legal aspects,[31] and on 16 January the Court voted by secret ballot on the question 'that it be lawful, this Court are of opinion, it is for the interest of this Company to licence the diamond trade'. The resolution was passed and a special General Court was convened to settle the problem.[32] The stockholders authorized the Directors to permit the diamond trade and to impose such conditions and restrictions as they considered appropriate. This authorization, however, was limited to a period of two years.[33] A few days later the Court of Directors formulated the conditions under which the diamond trade was to be carried on, having been requested to do so by the merchants Bradyll and da Costa.[34] This resolution was more in the nature of a confirmation of old rules than a promulgation of new ones. Duties were slightly lowered, and it was hinted that the issue of licences for the export of silver would be renewed.[35] The new arrangement was put into force in February, when instructions were given to the Committee of Shipping to issue licences for the export of silver for the purchase of diamonds in India.[36]

This was not the end of the restrictions. The authorization given to the Court of Directors was renewed from time to time by the General Court, but only in 1718 was the time limit abolished. When the original authorization came up for renewal in 1715 the Directors recommended strongly that the issue of licences be continued:

> That it be represented to the Generall Court as the unanimous opinion of this Court, that the licencing of the trade in diamonds on the Company's ships, is of advantage to the nation in generall, by the making it the centre of the diamond trade, which other nations would be glad off, and very beneficiall to the Company.[37]

The strong support which was thus given to the diamond merchants may well have been motivated by a French attempt to gain a foothold in the Indian diamond trade in which at least two Jewish diamond merchants of London were involved.[38] The total quantity of silver which the diamond merchants were allowed to export remained limited, for another decade, to between £40,000 and £50,000 per annum. But the fact that the merchants did not protest may have meant that this amount was sufficient, in addition to the money which became available from the sale of coral and precious stones in India.[39]

After 1720 the relations between the East India Company and the private merchants were finally stabilized. From now on, silver, coral and precious stones were sent to India, and diamond imported from there without hindrance. The legal framework which had been fixed for the trade was to remain substantially unchanged till the beginning of the nineteenth century. But it was at this moment, when the long struggle for freedom of trade was at last crowned with success, that the Anglo-Indian diamond trade suffered a setback which almost completely paralyzed it for a period of ten years: diamonds were discovered in Brazil.

B. THE CORAL TRADE

The jewellery trade between India and Europe has always been a two-way business. India supplied Europe with diamonds, garnets, rubies, and eastern pearls, and Europe exported to India coral and amber; later Europe also exported emeralds and western pearls from South and Central America. After the early sixteenth century diamonds were the main item in jewellery imports from India, and coral took first place in exports to the East, for a long time being an essential commodity in all trade with India.[40] The western Mediterranean was the only source of red coral, the kind needed for the Indian market. Marseilles, Leghorn, Genoa, and Naples were centres of coral fishing and coral industries. Most of the coral produced there was sent to India and only a small part was sold in Europe and Africa. In India it was used for jewellery and in cremation ceremonies, and served also as a symbol of social standing. In 1613 William Biddulph reported to the East India Company from Surat: 'Coral . . . a chief commodity here . . . being a custom in Decanie [i.e. the Deccan] . . . for to buy as much of it as they can, and hoard it up as it were gold, and the more they have of it in their house the greater honour it is for them, and when they die they burn it all with them.'[41] Towards the end of the eighteenth century Lyon Prager wrote to his uncle about the market for coral beads in Calcutta: 'they are much worn by the Indians here and in Benares too. I should like very much to get some in commission from the Portuguese [Jews].'[42] Streeter describes the use of coral: 'In India the dark variety has always been valued. Every oriental strives to get a string of Coral to his turban, or at least sufficient to decorate the handle of his sword. They think that to leave their dead without ornament of coral is to give them over to the hands of mighty enemies. There is scarcely an Indian to be found without at least one or two rows on one of his arms, and the rich wear red coral on head, throat and legs.'[43] The use of coral for funeral purposes was prevalent only in Western India. In Bengal and on the Coromandel Coast coral served only for personal ornament, and as a consequence the demand there was solely for coral beads, not rough coral.[44]

Till the discovery of the direct sea route to India, coral was usually sent to Alexandria and from there consigned to India by Arab merchants. Later coral became an important commodity in the Portuguese trade with India[45] and Goa became the centre of the coral trade. Goa was still a central market for coral in the middle of the seventeenth century, and the English factory at Surat sent coral there for sale.[46]

The chief centres of the coral industry in Europe were Marseilles and Leghorn, from where, and from the secondary fishing centres of Naples and Genoa, boats sailed to the shores of

North Africa in search of red coral. The coral industry of Marseilles reached a high stage of development in the sixteenth and seventeenth centuries, and a great coral company was established there.[47] In the eighteenth century, however, Leghorn surpassed it as a centre of the coral industry. Coral fishing continued at Marseilles, but most of it was sent to Leghorn for working. Leghorn's importance as a centre of the coral trade and industry was described by a Jewish coral merchant from that place named Abraham de Castro:

> it is common for the coral fisheries to bring from the islands adjacent to Leghorn from six to eight thousand pounds weight of coral each boat . . . about three hundred of such boats are employed in collecting in each of the coral fishing seasons for the market of Leghorn, besides which great quantities of coral are from time to time imported at Leghorn from France . . .[48]

Coral was one of the principal commodities exported to India by the English East India Company during the seventeenth century. Amber was frequently sent to India, but it was much less important than coral.[49] It does not follow that the coral trade of the Company assumed very large dimensions: till the eighteenth century European exports to India were limited by the lack of demand for European goods in the Indian market, and the value of commodities exported was always much lower than that of coins or precious metals consigned to India. It was precisely for that reason that the Company was interested in a product which enjoyed a natural demand in India and which had not to be 'forced' on the market there.

The Company embarked on the coral trade with great expectations, and encouraging reports reached London from the Company's agents in the East.[50] The Company bought the coral at different places: Marseilles, Leghorn, Genoa, Florence[51] and even through a Venetian firm. During the 1620s and 1630s the coral business of the Company was under the supervision of the famous mercantilist writer Thomas Mun, who was a director of the Company.[52] The coral was brought to England, usually by sea, and was then loaded onto ships sailing to India. For a time there existed a two-way trade between Leghorn and India, which passed London in both directions: the English Company used to send Indian pepper to Leghorn and to invest the proceeds in coral destined for India.[53]

Despite relatively favourable market conditions[54] and occasional high profits, the initial expectations were not fulfilled. The Company encountered continual difficulties in its coral trade, and it was the cause of a long series of disappointments. The reasons for this were varied. The Company had to compete with the Dutch and even more with the Portuguese.[55] Portuguese competition increased after Portugal regained her independence in 1640. After the Portuguese victory over the Spaniards in 1644 the chief of the English factory at Surat reported his anxiety lest they should now supply the coral market of Western India. In fact the English had difficulties in selling their coral during the following years because of the great quantities brought by the Portuguese to Goa. A few years later the coral market was oversupplied by the Dutch. Coral was also imported into India by way of the Red Sea and Mecca.[56] As a result supply often exceeded demand and prices were low. After 1620 English coral exports to India encountered strong opposition from local merchants at Surat, and were prohibited by the local ruler.[57] The prohibition was first imposed in 1619, when the Surat factory reported to London: 'the Governor and merchants consultinge together, prohibitt us to sell'. The difficulty was removed only in 1621; Thomas Kerridge and his Council reported 'Our Corall found such opposition that we were informed to give the Governor 1,100 r[ial]s of eight and 2000 mam[udis] more in the under price of lead ... upon the foresaid bribe we obtained proclamation for our free trade'. But even thereafter the local authorities and merchants continued to hamper the Company's coral trade. An Indian coral merchant by the name of Verge Vora completely monopolized the local market and retained this dominant position for 30 years. The agents of the Company reported from time to time that they had succeeded in bypassing Verge Vora's monopoly, but they never managed to effect it permanently.[58]

Verge Vora is first mentioned in the Journals of the Surat Council in April 1634, when an attempt to break his monopoly is reported, he having 'become the sole monopolist of all European Commodities'. But in this they failed dismally. Brokers employed by the Company were intimidated by the monopolist, and in 1636 the Council was still unable to sell its coral. 'There has not been in all this time one man that hath desired to see or buy it, but here it lies still, unrequested and unregarded.'[59] Verge Vora still dominated the Surat coral market in the 1650s and early

1660s. In 1655 the Company sent him a present in order to conciliate him after he had complained about the low quality of coral which they delivered to him, and in 1662 Oxenden was asked to express the Company's 'love' to Verge Vora. This gesture did not, however, prevent him from impeding the Company's coral sales, 'threatening all other buyers from dealing with us for it, whose greatness awes them all'.

After 1650 a coral market with apparently good prospects developed at the Company's new base at Fort St George. The Company first sent coral to the Coromandel Coast in 1624. It seems, however, that regular consignments to that part of India began only after the foundation of Fort St George in 1640. Success was limited at first because of local wars, but the reports of the Fort St George factory became more optimistic after 1641, and in 1654 London was informed that, unlike other European goods, coral was in great demand there. In 1661 the agents there reported to the Company: 'We know no more staple commodity for this country'.[60] Two years later Fort St George informed India House that several coral merchants had moved from Goa to Madras and were willing to buy coral to the value of 13,000–14,000 pagodas per annum.[61] In 1665 the agents again reported a large demand for coral: 'If you were constant in sending of it, this towne would take of 40,000 pagodas yearly, for a multitude of people would come and live here, only for the work of it.'[62] The agents, however, pointed out on every occasion that the market could only be mastered if the quality of the coral was improved.

Encouraged by these reports the Company placed large orders for coral at Leghorn, demanding at the same time a better quality. Results, however, were not very promising: letters to the agents at Leghorn are full of complaints concerning bad quality, high prices, delays in shipment of the coral (as the result of which it reached England after the East India ships had sailed), deficient packing, and the like.[63] Coral was offered to the Company in London for lower prices than those demanded at Leghorn and rumours were spread that its agents there were not familiar with local market conditions, bought at second hand, and allowed brokers to fool them. At the same time coral was being smuggled to India. The Company's agents at Surat wrote in 1663 that the prospects for the coral trade were good, provided the Company could manage to keep smuggling within bounds, as it had assumed unbelievable proportions.[64] A few years later the chief of the Company's factory at Fort St George was himself accused of private dealings in coral.[65]

In view of these difficulties it is not very surprising that after 1670 the Company allowed the coral trade to pass gradually into the hands of the diamond merchants.

There cannot be much doubt that the Jewish diamond merchants of London, with their close connections with Leghorn and India, always had a considerable interest in the coral trade. We have seen that the Jewish correspondents of Oxenden consigned to him, among other things, coral destined for Goa. Very likely the large-scale smuggling reported in 1662 was a manifestation of the commercial activity of the Jewish immigrants, no less than was the diamond smuggling which resulted in the liberalization of the diamond trade.

The Company was not so quick to give up the coral trade on which it still pinned great hopes. But when these hopes were disappointed the Company began to make concessions to the diamond merchants in this field too, and it finally relinquished the trade at the beginning of the eighteenth century. The first indication of the new policy came in 1668, when the Court of Directors allowed Fernando Mendes da Costa, well known for his plan to settle Marranos in Italy and England, to consign two chests of coral beads to Goa through Sir George Oxenden at Surat. A similar permission was given to him in the following year.[66] This concession, however, did not yet bear a general and permanent character. In the following years licences were granted or withheld as was thought best for the Company's own trade; in 1671 the Court decided not to issue any more licences for the export of coral, but in 1672 exports were permitted again because the Company consigned no coral of its own.[67] Three years later the export of coral beads was permitted and rates of payment for licences and transportation were fixed.[68]

It is not clear whether the arrangement was meant to be permanent or just for that year.[69] Ten years later we find a resolution of the Court stating:

Mr. Alphonso Rodrigues and Alvaro d'Acosta moving the Court for liberty to export corall beads to India. On Consid[era]con thereof had, it is ordered that permission be granted to them and all other merchants to export on the Company's ships to India such quantities of corall beads as they shall think fit.[70]

Rather severe conditions were however imposed which considerably restricted the freedom of trade which had been granted. Exporters had to pay the Company 10 per cent of the value of the coral consigned and to sell it to the Company after its arrival in India. They were promised a profit of 10 per cent and the return of the 10 per cent paid in London, according to a fixed rate of exchange.[71] A profit of 10 per cent in the East India trade was considered small, because of the slow turn-over. In fact, the business under such conditions could only be worthwhile if the diamonds purchased with the proceeds of the coral produced a much bigger profit. The stipulation concerning the 10 per cent which had to be paid to the Company in London for repayment in India was evidently meant to insure that the coral would really be sold to the Company after its arrival in India. The regulations represented an attempt to prevent coral smuggling – by making some concession to the private merchants – and at the same time to enable the Company to enjoy the trade in coral beads to India, without incurring the trouble and risk of its purchase in Europe, by using the connections of the Jewish diamond merchants at Leghorn. The Portuguese Jews had undoubtedly considerable advantages in this field, even before the immigration of Livornese Jews at the beginning of the eighteenth century tightened the relations between the Jewish communities of London and Leghorn.

This arrangement was too clever and too complicated to last. Three years later, in 1688, duties on coral exports were reduced 'in regard five percent custome is to be paid for the same in India'.[72] But full and permanent freedom of trade in all sorts of coral was granted only in 1709 in order to compensate the diamond merchants for the refusal to issue licences for the export of silver.

Two points should be noted in the resolution of 1709; it applied to rough coral as well as to coral beads, and the connection between the coral and the diamond trade, which had always existed, was officially recognized and made obligatory. The Court of Directors approved the recommendations of the special committee which had been appointed to consider the problem:

> That licence be granted for exporting to Surrat, Fort St. George and Borneo all sorts of Corall, corall beads, amber, amber beads, pearl, emeralds or any sort of precious stones, the

exporters giving security, if required, that the produce be brought home in diamonds, diamond boart, musk, ambergreece or bezoar, and in no other goods whatsoever.[73]

The same resolution fixed rates of payments for licences and transportation, the obligation to pay a commission to the Chief of the Company's factory in India, and to register the diamonds, which were to be returned for the coral, in the Company's books. It was also specified how the diamonds should be sold on arrival in London. These rules remained in force during the whole of the eighteenth century.

The resolution was passed in November 1709. On examining the Company's accounts[74] for December of the same year we find the names of three exporters of coral who paid licence fees during that month. Two of them were Jews: Abraham Franco and Josua Gomes Serra. Abraham Franco and his brother Jacob were to become the biggest exporters of coral and importers of diamonds in London during a large part of the century. In the following years the names of many other merchants appear in the Company's Cash Journals, representing the foremost Jewish-Portuguese families of London: Aaron Pacheco, Isaac Alvares, Alvaro Mendes, Francis and Isaac Salvador, Moses Blaw (Azulai), Jacob Fernandes Nunes, Moses Abendanon, Joseph Perreira, Jacob Rodrigues Silva, Isaac Portello, Jacob Mendes da Costa, Solomon and Moses de Medina, John Mendes da Costa, Judah Supino, Abraham Lopes Mendes, and others.

The coral trade grew rapidly after 1720 and assumed dimensions which the Company could never have hoped to achieve when it held the monopoly. The concentration of diamond imports from India in the hands of London's Jewish merchants, the connection of these with Leghorn, and the gradual displacement of England's competitors in India gave London a dominant position in the Italian–Indian coral trade.

Chapter 7
Competition from Brazilian diamonds 1730–1740

India's monopoly on the supply of uncut diamonds to Europe was broken in 1728.[1] A few years before, diamonds had been discovered in Brazil. The discoverers did not at first realize the nature of their find; a consignment of stones from Brazil is said to have reached the Dutch consul at Lisbon, who sent them to Amsterdam, where they were recognized as diamonds.[2] The diamonds were found in the area of Minas Geraes, north of Rio de Janeiro, where many goldmines were also located. A diamond rush soon developed and large consignments of stones reached Lisbon.

The diamond, being a typical item of luxury, is extremely sensitive to the fluctuations of supply and demand. In times of adversity the demand for jewellery naturally drops sharply and people will even tend to sell what they possess. On the other hand the value of the diamond stands in direct relation to its scarcity, and any sudden increase in supply brings prices down. Until the discovery of diamonds in Brazil there was a natural regulation of supply, resulting from the limited output of the Indian mines and from the concentration of diamond imports in the hands of a small group of London merchants, the size of whose orders were determined by the demand for stones in Europe. It may be assumed that the gradual increase of imports from India was balanced by a growing demand for diamonds and precious stones in Europe, with its increasing affluent middle class. But the great quantity of diamonds which suddenly reached Lisbon in 1728[3] threw the European market into a turmoil and played havoc with the Anglo-Indian diamond trade. Twenty years later a diamond expert, David Jeffries, commented[4] on this event as one 'which occasioned many, even of the most capital traders in *London*, to believe that diamonds were likely to become as plenty as transparent pebbles; and they were so far influenced by this opinion that most of them refused to buy diamonds on any terms'.

His comment finds support in the letters of Sir James Tobin of London to Major John Roach of Madras, in which the development of the crisis is fully reflected. In January 1730 Tobin informed Roach that he had difficulty in selling his diamonds:

> here has great quantities lately come from Lisbon, and it is advised from thence, both privately and publicly, that there is a diamond mine discovered in Brassile near Rio de Janeiro, the truth of which time must discover. Be it true or false, it affects the price of diamonds here.

During the following days the crisis developed rapidly, and on 10 February Tobin reported: 'The diamond mine discovered in Brasille has caused an entire stagnation in that commodity, and still there are an abundance that doubt its veracity.' In autumn, according to Tobin, the situation was bad, and worse was expected: 'for it is now certain there is a diamond mine in Brasille discovered and a second cargoe is arrived from thence of different sizes.'

Tobin's letters show that the standstill in the trade continued, though many still doubted the authenticity of the Brazilian discoveries. In February 1732 Tobin reported that a new consignment of diamonds had reached Lisbon by the latest fleet from Rio de Janeiro, so that even the sceptics were now convinced. Tobin concluded this piece of news with the words: 'and leave you to judge the consequences to Madrass etc.'[5]

News from Lisbon was not very encouraging. According to the estimate of the British Consul, given in April 1733, the value of diamonds which had reached Lisbon recently amounted to £500,000–£600,000. This was more than five times the average quantity imported from India in the later 1720s.[6] Compton, the consul, thought that a further increase in consignments had to be expected; diamonds were found together with gold, and gold imports were rising, 'which makes me inclined to believe that this trade cannot last always, especially considering that diamonds are no consumable commodity, and that Europe is already stocked with them.'[7]

In India, too, the shock was soon felt. After the arrival of the first diamond consignment from Brazil most London merchants instructed their agents at Madras to buy diamonds only for half the usual price.[8] The crisis in the diamond trade coincided with serious difficulties in the sale of coral in India. John Roach reported in this same letter:

If you have not as yet purchas'd Coral I beg you will lay aside the thoughts of it, for the price of that commodity here is fallen prodigiously and great quantity remain now unsold, that have been two years in the place, and I have reason to believe that the Franco's, who consign largely hither yearly ... must be considerable losers.

The Indian sellers refused to lower their prices, as a result of which a complete deadlock ensued at the Indian end of the trade.[9] John Roach wrote to Sir James Tobin: 'the diamond trade is entirely at a stand here', and to Aaron Franks: 'The diamond trade must in a short time ruin many of the merchants here for being unwilling to credit the report of the Brazil mines. They keep up their prices as high as ever and nobody buying their goods must of course eat them out bye interest.'

The same situation was described by Jeffries in his book: 'Notwithstanding the India people knew what despisable prices Brazil diamonds sold for in Europe ... they kept up their price of the diamonds.'[10]

This lack of flexibility was typical of the Anglo-Indian diamond trade – low prices in Europe often went together with high prices in India. The great distance between the source of supply and the market prevented a rapid reaction of the former to the fluctuations of the latter, and the short sailing seasons and the limitations imposed by the Company restricted the manoeuvring capacity of the European diamond merchant. These factors as well as the activity of unprofessional elements – officers and officials of the Company – in the trade encouraged the Indian sellers to adopt a rigid price policy. On the other hand it would seem that the European merchants had more staying power, which was amply demonstrated when they brought about a virtual standstill in the trade lasting ten years. The situation was reflected in a reply made by Marcus Moses in a case heard by the Mayor's Court of Madras. Speaking about a diamond which he sold to a certain person who then refused to accept it, Moses maintained that 'the Brazil mines have since effected the diamond trade so much that the defendant [Marcus Moses] has no prospect of disposing the diamond aforesaid.'[11]

The figures of diamond imports during the 1730s reveal a virtual standstill in the trade. Between 1724 and 1730 registered imports had amounted to about £100,000 a year. In 1731 – the first year in which a reaction to the Brazil discovery could be expected – imports fell to £58,000, and in 1732 no more than £2,900 worth of diamonds were imported from India. Thereafter import figures remained very low till 1740, the largest yearly quantity imported during this period being just over £17,000 (in 1735). Only the biggest importers continued to do business, and they, too, on a much reduced scale; the Portuguese Jews Abraham and Jacob Franco and the Ashkenazim Aaron and Isaac Franks imported most of the diamonds bought from India during those years.

The flooding of the European market with Brazilian diamonds threatened to destroy the diamond trade, or at least England's dominance in that trade. Not only was the flow of stones from India to London almost stopped, but it could reasonably be expected that supplies from the new source would bypass the London market. The East India Company and other authorities in London showed full understanding of the problems which the new situation presented, and took steps calculated to help the merchants overcome the difficulties. The Portuguese government, too, was interested in the stabilization of the diamond trade, without which it would have lost a great part of the benefit which could be expected to accrue to the country and the Treasury from the discoveries in Brazil.

The danger to London's position in the diamond market was potential rather than immediate. The commerce of Lisbon was very closely tied to that of London, and the English had a specially large stake in the import of Brazilian gold.[12] It was only natural that the diamonds which were now arriving from Brazil were sent on, together with the gold, to the central diamond market at London. The British Ambassador at Lisbon reported on the situation, as it had been described to him by an English merchant:

> when diamonds were only found in the East Indias the settlement which our Company had at Fort St. George had almost brought the whole diamond trade into the hands of the English, so that London, within these thirty years, is become the first market for them in Europe ... The discovery of diamonds in the mines of the Brasils, has put a stop, for the present, to the trade from the East Indies, tho' not to the London market, on accompt of the advantage which England has over its neighbors in the trade with Lisbon, with packets, men of war and

merchant ships, which are constantly going backwards and forwards between the two countries, so that the much greater part of the diamonds that come from the Brazils have hitherto gone to London, from whence they are distributed to the rest of Europe.[13]

The diamond merchants, however, feared that things might take a different turn. In the beginning of 1732 the customs authorities at Falmouth – the home port for the Portugal packet-boats – seized a consignment of diamonds which had arrived from Lisbon for a number of London merchants. The diamonds were apparently impounded because no declaration had been made and no duties paid. It is not clear whether there was an intention to break the law: diamond imports from Portugal were just beginning and there was no established procedure for dealing with them. (Gold, the main import item at Falmouth up to that time, was duty free). Diamonds had been imported regularly either through India House or the London Post Office; at both places the importer's declaration concerning value was usually accepted as *bona fide*, and the authorities did not insist on inspection. The owners, including some of the foremost Portuguese merchants of London, insisted that steps be taken to remedy the situation: that the impounded diamonds be returned, that the publication of import and export figures of diamonds be discontinued, and that the Crown duties on diamonds should be abolished.

The customs authorities were approached by 25 merchants, of whom ten were Jews. The Jewish signatories were Frances Salvador Jr, Jacob Fernandes Nunes, Benjamin Mendes da Costa, Alvaro Lopes Suasso, Jacob Mendes da Costa Sr, Jacob Mendes da Costa, Isaac Franks, Abraham Franco, Jacob Franco, Joseph and Daniel Vianna. The unusually small number of Jewish signatories (less than half of the total) is easily explained by the fact that as a result of the discovery of diamonds in Brazil a new element appeared among the English diamond importers, namely the Portugal merchants. Among the non-Jewish signatories, only one was a long-established diamond merchant (Thomas Godfrey). The Jewish petitioners, on the other hand, had all been active in the Anglo-Indian diamond trade. It is possible that many of them switched to Brazilian stones during the stand-still period in the India trade. These merchants explained that in no other country was the volume of diamond imports made public, and unless publication was stopped in England its position in the trade would be endangered.[14] They also requested that henceforth the importers' declaration, concerning the value of diamonds imported, should be accepted as *bona fide*, and that the authorities should not insist on inspecting the stones, a procedure to which the East India Company had already agreed. The merchants also gave notice of their intention to approach Parliament with a request for the total abolition of Crown duties on diamonds.[15]

The merchants were strongly supported by the Ambassador and Consul at Lisbon. The arguments of the English merchants at Lisbon were reported to London by the Ambassador there, Lord Tyrawley:

> even the laying any duty upon the importation of rough diamonds is destructive to it, since the greater quantity of rough diamonds are imported – the greater the benefit of the nation, and that the duty upon them, with the penalty of confiscation, if not taken off very soon, will turn that rich channel out of ours into our neighbors' country, and give them the advantage which we now have in that trade over all the rest of Europe.

Tyrawley pointed out the danger of competition by countries with freedom of trade in diamonds:

> and particularly Amsterdam seems to stand the fairest to rob us of that trade, if any hardships are laid upon it in England, as being better situated by far than London to circulate them through the rest of Europe.[16]

The Consul supported the merchants even more decidedly than the Ambassador. He argued that the imposition of import duties on diamonds was economically harmful, especially as far as uncut diamonds were concerned;[17] in view of the ease with which diamonds could be smuggled, the Crown's income from custom duties was bound to be negligible, compared with the damage which would be caused to the national economy.[18]

By bringing pressure to bear, or perhaps by the sheer force of their arguments, the merchants were able to attain fulfilment of all their demands. The customs authorities permitted the import and export of diamonds by the packet-boats which plied between Lisbon and Falmouth, and the publication of import figures was discontinued.[19] Parliament soon thereafter abolished the duties, expressing the hope that the encouragement of imports would result in an extension of the diamond trade.[20] The external obstacles which had confronted English trade in Brazilian diamonds were thus removed. Brazilian diamonds continued to flow to the London market throughout the eighteenth century, though they were never an English monopoly in the way that Indian diamonds were.

The Indian trade presented a special problem. The immediate danger was that the complete standstill in the diamond trade would similarly affect the coral trade. The two branches had been closely connected since the beginning of the century; they not only represented two sides of what, in effect, was a single trade, but the licences for the export of coral issued by the East India Company were granted on the explicit condition that it was to be sent 'for the purchase for diamonds'.[21] This condition had now to be annulled if the coral trade was to be continued.

Once the magnitude of the crisis had become clear, the merchants requested the East India Company to be allowed to return the proceeds received from the sale of coral in India by bills of exchange drawn by the Council at Fort St George on the Company in London. On the recommendation of the Correspondence Committee the Court of Directors gave the required permission, and in the autumn of 1731 Fort St George was instructed to issue bills of exchange on London to the agents of the coral merchants.[22] The agents were now able to pay the money received from the sale of coral into the Company's treasury at Fort St George, and receive bills in return.

The Company was helpful, but in making concessions to the merchants it did not sacrifice any of its own interests. The Company's main concern was to prevent private merchants from infringement of its monopoly, and consequently the possibilities of investing the proceeds of coral in goods destined for England were very limited. The issue of bills of exchange to the agents of coral merchants, if kept within bounds, could even benefit the Company, enabling it to reduce its silver exports by the amount it received for its bills in India. This situation changed when the rate of exchange became less favourable to the Company, and in 1737 the Court of Directors stated that 'the exchanges are in favour of those who remit their money by bill on the Company compared with what the Company would get by sending out silver'. It was therefore ordered that the bills issued in India should be paid only 90 days after presentation instead of after 61 days as before.[23]

The concession, however, remained in force throughout the period of the crisis. The formulation of the licences was changed, and permission for the export of coral was now granted 'on the Company's usual conditions' instead of 'for the purchase of diamonds'. Only after the passing of the crisis was the old condition reintroduced. (The merchants again began to use Company bills for remitting back the coral proceeds during the Seven Years War. At that time the Company gave its tacit consent.) The Company thus made it possible for the coral trade to continue to flow through the London channel. This does not mean that the trade remained unaffected by the crisis. It is doubtful whether the coral trade could have been carried on independently without the additional profits derived from the importation of diamonds. It is nevertheless true that the coral trade began to recover some five years before the diamond trade (see Appendices I and K).

The new arrangement which enabled the coral merchants to return the proceeds to England by bills of exchange issued by the Fort St George Council did not work smoothly because of the unstable monetary situation at Madras; the local ruler issued debased coins and the Company Council at Fort St George had to decide whether it would accept these new 'current pagodas' in payment for the bills issued to the coral merchants; it decided in the affirmative, but at the same time announced that in future it would accept only the old 'Madras pagodas'. The discussions relating to this problem are recorded at length in the journal of the Fort St George Council. They reflect the difficulties which were caused in the conduct of the Company's affairs in India by the great distance of its establishments there from the headquarters in London, and the impossibility of rapid consultation. The Fort St George Council had to decide on its own responsibility whether the changed conditions justified a deviation from the instructions received from London, and they had to meet in advance all possible arguments which could be expected to be made in England against their decision. In fact, the coral merchants in London lodged a strong protest, maintaining that the new arrangements made by Fort St George were detrimental to their business, and submitting an account of the profits which had accrued to the nation and the Company from the coral trade. After a copy of the Fort St George report had been distributed to the Directors and a review made of the licences for coral exports issued during the preceding five years, the Court of Directors met to discuss the question. The Directors sustained the decision of the Fort St George Council, and fixed a lower rate of exchange for bills issued in return for the debased 'current pagodas'. They also suggested that the coral merchants could remit the proceeds in gold bars or coins, but this alternative was never much used.[24]

The merchants also endeavoured to bring about a reduction of the Company duties in India, which the trade could bear in normal times but which hampered recovery. In October 1733 Isaac Salvador approached the Court of Directors with the request 'to take into consideration the hardships that their trade lyes under, and to indulge such conditions as may ease it, as they shall think reasonable'. The request was referred to the Committee of the Treasury which recommended the reductions of duties on the import of coral at Madras from 5 to 4 per cent, and of the commission due to the Governor, and to the other agent concerned, from 2½ per cent to 2 per cent.[25] The duties in London and prices of freight were not changed. These constituted between 2 and 4 per cent of the value. Payments were thus lowered from 10 to 8 per cent. The Directors consented to this concession, which was however revoked later.[26] In 1735 the Fort St George Council decided on its own initiative to reintroduce the higher duties which had been customary up to 1733. The Council argued that as the duty of 2½ per cent imposed on transfers of money by bills of exchange had been abolished by India House, they were now entitled to insist on payment of the former duties at Madras. The London merchants protested against the Council's action, arguing that 'as trade is dull, the said difference lies heavy on us', and demanding the refund of the difference. (The petition was signed by six firms, four of them Jewish: Abraham and Jacob Franco, Jacob Fernandes Nunes, Anthony da Costa, Judah Supino and Son). The Court of Directors' decision is not recorded, but it seems that later the old duties were again in force.

A permanent reduction of duties was achieved for the diamond trade. The developments which had taken place since 1730 gave Brazilian diamonds a distinct advantage over Indian stones. The importation of the latter was regulated and controlled by the East India Company, which also levied duties from which Brazilian diamonds were free. A petition concerning this difficulty was submitted to the Directors by six diamond merchants: they mentioned the hardships which had beset the trade since the discovery of diamonds in Brazil, and asked for a reduction of duties in order to enable Indian stones to compete with Brazilian ones:

> That since the discovery of the Brazill diamonds, the importing of them from India labours under many discouragements, and submit it to Your Honours' consideration to mitigate the dutys payable to the Honourable Company, so as it may bear a proportion with the charge from Brazill to Lisbon and thence to London, and to give such encouragement to the importation from India as to Your Honours shall seem proper.[27]

The petition is signed by six firms, four of them Jewish. These were Francis Salvador Jr, Abraham and Jacob Franco, Judah Supino, and Aaron Franks. The matter was referred to the Committee of Correspondence, which received a delegation of merchants headed by Isaac Salvador, who obviously was serving at that time as a sort of 'official spokesman' for the diamond merchants. Salvador explained that, while 5 per cent was due to the Company for diamonds imported from India, charges on Brazilian diamonds amounted to no more than 1½–2 per cent. He therefore requested that duties be reduced by half.[28]

Though the Company was willing enough to help, adoption of the proposed measure presented grave legal difficulties, the Company not being entitled to abolish the 5 per cent duty which had been fixed by Act of Parliament.[29] The percentage could therefore formally be reduced only by another Act of Parliament – a complicated and uncertain procedure. The problem was discussed by the Court of Directors and the Committee of Correspondence, and the Company's lawyers were consulted. They finally hit upon a solution which enabled the Company to grant the request of the merchants, while adhering to the letter of the law: the diamond merchants were to receive a subsidy of 2½ per cent on the value of all diamonds imported from India, which in reality meant a reduction of duties from 5 to 2½ per cent.[30] The Committee of Correspondence advised the Court to grant the subsidy 'for recovering as far as possible the diamond trade to this Company and recovering their servants and others to make returns of their effects in that way and thereby preventing such great sums being remitted by bills of exchange on the Company'.[31] During the 30 years following, payments by the Company to diamond importers of the 2½ per cent 'subsidy' were regularly registered side by side with payments of the 5 per cent duty by the merchants to the Company. Only in 1763 was this complicated method of registration abolished and thereafter the duty was registered at its true rate of 2½ per cent.

It is impossible to say to what degree the various concessions helped the recovery of the trade. Probably they did no more than encourage and accelerate a natural process of recuperation. The panic subsided gradually and the Portuguese government adopted measures for the regulation of supply, while merchants and public realized that the output of the Brazilian mines was not boundless and that diamonds did not become 'as plenty as transparent pebbles'. The idea soon spread that the quality of Indian stones was better than that of Brazilians. Both Robert Southey and John Mawe maintained – some 70 years after the event – that at the time of the crisis the diamond merchants had spread rumours about the inferior quality of Brazil stones. Mawe wrote: 'the diamonds arrived in Europe in such abundance as to excite an apprehension that these valuable gems would be greatly depreciated. To counteract this, a report was industriously circulated, that the Brazilian diamonds were decidedly inferior to the oriental.'[32] Be that as it may, the European diamond market eventually adapted itself to the new conditions, and a balance was achieved between the two sources of supply. Diamond imports from India were renewed on a large scale after 1740 and, despite a provisional setback caused by the occupation of Madras by the French in 1745, it reverted gradually to its former proportions.

At this point it is necessary to digress slightly from the main theme – the diamond market of London and its connection with India – in order to survey the development of Portugal's diamond trade and its regulation by the Portuguese government. The discovery of diamonds in Brazil might be expected to improve Portugal's balance of trade considerably, and supply a new source of income for the Crown. But it was first necessary to overcome the crisis which had been caused by this discovery, the price of diamonds having fallen from 8 to 2 milreis a carat within two years.[33] (A milreis was equal to 5 shillings and 7 pence.)

The Portuguese government had to regulate the supply of diamonds by one means or another. Several proposals were submitted to it, and handed on to various businessmen for their opinion. Southey gives *in extenso* the memorandum of a certain Dr Juan de Almeyda. His remarks concerning a proposal to establish a diamond company are of interest in as far as they reflect the fears of Jewish dominance which were apparently prevalent in Portuguese circles. De Almeyda considered the proposal to be a plot hatched by 'certain foreigners and Jews in the north of Europe' and put forward through their agents at Lisbon. He maintained that these merchants had hoarded a large supply of diamonds and were endeavouring to prevent the sale of Portuguese diamonds till they got rid of their own; the directors of the proposed company would all be connected with these foreigners and Jews and would further their interests instead of those of the company.[34] De Almeyda suggested that the Brazilian diamonds should be made a monopoly of the Crown, which would regulate the supply in accordance with the state of the market. The Portuguese government, however, decided to lease the right of mining, and only in 1771 was mining itself taken over by the Crown.[35] The sale of the stones was made a government business from the start. A contract was signed with a single merchant, who undertook to buy from the government, during an agreed period, a certain quantity of diamonds for a fixed price.

The contractors were always foreign merchants. Lisbon had lost its former importance as a market of diamonds and precious stones – there can be no doubt that this was at least partly due to the persecution of the Marranos and the escape of the richer among them to England and Holland – and it was impossible to raise the capital required by such a large business in Portugal itself.[36] These contractors were usually Dutch. It was only during the 1750s, after Pombal had come to power, that the contract was given, for a few years, to English merchants. Interesting information about the Portuguese diamond contract is revealed in a letter from an English merchant, Matthew Carrett, to Yehiel Prager.[37] The contract was held by Vanderton till he was deprived of it in 1752 by the new Chief Minister Carvalho (later Marquis de Pombal), apparently as part of his policy aimed at strengthening Portugal's economy. Vanderton was thrown into prison and the contract transferred to John Bristow – an Englishman. When Bristow left Lisbon after the earthquake of 1755, the contract passed into the hands of another Englishman by the name of Bury, who held it only till 1758, when it was again granted to a

Dutch merchant – Gildemeester, who held the contract for 30 years. The Prager letters often mention his periodical distributions of Brazil diamonds to Dutch merchants at Amsterdam.

After Pombal's downfall Vanderton was freed and tried to regain the contract. His friend Carrett tried to interest Prager, but the latter hesitated. His reluctance was fully justified when even the great Dutch house of Hope failed to wrest the contract from Gildemeester,[38] who was to hold it for another ten years. In 1788 the well-known Dutch-Jewish merchant Benjamin Cohen (known as Benjamin Amersfoort among Jews) wrested the contract from Gildemeester, but he apparently derived no great profits from it. As early as August 1788 David Prager reported from Amsterdam that most of the merchants refused to accept Cohen's diamonds because they had lost on the stones received in his first distribution, adding: 'it looks as if he will not have much success in this enterprise and is going to suffer severe losses'. Cohen had to give up the contract after two years.

Normally the diamonds sold by the Portuguese Crown were sent from Lisbon to Amsterdam, and London lost the virtual monopoly it had formerly enjoyed as a supplier of uncut diamonds to Europe. Nevertheless, London remained the chief market: it continued to import most of the Indian diamonds, and also attracted a considerable proportion of Brazilian stones.[39] The Portuguese government was unable to prevent large-scale smuggling, and it seems that many, if not most, of the smuggled diamonds found their way to London. Smuggling started immediately after the discovery of diamonds in Brazil, and large quantities of smuggled stones were seized by the Portuguese authorities as early as 1731. Pombal tried to stop the illegal trade by draconic regulations, but without success. According to Southey there existed a close co-operation between the smugglers and the mining contractors in Brazil. Mawe pointed out that because of the greater flexibility of the private trade the smuggled stones were usually sold more easily than those belonging to the government, and this statement is fully substantiated by the information supplied by the Prager brothers of Amsterdam in their letters to London, concerning the distribution of the 'official' diamonds at Amsterdam. According to Mawe almost one half of the Brazil diamonds were sold through unofficial channels.[40]

For a period of about 75 years Europe drew its diamonds from

India and Brazil. Statistical data relating to imports of Brazilian diamonds during the whole of that period are not available, and it is therefore difficult to compare the importance of the two sources of supply. In the 1750s the value of official sales of Brazilian diamonds was slightly higher than that of registered imports from India to England.[41] Eschwege gives the values of diamond sales by the Portuguese Crown during the years 1775–88; a comparison of these figures with those relating to diamond imports from India tends to show that during that period imports from India were larger, at least till the 1780s.

	Diamond imports from India (according to the General Cash Journals of the East India Company) £	Diamond sales by the Portuguese Crown (according to Eschwege)
1775	158,000	52,000
1776	279,000	44,000
1777	209,000	160,000
1778	188,000	165,000
1779	85,000	110,000
1780	106,000	96,000
1781	89,000	52,000
1782	41,000	51,000
1783	72,000	–
1784	132,000	103,000
1785	120,000	32,000
1786	69,000	101,000
1787	83,000	27,000
1788	117,000	74,000

(Eschwege gives the value in milreis, which was at that period worth 5 shillings and $7\frac{1}{2}$ pence)

In drawing conclusions from these figures the factor of smuggling must not be forgotten. The official figures, relating both to Indian and Brazilian diamonds, do not represent the total value of imports.[42]

After the late 1780s the importance of India as a source of diamonds began to decline rapidly. By 1823, as reported by Mawe, Brazil was almost the only supplier of diamonds to Europe, and for another 50 years it remained so. Only around 1870, when diamonds were discovered in South Africa, was Brazil relegated to a place of secondary importance.

Chapter 8

The diamond and coral trade at its zenith 1700–1770

We have seen that the merchants of London consigned to India coral, precious stones, and silver, for the purchase of diamonds. (After 1750 another method was evolved of transferring to India the means needed by the trade: we shall return to this later.) Every year, between November and March, the period preceding the sailing season to India, a group of merchants applied to India House for permission to transport coral, silver, and precious stones to India for the purchase of diamonds. After 1720 the handling of these applications became a matter of routine. Rarely was any limitation imposed. In 1755 Moses Montefiore was allowed to export a quantity of coral on condition that there was enough shipping space, and a similar condition was attached to all licences issued that year and again in 1760.[1] Generally there was no need for such a qualifying clause because ships used to sail to India half empty. In this respect too the coral-diamond trade fitted in well with the interest of the Company – the bulky coral was taken on the outward journey, when ships had space enough to spare, while the diamonds, taken on the return journey, when ships were fully laden, presented no problem of storage. Normally the applications were approved without exception, and the names of the exporters and the contents of the licences were registered in the minute books of the Court of Directors. After receiving the licence, the exporter paid the usual fees and sent his goods or silver to India House in Leadenhall Street. There they were examined and sealed and the sign of the exporter – often consisting of his initials enclosed by a Shield of David – was put on the boxes.[2] The consignments were then loaded on East Indiamen which sailed to India in early spring, arriving there during the summer.

The coral needed for the India trade was usually bought at Leghorn; often it was the property of Leghorn merchants who sent it to India through their agents at London. Consignments consisted of rough coral, polished coral, and coral beads. In the seventeenth century the classification seems to have been according to quality, but in the eighteenth century according to the stage of the finish. The silver had to be in foreign coin because export of English money and of silver bars was prohibited. Most of the silver exported to India consisted of Spanish 'pieces-of-eight', a steady supply of which reached London from Cadiz. Many of the Jewish diamond merchants were also importers of precious metals – a particularly convenient combination which must have saved many of them the additional expenses involved in the purchase of silver.

Consignments to India consisted of coral, precious stones, and silver in varying proportions. *Prima facie* it should have been more profitable to send goods than silver, but silver coins were really in the nature of goods, and sometimes it was the silver which yielded a fair profit, while coral consignments proved a disappointment. At other times coral was a better investment.[3] The supply of coral was also more certain than that of Spanish coins, which was dependent on the irregular sailings of the Spanish-American fleet and on the state of relations between England and Spain. Till 1725 silver consignments by far exceeded those of coral, but thereafter coral became the more important export item. This development was encouraged by the migration of several Jewish merchants from Leghorn to England; the Francos, in particular, had a large part in increasing the English coral trade with India. Another factor may have been the Anglo-Spanish war of 1727–9 which caused a lack of Spanish coin in London. During the 1730s, when the Brazilian diamond crisis almost brought diamond imports from India to a stop, there was no point in sending silver in considerable quantity, while the export of coral, though reduced for a time, was continued, and the proceeds returned by bills of exchange. After the crisis had passed the export of silver was resumed. Large quantities were sent out between 1743 and 1752, and during three consecutive years their value exceeded that of coral exports[4] – a natural development, in view of the growing diamond imports during that period. We also have to keep in mind that during those years Ashkenazi houses were beginning to play an increasingly significant role in the Anglo-Indian diamond trade. The Ashkenazim had few connections with Leghorn and were not familiar with the coral trade, and their consignments were chiefly made up of coins and precious and semi-precious stones, especially emeralds, polished diamonds, pearls, amber and amber beads, and also glass beads. These kinds of jewellery were of secondary importance, but they formed a constant item in the trade during the whole of the eighteenth century.

After 1752 the importance of silver again decreased, and thereafter consignments were usually small.[5] The immediate cause of this development was, apparently, the flooding of the Madras market with silver coins and the consequent fall in their price. But in the long run it was undoubtedly connected with a new method of transferring to India the means needed for the purchase of diamonds, evolved during the 1750s by the diamond merchants. They started giving respondentia loans which combined elements of loan business and maritime insurance. It can be assumed that some of the diamond merchants had always been used to making indirect investments in the India trade by giving loans to captains and officers of East Indiamen. The merchants now discovered that it was possible to make use of a modified form of this kind of loan in order to transfer means to India without having recourse to the East India Company.

We have the texts of two respondentia bills given in April 1760 by Charles Mears, Captain of the *Egmont*, for a loan of £1,500 received from the Sephardi merchant Ephraim d'Aguilar, and for a loan of £3,000 received from the Ashkenazi Joseph Salomons.[6] The contents and formulation of the two bills are almost identical, showing that a certain routine had already been developed. D'Aguilar's money was lent jointly to Mears and to a certain Thomas Hindman – apparently one of Mears' officers. It is stated in the bill that d'Aguilar had lent to Mears and Hindman the sum of £1,500 'upon merchandise and effects of that value laden or to be laden upon their or one of their accounts on board the said ship *Egmont* now in the River of Thames'. The conditions of the contract were: the ship was to sail 'with all convenient speed' to Bombay or to any other port east of the Cape of Good Hope;[7] within 30 days after the ship's arrival at Bombay Mears and Hindman were to pay to Governor Richard Bourchier, who acted as d'Aguilar's agent at Bombay, a sum of rupees equal to 4,617 Madras pagodas (£1,770); the rate of exchange was fixed in the bill at 7 shillings and 8 pence the pagoda. The premium therefore amounted to £270, or 18 per cent.

In formulating the bill the possibility was taken into account that the ship might reach a port other than Bombay, that it might be ordered to sail from Bombay before the expiration of 30 days, or that Bombay might be in enemy hands. In such event Mears and Hindman undertook to see to it that the money would reach Madras, where it was to be paid out to Charles Bourchier or, in his absence, to Daniel de Castro – an Anglo-Jewish diamond merchant of that place. The final part of the bill contained the insurance side of the transaction; Mears' and Hindman's obligations were to be null and void should the ship be lost 'by fire, enemys, pyrates, men of war or any other casualty'. Although the loan was given on a voyage to Bombay, which had no diamond market, there can be no doubt that the purpose was to transfer money for the purchase of diamonds. The respondentia bill shows that Madras was the final destination of the money, but it was sent through Bombay because that port was a better market than Madras for European goods and it was easier and more profitable to lend money on voyages to Bombay.[8]

Why was this new method of transferring money for the purchase of diamonds evolved, and what was its importance as compared with consignments of coral, silver, and precious stones? Two interests were involved, the merchants and the ships' officers. The mere existence of an alternative method for the transfer of money to India was obviously useful to the merchants, particularly as this channel was not subject to control by the East India Company. It is perhaps no accident that instructions for smuggling diamonds into England are found originating from two merchants who employed the respondentia method of transferring money to India for the purchase of stones. Transfer by respondentia had the further attraction that it yielded a fairly safe profit and was not subject to the fluctuations of the market like coral and silver. It seems that the method was used mainly by Ashkenazim who had formerly chiefly consigned silver, because they lacked the connections with the coral trade which their Sephardi brethren enjoyed. At the time when respondentia loans were first employed by the diamond merchants the prices of silver at Madras were very low, and it was perhaps this state of affairs which was the initial cause for the development of the new method of transfer.

The advantage of this method to the ships' officers involved lay in the capital which it provided for their purchase of Indian goods. The officer used the loan to buy goods in England, the 'merchandise and effects of that value' referred to in our example.

These he sold in India, and from the proceeds paid over the loan plus premium to the lender's agent. The profit which he made on the transaction could then be used, together with additional sums borrowed in India from persons anxious to transfer their fortunes to Europe, to buy goods in India for his homeward journey.

It is more difficult to give a satisfactory answer to the second question: how important was the new method of transfer, as compared with the traditional consignments of silver and coral. The East India Company Court Books and Cash Journals supply accurate data relating to the annual value of these consignments. Naturally the respondentia method is never mentioned in the books of the Company, and we would not even know of its existence if it was not referred to in numerous legal documents of London and Madras. One of these documents gives a certain basis of comparison, though it relates only to the business of a single merchant. We know the amounts which were transferred to India by Joseph Salomons, one of the great Ashkenazi merchants of the City, to his agent Peter Mariette at Madras, in the period 1754–8. Salomons transferred to Mariette over £34,000 by respondentia; during the same period he consigned to India coral and coral beads to the value of £14,370 and silver coins worth £4,000.[9] Out of a total amount of £53,000 which Salomons transferred to India within those five years for the purchase of diamonds some 65 per cent was by way of respondentia.

It is instructive to compare these figures with others, relating to Salomons' business in an earlier period, before the diamond merchants switched over to respondentia loans as a method of transfer. In the five years 1746–50 Salomons consigned to India (usually in partnership with other merchants) £86,700 in silver coins and £800 in coral and precious stones.[10] The comparison shows that Salomons, who was one of the few Ashkenazim who managed to gain a foothold in the coral trade, partially replaced silver by coral consignments after 1750, but made even greater use of respondentia loans. The business of Michael Salomons – Joseph's son – shows a similar trend. Between October 1759 and October 1761 Salomons junior transferred to John Debonaire, his agent at Madras, £7,076 by respondentia, while the value of coral and coral beads consigned by him during the same period amounted to only £1,540.[11] He did not send silver.

Though one should beware of drawing far-reaching conclusions from the business of a single merchant, the case of Joseph Salomons and his son probably represents a general trend, particularly in as far as Ashkenazi diamond merchants are concerned. At least three of the great Ashkenazi houses – those of Joseph Salomons, Aaron Franks, and Levy Norden – transferred money by respondentia.[12] The importance of the new method is also indicated by the fact that silver consignments for the purchase of diamonds stopped almost completely after 1751, and were resumed only for a short time, between 1764 and 1766. Respondentia loans evidently served as a welcome substitute for silver. Were it not for the unknown factor of smuggling it would have been possible to compare the figures of silver and coral exports with those of diamond imports, and to have regarded the difference as representing the amounts remitted by respondentia. But smuggling was probably encouraged by these remittances, which were outside the Company's control, and as far as diamond imports are concerned the official figures are even less a reliable guide to the true state of affairs than before.

For about two-thirds of the eighteenth century Madras enjoyed an almost complete monopoly in the export of diamonds to Europe, and was the receiving end for the stream of silver, coral, and precious stones sent out to the East by London diamond merchants. Certain quantities were usually sent to other English factories – Bombay, Surat[13] and Calcutta[14] – and after 1760 a new market for coral was found in China,[15] but there can be no doubt that the major part of the consignments was destined for Madras.[16] The goods were sent to the agents of the exporters at Madras. The East India Company obliged the merchants to employ the Governor of Fort St George as a second agent who, of course, rendered no real services, but received a commission of 2 per cent.[17] On occasion, however, the Governor could play an active role.[18] The silver usually consisted of Spanish or Mexican 'pieces-of-eight'. These coins did not pass as cash at Madras and had to be sold like any other goods, their value in relation to the local pagoda varying in accordance with the state of the market. When there was a glut, prices fell and the coins sometimes remained unsold for a considerable period. In 1750, after several years of unusually large silver consignments, there was a loss of 12 per cent on the price of silver in Europe, but on the whole silver seems to have yielded a small profit. One way of overcoming sales difficulties was to recoin the silver at Madras into Indian rupees.[19] Coral and precious stones were sold to Indian merchants at Madras, usually at a credit of between two and four months. If the sum due was not paid by the end of the agreed period, the buyer was obliged to pay interest on the debt.[20] These credit arrangements were a cause of difficulties, as we shall see later.

Under favourable conditions coral exports yielded good profits. A box of coral worth £900, sent to India in 1729 by Jacob da Costa, was sold in Madras for 3,000 pagodas, the profit amounting to 33 per cent.[21] However, the frequent glutting of the Indian market, which had caused trouble to the Company in the seventeenth century, did not disappear after the coral trade had passed into the hands of the private merchants. In 1729 matters reached such a state that the Madras Council began to insist that customs duties on imported coral had to be paid even before it was sold, in view of the fact that large quantities which had arrived from London in 1728 were still unsold and an early sale was not expected.[22] Though the coral trade to India was now almost exclusively in the hands of London's diamond merchants, and the foreign competition which had hampered the trade in the seventeenth century had almost been eliminated, glutting of the Indian market was still a recurring phenomenon. Supply could have been easily regulated by an agreement among the major exporters of the City, but no arrangement of this kind seems ever to have been achieved.

The diamond mines were spread over a wide area, north and north-west of Madras. Stones were found in the riverbeds of the Penner, the Kistna, the Godavari, and the Mahanadi, and in the neighbouring areas.[23] In the middle of the eighteenth century a new source was discovered further north, in the vicinity of Panna in Bundelkhand.[24] The mines were leased by the local rulers, who usually retained the right to claim stones of exceptional size for themselves. The Indian diamond merchants were Banians, natives of Gujarat, who bought the diamonds at the mines and sold them to the European agents. In the seventeenth century there was an important diamond market at Golconda, some 300 miles north-west of Madras, but later there was a tendency to develop direct links between the mines and the port of export. We know of three Anglo-Jewish diamond merchants – Rodrigues Salvadore, Isaac Abendana and Marcus Moses – who used to travel from Madras to the diamond mines at the beginning of the eighteenth century. Generally, however, the European merchant preferred to have the stones brought to him at Madras or to order in advance certain quantities from Indian merchants or agents.[25] The roads to the diamond mines were often unsafe, a state of affairs which frequently resulted in a considerable difference between prices paid for diamonds at the mines and those demanded from the European agents at Madras. Dealings at the mines had a surreptitious character, as we know from evidence given by Marcus Moses – Glueckel of Hameln's son-in-law – who had an intimate knowledge of the business transacted in the diamond mines. According to Moses, the Indian diamond merchants at the mines never negotiated with the buyers themselves, but employed a coolie, 'who would not tell me his [the employer's] name even if I should desire such an out of the way thing'. We also have it, on the authority of the Council of Fort St George, that the purchasing of diamonds at the mines was 'a clandestine trade in which the persons concerned run the risque of life and estate if discovered'.[26] It may well be that the cause for this secrecy were the big stones which by law were the property of the Indian ruler, but in fact found their way to Madras and from there to London, where they were usually bought up by Abraham Nathan, a friend of Marcus Moses. The Indian diamond merchants usually demanded cash payments.[27] This was natural because, even if the stones were sold on credit, the purchaser could not hope to sell them before the day of payment. The insistence on cash payments, however, often caused difficulties to the European agents, who had to sell their coral at several months' credit, and were thus liable to miss opportunities of purchasing diamonds. This situation was made even more difficult by the irregular supply of diamonds. Supplies were dependent on more than one factor: the output of the mines, the state of security in the area of the mines, the safety of the roads, and also on the commercial tactics of the Indian merchants who often brought their stones to the market just before the sailing of ships, in the hope of creating favourable sale conditions for themselves.[28]

The ability of the European merchant to overcome these obstacles was limited. It seems that one way to tackle the problem which confronted the merchant, who had to sell coral on credit and pay cash for diamonds, was to give a discount on the price of the coral in return for early payment.[29] It is also possible that exchange dealings of diamonds for coral helped to bridge the gap.[30] An attempt was made to frustrate the tactics of the Indian merchants and prevent them from dictating their terms to the European buyers, by means of an administrative measure. This consisted of a strict prohibition on the registration of diamond consignments to Europe after the register had been formally closed, in order to make it impossible for the Indians to offer their stones for sale at the last moment.[31] The bargaining position of the Europeans was also strengthened by the possibility, which existed from 1733, of returning the proceeds of the coral by bills of exchange instead of diamonds.

All these, however, could be no more than partial palliatives. It might seem that the best way to bring the Indian merchants to reason would have been the formation of combinations by the European sellers. Evidence of only three such combinations has come to light, and of these, two belong to the period after 1765, when the bargaining power of the Indians assumed alarming proportions.[32] It therefore seems that associations of this kind were not very common, and Jeffries was probably not very far from the truth when he maintained that the Indian diamond merchants imposed their will on the market.[33]

The London merchants had even less control of the Indian diamond market than their agents in India. The City merchant was unable to anticipate the Indian market conditions which would prevail at the time his instructions reached Madras, nor the state of the market in Europe when his diamonds arrived, a year or more after he had ordered them. The few surviving business letters seem to show that the London merchants usually let the agents at Madras decide on the assortment of stones which they purchased.[34] In 1753 Thomas Godfrey of London wrote to Governor Saunders and to Solomon Salomons at Madras:

I send you the prices of diamonds as given me some time ago, but may not be quite so exact as I could wish. Stones of a mangelin weight [an Indian measure, equal to about 1.4 carat] and upwards, this season, were most in demand. But things alter, and the price with you must be considered, as well as price here, and sometimes when all run on one thing it enhances the price abroad, and quantity affects the same here. Of all these things you are better judges than I am.[35]

The element of gambling was even more pronounced in the Anglo-Indian diamond trade than was usual in other branches of commerce at that period.

The diamonds were sent to London in ships sailing in the service of the East India Company. They were packed in 'bulses' – leather purses inside cloth-wrapped boxes – each accompanied by a bill stating the number and assortments of stones and their value in pagodas. The diamonds sent to London had to be registered at the Company's offices at Fort St George, and after the register was closed for the season, it, too, was sent to India House. The register served as a basis for calculating the dues which the importers had to pay to the Company (5 per cent up to 1733, $2\frac{1}{2}$ per cent thereafter). The diamond consignments were entrusted to the care of the captain, who received 1.4 per cent of their value for his trouble. The chief aim of this payment, which was obligatory according to the rules of the Company, was to give the ships' captains a personal interest in the legal trade and to reduce the temptation of smuggling.

On arrival of the ships in London the diamond bulses were brought to India House. An Act of Parliament dating from 1699[36] prescribed that all goods imported from India, including such as were the property of private merchants, had to be sold at the public sales of the East India Company. This rule applied to diamonds too, and the Court Books of the eighteenth century include many instructions for the public sale of diamonds.[37] On the other hand we also find instructions for the delivery of stones to the importers to whom they were addressed, and requests by importers that their diamonds be delivered to them.[38] Sometimes the Court ordered the public sale of diamonds, and at the same time had them delivered to their owners.[39] The contradiction between the first and the second part of such instructions is obvious: how could the stones be delivered to the owner after they had been sold at the Company's public sales?

Here we are confronted with a rather baffling problem: did India House have a routine procedure for disposing of the stones? Were they sold at public sales, as prescribed by law, or delivered to their owners? Is there any way of explaining the apparent contradiction? The key to the solution of this riddle is supplied by a letter-book of the firm of Mocatta and Goldsmid, dating from the beginning of the nineteenth century. In this book there is a copy of a letter to N. Vansittart, signed by several precious stones merchants of London, and also a memorandum submitted by importers of pearls. Both relate to the method of delivery and sale of pearls received from India, and were occasioned by a new Act of Parliament enforcing the public sale of Indian pearls.[40]

These documents make it abundantly clear that the public sales of pearls were nothing but a farce, and there can be no doubt that the same applied to diamond sales.[41] A public sale was always held *pro forma*, but the 'buyer' was invariably the importer himself, who was represented at the sale by an agent of the Company.[42] The merchants, with the connivance of the Company, thus by-passed the law which would otherwise have ruined the diamond trade, as no merchant would have taken the risk of importing diamonds if he did not have the certainty of being able to sell them himself, in a manner and at a time he thought fit.[43] These documents also supply the key to the solution of another perplexing problem. Between 1719 and 1729 the diamond merchants repeatedly requested the Company to grant them a more favourable rate of exchange (£ : pagoda) for their diamonds sold at the public sales of the Company. Had there been a *bona fide* public sale the problem of the rate of exchange could not have arisen, because the stones would have been sold freely, without regard to the price paid for them in India. The true purpose of the request was, however, to obtain a reduction of the duties levied on diamonds. The declared value of the diamonds was stated in pagodas, and consequently it was in the interest of the merchants that the rate of exchange, according to which the duties were calculated, should be as much as possible in favour of the pound sterling. Between 1720 and 1730 the value of the pagoda declined, and the merchants naturally pressed the Company to alter its calculation of duties accordingly.

The maritime insurance of diamond consignments presented a special problem. In times of peace insurance premiums did not constitute too heavy a burden, though even then the rates demanded for voyages to and from India were considerably higher than what is considered reasonable today. In war-time, however, insurers charged up to 25 per cent of the value of goods, and under such conditions the profitableness of the trade was very doubtful.[44] A further difficulty was caused by the necessity of insuring the diamonds in London, as only in the second half of the eighteenth century were European insurance companies established in India. The London merchants had to decide whether to insure only after they received news that diamonds had been sent to them and in what ship, or whether to insure an estimated value, without awaiting definite information about the consignments. If he waited, the merchant ran the risk that the loss of the ship carrying his goods would be known in London before he had time to insure them.[45] On the other hand, the insurance of an estimated value of diamonds, to be carried by unspecified ships, was naturally dearer, and the merchant could not have absolute certainty that his agents in India would in fact be able to send him stones for the full value he had insured. It seems however that when consignments did not come up to expectations, the insurers in London, or at least insurance companies, used to refund part of the premium.[46]

The East India Company perfected a system of controls designed to ensure compliance by the merchants with the Company's regulations and regular payment of licence fees and other duties payable to the Company. India-bound consignments of coral, precious stones, and silver were inspected and sealed at India House before loading. Exporters were obliged to sign a declaration stating that the proceeds would be used for the purchase of pearls, diamonds or other kinds of precious stones. These were to be returned to England within three years after the consignment's arrival in India, in the case of silver, or after sale, in the case of coral.[47] This represented an improvement on earlier regulations – till 1730 the period within which the proceeds of coral and silver had to be returned was only a year and a half after the arrival of the silver in India and one year after the sale of the coral. In 1729 the merchants complained about 'the hardships they labour under by the shortness of time hitherto allowed for the investment of their money in India'. The Company agreed to their request and extended the period to three years.[48] Diamond consignments were entered in the Company's register at Fort St George, and the register was also sent to London. Only after full returns had been made were the declarations handed back to the merchants. Unregistered diamonds were liable for a further payment of 5 per cent. Despite these precautions the diamond trade was never free from smuggling. Controls were not as efficient in fact as they looked on paper, and diamond smuggling is notoriously easy.

The motivations for smuggling were not necessarily pecuniary, though when profits were low, duties could be an onerous burden. This was especially true before the Company's import duties were reduced from 5 to 2½ per cent in 1733. It seems that the captains of the Company's ships, through whom most of the smuggling was done, used to charge 2 per cent for their services,[49] which was only a little more than they received for registered diamonds consigned on their ships. Although the temptation to smuggle was lessened by the reduction of duties in 1733, non-monetary motives remained. For one, there was the trouble and waste of time involved in having the stones handed out by the Company in London; but a more important motive for smuggling existed during wartime: if anything happened to the ship there was a much better chance of the diamonds being saved if they were entrusted to the personal care of the captain.

Smuggling seems to have been on the increase after 1760. While formerly isolated cases had been discovered from time to time, we now find complaints about large-scale smuggling, even though nothing definite was found out.[50] Instructions for smuggling have been preserved from this period in which two of London's biggest diamond merchants – Aaron Franks and Michael Salomons – ordered their agents in India to consign their diamonds without registration.[51] In 1765 a case of large-scale diamond smuggling was discovered in which many diamond merchants were involved. Of the 19 firms involved eight were Jewish: Levi and Ruben Salomons, Herman Hendricks, Joseph Gompertz, Gompertz and Heyman, Abraham Heyman Levi and Aaron Levi, Philip Salomons, Henry Moses, and Michael Salomons – all of them, by the way, Ashkenazim. The agents at Madras who sent the stones were Nicholas Morse, Samuel Moses and Daniel de Castro. The blame, however, was put on their agents at Madras and on Governor Palk.[52] In 1774 Jacob Prager assumed as a matter of course that part of the diamonds which were expected from India would arrive by private hands.[53]

The causes of the increase of smuggling must be a matter of conjecture. The new method of transferring money to India by respondentia loans was probably one of them. This channel was outside the control of the East India Company and it could be a matter of dispute whether it was legal at all. It was more than probable, therefore, that respondentia transfers not only facilitated, but actually encouraged, the smuggling of diamonds. The merchant who imported stones purchased with the proceeds of respondentia transfers was unable to have them checked off at India House against legal exports of silver or coral. He may therefore have been well advised not to let them pass under the scrutiny of the Company's officials. Another factor which probably contributed to the growth of smuggling was the large-scale transfers of fortunes from India to England, which were partly effected through diamond consignments. The captain or the Company official who brought the diamonds to England unregistered saved a sum equivalent to 2½ per cent of their value. Considering the small risk, there can be no wonder that many were tempted to disregard the law.

Smuggling must be borne in mind when evaluating the statistical data. The precise registration of duties paid by merchants, in the books of the East India Company, enables a calculation to be made of the volume of exports and imports throughout most of the eighteenth century, and of the individual transactions of every merchant. Because of smuggling, however, it is difficult to tell how far these figures represent the true volume of the trade. As the extent of smuggling can never be known, the official figures must be regarded with some reserve. They probably are not far from the truth where the export of coral, precious stones and silver to India are concerned: the papers of the East India Company mention only one case of coral smuggling during the whole of the eighteenth century.[54] These goods were much more difficult to smuggle than diamonds, and they were usually the property of merchants who, to all appearances, were less inclined to smuggling than the Company's people. With diamond imports things stood differently: here the official figures probably never represented the full volume of the trade, and at certain times, as in the first decade of the eighteenth century and during the period 1760–80, diamond smuggling must have attained considerable proportions.

There were three kinds of diamond merchants in London. The importers sold the stones to the big dealers in the City, who were the wholesale merchants of the trade; they had the stones cut and polished or sent them to Amsterdam or Antwerp for that purpose. The third class consisted of jewellers – people of lesser means who bought finished stones or polished them themselves and manufactured all kinds of jewellery. They were therefore craftsmen and retailers rather than merchants and it was they who sold the finished product to the public.[55] Though the functions of the three classes sometimes overlapped, the distinction between them was quite clear. The jewellers were naturally the social inferiors of the merchants. It is true that a jeweller like Disraeli's

great-grandfather, Isaac Siprut de Gabay, used to import small
quantities of diamonds from India on his own account, but when
he dared to provoke the great Francos he brought upon himself
quick ruin. He used to buy uncut diamonds on credit from
Abraham and Jacob Franco. In August 1756 he decamped with
diamonds for which he had not yet paid and with a large sum of
money which he had received for other, unpaid, stones. De Gabay
got to Holland, but the Francos acted swiftly. They sent a description of the malefactor to their agents in Germany, France, Italy
and the Netherlands, with the numbers of the bills of exchange
which he had with him and the names of the persons on whom
they were drawn, requesting them to publish the affair in the
newspapers. De Gabay was thus effectively prevented from selling the diamonds and disposing of the bills and was obliged to
return to England where he was immediately arrested at the
Francos' request.[56]

The importers and the wholesale merchants belonged to the
same social class, though the Jewish importers were predominantly
Sephardim – at least till the second half of the eighteenth century
– while the wholesalers mostly belonged to the Ashkenazi community. There was, however, a sharp distinction between the
economic functions of the two classes, and there are indications
that the wholesalers jealously guarded their sphere of activity
against any penetration by the importers. Esther Prager explained
to her brother-in-law at Amsterdam that she did not send him the
diamonds which she had received from India because this would
have annoyed the London diamond merchants: 'They do not
want, so they say, that I should send diamonds to Amsterdam.
I must leave this market to them.'[57]

The diamond bulses were usually sold unopened, as they
arrived from India, according to the bill enclosed by the consigner
there. We have reliable evidence for this custom from the leading
merchants Abraham and Jacob Franco:

> it is usual and customary for diamonds imported from the East
> Indies for sale, to be sent over in several different parcels,
> sealed up in bags or bulses, and that it is usual to send over
> therewith an invoice of the prime cost, weight and value of each
> parcel, sealed or stamped with the same seal with which the
> bulses it relates to is sealed up, and that it is frequent, usual and
> customary for dealers in diamonds to buy and contract for the

purchase of all or such parcels of diamonds as they chose and can agree for, on the sight and examination of the invoice only, before the bulse is opened and before first seeing the diamonds, reliance and regard in these cases being had to the judgment, credit and integrity of the person abroad by whom such diamonds are sent to Europe and by whom such invoice is made.[58]

The bill was made out in Madras pagodas, and the rate of exchange had to be negotiated between seller and buyer.[59] It was determined not only by market conditions, but also reflected the degree of trust which the consigner in India enjoyed in the City: the difference could amount to one shilling in the pagoda, or about 10 per cent.[60] Bulses consigned by merchants who were known to be unreliable could not be sold unopened at all.[61] Once a bulse of diamonds had been sold unopened, the purchaser had no ground for complaint, even – in the words of a person acquainted with the trade – 'if the bulse was filled with sand and gravel'.[62] If the seller opened the bulse before he sold it, or if it was opened at the insistence of the buyer, the diamonds were sold, like any other goods, for so many shillings per carat, without regard to the enclosed bill. As a rule cash payment was demanded.[63]

Diamonds were usually sold from hand to hand, but public sales were sometimes resorted to, when chances seemed better that way.[64] Under normal conditions the merchant preferred to sell privately, mainly, it seems, in order to avoid the risk of a combination of buyers which a public sale entailed.[65] The same preference for direct contact with the buyer was also reflected in the attitude of diamond merchants towards brokers, with whose services they gladly dispensed. It is quite possible that the average diamond merchant was much more of an expert in his field than other merchants in theirs, and was therefore less dependent on brokers. The relatively insignificant role which the brokers played in the trade can, however, be better explained by the fact that it was impossible to sell diamonds by samples. If the merchant wanted to avail himself of the services of a broker, he had to entrust him with the diamonds he wished to sell – no wonder the merchants were reluctant to trust brokers to such an extent.[66] Diamond brokers like Moses Machoro, Abraham de Paiba, and the firm of Mocatta and Goldsmid probably did most of their business with people from outside the trade.

The value of the diamonds in the London market was, of course, determined in the first place by their quality. Transparency, spots and flaws, possibility of cutting and polishing and the size of stones were the important factors.[67] Diamonds were classified according to their quality, and were sorted in India before being sent to Europe, into five groups, ranging from fine to boart. The 'fine' stones were usually made into brilliants, the middle sorts were cut into less expensive stones, while the boart seems to have served mainly for cutting other diamonds. It was also used for cutting glass.[68] There was little demand for industrial diamonds. In the 1770s and 1780s the price difference between the highest and lowest quality was about five to one,[69] but a table of prices in India, c.1746, shows a difference of about eight to one.[70]

In addition to the usual categories of diamonds there was a sort known as lasks – stones already worked in India. Because Indian workmanship was bad, these stones were always recut and polished in Europe, usually into cheap diamonds like those produced from 'refuge' and 'turn out'. The lasks differed from the other sorts in that their quality varied widely, their values in Holland ranging between 15 gulden and 40 gulden per carat.[71]

These ratios, like the absolute values of diamonds, were liable to change in accordance with market conditions. The diamond trade was always quick to react to changes in supply and demand, to fluctuations caused by the international situation, and to alterations in fashion.[72] Unusually large consignments could mean disaster, because, in the words of Jacob Prager, 'this diamond trade only serves pomp and luxury'. The trade could flourish only during times of peace and prosperity, generally because such conditions were vital for a steady demand, and in particular because of the steep rise in insurance premiums which was the inevitable result of war.[73] The defeat of the allies in the Battle of Almanza and Villars' raid into Germany in 1707 had an immediate effect on the German market for large diamonds,[74] while the Russo-Turkish war in the 1780s resulted in a steep decline in the demand for cheap diamonds.[75] We may quote the Parisian jeweller Philip Masson:[76] 'In order to sell diamonds people must be at their ease, money must circulate and trade must be settled, and there must be, as t'were, a superfluity.'

Although the relative importance of royal courts as customers for jewellery was declining, they could still influence the diamond market. A coronation, a royal marriage, or even the return of the king from London to Hanover or his recuperation from illness could increase the demand for diamonds and bring about a rise in prices.[77] After the French Revolution it was feared that the abolition of monarchy in France would cause a grave setback to the diamond trade.[78]

In view of the special character of the diamond trade, some indication of the developments which later resulted in the formation of the London diamond syndicate could have been expected to be evident by the eighteenth century. In fact this was so only in one respect – the concentration of the trade in London. There is no evidence whatsoever for a permanent organization of the market or for the regulation of supply by a group of merchants. There were, of course, temporary combinations of buyers, but there appears to be only one single allusion to a general combination of dealers, and even here the evidence is of a rather doubtful authenticity.[79] Indeed we have more than negative evidence for the absence of any sustained attempt to regulate the diamond market. The Prager Papers show that fierce competition, rather than regulation, characterized the London market, and caused great harm to the trade. It is of course possible that this state of affairs developed only after 1770, when diamond imports grew by leaps and bounds, and it was perhaps only then that the necessity of regulating supply first made itself felt. It is not clear whether the cessation of diamond imports from India after the Brazil discoveries was a spontaneous action or resulted from an agreement between the merchants.

After the Jewish merchants moved the international diamond market to London in the second half of the seventeenth century the commercial and industrial centres of the trade were at different places. While the one had moved to London, the other stayed at Amsterdam. Antwerp retained some importance as a secondary centre of the industry, cutting only cheap stones. Diamond cutters could be found in London too, and there is certainly much evidence for the existence of a diamond industry in London. The famous Pitt diamond was cut in London by Joseph Cope, whom Alvaro da Fonseca considered as the only person in England who could be entrusted with this task.[80] We know the names of Jewish diamond cutters of London like Isaac Robles and Abraham Levy.[81] Levy Norden described himself in 1764 as 'an opulent and very considerable jeweller in London ... having diamond

mills in Wheeler Street, White Chapple'. He employed journey-
men and apprentices, the names of two of these being known:
Solomon Joseph and Eleazar Hart.[82] There were also diamond
cutters among the Huguenots who settled in England and it is
quite possible that many of the London jewellers not only sold
but also cut diamonds. The British Ambassador in Portugal, who
received the information from English merchants resident there,
maintained in 1732 that the best diamond cutters were to be
found in London, and a similar statement was made by the British
Consul in Portugal, Charles Compton.[83] The preamble to the Act
of Parliament which abolished the duties on diamonds in 1732
also stated that 'great numbers of rough diamonds are sent from
abroad to be cut and polished here'.[84] Philo-patriae (Joseph
Salvador) wrote in 1753 that the concentration of the diamond
trade in London was 'retaining' there 'a great part of the polishing trade which is a considerable manufacture'.[85] When in July
1787 Lyon Prager protested to the Board of Trade at Calcutta
against the diamond cutter Evan Bowen establishing himself in
the town, he argued that 'this might, if carried on to a large
extent, not only injure many families in England who carry on
that manufactury for the support of themselves and many poor
labourers, but it might materially interrupt my endeavours to
re-establish that trade'. On the other hand, although these quotations show a diamond industry of some significance in London its
importance must not be overrated. London's industry could never
compare with that of Amsterdam, and its importance seems to
have declined even further in the course of the eighteenth century.
At the time of the Pragers diamonds were usually sent from
London to Amsterdam for cutting and polishing.

   Why did no big diamond industry develop in London after it
had become the foremost commercial centre of the trade? Jeffries
ascribed it to the cheaper labour available on the Continent;[86] it
seems, however, that a better explanation can be found in the
very nature of the diamond industry with its high degree of
specialization. Its transfer from Amsterdam to London could not
have been accomplished unless a considerable number of experts
emigrated in the same direction. There was no cause for such
emigration, and it did not take place. Thanks to the ease and
frequency of communication between England and Holland, the
separation of the industrial from the commercial centre presented
no serious difficulties and close contacts were further facilitated

by business and family ties which united the Jewish communities of London and Amsterdam.

For a century and a half the diamond trade constituted one of the main economic pillars of the upper strata of London's Jewish community, Portuguese as well as Ashkenazi. We must therefore try to form an idea of the profits that could normally be expected in the trade, although, in view of the meagreness of sources relating to individual business transactions, we cannot hope to arrive at any firm conclusions.

There are three extant accounts relating to the sale of diamonds in London on behalf of Thomas Pitt, all dating from the early years of the eighteenth century. The first sale, in 1701, resulted in a loss of 13.9 per cent on the price paid for the diamonds in India; the second sale, in 1705, yielded a profit of 89.6 per cent, while a profit of 34.7 per cent was achieved in the third.[87] It seems that these figures were not untypical both as to the average profit and the big differences between the results of the individual trans-actions. One person well acquainted with the diamond trade wrote in 1721 that a profit of between 30 and 40 per cent could usually be expected from diamonds.[88] This estimate is confirmed by an interesting document dating from the 1740s. It contains the resumé of accounts relating to consignments of diamonds sent by George Jones and his partner Levy Moses of Madras to John Goddard and Henry Moses in London, between 1744 and 1746 (see Appendix K). On the basis of the subsidy of $2\frac{1}{2}$ per cent paid by the East India Company to the importers, it is possible to calculate the declared value of the diamonds[89] and to compare it with the price received for the same stones in London. The total purchase value of the diamonds was £13,504 and they were sold in London for £19,722. There was thus an overall profit of £6,218 or 46 per cent, while profits of the individual transactions varied between 28 and 124 per cent. This must be considered a fair profit, even if we take into account, as we must, the long time which was required for the completion of a transaction in the Anglo-Indian trade. If three years was the usual time needed to complete such a transaction then a profit of 15 per cent was needed to cover the interest alone. This includes of course any profit in consignments *to* India. If Jones and Moses achieved a similar average profit on the rest of their transactions between 1744 and 1749, their net gains during that period must have amounted to something like £7,000. This was a considerable sum for a firm of medium size whose consignments during the period under consideration added up to no more than the quantity which one of the bigger firms used to consign in a single year.

In addition to the profits on diamonds sent to England, consignments of silver and coral to India must normally have yielded some gain. Here again we have few details of individual transactions, the most conclusive information being that which concerns the business of Moses Mendes da Costa. During the 1750s da Costa sent £4,529 worth of coral to India, which yielded a profit of about 18 per cent.[90]

In conclusion it can be said that in good times the diamond trade yielded considerable profits. It must be remembered, however, that this trade was even more susceptible than others to the influence of unforeseeable factors like fluctuations of supply and demand, fashions, war and peace, and so on. As a result, there were frequent periods when business was slack, and at such times the situation was aggravated by the fact that the duties imposed by the East India Company remained constant and constituted a relatively much heavier burden than when trade was flourishing. Thus we find that diamonds to the value of £11,329, consigned around the year 1700 to Moses Barrow (Barukh Lousada) and Joseph Gomes yielded a profit of 9.8 per cent in London; the net gain, however, amounted to no more than 2 per cent, after deductions of duties. This meant, in fact, that the transaction resulted in a considerable loss, the profit being much below common interest.[91] In view of the considerable risks involved it is only natural that a large part of the diamond trade was concentrated in the hands of a few big merchants.

There was hardly a firm in the Jewish-Portuguese community of London which did not, at one time or another, have a stake in the Anglo-Indian diamond trade. Not all of them, of course, played an important role. There were houses like those of Espinoza, Lindo, de Mattos, Mocatta, Gideon, Bernal, and Brandon which, while very prominent in other branches of trade and finance, had only a fleeting interest in the diamond trade. On the other hand there were families whose members imported large quantities of diamonds every year over long periods of time, sometimes for generations. To this group belong the firms of Franco, Salvador, Mendes da Costa, de Castro, Aguilar, and also some smaller firms:

Serra, Supino, Levy Sonsino, Montefiore, and Modigliani. During the eighteenth century several diamond importers belonging to the Ashkenazi community established themselves in London. Among them we find the Franks, Moses, the various Salomons families, Isaacs, Elias, Gompertz, Heyman, and Goldsmid. Diamonds figured prominently in the business of each of these merchants.

Much of the trade was concentrated in the hands of a few big merchants. A small group of between three to five houses usually imported more than half the yearly quantity of diamonds brought from India. The following table shows the percentage of diamonds imported by those Jewish merchants whose share exceeded £5,000 during four years.

1730: out of 21 Jewish merchants 5 imported 73.6%
1744: out of 20 Jewish merchants 3 imported 69.9%
1760: out of 28 Jewish merchants 2 imported 24.6%
1770: out of 28 Jewish merchants 8 imported 78.2%

The difference between big and small importers was less marked in 1760 because in that year the leading firm of the brothers Franco imported far fewer diamonds than it usually did.

The most prominent firm, for a period of some 40 years, was that of the brothers Abraham and Jacob Franco, who had come to London from Leghorn early in the eighteenth century. Abraham Franco began to import diamonds about 1710 and was joined by his brother shortly after. From that time, until their deaths in 1758 and 1777 respectively, they remained active in the coral-diamond trade with India, rapidly rising to the top. I have examined their relative importance as importers of diamonds during two periods of five years each: on the eve of the Brazilian diamond crisis and during the period immediately following it. From 1725 to 1730 between 11 and 24 per cent of the yearly quantity of registered diamonds were imported by the Francos. Their prominence was even greater after the crisis had passed, perhaps because of the role they played in reviving the trade. In the period 1741 to 1744 between 54 and 58 per cent of the annual value of diamonds imported were the property of the firm.

The pre-eminence of the Francos was still more marked in the coral trade. If we again take two periods of five years each as samples, we find that of the total value of licences issued by the East India Company to Jewish merchants for the export of coral, during the years 1733/34–1737/38 and 1753/54–1757/58, 38 and

The share of the firm of Abraham and Jacob Franco in diamond imports from India

Year	Imported on the firm's own account £	Imported in partnership with others (non-Jews)	The firm's share in overall diamond imports* %	The firm's share in diamond imports by Jews (without partnerships)
1725	14,100	1,600	13.4	16.4
1726	12,100	–	11.5	19.1
1727	9,000	5,900	11.9	18.4
1728	12,200	2,200	15.2	34.4
1729	10,200	1,200	12.8	20.9
1730	24,600	4,900	24.8	33.3
1741	32,500	–	57.6	68.1
1742	35,500	–	60.0	67.9
1743	48,300	–	50.4	56.8

* In compiling this column 50 per cent of amounts appearing in 'partnerships' were regarded as attributable to the Francos

28 per cent respectively belonged to the Francos. As the English coral trade was mostly carried on by Jews, there was no great difference between the relative share of the Francos in the total of coral exports, and their relative share in Jewish exports. The figures given here relate to their share in Jewish exports because in the 1730s some licences were issued to non-Jewish merchants in which not the value but the weight of the consignments was stated, so that it is quite impossible to take them into account.

Year	Licences issued to Francos £	Licences issued to Jews	Percentage of licences (value) issued to Francos %	
1733/4	3,500	16,800	20.8	
1734/5	14,500	34,000	42.6	*Periodical average*
1735/6	21,100	49,300	42.8	*over the years*
1736/7	14,000	47,200	29.7	1733–1738
1737/8	19,000	43,600	43.6	37.7%
1753/4	14,000	58,100	24.1	
1754/5	15,200	53,900	28.2	*Periodical average*
1755/6	12,000	43,800	27.4	*over the years*
1756/7	12,000	29,000	41.4	1753–1758
1757/8	5,000	19,000	26.3	28.5%

The General Cash Journals of the East India Company supply the data for an accurate estimate of the Jewish share in the coral–diamond trade. The duties paid for the export of coral and import of diamonds were registered, and these figures enable us to calculate the volume of business done by each individual merchant throughout most of the eighteenth century. By adding up the figures relating to Jewish merchants we arrive at the sum total of Jewish business. In considering the resulting figures it must be remembered, however, that the Anglo-Indian diamond trade always had a dual character: part of it – usually, without doubt, by far the more important part – was carried on by the professional importers of London, but part also served as a channel for the transfer of fortunes by, and as a sphere of investments for, the Company's people in India. The 'professional' part of the trade was dominated by Jews throughout the eighteenth century. Their part in the general import of diamonds varied, and was determined to a large extent by the activity of the 'non-professionals' in the trade: when this activity was on the increase, the share of the Jews in imports decreased and vice versa. During half a century, between 1717 and 1766, there were only four years in which the total of imports by non-Jews exceeded that of Jews – 1720, 1728, 1734, and 1745 – and of these four years three – 1720, 1734, and 1745 – were in some way irregular, with much reduced imports of diamonds. During the rest of the period the Jewish share of the trade always exceeded 50 per cent and sometimes was more than 80 per cent. In the decade 1749–58 it was never below 67 per cent, and during four years rose to over 80 per cent. The situation changed completely after 1765, and for nearly 20 years the majority of registered diamonds were imported by non-Jews. This was one aspect of the great crisis which overcame the diamond trade at that time, and which will be considered in the following chapter. From 1786 onward the Jews' part in the trade again increased, mainly as a result of Lyon (Leib) Prager's activity.

The coral trade was Jewish to an even greater extent than the diamond trade. Although there were some non-commercial elements – largely officers of East Indiamen trading on their own account – they played only a negligible role, and were never able to rival professional (mostly Jewish) merchants. It is impossible to make an accurate comparison for the period before 1750 between the value of licences for the export of coral issued to Jews and those issued to others. The figures relating to licences granted before 1730 are not reliable, while between 1730 and 1750 a small part of the licences stated the weight instead of the value of the coral, so that they cannot be correlated to the other figures. But during the 25 years between 1750/51 and 1774/75 the East India Company granted licences for the export of coral amounting to £1,596,000, of which £1,217,000 (76.2 per cent) went to Jewish merchants. Even in 1768/69, when the Jews' part was lowest, they had 63½ per cent of the value of licences, while in the year 1761/62 94 per cent of the licences were taken out by Jews (see Appendix J). Though the later part of the period coincided with the first stage of the crisis in the diamond trade, when the Jewish merchants were eclipsed by non-professional intruders, their pre-eminence in the coral trade remained unimpaired.

Partnerships between Jews and non-Jews were frequent, especially among the bigger merchants. Among partnerships of more than a transient nature were those of Alvaro da Fonseca and Roger Bradyll in the 1720s, between the Francos and John Cook in the period 1715–30, of Henry Isaac and Alderman George Arnold in the 1740s, of Joseph Salomons and the brothers Muilman in the 1750s,[92] and of the brothers Modigliani and Daniel Bradley after 1770. The basis for these partnerships was one of mutual benefit. The connection with a prominent gentile house must have been a distinct advantage for a Jewish merchant; it added to his prestige and may have enhanced his position vis-à-vis the East India Company, in which he could not hold an official position. The non-Jewish partner, on the other hand, would benefit from the expertise of the Jew and his international connections in the coral and diamond trades. There is no evidence that partnerships extended beyond these branches, except in the case of Modigliani and Bradley who were also partners in the silk business.

The Jewish hold on the diamond trade was even stronger than is indicated by the figures relating to imports. Many of the diamonds which were imported by non-Jews were sold to Jewish merchants in London. This was the case in three public sales of diamonds, early in the eighteenth century, of which we possess detailed accounts. In March 1700 diamonds sent to London by Thomas Pitt were sold to 33 buyers, 17 of whom were Jews.[93] In 1702 John Pitt, Lewis de Paz, and Isaac Abendana consigned stones to ten London merchants.[94] They were sold in the City to 15 persons, including 11 Jews.[95] Diamonds belonging to Pitt were again sold in 1705; on this occasion six out of eight buyers were

Jews, and they bought the bulk of the stones put up for sale.[96] The value of diamonds purchased by named buyers was 17,529 pagodas, of which 15,102 worth were sold to Jews. A similar impression is gained from the Prager letters, written in the 1770s and 1780s, which clearly indicate that most of the major buyers of diamonds in London were Jews, some of them acting as agents for Jewish houses in Holland.[97] Yehiel Prager himself used to buy diamonds in London long before he started to import them himself, and he purchased most of the stones brought to England by Robert Clive and Harry Verelst.[98]

In this context the name of Abraham Nathan must not be omitted. Nathan, originally from Hamburg, and one of the first Ashkenazi diamond merchants of London, said in 1721 that he 'had always dealt in great diamonds and bought the largest diamonds that have come to England for these forty years'.[99] For a time Nathan had to compete with Sir Francis Child of the East India Company, who also purchased large stones. Around the turn of the century, however, Nathan acquired a virtual monopoly in this hazardous speciality; Thomas Marshall in London wrote to Thomas Pitt in 1709: 'Nathan is the only purchaser at present of any large stones, which he is sensible of and doubtless makes what advantages thereby he can.'[100] He put to good advantage his connections with Germany, which was the foremost market for large diamonds,[101] and with the German court-Jews. He was the London agent of the court-Jew Leffman Behrens (Lipman Cohen) who supplied jewellery to the court at Hanover.[102] As a result however of the economic depression which followed the South Sea Bubble he was ruined. There was no demand for big diamonds and he had to return to his family at Hamburg, 'where he could live much cheaper'. It would seem however that the real reason for his departure from England lay in his inability to pay his debts.[103] There were considerable risks involved in dealing in big diamonds which were difficult to sell. Often there was a considerable lapse of time between the purchase of a stone and its sale.[104] His case illustrates in a striking manner the Jewish hold on the trade, from the Jewish agents at Madras through the Jewish importers and big dealers in London (Nathan stated that in a period of 20 years he had bought diamonds worth £100,000 from the importer Alvaro da Fonseca), to the German court-Jews who usually functioned as agents for precious stones on behalf of their masters.[105]

The degree to which laymen dealing in diamonds were dependent on the advice of experts – usually Jewish – is clearly seen in the history of the famous Pitt diamond. Four Jewish experts – the Portuguese Alvaro da Fonseca and Isaac Abendana, and the Ashkenazim Abraham Nathan and Marcus Moses – were, at one time or another, connected with the case. Thomas Pitt consigned the diamond, weighing 426 carat, to London in October 1702, addressed jointly to his son Robert, his agent Sir Stephen Evance, and Alvaro da Fonseca.[106] The latter was clearly a personal friend, being the only one of Thomas Pitt's correspondents whom he addressed as 'Dear Sir and Friend' instead of the formal 'Dear Sir'. Both had been 'interlopers' in the East India trade and da Fonseca had returned to London from Madras shortly after Pitt became Governor there. Pitt asked Isaac Abendana at Madras to make a model for the cutting of the stone, and this too was sent to London together with Abendana's opinion of its value. Isaac Abendana came to Madras from the New Company's factory at Masulipatam after the merger of the two Companies in 1702. Alvaro da Fonseca had no great esteem for him, and Joseph Cope, who cut the Pitt diamond, maintained that he had never seen a model as bad as that which Abendana made for the famous stone. Pitt, on the other hand, trusted Abendana.[107] Da Fonseca, who mistrusted Sir Stephen as well, refused to share responsibility for the stone, but promised to advise the two others. Pitt wrote:

> Mr. Alvarez de ffonseca . . . did . . . decline concerning himself therewith any otherwise than by giving his advice about the cutting thereof . . . Mr. Alvarez excuseing himself from acting as a consignee was occasioned by the dislike he had conceived against being concerned with the said Sir Stephen Evance, as not approving of his conduct in things of that nature.[108]

Subsequent events justified da Fonseca's attitude – it was with great difficulty that the stone was extracted from Sir Stephen just before he went bankrupt. The stone was cut according to da Fonseca's instructions, and he arranged the sale to Abraham Nathan of the parts which were cut off. The sale of the polished stone represented even greater difficulties than the cutting; it was not easy to fix a price because the stone was so much bigger than anything usually offered for sale that the accepted rules for determining the value could not be applied. Robert Pitt consulted several Jewish experts at Amsterdam, but when his father returned from India seven years later the big stone had still not been sold. Marcus Moses took with him a replica of the diamond when he went to France in 1712 but he too failed to sell it. Only in 1717 was it finally sold to the French Regent by Thomas Pitt's son, Lord Londonderry, though the full purchase price was never paid.

Although the major part of the coral and diamond trades was concentrated in the hands of London Jews by the early years of the eighteenth century, the investments were not entirely on their own accounts. It seems that part of the trade was always financed by foreign Jews, especially by merchants of Leghorn. There is no way of determining what share these people had in the trade, because exports and imports were registered in the East India Company books under the names of their London agents. There is, however, definite evidence that the Leghorn coral merchants were not always content to sell their goods to London, but traded to India on their own account, employing Anglo-Jewish merchants as their agents. The earliest indication that foreigners had a permanent footing in the trade dates from 1714–15. In December 1714 the East India Company obliged merchants who made consignments to India for the purchase of diamonds, to declare on oath who were the proprietors of the goods or bullion exported by them.[109] In the only declaration of which a record has survived Isaac de Medina affirmed that the coral and coral beads he was about to send to India were the property of Bentura and Lope[s] de Morales of Leghorn.[110] This regulation was abolished by the General Court less than a year after it had been passed because, as the Court of Directors stated,

> the requiring an oath for whose accompt effects were sent to purchase diamonds withall may prove prejudicall to the Company because some person abroad or in England have been and may be unwilling to discover their correspondents concerned with them in those effects and if the oath be insisted on may be tempted to drive that trade another way for which they have great offers of encouragement.[111]

It is evident from the speed with which the secrecy of the foreign proprietors' identity was restored and from the reasons given, that the foreign investment in the Anglo-Indian coral and diamond trade was a factor to be reckoned with. This impression is confirmed by other evidence. When Jacob Salvador represented to the East India Company claims for diamonds lent by his agent to the Council at Fort St George in order to ransom Madras from the French in 1745, he disclosed the names of persons who had a share in the consignments sent under his name. These included several Livornese Jews: Francis Bianchi, Emanuel Ergas, Raphael Ergas, and Alessandro Henriques.[112] The same Raphael Ergas and a certain Salvadore L. Recanati consigned coral through London to Solomon Salomons at Madras, and were named among his creditors after he went bankrupt.[113] The importance of Livornese investments in the English coral-diamond trade is also confirmed in Joseph Salvador's survey of Jewish trade written in the middle of the eighteenth century[114] and by a letter written in 1800 by the firm of Mocatta and Goldsmid.[115]

The growing importance of the Ashkenazi community of London during the eighteenth century was reflected in the diamond trade. During the first 50 years of its existence, the trade had been almost exclusively in the hands of Portuguese Jews. The Ashkenazim, who came to England from Holland and Germany, brought with them an old tradition of trade in jewels, but they were used to dealing in finished products, selling and buying at fairs and supplying princely courts, rather than to the business of importing uncut stones from overseas. It therefore took some time before they began to play a significant role in the Anglo-Indian diamond trade.

The early Ashkenazi merchants, men like Abraham Nathan and Marcus Moses, both from Hamburg, were at first content to buy the Indian diamonds after they had arrived in London (Moses was at that time connected with the goldsmith-banker Sir Richard Hoare, who dealt in jewellery with Germany and France). Later Moses became the first Ashkenazi to participate directly in the Indian diamond trade, when he went to Pondicherry in 1713, induced, as it seems, by French offers designed to make a breach in England's monopoly of the trade. This attempt, however, ended in complete failure, and in 1715 Moses went over to English Madras.

In the same year the 19-year-old Aaron Franks sailed to Madras from England and remained there until 1727. The families of Moses and Franks were to keep up the connection with India during the greater part of the century. It became a tradition in both families to have one of their members permanently stationed in India, and the Franks soon rivalled the greatest Portuguese houses in the volume of their trade. The family became one of the leading Jewish families; Abraham Franks was among the first

Ashkenazi sworn brokers in London in 1697, and he and his son Isaac were among the early Wardens of the Ashkenazi synagogue. Isaac's brother, Aaron, who was English-born (1694–1777) became head of the family after Isaac's death in 1736 and a leader of the Ashkenazi community. There were two other brothers: Moses, an insurance broker who died in 1715 or 1716, and Jacob, who emigrated to New York. Two of Jacob's sons, Naphtali and Moses, returned to London and were active in the diamond trade. Abraham and Isaac Franks began to import large quantities of diamonds a few years after Aaron established himself in India. Isaac's marriage in 1719 to the daughter of the rich broker Moses Hart gave a further stimulus to their business, and the *Original Weekly Journal*, reporting this intended marriage, commented that these two had won the great lottery prize of £20,000 in 1719;[116] this would fully explain the Franks' sudden emergence as major diamond importers. In 1724 they imported £27,000 worth of diamonds, about 40 per cent of the total brought from India in that year. Although this was exceptional, they kept up a flourishing trade, importing about £10,000 *per annum* during the following years. The following table illustrates their significance.

Diamond imports of the Franks family

Year	Value of diamonds imported by members of the Franks family £	Percentage of value of diamonds imported by Jews %
1723	13,600	28.5
1724	27,400	38.4
1725	10,000	11.6
1726	8,800	13.9
1727	11,300	23.2
1728	–	–
1729	11,100	22.8
1730	10,200	13.8
	92,400	19.4

During the crisis caused by the discovery of diamonds in Brazil, the Franks were foremost among the few who did not panic and continued to trade, though on a reduced scale. After the passing of the crisis Aaron Franks continued for many years to figure among the more important merchants.

During the 1740s many more Ashkenazi families began to take part in the trade. The firms of Isaacs, Salomons, Levy, Gompertz, Norden, and Goldsmid became importers of diamonds from overseas, and took over a large part of the trade. All these people had the advantage of close family connections to Holland, the great centre of the diamond industry. Ashkenazi late-comers were the Pragers, who entered the Anglo-Indian diamond trade in the 1770s and became the most important firm in the branch after 1786. They deserve a special chapter.

Despite their growing importance as importers of diamonds, few Ashkenazim gained a foothold in the coral trade, and only one – Aaron Franks' nephew Moses Franks – exported coral on a large scale. The brothers Aaron and Solomon Norden, who consigned coral to India in 1765, wrote to their agents at Madras (Moses and Daniel de Castro): 'The coral which is for our account we bought of your brother Mr. Samuel de Castro who warranted us that it would do for your place, as we know nothing of the coral trade and are no judges thereof.'[117] This was written at a time when the firm of Norden had already been importing diamonds from India for about a generation (formerly under the name of Levy and Ruben Salomons). The Ashkenazim did not have the advantage of long-standing connections with Leghorn, which enabled the Sephardi coral traders of London to dominate the trade. This was a distinct disadvantage in view of the fact that coral had become an indispensable commodity in the Anglo-Indian diamond trade, and it is quite possible that it slowed down the penetration of the trade by members of the Ashkenazi community.

The Ashkenazi merchants, however, overcame the difficulty in various ways. Abraham Franks had a share in the coral consignments of the Francos and of the English merchant Thomas Godfrey, and others, perhaps, entered similar partnerships.[118] The firms of Henry Isaac, Joseph Salomons, Levy and Ruben Salomons, Aaron Goldsmid, and Gompertz and Heyman consigned large quantities of silver and precious stones, and after 1750 they developed the system of respondentia loans as a new method of conveying means of the purchase of diamonds.

In 1685 James de Paiva left London for Madras, accompanied by his newly-wed wife, three servants (one Jewish), and a maid. He took with him 12,000 pieces-of-eight – the property of Jewish merchants of the City. He was in debt when he left London, and he no doubt hoped to mend his fortunes in the East, but he died after two years in India, having fallen ill on a visit to the diamond merchant at Golconda.[119] He was the first of many English Jews who went to India with the permission of the East India Company, and who carried on the diamond trade at its Indian end during the following century. Between 1686 and 1786 there were only a few years without at least one Anglo-Jewish diamond agent at Madras, and for several years, around 1750, there were nine of them at a time.

Shortly before the arrival of de Paiva from England, the Company gave permission to a number of English Jews, former interlopers, to settle at Madras. They were Alvaro da Fonseca, B. Rodrigues and D. de Porto.[120] Another English Jew – Rodrigues Salvadore – arrived in India without the Company's permission early in the 1680s and settled at Golconda – the famous centre of the diamond trade. He had connections with the East India Company's people at Madras, but apparently never became a permanent resident of the English colony. He was not particularly successful in business, and died in 1706, after having cut himself off completely from the Madras colony and from his brother in London.[121]

Of the early Jewish settlers, Alvaro da Fonseca stayed longest in the East. He returned to London in 1700, after having been away 19 years, and he still had before him 40 years of diamond trading as a City merchant. Two years later Isaac Abendana, a Dutch Jew, settled in Madras, after having resided for some time at Masulipatam together with Rodrigues Salvadore. He now became Governor Pitt's adviser in his diamond business.[122] Opinions on Abendana differed, people on the whole trusting his judgment but doubting his integrity. Alvaro da Fonseca, who was annoyed by Abendana's advice concerning the cutting of Pitt's big diamond, wrote to the latter: 'Mr. Abendana ... whom I never knew nor his name but have heard such a character of him that he is not worthy to be trusted by anybody, nor in what he says.' But about the same time the merchant Francis Chamberlayne wrote to his agent Robert Nightingale about the purchase of diamonds in India: 'Your cheife care must be in employing a man of judgment in this commodity, who has such a reputation as Isaac Abendana, who has not sent home many this yeare, yet those he has are verry good and well bought', to which Nightingale replied: 'Mr. Abendana carrecter, they say, begins to faile, I mean not as to his judgement, but to his honesty. However have employed him this season.' A year later, however, Nightingale again expressed trust in Abendana: 'Abendana, I believe is a verry honest man, and hope shall find him so by the diamonds sent home.' Yet, when Nightingale visited Amsterdam in 1709, he found that others shared da Fonseca's unfavourable opinion: 'Abendana carrecter – in part you are in ye right, for he understands them as any man, but for ye other, of late his friends here are grown verry doubtful as to his integrity.'

Abendana died in 1709, and for some years there was no diamond agent at the place – presumably the need for one was not keenly felt in view of the depression which the war had caused in the diamond trade. Only after the Peace of Utrecht was the tradition of keeping diamond agents at Madras resumed, when Moses Marcus and Abraham Franks settled there in 1715. Of the 21 Jewish agents resident at Madras between 1715 and 1786 14 belonged to three families: Moses, Franks-Salomons, and de Castro. The Moses family alone supplied seven agents: Marcus Moses, his sons and grandsons, and another agent – Ephraim Isaacs – who was connected with them by marriage. The three families saw to it that they were always represented in India by one of their members. When one representative returned, a brother, son, or nephew was sent out to take his place. Before Aaron Franks returned to Europe in 1727, his brother Isaac sent their nephews Henry and Abraham Salomons to carry on the business at Madras, and when Henry died in 1737, his brothers Solomon and Moses sailed immediately to India, Solomon staying till 1758. Abraham, Henry, Solomon, Moses, and David Salomons were the sons of Benedictus Salomons and Abigail née Franks. Benedictus Salomons had business connections with Abraham Nathan and was one of the first Ashkenazim who imported diamonds from India, though small quantities only. In 1726 Isaac Franks was permitted by the East India Company to send his nephew Abraham Salomons as a 'menial servant' to his brother Aaron in India, but in fact the intention was that Abraham, together with his brother Henry, should relieve Aaron Franks at Madras and enable him to return home. John Roach, who was a member of the Fort St George Council, used to send the brothers Franks reports on their nephews, evidently having been requested to do so. In the autumn of 1730 Roach wrote to Isaac Franks:

'Abraham seems to me a sober, and well disposed young man. Harry is guilty of no remarkable vice that I know of, but being master of most of the languages and pretty well acquainted with the customs of the country, loves rambling about, as his brother does the attending more closely to business.'

Next summer Roach wrote to Aaron Franks:

> Your nephew Abraham behaves exceedingly well, but Harry's extravagant deportment is not only very inconvenient to his brother, but has carried him into an affair with Messrs. Peers and Foxley which has got him ordered home, but I think the order will not be put in execution on your and your brother Isaac's account to whose interest he may be usefull in case of accident to Abraham, whom he uses very ill.

The brothers Salomons did not meet with a success like that enjoyed by their uncle Aaron, who was perhaps the richest Ashkenazi in London. Abraham indeed left a certain fortune to his brothers Solomon and Moses who followed him to India, but they both went bankrupt. Another brother, David, who was a broker in London but also imported diamonds from India, went bankrupt in 1762.[123]

The Moses' representation at Madras was almost as continuous as that of the Franks, and was maintained for a longer period. As already mentioned, Marcus Moses moved from Pondicherry to Madras in 1715, after the failure of the French attempt to gain a foothold in the Indian diamond trade. Marcus Moses, the son-in-law of Glueckel of Hameln, was connected with Sir Richard Hoare, the banker, during most of Moses' first stay in England (1701–12). They dealt jointly in diamonds and it seems that while Hoare supplied the necessary means, Moses provided the expert knowledge. In 1712 Moses went to Paris taking with him a model of the Pitt diamond. Pitt arranged for Moses to meet Pierre Dulivier, the Governor of Pondicherry, who was then in Paris. Dulivier suggested to Moses that he should come with him to Pondicherry and engage in diamond business jointly with him. Several people in France and England ordered diamonds through Moses, and one of them permitted Dulivier to draw on him up to 30,000 pagodas (approximately £13,000) for diamonds consigned to him. The London merchants who supported this venture evidently hoped to evade the strict limitations imposed by the East India Company during the war on the export of silver for the purchase of diamonds, and the undertaking was supported by the French East India Company, who offered favourable terms to the participating merchants permitting unlimited exports of silver for the purchase of diamonds. The English East India Company became alarmed and more inclined than before to make concessions to the diamond importers.

Moses remained at Pondicherry for two years and in 1715 diamond consignments made by him reached France (it is known that they included stones destined for Isaac Franks in London). The consignments caused a general disappointment among the consignees in France, but it seems that Moses himself had already despaired of the French plan. At the end of 1714 he had received permission to settle at Madras, and once there he broke off his connections with France. A bill of exchange drawn by Moses in India on his wife Joy (Freudchen) and his son Moses in London is extant. The bill has a double signature 'Marcus Moses' in Latin characters, and 'Mordecai Hamburger' in Hebrew.[124] He stayed five years at Madras and apparently grew quite wealthy during this time. In 1720 he returned to his wife and children in London, after an absence of seven years. and became famous as the founder of the dissident ('Hamburg') Ashkenazi community. At the same time, however, he squandered whatever wealth he had amassed in India, and in 1728 he went bankrupt.[125] He was compelled once more to try his fortune in the East, but unfortunately his second arrival in India coincided with the beginning of the long crisis caused by the discovery of diamonds in Brazil, and he died penniless at Madras in 1735. The family, however, maintained its connections with India. Levy Moses had joined his father a year before his death, and he now took over the family's business at Madras, where he stayed for almost 20 years.

In 1743 Levy Moses entered a partnership with George Jones in Madras. The partnership comprised all the business activity of both merchants and its terms were laid down in a written contract valid for five years. The contract was renewed for a similar period in 1747. The business suffered severe losses when the French took Madras in 1745 and the diamonds which Moses had hidden were discovered by the occupation authorities. According to Jones the loss amounted to £9,500. The partnership came to an abrupt end in 1750 when Moses and Jones became embroiled in a quarrel which brought about a series of law-suits in Madras and London.[126]

In 1747 Levy invited his brother Samuel to join him in his business. Samuel Moses told about the invitation extended to him by his brother Levy to come out to Madras:

> Levy Moses then was and for several years . . . had been a large trader and dealer in the mercantile way and was desirous before he quitted the same, for the brotherly love and affection which he bore to this defendant [Samuel Moses] and for . . . his advancement in the world, to introduce him into the said trade and had agreed to allow him a joint concern with him . . . of . . . half of all profits that should arise . . .[127]

Samuel, in his turn, was joined by another brother – Joseph – who came out to India after Levy's death in 1753. Samuel returned to England in 1755, but Joseph remained in Madras where he died in 1761.

For three years the family was unrepresented in India, but in 1764 Samuel returned, bringing with him his nephew Eleazar, thus initiating the third generation of Moses into the Indian diamond trade. When Samuel returned to London in 1771 in order to marry his niece, Eleazar asked his brother Levy to come out to India, but he was refused permission by the East India Company, and Eleazar was to be the last of diamond agents who represented the family at Madras. He returned to Europe in 1777 – 64 years after his grandfather had first arrived in India.

The third family to be represented in Madras by a consecutive line of agents were the Sephardi de Castros. They came to Madras in the middle of the eighteenth century and were represented there by one generation only; still, their activity in India covered almost 40 years, and Moses de Castro, who returned to England in 1786, was the last of the Jewish diamond agents at Madras. The family had been active in the diamond trade for a long time before Samuel de Castro sailed East in 1749. Samuel's father – Solomon de Castro – was already importing small quantities of diamonds around 1720,[128] but in the 1740s the house suddenly became a major exporter of coral to India, rivalling the Salvadors and the Francos. They maintained their apparent importance till about 1760, when their exports diminished as suddenly as they had expanded some 15 years earlier.

It was not a matter of fluctuating fortunes or of switching to another branch of commerce; the de Castros continued to be active in the coral-diamond trade for another 25 years, but mainly as agents in Madras, not as importers in London. It appears that the large quantities of coral exported by the de Castros in the 1740s and 1750s were not their property, but belonged to Benjamin Mendes da Costa, one of the wealthiest Jewish merchants of London. This is shown, in the first place, by the fact that, while the de Castros exported large quantities of coral, they imported only an insignificant quantity of diamonds. Benjamin da Costa, on the other hand, was one of the greatest importers of diamonds throughout this period, although no corresponding exports can be traced. A very plausible explanation for this state of affairs is that the coral really belonged to da Costa, who was perhaps making use of the de Castros' connection with Leghorn[129] in order to purchase his coral on favourable terms, and so had to re-export it to India under their name in order to get the drawback.[130] This arrangement seems to have come to an end in 1761, when, on the death of David de Castro, Benjamin's nephew Hananel began to export coral under his own name.

That there was in fact such an arrangement is all the more likely in view of the close ties that existed between the Mendes da Costas in London and the de Castros in India. The last named functioned primarily as the India agents of the house of Mendes da Costa. When Samuel de Castro and David Lopes Fernandes applied to the East India Company in 1749 for permission to settle at Madras, the required security was given by Benjamin Mendes da Costa and David de Castro.[131] Out of 30,830 pagodas worth of diamonds sent to England by Samuel de Castro and David Lopes Fernandes during their first year in India, over 80 per cent was consigned to Benjamin Mendes da Costa.[132] When the 24-year-old Daniel de Castro relieved his brother in India in 1757, the security was again given by Benjamin Mendes da Costa and David de Castro.

In 1763 the two firms sent out a certain Joseph Dias Fernandes to relieve Daniel,[133] who wanted to return to England in order to marry the daughter of his deceased brother. But Dias Fernandes died during the voyage and the houses in London had to find another agent. They came to an agreement with Moses de Castro – apparently a nephew of Daniel – and signed a contract with him, in Daniel's name, promising him a gradually increasing share in the latter's business. Samuel de Castro wrote to his brother, Daniel, on 10 December 1765:

Dear Brother Daniel de Castro,

By last year's shipping I wrote you several [letters] which I hope you received. Since which I received yours of the 25 October, 12 and 29 January, 6 February and 26 March. I was very sorry to hear of the death of Mr. Dias, your intended partner, as I thought him to be a very good young man, and of a temper that I know you would agree with. But man proposes and God disposes. We must have patience and hope that this that goes, Mr. Moses de Castro, may have better luck, and that you may approve of our choice, for he is really, I believe, a worth[y] young man, good natured, and with a little of your polishing will be in time, please God, almost as clever a fellow as my Danny. The agreement: a copy goes inclosed, by which you'll see it is made to your desire, except the article you objected to, that in case of death to lose all share of commissions, which he could not with any conscience agree to, as if so in the case of Mr. Dias, his friends will not only have the great loss of their relation, but would also be behind hand the charges of the voyage, and upon which footing, you may be sure, no body would venture. So I don't doubt you will consider it and think that I am a brother, and Mr. Hananel Mendes Da Costa as a true friend that you'll always found him [sic], have done what in justice we thought right.

Whenever you come to England, you may be sure I shall be glad to see you, but for all that I must advise you to have a year or two more patience, that your partner who goes out by these ships may, please God, have time to have some experience of the trade, as also that, as we have wrote you last year, we wait for an answer which we expect by first ship from home for to get another person to send out, as trusting to one person alone is not satisfaction to our friends, so I hope you'll consider this, that the future character of your house may not suffer. To be sure, thank God, you have a handsome fortune but for all that, as I say above, a year or two more will not hurt you, your age to [sic] is not so far advanced neither.

Samuel de Castro.[134]

Their associate, Hananel Mendes da Costa, wrote the next day:

Dear Friend Daniel de Castro,

By my former letters you will find the resolution your brother Samy and myself took to send Moses de Castro for to be your partner, and he is ready to sail in the *Lioness*, Captain Larkin, within this month. God send him a good and safe voyage.

Now my dear friend, you may think that I should be glad to have your Company, but I must beg of you, as well for his sake as ours, that you would defer it a year longer, for by your good advice and councils I don't doubt but he would understand the trade and give content to all, and we intend to send out some worthy person to be joined with him. Therefore hope you'll consider it well and confirm to it [sic] as it may be the making of many, as you will find by the large consignments by these ships of sundry persons that never sent to your house, that he has brought himself to be esteemed by his good behaviour etc.

By these ships I consign to you both 9 chests of coral beads, as per invoices and bills of lading I send in another letter amounting to near £5,000, and have the same quantity for next shipping and inclosed is invoice for a box of Jewels in the *Neptune*, which goes in a chest of coral, Messrs Norden send, and inclosed they send the large diamond, in which I have no concern but the remainder of the jewels you will make the returns to me, and 1/3 of them are for account of Abraham Gomes de Mesquita.[135]

The contract is also preserved. It was signed by Moses de Castro on the one hand and Samuel de Castro and Hananel Mendes da Costa on the other. The main terms were:[136]

1. Moses de Castro is to proceed to India and be received in partnership by Daniel de Castro.
2. Moses de Castro is to receive a gradually increasing share of the partnership commission business, starting with one-sixth in the first year and reaching one-half in the sixth year.
3. Each side can cancel the partnership after giving six months notice.
4. In case of dispute between the partners the case shall be arbitrated by Hananel Mendes da Costa and Samuel de Castro.
5. Each partner is to be entitled to conduct his own private business in India, provided he does not use the partnership capital for this purpose.

Hard as the others tried however they failed to persuade Daniel to stay at least until Moses de Castro had gained some experience in the trade. Daniel did not even await his arrival, but hurried back to Europe. He returned to India in 1768, bringing with him his young wife, and so breaking a long tradition of bachelordom maintained by the Jewish diamond agents at Madras. This time Daniel stayed for only three years, while Moses de Castro remained in India till 1786, being the last of the Jewish diamond agents of Madras. Two years before he had married Judith, the daughter of Hananel Mendes da Costa, and so sealed the long standing business connections between the two families by a bond of marriage.

The right to reside in one of the English 'presidencies' in India was subject to the consent of the East India Company. Apart from its own officials, the Company permitted a limited number of businessmen to reside in the presidencies, as 'free merchants'. They were allowed to trade in the East, and to do a certain amount of business with England. Before sailing to India, the person had to apply for a permit from the Court of Directors, specifying the number of persons – wife, children, servants etc. – which he intended to take along. He had to pay a fee of £12 for the licence, to declare on oath that he would observe the regulations concerning 'free merchants', and to produce two people of means who were prepared to guarantee his good behaviour. When all these formalities had been completed, he was free to proceed to India on one of the ships sailing in the Company's service. It seems that up to 1770 permission to settle in India was granted to any applicant who had some backing among the Company's stockholders. Usually at least one of the guarantors was a person of standing in the City, whom the Company could accept without hesitation. There were exceptions, however; when Levy Moses in 1733 offered his brothers Haim and Moses as guarantors the Court of Directors asked the Company Secretary 'to inquire into the circumstances and ability of the said persons'. Only on a favourable report being received did the Company agree to accept their security. But since the Jewish diamond merchants usually went to India as agents of respectable firms in the City, the Company did not, as a rule, make any difficulties about granting a licence. There is only one recorded case of a refusal to grant a licence (to Abraham Elias in 1729), the Company's Committee of Correspondence having advised that it should not be given because Elias had explained that he wanted to proceed to Madras 'to follow the business of dealing in diamonds only', while the

Committee maintained that 'there is no difference between a diamond merchant and a free merchant' so that 'his petition cannot be granted without opening the door for many more of the same nature'.[137] This might or might not have been the true reason for the refusal, and it is quite conceivable that Elias, lacking the right kind of support, tried to get the permission by renouncing in advance the right to trade in any article but diamonds. There was indeed no recognized status of 'diamond merchant' in the Company's presidencies, and the Jewish agents enjoyed all the privileges, and had to undertake all the obligations, of 'free merchants'.[138]

The Company's attitude became less benevolent after 1770, perhaps because the increase in private trade made her fear competition with her own business. In 1772 the Committee of Correspondence advised the Court of Directors to reject the applications of David Levy and of Levy Moses, who had asked for permission to settle at Madras, because 'it appearing that the practice of permitting persons to repair to the East Indies under free merchant covenants, from the inconveniences attending it, has been discontinued'.[139] The difficulties which Yehiel Prager encountered when he tried, 14 years later, to get permission for his nephew to settle in Bengal show that the Committee's reasoning reflected a fixed and consistent policy.

The Jewish merchants who went out to Madras were usually young people, who were just starting to make their way in business. Most of them were Ashkenazim and none belonged to the leading commercial families, who preferred to keep their sons at home and not expose them to the hazards of the East. As a result most Anglo-Jewish merchants at Madras did not have any extensive diamond business of their own, but acted as commission agents for London houses. For their trouble they received a commission of $2\frac{1}{2}$ per cent from their principals, and an additional 2 per cent from the Indian merchants from whom they bought the stones.[140] Their income therefore depended on the size of consignments sent to them from England, or, in other words, on the volume of business done by the firms they represented, and on the number of houses which could be persuaded by their principals or relations to entrust them with their business in India. Obviously one could not get very far if one depended solely on this kind of business. It is true that, except in the 1740s and 1750s, there were usually no more than two or three Jewish agents at

Madras, but they were not alone in the field. Non-Jews – 'free merchants' or members of the Fort St George Council – also had a share in the consignments sent out by the London diamond merchants.

The only period for which the agents of the various London firms can be identified is 1748–50. At that time the Company's presidency was at Fort St David, where it had moved after Fort St George fell to the French. Among the Fort St David papers there were preserved lists of diamond consignments with the names of the consigners in India and of the consignees in London. There were seven Jewish agents at Madras, but a considerable part of the consignments went to non-Jews like Nicholas Morse and Joseph Fowke. It may well be that at times when there were fewer Jewish agents at the place non-Jews had an even bigger share in the trade.

This is a proper place to examine more closely the connections of the seven agents who were active at Madras between 1748 and 1750. Four of these were Ashkenazim and three Sephardim, two of the latter being partners (Samuel de Castro and David Lopes Fernandes). The Ashkenazi agents usually served Ashkenazi firms, while the Sephardim acted on behalf of Sephardi houses. The Ashkenazim Moses Berend Heyman, Levy Moses, and Ephraim Isaac received no commissions from Sephardi houses, and the Sephardi Solomon Franco had only one Ashkenazi correspondent in London – Joseph Salomons. The only one who did not conform to this pattern was the Ashkenazi Solomon Salomons, who acted for nine Sephardi and six Ashkenazi firms of London. Perhaps his wider connections were due to the influence of his uncle, Aaron Franks, who was associated in his coral and diamond business with the great Sephardi house of the Francos. Solomon Salomons was in fact described at that time as the most important Jewish merchant at Madras.[141] The limited and uncertain income from commissions on diamond purchases could hardly have induced English Jews to reside for years far from their homes and to expose themselves to all the dangers of the East. In fact the agents had their own businesses in India, which offered abundant opportunities for Europeans to make substantial profits in local trade.[142]

Fischel has already pointed out the business connections which the early Jewish settlers at Madras had maintained with China.[143] In the eighteenth century, however, the Jewish merchants seem, on the whole, to have preferred indirect participation in the local trade by giving respondentia loans, which were a combination of lending and maritime insurance business. Jews coming from London must have been familiar with this sort of business, and the high interest and insurance rates in the East – 12 per cent in India as compared with 5 per cent in England – made it specially attractive. We have details concerning the local trade of Abraham and Henry Salomons, Solomon Salomons, Levy Moses and Solomon Franco. They made respondentia loans to European and Armenian merchants who needed money to finance voyages to Persia, Calcutta, Canton and other ports in the East.[144] A list of debts owing to Solomon Salomons in 1755 has been preserved; there were debts for respondentia loans made by Salomons between 1750 and 1755, amounting to 2,416 pagodas. The recipients of these loans were mainly local merchants who invested them in voyages to China, Manila, Cochin and Siam.[145] The list probably does not show all respondentia business done by Salomons during that period, as it must be assumed that some of the loans were repaid before the list was compiled in 1755.

An intense activity in Eastern trade is also shown by the balance of investments of Levy Moses, drawn up after his death. Moses, together with his gentile partner Jones, was perhaps the only Jewish merchant of Madras in the eighteenth century who consigned considerable quantities of diamonds to England on his own account.[146] Henry and Samuel Moses described the business of Levy Moses and George Jones as falling into two categories: consignment of diamonds and the like to Europe on their own account, and commission business on behalf of merchants in Europe and in India. In a reply made by Jones in 1752 to a questionnaire concerning a loan he and Moses had made to the Fort St George Council after the fall of Madras in 1745, he stated explicitly that the money lent was their own, while the loans made by other merchants 'were . . . lent by them for sundry Jewish and other merchants in Europe, consigners of coral and silver to those Gentlemen'.[147] In addition he made extensive investments in Eastern trade: at the time of his death he had 9,328 pagodas invested in diamond consignments to London, and 11,206 pagodas in voyages to Manila, Bengal, Surat, Batavia and Persia.[148] Unlike Solomon Salomons, Levy Moses made many direct investments in Eastern trade, only one-third of his total investment being in respondentia loans.

The possibilities of amassing wealth in the East were therefore much better than could be expected in view of the limitations of the diamond trade. It cannot be said, however, that the activity of those young Anglo-Jewish merchants in the East often resulted in the foundation of great fortunes. In fact only two of them later became heads of big houses in the City: the Sephardi Alvaro da Fonseca and the Ashkenazi Aaron Franks. Alvaro da Fonseca went East in 1681, at a time when some of the first Jewish diamond merchants, who had settled in London around 1660, were still active. He was an adventurer, like his friend Thomas Pitt, and like Pitt an 'interloper' – trading in the East without the permission of the East India Company. Like Pitt too, he made his peace with the Company and settled at Madras, where, it seems, he was accepted as an equal despite his religion – differences between Europeans tended to get blurred in the East. Da Fonseca was probably a wealthy man when he returned to England in 1700, and he soon became one of the great diamond importers, acting in partnership with the Christian Roger Bradyll.

Alvaro da Fonseca was the only one of the diamond merchants who made his fortune in the East. Aaron Franks, in all probability, would have had to content himself with the sort of modest commercial career which was the lot of other diamond merchants in India, had it not been for an extraordinary stroke of luck which was put to extremely good use by the Franks family. Four years after Aaron left England, his brother Isaac won the great lottery prize of £20,000.

Although none of the other agents achieved prominence in the City, some of them were quite successful in business and became very respectable merchants in India. Abraham Salomons left a considerable estate to his brother Solomon,[149] and the latter lived in affluence, keeping two houses, a billiard house and stables, having also given a further house to his Indian mistress.[150] Levy Moses turned the bankrupt undertaking which his father had left him into a prosperous business and could afford to employ several servants.

The Jewish merchants usually took with them a Jewish servant to India, who probably also cooked for them. These servants were in most cases Ashkenazim. We know something about the contracts made by two merchants with the servants who went with them to Madras. One contract was between Marcus Moses and his servant Lazarus Simons. Moses undertook to pay Simons 50 pagodas (approximately £20) p.a. and to pay his return voyage to England after three years if Simons requested it.[151] The other contract was between the merchants Samuel de Castro and David Lopes Fernandes and their servant Abraham Jacobs. Jacobs was engaged in England in 1748 as a cook. He was to receive £20 for the expenses of the voyage and £20 p.a. in India or £15 plus clothing. He was to enjoy all terms granted to his servant by Isaac Cohen Delmonte (who had been sent out the year before by the Francos and perished when his ship sank). De Castro and Lopes Fernandes also promised to send Jacobs home at their expense 'if the climate of the country does not agree with his health', or should they discharge him within three years. Because the contract was not throughout specific as to the terms agreed on – referring, as it did, to the late Delmonte's contract – a dispute arose between Jacobs and his masters. The case came before the Mayor's Court of Madras, and in the course of the proceedings an interesting custom came to light, namely that the Jewish merchants at Madras used to deduct one-quarter of the brokerage fees due to the Indian diamond broker for stones purchased through him, in favour of their Jewish servant. It was stated explicitly that this was only done when the servant was a Jew.[152]

Even after the losses which Levy Moses and his partner Jones suffered when Madras was occupied by the French in 1745, they still had £6,000 left between them.[153] They recovered so quickly that within a few years they were able to make extensive purchases of stock in London, acquiring £6,400 worth of Bank of England and Government paper.[154] The house of de Castro, too, seems to have benefited by the activity of its members in India. Daniel de Castro was described by his brother as having a fair fortune – eight years after he had come to India at the age of 24. Moses de Castro, who took Daniel's place when he returned to Europe, became a partner in one of the best Madras houses,[155] and the firm of de Castro in London was described as 'very respectable' by David Prager in 1787 – a serious compliment, coming, as it did, from a quarter where it was usual to regard Sephardi houses with a mixture of contempt and suspicion. Thus, although the commercial activity of English Jews in India did not lead, in most cases, to the establishment of great fortunes, it nevertheless offered to young people of modest means opportunities of economic advancement, which they would not, perhaps, have found had they stayed at home.

Chapter 9
The collapse of the Anglo-Indian diamond trade 1765–1793

In the 1760s the Anglo-Indian diamond trade became involved in a crisis which lasted for 25 years and from which the trade never recovered, although a semblance of normality was re-established in the last decade of the century. The crisis had two aspects: on the one hand the East India Company again limited the amounts which its presidencies in India were allowed to draw on it, thus partly closing an alternative channel by which the proceeds from coral sales could be returned to England and weakening the position of the European diamond merchants in India in their dealings with Indian sellers. On the other hand many more Englishmen in India were looking for ways of transferring home fortunes acquired in the East, and consequently the diamond trade was being constantly penetrated by non-commercial elements and the European market was flooded in an unprecedented manner.

We have seen earlier that during the crisis which followed the discovery of diamonds in Brazil in 1728, the East India Company agreed that the proceeds received in India for coral consigned from England could be remitted home by bills of exchange drawn on the Company by the presidencies in India, instead of being invested in diamonds. While the crisis lasted the agents in India made extensive use of this concession, but later the trade resumed its normal course, most of the proceeds being again invested in diamonds. After 1755, however, diamond imports were considerably reduced,[1] probably as a result of the general stagnation which afflicted British trade during the earlier stages of the Seven Years' War. Most of the Jewish diamond agents left Madras, and an increasing amount of bills of exchange from Fort St George began to arrive in India House, drawn to the order of the City's coral exporters. This in itself would probably not have caused difficulties, had it not coincided with a general increase in sums drawn on the Company by presidencies in India.

Europeans in India were amassing wealth as never before, and were looking for means to transfer their newly-acquired fortunes home. A very convenient way of doing this was to buy bills from the local authorities of the East India Company, which could be cashed at India House 90 days after presentation.

The flood of bills caused concern in Company circles, for it was feared that they might not be able to meet all the demands for payment. At first the Directors only warned the Council of Fort St George not to give bills for amounts larger than what was absolutely needed, and reminded it that remittance by Company bills was not a privilege of the coral exporters, but a favour granted to them 'as very beneficial traders'. 'We are still willing', they added, 'to oblige those gentlemen and all others under our protection, so long as such occasional kindness does not embarrass or prejudice us'.[2] For a few years matters were left at that, but the resumption of large-scale drawing in 1766 caused renewed anxiety in Leadenhall Street. The Directors found themselves in a dilemma: on the one hand they feared that the financial burden imposed upon them by continuous drawing from India might prove too heavy, but on the other hand they hesitated to put a limit on the amounts which the presidencies were allowed to draw lest people seeking ways to remit money to Europe should turn to other East India Companies, especially the Dutch and the French ones, thus supplying them with means to finance their trade.[3] Under these conditions it was only natural for the Directors to try to enforce the clause which obliged the coral traders to make returns in diamonds, and so remove at least one of the causes for the inflated stream of Indian bills. The Committee of Correspondence advised that the return of proceeds from silver and coral by bills of exchange should be prohibited 'it appearing from the late advices received from the Presidencys that in all probability there will be in their respective treasurys larger sums received on the Company's account than can be invested in goods to be sent to England'.[4] The Court of Directors agreed with this view, and decided to insist on fulfilment of the exporters' undertaking to make returns in diamonds.[5]

The merchants did not acquiesce in this decision. In a petition submitted to the Company they asked that the ruling be revoked.[6] The original petition is signed by 23 merchants or firms, 13 of them Jewish – Jacob Moses and Raphael Franco, Hananel Mendes da Costa, Isaac Mendes da Costa, Judah Supino, Phineas Serra,

Michael Salomons, Samuel de Castro, R. Franco for Joseph Salvador, Ephraim de Aguilar, Isaac Jessurun Alvares, Moses Montefiore, Gompertz and Heyman, Aaron and Solomon Norden. Joseph Salvador – who enjoyed a special degree of influence in the Company as one of the leaders of the Clive faction[7] – addressed a personal letter to the Directors with a similar request. The merchants pointed out that the Court's decision endangered the trade, and that, while normally not much use was made of the right to remit by bills of exchange, the denial of this right would enable the Indian diamond merchants to exert pressure and practise blackmail on the European buyers. The fact was also mentioned that coral exports were being extended to regions like Bengal, Bombay, and China, where there was no possibility of investing the proceeds in diamonds. The Directors, either seeing the logic of the merchants' arguments or giving way to pressure, agreed to restore the merchants' right to buy bills from the presidencies, although it was stipulated that they should be payable after one year instead, as formerly, after 90 days, and that no interest should be paid for this period.[8]

The merchants' victory was, however, short-lived. Although one would have expected the Company to welcome the possibility of getting funds needed for its Indian purchases on the spot, thus being able to reduce its silver exports, limitations were imposed on the issue of bills. In fact a paradoxical situation developed: the presidencies complained that they did not have sufficient money for their investments and that, by fixing a low rate of exchange and limiting the issue of bills, the Company was preventing people from supplying them with the needed sums,[9] while the Directors upbraided the presidencies for receiving more money than they needed, thus imposing an unbearable financial burden on the Company. The explanation of this apparent paradox seems to be that the presidencies used a considerable part of their money for administration and military expenses rather than for commercial purposes, an 'investment' producing no immediate returns which would have enabled India House to repay in England money received by its people in India.[10]

In 1775 the coral exporters – Jacob, Moses, and Raphael Franco, Nathan and Hananias Modigliani and D. Bradley, Phineas Serra, Ephraim de Aguilar, David de Aguilar – again complained about the restrictions,[11] but by this time the policy of the East India Company had become a factor of secondary importance.

Circumstances quite independent of any decisions by the Directors had developed, and were undermining the whole structure of the coral-diamond trade. The pressure on the means for transferring money to Europe was causing damage to the trade not only by inducing the Company to limit the issue of bills in India, but also directly, by bringing about an increasingly serious penetration of the diamond trade by people who wanted to transfer money to Europe.

There were four ways of transferring money: Company bills, transfer through foreign East India Companies, purchasing the 'privileges' of ships' officers, and diamonds. The 'privileges' served as a convenient channel, but the amounts which could thus be transferred were of course limited. By far the least complicated method was to buy Company bills drawn on London, but the restriction imposed by India House on the issue of bills and the low rate of exchange prescribed by it put a limit to the sums which could be sent to England by this channel and made it less attractive. People were therefore looking out for alternative ways; they turned to other East India Companies, and they made use of the possibilities offered by the diamond trade. It was apparently Robert Clive who first used diamonds on a large scale as a means for remitting money to England. Shortly after Clive returned to India in 1765 he sent Thomas Motte to the diamond mines. In Motte's own words: 'His Lordship being then at a great loss for means of remitting money to England, proposed to me to return with the Vakeel to the mines and to endeavour to open the diamond trade. He offered to make it a joint concern, in which I was to hold a third, he the other two.'[12] A year after Motte went on this mission the great flow of diamonds 'outside the trade' began, and according to Harry Verelst, Yehiel Prager bought almost all the diamonds which were sent to London on his own and on Clive's account.[13] Warren Hastings also made extensive use of diamonds as a means of transfer. In April 1770 Hastings wrote to Robert Palk concerning diamonds which he had sent to London: 'It was the only way I had of complying with the pressing solicitation of these gentlemen Mr. Hancock and Lieut. General Ironside to remit money for the use of their families, as they had been disappointed of bills in Bengal', and in 1774 he informed John Woodman: 'My best and speediest remittance will be in diamonds.'[14]

Diamonds could be used in two ways for the transfer of money.

They could be purchased in India, and taken or sent to London for sale there. Another method was to buy bills of exchange from a European diamond merchant in India, drawn on a diamond merchant in London. As a security for the payment of the bill a quantity of diamonds were attached, of a value slightly greater than the bill, to be handed over to the merchant in London on his honouring the bill of exchange. The first method was the most obnoxious, from the merchant's point of view, because it bypassed him completely. The second method, which may have started as an attempt by the merchants to adapt themselves to the new conditions, left them large scope for playing an active role in the importation of diamonds to England; in one respect it even had a distinct advantage, because it enabled the merchant to get in India at least part of the money he needed for the purchase of stones. In the long run, however, the results of this intrusion of outsiders into the trade proved disastrous: it not only completely upset the balance between supply and demand, making the Indian diamond market into a typical sellers' market, but also – and this was even more serious – made the trade dependent on outsiders over whom the merchants had no control, and who acted according to their own interests, which often were not identical with those of the merchants.

The crisis is reflected clearly in the figures of diamond imports, which jumped to the unprecedented value of £300,000 in 1767. During the following decade the yearly average of diamond imports stood at £209,000, as compared with £71,000 in the preceding decade. Together with the enormous inflation of diamond imports, there was a sharp decline in the share the professional merchants had in them. This is best demonstrated by the much diminished importance of the Jews, who had always constituted the bulk of the merchants active in the diamond trade. During the 50 years preceding 1767 there were only four years in which the share of Jews in diamond imports fell below 50 per cent, but from 1767 onwards, for 19 consecutive years, this share never reached 50 per cent. It was in fact continually declining, until it reached a mere 10 per cent in the early 1780s. Only after 1785 did the Jews re-establish their old paramountcy in the importation of diamonds from India, though by then the trade was already entering the stage of its final decline. The diminishing importance of the Jews illustrates in a striking manner the temporary eclipse of the professional element.[15]

It has already been mentioned that one of the symptoms of the crisis was the creation of a sellers' market in India. The European buyers attempted at least twice to break the stranglehold of the Indian merchants by forming combinations among themselves, but the Indians, who were quite aware of their strong position, just stopped sales. The situation was summed up, in an early stage of the crisis, in a petition presented to the East India Company by the diamond merchants of London:

> By the considerable returns that are become necessary to be made for account of individuals, the diamond trade is becoming greatly extended, and the profit thereon made reduced, owing to the advantage the natives have taken of this particular situation, enhancing the price, though there has been no considerable increase in the quantity of diamonds, and by the methods in which they carry this trade on.[16]

Of the 16 merchants and firms who signed the petition eight were Jewish: Jacob, Moses and Raphael Franco, Joseph Salvador, Phineas Serra for himself and the late Judah Supino, Aaron and Solomon Norden, Michael Salomons, Benjamin D'Israeli, Nathan and Hananel Modigliani, Moses and Joseph Norsa.

The merchant who tried to adapt himself to the new conditions by combining his diamond business with transfer transactions had no easy task. This is illustrated in detail by the letters which Jacob Barnet wrote from India between 1777 and 1785. Barnet seems to have been a protégé of Moses Franks, and through him became connected with two other diamond merchants, Yehiel Prager and Solomon B. Gompertz. It seems that throughout most of Barnet's stay in India Prager was his main London correspondent, and all or most of Barnet's letters have been preserved among the Prager Papers.

Barnet started to do business at Madras, but soon discovered that this was no longer the best place for purchasing diamonds. As a result of the crisis the centre of the trade had shifted from Madras to Benares which was closer to the mines at Patna and also to the main English centres in the North.[17] He stayed in Benares from 1778 to 1785. On arriving, he offered his services to persons desirous of transferring money to England.[18] He agreed to buy diamonds on commission taking 5 per cent for his trouble. For a further 2½ per cent, and on condition that the stones be consigned to one of the London firms he was connected with, he would guarantee a minimum price for the diamonds in England – equivalent to the price paid in India including commission, at a fixed rate of exchange. To people wanting to purchase bills, Barnet offered bills (drawn on his correspondent in London) at the same rate of exchange. As a security for these bills, diamonds would be attached to be consigned jointly to the representative of the purchaser of the bills and to one of Barnet's correspondents in London. Barnet therefore offered his services both to people who wanted to transfer their money by purchasing diamonds and sending them to England, and to such who did not intend to invest their money in diamonds, but wanted bills drawn on London.

Barnet's project failed completely. He was probably ill-adapted personally to fight against adverse circumstances and lacked experience,[19] while the international as well as the local political situation were unfavourable;[20] but it is extremely doubtful whether Barnet could have succeeded even if all these adverse factors had not existed. The elementary requirements for a successful business were lacking: extensive orders for diamonds from various English centres in India caused a scarcity and inflated prices. Orders were given to Barnet only a short time before the sailing of the ships to Europe, thus weakening further his position with the Indian sellers. Barnet had no means of his own, and so was completely dependent on whatever sums he could acquire by offering his services in the transfer business. To crown it all, the Company sold a large quantity of bills drawn on London in the years 1782 and 1783 in order to finance its war against Hider-Ali,[21] and it is not surprising that many people preferred Company bills to those issued by Barnet.[22] In short, business was too dependent on outside factors and the merchant's capability to control his affairs was drastically reduced.

The situation is similarly reflected in the letters of Joseph Fowke, who was still dealing in diamonds, this time at Benares and Calcutta. In September 1784 he wrote to his son Francis:[23] 'I see not the least likelihood of the market mending here or at home ... all modes of remittance being now thought hazardous, people will buy diamond, I am afraid, at any rate'. In June of the following year the firm of Pelling and de Fries – the foremost diamond merchants at Madras – reported to Yehiel Prager, describing the pressure exerted on the market by people who were only interested in transferring their fortunes to Europe, and with whom the merchant, who had to make profits, could not compete:

> Lord Macartney applied to us for our opinion of the diamonds he was going to purchase. We told him they were indifferent, but as he could not get better, and was determined to remitt for the money in his hands, he was under the necessity of purchasing such as he could get[24]

and in January 1786 they wrote:

> As to our trade of rough diamonds, it was never so bad in the course of our experience as at present. The troubles subsisting in the country of the mines have occasioned the working of them to be discontinued, and our market here has been so much inflamed by some new purchases out of the trade, that in our opinion the business is wholly ruined.[25]

Among the Prager Papers which have been preserved in the Public Record Office there are dozens of letters written from India by Yehuda Leib (Lyon) Prager to his uncle Yehiel and, after the latter's death, to his own sister Esther (Yehiel's widow) and to his nephew Mark (Mordecai) in London. These letters are of the utmost importance for the history of the diamond trade, containing, as they do, the full and consecutive business reports by a diamond merchant in India who, writing to his own firm and family, had nothing to hide. The correspondence throws an invaluable light on the final stage of the Anglo-Indian diamond trade, in which Prager tried, to some extent successfully, to play a central role.

The firm of Yehiel Prager (Israel Levin Salomons, as they were known in the City) entered the diamond business at a comparatively late date. The parent firm at Amsterdam specialized in Anglo-Dutch trade, and Yehiel Prager did the same for some years after he had established himself as an independent partner in London (1762). In the 1760s he made several attempts to enter the diamond business between London and Amsterdam, but without noticeable success. His luck changed, however, after 1770, probably thanks to the growing reputation of his own firm, and that of his brothers in Amsterdam. For some years before he began to import diamonds himself he was purchasing large quantities of uncut stones in London, especially from 'non-professional' importers like Robert Clive. When Jacob Barnet went to India in 1777 Yehiel Prager became an importer. By this time the character of the trade had been changed out of recognition, and Prager adapted himself from the start to the new conditions, combining the business of importing diamonds with that of money transfers from India. Prager was soon disappointed by Barnet's way of conducting business, and by 1780 he was planning the dispatch of one or two members of his own family to India. In fact, if he wanted to realize his ambitions, which were no less than the achievement of a dominant position in the trade, he could not rely on strangers. That this was indeed his ambition there can be little doubt; and why not? – a monopolization of the Anglo-Indian diamond trade was not beyond the reach of a merchant like Prager, with the experience he had gained in diamonds, his entrenched position in Anglo-Dutch trade, his standing with the East India Company, and, above all, his readiness to put the new conditions in India to his own use.

In 1785 Prager put his plans into action. His nephew and brother-in-law Leib, who had been his chief assistant in London since 1763, agreed to go to India, in face of strong opposition of his father Jacob – the brother of Yehiel and head of the Amsterdam house. Yehiel exerted all the 'interest' he had in India House in order to procure the consent of the Directors for Leib's voyage and recognition of his monopolistic status. In his formal request Yehiel Prager dwelt on the decline of the diamond trade, which, he maintained, had caused serious damage to people who wanted to transfer their fortunes to Europe, and he suggested that he would be able to arrest the decline, re-establishing the trade on a firm basis.[26] Prager achieved some of the things he wanted to get, though only in the teeth of opposition which apparently originated in the circles of importers of Indian diamonds.[27] Leib was permitted to settle in India and carry on a trade in diamonds, but he was refused the status of a Free Merchant. The Company also rejected the idea of a monopolistic status, though they wrote to Calcutta that they did not intend to grant a similar permission to any other person during the period of seven years for which the contract with Leib Prager was to be in force.[28] The Directors also agreed that Prager should purchase 'drugs' for the Company, receiving a 10 per cent commission.[29]

Leib Prager enjoyed most of the advantages which Jacob Barnet had lacked: although he was not a diamond expert in the strict sense of the word, he was not a novice in the trade and was an experienced merchant, he had the backing of a respectable house in the City, possessed many reliable connections in the East India maritime service, and had an officially recognized status. Those advantages saved Prager from the ruin which had overtaken Barnet, and his abilities and adaptability enabled him in the end to achieve a moderate degree of success in business. But Prager, too, failed in the main task which he had set himself, the restoration of normal conditions in the Anglo-Indian diamond trade and the concentration in his own hands of the transfer business based on diamond consignments.

The causes for Prager's failure were in all essentials the same as those which had frustrated Barnet's endeavours. The conditions created by the transfer rush did not leave the merchant enough ground for manœuvring; the Indian diamond merchants were well aware of their power – when Prager arrived they immediately raised their prices by 50 per cent and, although he managed to bring them down to their former level, they remained higher than what he had intended to pay.[30] About half a year after his arrival in India Prager explained to his uncle why he had decided to buy stones, despite the fact that no substantial profits could be expected; writing, as usual, in Yiddish, he said:

> In view of what I reported to you last season you could not have expected any profits on the stones which I sent from here. It was a forced thing and was only done in order to make good my expenses here, especially those incurred by travelling to and fro between here [Calcutta] and Benares. On my arrival here, and for a long time afterwards, prices were 50% too high, and I should certainly not have given such prices but for the consideration that if I had not begun to buy, people would have thought that our plan of remittance cannot be realized. How does it happen that I advertise a plan in the papers [people would say] and no one can get bills of exchange! Many have already begun to murmur that instead of serving people I was disappointing everyone. Furthermore I thought it may be useful to try in this way [by buying at high prices] to throw others here . . . out of business. So I had no alternative, if I did not want to sit idle, and I am certain that had you yourself been here, you would also perforce have acted similarly . . . in a month's time I intend to go again to Benares, and I am deter-

mined not to buy without better profits. Therefore, dear Yehiel, you must be satisfied till I can show you my ability to achieve good profits.[31]

These hopes were not to be realized. Although Leib Prager succeeded in concentrating a large proportion of the diamond imports in the hands of his London firm,[32] profits remained low. The net gain on diamonds worth £25,000, which Leib Prager sent home during his first year in India, was £55! 'That is the result of a year's residence in India, for which I had to undergo so many nasty troubles', he remarked bitterly in a letter to London.[33]

Prager failed to master the abnormal conditions which had prevailed for 20 years. He had to adjust his terms to the possibilities offered by other channels of remitting money. Thus it was now possible, as a result of the growth of the China trade, to send goods from India to China and to invest the produce in bills drawn on the East India Company in London. Prager could not possibly sell bills on less advantageous terms than those of the China bills.[34] The orders for diamonds which Prager received were usually made a short time before the sailing of ships to Europe, and he had to borrow money at 10 per cent interest in order to get the required diamonds in time.[35] Frequent orders for diamonds reaching Benares from Madras – on behalf both of people interested in remitting and of regular merchants – interfered with Prager's purchases. He was also hampered by the necessity of sending all his stones from Benares to Calcutta, which entailed further expenses for transport, insurance, and commission fees for his Calcutta agent, all of which were a severe burden for a business which in any case yielded only meagre profits, at best.[36] On top of it all an unfavourable rate of exchange for bills drawn from Benares on Calcutta was brought about in 1788 by a decline in the value of gold in relation to silver. Consequently there was a loss of 7 per cent on every drawing.[37]

Not unnaturally a scarcity in bills payable in Europe was usually connected with a scarcity in diamonds. When bills were in demand, diamonds could not be got, and when the demand for bills decreased, diamonds again appeared in the market. The general trend, by the late 1780s, was one of decline both in the demand for bills and the supply of diamonds. In the summer of 1788 Leib Prager reported: 'Remitters for Europe are now very scarce, because the people possessing the biggest fortunes have returned to Europe';[38] in the autumn of 1789 he wrote home: 'diamonds are very scarce because, as I hear, the mines have produced less than usual'.[39] In a letter to an unknown person, written in November 1791, Leib Prager himself summed up the causes of his failure in the diamond trade:

> I must own to you, when I left Europe, that I was in hopes to have been able by my exertions to accomplish as well the expectations of the Company within seven years, as also to obtain sufficient addition to my fortune, so as to enable me to return to England to pass the few years I may have to live in comfort, and to do some good to some of my friends. But to my great disappointment the high price at which the natives value their diamonds has prevented my making considerable purchases, and the profits on those I have hitherto purchased were too trivial.[40]

These quotations indicate future developments. The remitting fever subsided in the 1790s, when the period of unrestrained acquisition of wealth came to a close while the India trade was gradually being thrown open to private merchants. The return of normal conditions, however, did not result in a new flourishing of the Anglo-Indian diamond trade. Although the old routine was resumed for a time, there was a rapid decline in the output of the Indian mines. By the beginning of the nineteenth century Brazil had become the main source of supply for uncut diamonds.

PART THREE

The House of the Prager Brothers (Levin Salomons) and the Anglo-Dutch Trade 1760-1796

Chapter 10

The firm and its business

During the closing years of the eighteenth century there was tried before the Court of Chancery in London a case concerning the estate of Israel Levin Salomons, known among Jews as Yehiel Prager.[1] In the course of the trial many thousands of documents were submitted to the Court: a considerable part of the archives of the firm of Israel Levin Salomons and successors, consisting of documents written in Yiddish, English, Dutch, French, Italian, and Hebrew, were handed into the safeguarding of the Court. There they remained until they were transferred to the Public Record Office, where they are kept in 18 boxes, many of them still bound together in the original bundles arranged by Yehiel Prager and members of his family between 1760 and 1800. The letters are sorted according to years, language and place of origin and marked in the handwriting of Yehiel Prager or Leib Prager. There are separate bundles for letters written in Yiddish and those written in other languages, and again for letters received from England and for correspondence with foreign countries.

Of special interest is the internal correspondence of the firm, about 1,300 Yiddish letters sent by the Amsterdam branch to the house in London. The firm was a partnership between Jacob and David Prager of Amsterdam and their younger brother Yehiel in London, dealing mainly in the export of colonial goods from England to Holland – one of the most important links in the international trade of that time. Their joint business was conducted by means of this correspondence. The majority of the Amsterdam letters were written by Jacob Prager, up to his death in 1787. Thereafter the Amsterdam letters were written first by David Prager – up to 1793 – and from 1793 to 1795 by David's son Isaac. A letter was sent regularly twice a week – on Tuesdays and Fridays – but if a Jewish holiday occurred on one of these days, the letter was written on the preceding day. Letters were written on the Sabbath and on Jewish holidays only when necessary, and by a gentile clerk.[2] The day of the week was always given at the head of the letter, as well as the Hebrew and the Gregorian dates. It is of some interest that the Hebrew date was always given in full, while in the general date only day and month were written, evidently reflecting the prejudice of Jews against the religious connotations associated with the Christian Year.[3] A strange riddle was posed by 9 letters, written by Jacob Prager and signed by him, but dated after his death. On closer examination, it turned out that the dates of these letters had been changed by Yehiel Prager, in an attempt to hide from his wife and niece the fact of her father's death. Esther learned about the sad event only nine months after it happened. During that time Yehiel had occasionally brought her an old letter of Jacob, the date of which he had changed, sometimes he added a few lines about personal matters, imitating his late brother's handwriting. Esther, who was unfamiliar with the firm's business affairs, obviously did not discover the deception.[4]

This correspondence is, because of its very nature, much more revealing than commercial letters usually are. The smooth conduct of the firm's business depended on the regularity and adequacy of the reports which the two houses sent each other, and there were usually no secrets between the brothers and partners. Since the partners on both sides of the Channel met only on rare occasions[5] all questions concerning the business had to be discussed and settled by letter. The letters, moreover, are not mere commercial documents; they are at the same time family letters, unfolding the history of a well-to-do Jewish family, with its moments of happiness and celebration, its worries and misfortunes, culminating in the final tragedy of the collapse of the London house. We learn about projects of expanding the business and about marriage plans, and we get an insight into the attitude of members of the family towards life, their views on Judaism and religion, and their opinions on the political events of the day. The letters bear the intimate character of a correspondence between brothers, and reflect the personality of the writers – Jacob Prager's intelligence and sense of humour, the good nature of his brother David, the arrogance of his son Meyer and the businesslike manner of Yehiel Prager in London. Some letters have postscripts by Jacob's wife Bela to her children Esther and Leib Prager and her brother-in-law and son-in-law Yehiel. Unfortunately only part of the internal correspondence has been preserved, although other sections of the firm's correspondence are extant in their entirety. The London branch of the firm was established in 1762 and liquidated in 1796, but the earliest extant letter of the Amsterdam to the London house is from 1772, and the earliest batch of continuous correspondence is dated July 1774 to May 1775. After that there is another interruption in the continuity, only a small part of the letters of 1776 and 1777 having been preserved. From 1778 onwards, however, we have an almost complete set of the Amsterdam letters, covering a period of exactly 17 years.[6] The last letter was written on 9 January 1795, a few days before the French occupation of the Netherlands.

Of the outgoing correspondence a much smaller part has been preserved. All except one of the copy-books of the London branch, from the time of its establishment up to the death of Yehiel Prager in 1788, have been lost, the exception being a book containing copies of letters sent by the London house to the firm's Philadelphia branch, from 1784 onwards. These are the only letters of Yehiel Prager which we have. We thus lack the great majority of the outgoing letters of the London branch written before the final period of stagnation and decline. The copy-books of the later years – from 1788 onwards – are all extant, including copies of the letters sent by the London house to the house in Amsterdam. To the firm's internal correspondence also belong the letters of the Ostend branch (1781–3) and that of the Philadelphia house (1783–92), mostly written by Meyer Prager,[7] as well as Leib Prager's letters from India (1786–93).

The external correspondence, which has been almost fully preserved, includes letters received from the English outports, from Jewish merchants of Amsterdam and Antwerp, from the Hanoverian banker Meyer Michael-David (Meyer Hanover), the Berlin merchant Aaron Meyer (Aaron Yoresh), and many other letters, from Petersburg, Copenhagen, Lisbon, Leghorn and other places. In addition, the papers include personal documents – receipts of the Jewish burial society, a carriage licence, a pocket diary, plans of the Prager house at Clapton and the like. We also have the firm's original partnership contract of 1762. Besides all this, there are the inevitable begging letters, from less fortunate members of the family and from other persons, partly written in Hebrew. Unfortunately the only account books preserved are those of the last period of the firm's existence, from 1788 onwards, and it is therefore impossible to determine the volume of its business and its composition before the decline set in. Some idea on the subject can be gained from the correspondence, but a full and accurate account of the firm's transactions is, of course, impossible. The papers, nevertheless, enable us to tell the story of a big Jewish firm during the greater part of the second half of the eighteenth century, and they also shed some new light on several incidents in the Jewish history of the period – the affair of Lord George Gordon and his conversion to Judaism, the self-defence of the Jews of Amsterdam during the revolt of the Patriots in 1787, and the problems of the Jewish charity in Hanover.

Little is known about the history of the Prager family before 1760. The father of the brothers Prager was called Yehuda Leib and died some time before 1745. The Amsterdam house probably existed already during Yehuda Leib's lifetime, as it was later known by the name of Weduwe Levie Salomons en Zoonen, but it seems that its beginnings were rather modest and that it rose to importance only after the three brothers, Jacob, David, and Yehiel, had taken charge of the business.[8] Jacob was apparently the eldest brother, while Yehiel was the youngest. In 1752 the latter went to London as representative of the firm.[9] He returned to Amsterdam ten years later, married his niece Esther – Jacob's eldest daughter – and returned to London with his young wife and her brother Leib (Lyon), after signing a contract of partnership with his brothers.[10] Its main provisions are that the firm's books, papers and cash will be kept in Jacob Prager's house; the division of profits and losses will be as follows: Jacob 36 per cent, David and Yehiel 32 per cent each; Jacob and David will have a common household, which will be maintained from the firm's cash, the expenses to be deducted from the net profits; Yehiel's household expenses will be deducted from the firm's profits; if a child of one of the partners marries, he will receive from the firm an amount of money to be fixed by common agreement; the contract is to be valid for the partners' lifetime, but any of them may break up the partnership by giving notice of his intention at least three months before 31 December; Yehiel agrees to sell his part in the brothers' real estate in Amsterdam, as well as his place in the synagogue, for 3,000 gulden. Yehiel, however, never regarded the partnership as a comprehensive one, and he undertook many independent transactions, especially in diamonds – there are frequent complaints by his brothers against his habit of selling diamonds in London instead of consigning them to Amsterdam. This private business enabled Yehiel to acquire a much larger fortune than his brothers, and in the mid-1770s he proceeded to establish an independent house in London bearing his 'business name', Israel Levin Salomons. A new contract was drawn up between the old Amsterdam firm, now headed by Jacob and David Prager, and Yehiel's new firm in London. The Amsterdam house as such was the senior partner, but Yehiel's personal share was now larger than that of either of his brothers. He was to receive 10,000 out of the first 22,000 gulden of the partnership's profits, while his brothers were entitled to only 6,000 gulden each. The rest of the profits, if any, was to be divided equally between the three brothers. On this basis the partnership functioned until Yehiel's death in 1788.[11]

The house of Prager became one of the foremost Ashkenazi firms of London and Amsterdam. Thanks to their caution, the Pragers survived the economic crises of 1763 and 1772,[12] thus making a name for themselves as one of the most stable of Jewish houses. The Prager's pride in their good reputation is often reflected in their letters. When Jacob visited London in 1786 he wrote home about Yehiel's excellent standing in London, to which his brother David replied on 20 February 1787: 'We here, too, are not in bad repute, thank God, especially among Gentiles.'

Nevertheless it looks as if the financial basis of the Amsterdam house was somewhat shaky. When Jacob died in 1787, his nominal share in the business amounted to 100,000 gulden (about £10,000, but of this sum, there remained in fact only about 65,000 gulden, because several of his children had already received substantial amounts before his death.[13] Yehiel's situation in London was by far better: his share in the partnership was larger, and his estate amounted to £48,000 – a far from negligible sum, especially in view of the modest financial basis on which most Ashkenazi houses stood at that time. The Amsterdam and London houses also differed in their style of living. While the Dutch Pragers were content with their house in Keizersgracht, Yehiel in 1781 moved with his family to a big house in Clapton, where he kept several servants, a gardener, a coachman, a teacher and a governess. Already three years before they settled in Clapton, on 28 August 1778, Jacob wrote about the impression which the London family made on his son-in-law Levy: 'As for my son-in-law Levy, he has English air in his head ... all his talk is of you, of the richness, the influence, and the pleasant life that you lead, thank God, unlike anyone in the world. May it continue like that and may God grant to you more, amen.'

In the course of the fourth Anglo-Dutch War a branch house was established at Ostend, which served as a commercial link between England and Holland during the war. As Jews were not usually permitted to reside at Ostend[14] a special permit had to be obtained from the Imperial authorities. When this was granted, the Pragers, in partnership with an Antwerp firm, established a house in Ostend, which existed from 1781 until 1783. It was headed by Jacob's eldest son, Meyer, who was helped by his brother Yehiel Jr and by his cousin, also called Meyer. It soon became clear that the branch's intended services, as a wartime link between the Amsterdam and London houses, could be dispensed with, because direct commercial connections continued to exist in spite of hostilities. The Ostend house, nevertheless, made good profits. Ostend, for a short time, was turned into an important commercial centre, and opportunities of doing business were never lacking. It attracted great quantities of colonial goods, like tobacco, coffee, hides, and rice, which in normal times could be found only in London and Amsterdam. During this period of poor business, Ostend was the only bright spot in the Pragers' affairs.

With the end of the war in sight, Ostend returned to the obscurity of a small seaside town. Already in the spring of 1783 the Pragers realized that the days of the Ostend branch were numbered, and Jacob suggested that their sons, who had conducted the business there, should establish a new house in Philadelphia. The newly-won independence of the United States opened promising prospects in the American trade, especially for the importers of tobacco, which had always figured prominently in the Pragers' business. Jacob hoped that it would now be possible to import American tobacco directly, without having recourse to English middlemen, and that the establishment of a house in America would help in providing a profitable occupation for the young men of the family. By June 1783 everything was ready[15] and in autumn the two Meyers and Yehiel junior sailed to America and established a house in Philadelphia, in co-operation with the Liebaerts of Antwerp, their old Ostend partner. Meyer and 'Yehielke' sailed from London, 'Meyerke' from Amsterdam. There is a list of the items with which the latter was provided for the journey, including kosher meat, live chickens and ducks, dishes, medicines, a table of prayers, prayer-books, etc.[16]

Although the young Pragers enjoyed the support of two substantial European houses and were provided with ample credit in Europe the first years were very difficult. North America was flooded with European goods. England regained much of the tobacco trade,[17] and the Pragers in Philadelphia were unable to consolidate their position in the trade. Their fathers and uncle in Europe more than once discussed whether it would not be better to recall them, but in the end they stayed, and it seems that after 1790 business began to prosper. After the termination of the partnership between the London and Amsterdam houses in 1793 the latter concentrated chiefly on American business.

The death of Jacob Prager in 1787 marked the beginning of a series of misfortunes which ended in the collapse of the London house. A year after Jacob's death his brother Yehiel, head of the English house, passed away, so that the partnership was all at once deprived of its two main supports. Yehiel's elder son, Mordecai (Mark), was an immature youngster of 20, not fitted to take his father's place. At the time of Yehiel's death his nephew Meyer was on a visit to the family in London, on his way back from the United States, and it was agreed that he should take over the conduct of the London house, together with his sister Esther, Yehiel's widow. The situation of the Amsterdam house was less desperate. It is true that David, the only surviving brother, had always played second fiddle to his brother Jacob, but he had taken part in the conduct of the firm's business from the very beginning, and was thoroughly acquainted with it. Here, too, there were several older children – David's sons, Isaac and Wolf, and Jacob's son Isaiah. Jacob had been something of an autocrat and had never allowed the second generation to take part in the conduct of affairs; after his death his brother David wrote about him: 'He, may he rest in peace, used to do everything himself and it was positively impossible to gainsay him, so that the children actually have no idea at all what goes on in the business.' Nonetheless there was not the same break in continuity as in London.

The London house might have been able to overcome the crisis, in spite of the unfavourable circumstances, but for two steps undertaken by Yehiel before his death – the sending of his nephew and brother-in-law, Leib, to India and an enormous speculation in drugs upon which he embarked in 1786. By these ventures Yehiel hoped to gain a monopolistic position in the diamond market, as well as in the drug market of London, but both attempts proved failures. Leib Prager's lack of success in the Indian diamond business did not cause serious financial loss, but his absence from London at the time of his uncle's death was a real disaster. Even before he left Europe, his father Jacob had warned Yehiel that, if Leib went to India, the London house might be left without a person capable of taking charge of its affairs. This is exactly what happened. Leib, who had been his uncle's chief assistant for almost 25 years, was in India while his brother Meyer, who became the *de facto* head of the London house, was a newcomer to the City, and had none of Leib's excellent connections there. In complete contrast to Leib, Meyer was an arrogant person and soon fell out with his sister Esther. After a few years the situation became unbearable and Meyer had to leave.[18] The speculation in drugs was connected with Leib Prager's journey to India. While visiting Capetown, on his way east, Leib, acting on his uncle's instructions, signed contracts with two ship captains for the purchase of great quantities of drugs to be delivered to Yehiel Prager in London. Shortly after, prices of drugs in Europe dropped sharply and during the year following Yehiel's death in 1788 the firm lost about £10,000 in this business – a sum equivalent to approximately one-fifth of Yehiel's estate.[19] Worse was to follow. In 1790 it was discovered that Yehiel's eldest son Mordecai (Mark) had been leading a licentious life and was deeply in debt. This affair cost the firm another £20,000, and in May 1792 the widow Esther wrote to her brother Leib in India: 'I sit down with an estate reduced from £48,000 to £9,153. Melancholy recital indeed, but nevertheless true!'[20]

None of the five surviving sons of Yehiel and Esther Prager was fit to take his father's place at the head of the firm. Mordecai was deprived of his share in the business[21] and was sent to join his uncle Leib in India. He was apparently not without ability and during his sojourn in Holland, between 1780 and 1783, had made a good impression on his uncles. George Elliot, who took over the management of the London house after Meyer Prager's withdrawal, wrote about him: 'Mark has great power and abilities, and with proper engine to direct them must do well'.[22] Hopes that may have been entertained that he would mend his ways under his uncle's supervision were, however, dashed when Leib died in 1793, and he returned from India in 1795, having incurred new debts to the amount of 35,000 rupees (about £3,500). In September 1796 his mother wrote: 'He is a most unhappy young man and is now a bankrupt in the King's Bench . . . whether he will ever be free, God only knows.'[23] This is the last information to be found in the Prager Papers about Mordecai. It is probable that the Anglo-Dutch writer Mark Prager Lindo (1819–77), the son of David Lindo and his wife Mathilda – the youngest daughter of Yehiel and Esther Prager – was called after his uncle.

Mordecai's brother Leib junior (Lionel), too, was a good-for-nothing. He was placed with his uncles in Philadelphia, who found him such a nuisance that even his nearest relations despaired of him. The third son, Simeon, was also sent to India and died there in 1794. His brother Henry went to Jamaica, accompanied by the family tutor. There he was to be initiated into business by the house of Lindo, but he, too, proved a sore disappointment to his mother. The youngest son, Joseph, stayed in London; he is known to have served later as an army officer in India, where he died in 1824. For several years Esther tried to save what remained of the business, assisted by George Elliot (an old friend of her brother Leib) and supported by her son-in-law Benjamin Goldsmid and his brother Abraham, who at that time was acquiring a dominant position in the London money market.[24] The business was now mainly limited to Indian goods and diamonds, but Leib Prager's death in Calcutta left the firm without a representative there and caused serious harm to its standing in this branch, and in 1796 Esther decided to wind up the business. She died two years later.[25]

Something should be said about the two business-houses of London and Amsterdam and how their affairs were conducted. Both houses endeavoured to employ, as far as possible, members of the family. The boys received the sort of education useful to men of business, with the stress on languages and mathematics. The London and Amsterdam houses even 'exchanged' sons for certain periods of time, in order that they should improve their knowledge of Dutch and English respectively. Mordecai Prager spent about two years at his uncle's house in Amsterdam, while his Dutch cousins, Yehiel junior and Isaiah, worked for a time in the London business. Their presence there was also meant to help Yehiel and Leib, who, in the absence of grown-up children, were often overwhelmed by the amount of work which had to be done; Yehiel did not consider it beneath him to sew sacks.[26] The daily routine consisted of writing letters and making copies, looking after goods stored in warehouses, loading and unloading of goods, seeing to the release of goods by the warehouses of the East India Company, and the like. The London business also required visits to the southern and western outports at which a considerable part of the West Indian and North American goods arrived. These journeys were usually undertaken by Leib Prager.

Negotiations with brokers and merchants were conducted in the firm's office, on the exchange, or in a coffee house. Yehiel and Leib Prager could be found regularly at Tom's Coffee House which was situated near the Royal Exchange and not far from the firm's offices.[27] These had originally been in Budge Row and later moved to Throgmorton Street. The partners usually worked in harmony and constantly consulted each other. This co-operation was made possible by the excellent personal relationship between Jacob and Yehiel, who were not only brothers but were further connected by Yehiel's marriage to his niece, Jacob's daughter. It was thanks to this relationship that the private business deals which Yehiel did in London, and the much greater success of the London house, did not cause excessive jealousy on the part of the Pragers of Amsterdam. Jacob could not but be happy about the prosperity of his eldest daughter and her family, and thus a rather delicate situation was prevented from developing into a major row, which would perhaps have been unavoidable under different circumstances.

Friction there was, from time to time, usually caused by Yehiel's aggressive nature. But these disputes never lasted long – Jacob's goodnatured resoluteness and his sense of humour took the sting out of them, and the none too frequent meetings between the brothers in London were always happy occasions. Even the Anglo-Dutch War did not spoil the fraternal relations. Yehiel was a loyal British patriot, but his brothers in Amsterdam sympathized with England rather than with her main enemies, the French and Americans. Their letters abound in comments on the international situation. In February 1778 Jacob Prager expressed anxiety about Howe's chances against Washington, concluding: 'May God, be He blessed, help England'.[28] Three days later he dwelt on rumours concerning French military preparations, which were said to be in progress:

In short, England will now find out that all French promises were nothing but trickery. And really, seeing that the villain Franklin of Congress has already been there [i.e. in France] for so long a time, how could one not see that they are reaching an agreement with the Americans?[29]

His attitude did not change when the Netherlands joined England's enemies, and in August 1781 he wrote: 'Why don't the English give the French a decisive beating? Then the end *could* come. We shall revenge ourselves, God willing; the wise will understand the hint.'[30] Earlier, Jacob had been somewhat sceptical about England's ability to overcome all her enemies:

Thank God you think England's power so great as to enable her to destroy all others. Reb Asher used to say: 'beeter hart geblaasen als het mond verbrand' ['better to blow hard than to burn one's mouth']. You are talking very big, may God grant it should be as you report.[31]

It was at this time that David wrote to Yehiel:[32] 'We have always lived, thank God, as brothers should live, not as other, unworthy families live together'.

Despite the firm's success and respectability, its capital was relatively modest[33] and much of its business was based on credit. Explaining the reasons for the restrictions imposed by Jacob's will on the withdrawal of capital from the business by his successors, David Prager wrote in 1786:

This has been arranged by your father, may he rest in peace, after having carefully considered the matter together with me, because we knew that our capital is much too small for honourably meeting our engagements and for sustaining our trade, as we have in fact sustained it, thank God, by many contrivances and much work and worries, and hope to continue to sustain it in future.[34]

Without the credit which it enjoyed, the firm could not have lasted a day. The Pragers were not prepared to adapt their business to the narrow basis provided by their own resources and could not bridge, unaided, the lapse of time between the purchase of goods – usually in England – and the reception of payment for the same goods after they were sold – usually in Holland. The credit, on which much of the firm's business was based, was not a regular bankers' credit, but a discount credit, which was very common in Anglo-Dutch trade, with its pronounced financial character. Big transactions in bills of exchange were constantly made between London and Amsterdam, which was an international centre of bills discount.[35] The discounters in effect also functioned as lenders, paying out the value of the bills earlier than they were due, less the discount fees. The ease of discounting bills in Amsterdam added a great measure of flexibility to commerce and enabled the merchants to increase the volume of their transactions. On the other hand, these credit facilities were liable to cause an unhealthy expansion of business activity. In the only extant letter of Jacob Prager written in 1772 – the year of the great economic depression – he quotes the head of the big house of Hope as saying: 'The English have for the last 4 to 5 years engaged in such extensive affairs, and all on the basis of bills' service [discount], that they are forced to send all goods here [to Amsterdam], and will ruin all business.'[36]

The advanced mechanism of discount at Amsterdam gave a marked advantage to houses with branches on both sides of the Channel; they could draw on each other to keep business going. Yehiel Prager usually seems to have paid for the goods to be bought by drawing on his brothers in Amsterdam. Often, however, the latter had not yet received the proceeds of the goods by the time payment fell due. At this stage the possibilities of discounting bills and of drawing bills on each other had to be exploited. The Amsterdam Pragers could now draw on the London house, or Yehiel, in London, would send them bills drawn on Amsterdam or other places which they could discount. The firm, of course, had to pay commission and discount fees for these financial transactions, and often suffered losses because of an unfavourable rate of exchange. In fact, the system was less elastic than appears at first sight, and David Prager's statement about their maintaining the business 'by many contrivances and much work and worries' was certainly well founded.

The exchange business between London and Amsterdam was the domain of specialized exchange merchants, most of whom were apparently Jews. The regular merchant did not have the knowledge and experience essential for successful operations on the exchange market, nor was he in a position to give a considerable part of his time to this sort of business, as the specialist could and had to. In addition, his transactions in goods severely limited his freedom of manœuvring on the exchange market – he was often not in a position to await a suitable opportunity for drawing or for remitting bills because his regular business might necessitate his doing so even under unfavourable conditions. If he was not careful or just not lucky, the regular merchant might lose all his profits by an unfavourable rate of exchange, coming on top of his expenses for commission and discount fees. He was heavily dependent on the bill brokers, who usually seem to have given preference to the exchange merchants with whom they worked regularly, over the ordinary merchants. It was not always possible to draw as the merchant would have liked to or to find bills for remission. In addition, it was very important not to arouse suspicion that the firm was employing a method of mutual drawing between its branches or was drawing below the current rate of exchange in order to get out of a difficult situation. In the long run, such a policy would be liable to ruin the house's credit and thus bring about its collapse. The London branch was able to draw on the house in Amsterdam without causing any misgivings because it regularly sent it goods, so that its drawings were considered as a legitimate part of the firm's business. But drawing in the other direction was liable to make a bad impression, especially if the receivers of the bills in London had to look for discounters and this became known in commercial circles.[37] The rate of exchange was considerably influenced by the rate at which the big houses of Hope and Muilman drew. Other houses, even those of good standing, had normally to draw somewhat below the rate of the big two, but they also had to be careful not to draw too much below this rate, if they did not want to damage their reputation.[38] Sometimes it was difficult to discount bills. A deficiency in coins would cause the rate of discount to rise from 3–3½ per cent to 4–4½ per cent, and even at that price it might be difficult to find discounters.[39]

Jewish houses were especially prone to suffer when such situations occurred. Because of the intensive activity of Jews in the exchange trade, they were the first to feel the approach of an economic crisis. Even a house like that of the brothers Prager, which shied away from uncertain financial transactions and enjoyed a good reputation, was not immune from the general distrust in the financial stability of Jewish merchants in times of crisis.[40] Because of difficulties of this kind, the Pragers sometimes found themselves in a precarious situation. Yehiel in London endeavoured to keep most of the firm's free capital in his own hands, and his brothers had frequently to make all-out efforts in order to honour the bills which he drew on them. It was always possible to get money by mortgaging the goods; however this was not only inconsistent with the standing of a reputable firm but it also prevented the sale of the merchandise.[41] The house was therefore obliged to look for other ways of increasing its financial resources and it found a partial solution to this problem in the maintenance of special connections with other firms: partnerships with other houses in mercantile transactions and exchange business with houses in Germany and France.

There were three reasons why the Pragers were prepared from time to time to undertake joint transactions with others. Firstly, the partner would advance to the Pragers their share of the outlay, repayable of course with interest at the rate, usually, of 4 per cent, though sometimes of 5. The Pragers had connections with several Dutch and Anglo-Dutch firms which from time to time agreed to take part in arrangements of this kind. Amongst them was Pieter de Wolff of Amsterdam (called 'Wolfkhe' in the Prager letters); despite occasional friction,[42] he was an important asset to the firm.

Secondly, joint transactions with reputable houses increased the possibilities of getting credit by the discount of bills. In May 1785 Jacob Prager recommended that they should agree to the request of a merchant called Francis Abrahams, who wanted to join them in a purchase of drugs in London, because they would thereby be able to undertake the transaction without having to make use of their free capital.[43] Again, though the Pragers disliked meddling in exchange business, they did maintain connections with such houses as Tourton and Baur in Paris,[44] because they could increase their financial flexibility by drawing on such associates. Indeed, if the rate of exchange were favourable it was sometimes possible to offset the loss on the discount against the profit on the exchange, thus obtaining working capital without interest.[45]

In the third place, partnership with others enabled the Pragers to buy greater quantities of the goods in question, thus strengthening their trading position in relation both to sellers and buyers. The most conspicuous example was Yehiel's great tobacco speculation of 1786: he could never have hoped to dominate the market without making common cause with other tobacco merchants.

The most frequent partners of the Pragers were Dutch and

Anglo-Dutch houses like those of De Wolff, De Bruyn, Grote, Van Notten, Reesen, Stapel and Abrahams. Second in importance were Jewish-Portuguese firms like those of Franco, Hananel Mendes da Costa, Brandon and Lara. Only on rare occasions did the Pragers share transactions with other Ashkenazim like Levy Cohen, Simon Tanhum (Simon Daniels), or the Goldsmids. Perhaps this order of preference reflected the relative importance of these groups in Anglo-Dutch trade (excluding diamonds and the exchange business). Another, perhaps complementary, explanation for the small number of Ashkenazi partners in the Prager business is to be found in the categories of goods in which the firm traded; all these goods, except diamonds, were not common in the business affairs of most Ashkenazim who were active in Anglo-Dutch trade. Partnerships with Ashkenazim like Levy Cohen and Simon Tanhum concerned goods in which the Pragers did not trade on their own account – cloth, china, etc. In transactions which the Pragers did in common with non-Jews and with Portuguese Jews they usually kept the conduct of affairs in their own hands, but it seems that when doing partnership business with Ashkenazim they were content to play the role of a passive partner. Some of the Pragers' partners were brokers, who could not trade openly on their own account and had to use the name of some firm as a cover.

By contrivances and partnerships of one kind and another, the firm succeeded in maintaining an adequate financial base for its operations. A mixture of daring and caution was needed, and a constant search for ways and means; it could not have been managed for any length of time without the excellent reputation, rare amongst Jews, that the Pragers had gained for themselves. So sound was this that when the London house collapsed after 1790, the Amsterdam business carried on, its credit unimpaired. Even as late as 1793, when it had become clear that the London house had little chance of surviving, Isaac Prager of Amsterdam could write that there were few Jewish houses whose bills were so easy to discount as their own.[46]

Factors have always played an essential role in international commerce – only a firm with branches in the places to which it traded could dispense with their services. In the trade between London and Amsterdam, with its emphasis on the re-export of English colonial goods, the principals were usually City merchants, who employed factors to take care of their affairs at the

Dutch end of the business.[47] The principals, naturally, preferred agents who had no considerable share of their own in Anglo-Dutch trade, and so were not tempted to further their own interests at the expense of those of their principals.[48] It is therefore not surprising that the Pragers, who invested mainly in the Anglo-Dutch trade, did not, at first, get much commission business. Till the late 1770s, the house acted as agents for a single merchant – Aaron Meyer of Berlin – and the transactions they did for him were rather small.[49] Only towards 1780, after the house had become known as a stable firm enjoying widespread connections, were the Pragers first entrusted with commission business in the Anglo-Dutch trade.[50]

There were four categories of commission business in this trade. The London house would sometimes act as factors for Dutch firms, buying goods in London for their account or selling goods consigned from Holland. The Amsterdam house could sell in Holland goods belonging to English firms or purchase goods ordered by them and consign them to England. All four kinds of transactions are encountered in the business of the Prager brothers, but as could be expected in view of the character of the Anglo-Dutch trade, most of the transactions they did as commission agents consisted of buying goods in London on behalf of Dutch principals, and of selling in Amsterdam by the order of English merchants.

In the 1780s the Pragers did a considerable amount of transactions as commission agents, but it is clear that in this field they were still hampered by their independent commercial activity. The orders which they received were usually either for goods in which they did not normally deal themselves or, on the other hand, for goods in which they specialized. In the first case there was no danger that they would give preference to their own interests to the detriment of their principals, in the second case they had a special advantage thanks to their expert knowledge and good connections. Into the latter category fell orders for the purchase of Indian thread and drugs in London and for the sale of dyestuffs and diamonds in Amsterdam. The excellent connections which Yehiel and Leib Prager enjoyed at India House gave them a great advantage in the purchase of Indian goods while their Amsterdam relatives were well acquainted with the local market for cochineal, indigo and diamonds. Although we lack numerical data which would enable us to determinate the place of commission business in the affairs of the Pragers during the 1780s, it seems that even at that time their independent transactions were more important by far. It is improbable that the Pragers' income from factorage was a very significant item in their balance-sheets, and it is doubtful whether it justified the trouble they took with these affairs. In 1786 – the only year of which a balance of profit and loss has survived – their income from factorage amounted to a mere 1,387 gulden, out of net profits totalling 14,168 gulden, that is to say, barely 10 per cent of their net income during that year.[51] This is not to say that the Pragers' commission business was not worth a great deal to them – they would certainly not have bothered with it, had it not been of some real advantage to them. In fact, these transactions enabled the house to extend the scope of its business, and it would seem that it was largely due to the big orders for drugs which it received from Holland that the firm succeeded in becoming one of the major firms on the drug markets of London and Amsterdam.

The partnerships and commission business of the firm enable us to gain an insight into the Prager's business ethics. Transactions of this kind presented great temptations because in their course the firm got possession of goods belonging to other merchants, who often were unable to exercise effective control over their partner or agent and, in the case of English merchants, were not familiar with conditions on the other side of the Channel. Although the Pragers apparently regarded themselves as honest persons, and were known as such, they were always ready to deceive their partners and principals if they thought that it could be done safely. If they decided against such a course, it was usually either because they feared that their dishonest behaviour might be discovered or because they hoped that honesty would be more profitable in the long run. Considerations of this kind are mentioned in letters of November 1780, which deal with a transaction in Spanish wool undertaken jointly with Pieter de Wolff. The wool was sent to London to be sold by Yehiel. Jacob told him that if he sold it for three shillings four pence, he should make up an account showing that he had sold it for three shillings two pence, or that perhaps it would be better to write three shillings three pence, so that de Wolff would not be discouraged from doing business with them in future. Yehiel, however, refused to accept his brother's suggestion, arguing that it would be too dangerous to falsify accounts.[52] It would seem, nevertheless, that, on some occasions, the nature of their personal relations with the partner or principal involved was of some importance in deciding their line of conduct. Jacob wrote about profits made on coffee which had been sold in common with Brandon of London. 'What account shall we now make up for Brandon? What should it amount to? Let us know. Whatever he gets is a sin.' The Pragers were not always so mean. When they bought goods for the London house of Hayter and Strong, Jacob assured Yehiel: 'Of course these are blessed people and we shall always do for them whatever will be to their advantage.'[53]

As partners and agents, the Pragers had frequent opportunities of practising deception in their reports on the sale of goods, and they were tempted to give preference to their own business over transactions the profits of which they had to share or those which they made on behalf of others. From the moral point of view, giving preference to their own business was perhaps the less reprehensible act. It is true that the Pragers did not hesitate to buy the best goods for themselves, if they could do so without the knowledge of their partners or principals, and they concealed from them transactions which they did on their own account, so that they should not demand a share in them. In February 1775, for example, Jacob suggested to Yehiel that they should use their Jewish name (Prager) in order to hide from their Christian partners that they were importing goods on their own account. In December 1777 Jacob suggested that Yehiel should secretly buy on his own account a part of the wool then available in London and consign it to Holland in such a manner that it would not become known what sort of goods he was sending: 'We promised de Wolfkhe to give him a share if we buy and he immediately agreed. But damn it, he need know nothing about it.'[54] But it can perhaps be argued that only an extremely naive partner or principal would have expected the Pragers to behave differently and that a merchant who employed as agents a firm having an extensive business of its own, or who entered a partnership with such a house, must have known the risks and been willing to take them.

Much more serious from the ethical point of view were the acts of outright fraud practised by the Pragers. They made up false sale-accounts and pocketed the difference,[55] and they bought goods for a lower price than the maximum price fixed by the merchant who had ordered them but reported that they had paid

the maximum price, retaining the difference.[56] When a merchant
sent them goods on commission but gave too low an estimate of
their value, they did not inform him about his mistake, hoping
that they would continue to benefit from his ignorance when he
sent them additional consignments.[57] They retained part of the
profits made on goods they sold on commission, although they
had no right to anything but their factorage.[58] On one occasion,
they sold in Switzerland goods received from a London principal,
and charged him with brokerage and weighing fees – although
these payments were usually not charged on goods sold abroad.[59]
The brothers in Amsterdam advised Yehiel Prager in London to
retain part of the drawback received for goods belonging to a
principal.[60] When, on another occasion, David Prager, who at
that time served as Parnas (community leader) in Amsterdam,
decided to make up a correct sale-account for indigo which they
had received from London on commission, he made specific
mention of his intention in a letter to his brother Yehiel: 'I'll duly
make it up correctly and honestly as becomes a parnas.'[61] It is
difficult to say whether this kind of behaviour reflected the prevalent ethical standards of English and Dutch commercial circles,
but it would seem that it was, at least, not uncommon. Westerfield has pointed out that the doubtful loyalty and integrity of
commission agents was one of the problems which beset international commerce at that period, although mutual confidence
among merchants was on the increase during the eighteenth
century.[62] Perhaps it is of some significance that the Pragers never
seem to have regarded their behaviour as disgraceful and did not
have any differences of opinion about its propriety.

During the eighteenth century the exchange of goods between
England and Holland remained stagnant and its volume even
decreased to some extent, while the relative share of Holland in
England's overseas trade declined sharply.[63] But although
Amsterdam's heyday as an entrepôt of international commerce
was over its importance as a financial centre was growing. Credit
and discount business was done on a large scale and the trade in
securities flourished.[64] This shift in the character of Amsterdam's
international trade was clearly reflected in Anglo-Dutch commerce by a marked increase in the relative importance of transactions in bills of exchange, precious metals and securities. Many
of the Jewish houses active in Anglo-Dutch trade were heavily

engaged in exchange business. Most of them seem also to have traded in goods, but the emphasis was decidedly on financial transactions. A firm like that of the Pragers, which dealt mainly in goods, was permanently confronted by the problem of whether, and to what extent, it should try to augment its profits by meddling in bills of exchange, precious metals and securities. It was not only a question of being tempted to make quick profits on short-term investments, but a cruel problem of survival – the result of the stagnation in the regular trade between England and Holland during that period. The Pragers were frequently in doubt whether the income from their regular business would be sufficient to keep it going, not to speak of its expansion, whether they would be able to continue the 'respectable' tradition of buying and selling goods or would be swept along by the rising tide of financial transactions.

Four kinds of financial business were open to the Pragers: they could deal in bills of exchange and precious metals, or in stocks and shares; they could become contractors for Government loans, or undertake to remit money to or from England. The Pragers were active, at one time or another, in all these fields; in fact the only sort of financial business at which they never tried their hand was that of real banking, including the discount of bills. But the brothers' attitude to financial transactions was usually equivocal and sometimes entirely negative. It is obvious that they always preferred a good transaction in buying and selling goods to financial affairs, which could, under certain circumstances, jeopardize the firm's standing. The Pragers had to deal regularly with bills of exchange – no merchant could avoid this – and in addition, as we have seen, the facility with which bills could be discounted in Amsterdam was exploited by them in order to get the credit which was essential to the smooth running of the business. But the Pragers from time to time also made transactions in bills which had no connection with their regular trade. The temptation to do this was particularly strong in Anglo-Dutch trade, with its pronounced financial character, and the Pragers sometimes tried to make use of favourable situations on the exchange market, in order to make quick profits by remitting large amounts of bills of exchange from London to Amsterdam or vice versa. Naturally, their tendency to undertake business of this sort increased when their own affairs looked unpromising and they were driven to find additional sources of income. On 9 March 1781 Jacob wrote about the trade in bills of exchange: 'Good business [in goods] is certainly better, but if there are good profits, one should take them – it is better than to let money lie idle.' On the whole, the Pragers' attitude to transactions in bills represented a mixture of greed for easy profits and a sound reluctance to get too deeply engaged. It was all summed up, on one occasion, by Jacob Prager: 'My dear Yehiel, let us not worry too much about the bill trade. If we can make some easy profits – very well. But to let ourselves get involved in this trade turns your brains and ours. Employ this work in trade.'[65]

A firm which dealt mainly in goods did not have the knowledge or the connections necessary for a successful pursuit of exchange business. The regular merchant was often utterly perplexed by it: 'At the moment the bill trade is like the play in shares, the devil can understand it.'[66] The exchange business was described by Jacob Prager as 'a dangerous trade' and 'a hazardous trade'[67] and in fact the firm profited little from its periodic attempts to meddle in it. It was impossible to carry on the regular trade in goods and, at the same time, to undertake exchange transactions on a large scale. A firm which tried it ran the risk of losing its regular business without succeeding in gaining a foot-hold in the exchange market. Taught by long experience, David Prager commented on the undependability of Yehiel's bill-broker in London: 'This trade is not for us, although many great households which do no other trade, amply subsist on it.'[68] Clearly only those firms which specialized in this business were able to succeed and prosper in it.

The Pragers' attitude to the exchange trade was also reflected in the instructions they gave to the youngsters who went to the United States in 1783, in order to establish a house in Philadelphia. They were warned not to do business in bills and their fathers and uncle in Europe were furious when they disobeyed. Yehiel threatened that he would not accept their bills – which would have spelt immediate ruin for the Philadelphia house – and added:

And I write you this in my own name and in the name of your parents: you must have no further dealings in bills and your abstaining from it will only bring you honour and renown. Respectable merchants do not concern themselves with it and you cannot get rich in one year. A merchant needs time and then respect comes of itself.[69]

The Pragers, nevertheless, not infrequently agreed to do ex-change business with other houses, like Michael-David of Hanover and Hamburg or the Sephardi houses of d'Aguilar, Mendes da Costa and Lindo of London. But their heart was never really in it and it would seem that in the case of the London firms, the Pragers' consent to undertake joint exchange transactions was mainly motivated by the hope that these partners would also give them a share in other business. On one occasion they told the d'Aguilars explicitly that they would only do exchange business with them if they let them have a part in their trade in goods and diamonds.[70] Two years later Jacob Prager wrote to Yehiel, in connection with a bill sent to him by Hananel Mendes da Costa: 'We do not want to have any bill business with him or with any [other] Portuguese, and neither must you, not even with Lindo.'[71]

There was a close connection between the trade in bills of exchange and the precious metals trade between London and Amsterdam. Although the profits made in precious metals – mainly by Jews – were regarded with envy by the Pragers, they appar-ently did not manage to do a single transaction in this field. It was obviously even more difficult than in the bills trade for per-sons from the outside to do anything in this branch. When the Amsterdam brothers, on one occasion, prompted Yehiel to send them silver from London, he replied that this trade was not for them, and when Esther Prager offered in 1793 to send silver to her brother Isaac in Amsterdam, he told her: 'One who has not been brought up in it and has no expert knowledge cannot do this.'[72]

While the Pragers were very cautious in their approach to the bill trade, they regarded the stock exchange with actual abhor-rence. Transactions in stocks were regularly done between London and Amsterdam. The London stock market was the most developed in the world and English paper was sold in Holland and was subject to speculations on the Amsterdam exchange. The Pragers of Amsterdam were always ready to act as agents in such trans-actions – there was no danger in this, and promising prospects would have opened before them had they succeeded in establish-ing a reputation as successful agents. Occasionally they tried to get stocks ordered from their brother Yehiel in London,[73] but they rarely succeeded. It was not easy for people from the outside, who could not make head or tail of the 'confusion de confusiones'[74] of the stock market, to find investors ready to entrust them with their investments and speculations. The Pragers were unwilling to get seriously involved in this kind of business, and when, at one time, Yehiel prevailed upon Jacob and David to try their hand at a transaction on the stock exchange, they thanked God for their failure to undertake anything:

> What a miracle that we could do nothing in stocks. There is a strange rise in [East India] Company [stock] because 7 ships are said to have arrived there [in England], and the 3% also stand at 64%. We hope that you, over there, also undertook nothing. From this it may be seen how one is liable to be endangered in this damned trade. God preserve [us]. An honest person must not go into this [business].[75]

During the following years, while the Amsterdam brothers tried to procure orders for stocks to be purchased by Yehiel in London, they kept on warning him against doing anything on his own account. Thus Jacob wrote in September 1781: 'Dear Yehiel, do no business in stocks, it may be disastrous for our trade. Heaven forbid.'[76] And a few months later he wrote, in connection with certain stock transactions of the London Lindos: 'Damn this cursed trade; by Heaven, it is a shame to speak with them and with all other stock brokers.'[77] The Amsterdam brothers apparently were at that time under the impression that Yehiel was not cautious enough where stock business was concerned. They told him that in Amsterdam a merchant was liable to ruin his credit if it became known that he dealt in stocks.[78] But Leib Prager, who was acquainted with conditions in England rather than in Holland, held a similar opinion. In 1792 he wrote from India to his brother Meyer in London, on hearing that the latter had been dealing in stocks:

> This would be the greatest misfortune that could befall you, because there is veritably no example that this has not meant certain ruin. I have had and seen such instances of it, that I avoid a stockbroker and do not give him a pound's credit, even if he is rich like a king.[79]

Connected with business in stocks, but of a different character, was the contracting of Government loans. The British Government used to divide the loans which it issued among businessmen of the City for marketing, and these loans were much sought after, especially during the American war which seriously impaired Britain's commerce and reduced profits in the City.[80] Yehiel Prager at that time made several attempts to get a share in such loans. For this purpose he made use of his connections with Anthony Bacon, a Member of Parliament and one of the biggest manufacturers of munitions during the American War.[81] But though he was a prosperous merchant, Yehiel never belonged to the City's upper strata, and the amounts he managed to get were small: £10,000 worth of Government paper in 1776 and £20,000 in 1778.[82] It is not clear whether his endeavours to obtain a share in the following years' issues were at all successful. In 1782 he was received by Lord North, 'together with other Gentile merchants',[83] but without result. In 1783 he was at first promised £15,000, but in the end obtained nothing. It seems that he was not powerful enough and, being a Jew, he could not hope for that seat in Parliament which was almost an essential in business of this kind. Yehiel's activity in this field caused serious dismay to his brothers in Amsterdam, who regarded the contracting of Government loans in the same light as all other financial business. It is true that they seem to have made a clear distinction between taking a share in a loan and speculating in stocks – a much more dangerous affair – but the two could not be held apart entirely. Thus Jacob Prager informed Yehiel in 1776, when it became known that he had obtained a share in the loan, that rumours had begun to spread that he was also dealing in stocks and that this might endanger their credit.

The following passage is taken from one of the two extant letters of 1776. It is reproduced here *in extenso*, as an example of the great sensitivity to rumours about a firm's dealings in stocks:

Reb Asher came to us yesterday – he says that he argued with Sluyter [of the house of Jan F. Sluyter en Zoon] in a coffee house. Sluyter told him confidentially that he was a very good friend of ours and that our house had a reputation among Christians similar to that of Hope's house, but that he would feel sorry for us if you and we engaged in stock dealings in London. (He thinks that you engaged in it, because you managed the last negotiation [concerning the Government loan]). That he should indeed have approached us and warned us to keep out of it, but that he was afraid lest we should abuse him, but that Reb Asher should tell us . . . and he answered him that we have no concern whatsoever in it and neither have you ... We tell you this only by the way, to show you that people, and especially Gentiles, must be talking about it, and if you do have some concern in it, God forbid, it is evidently being reported here and may harm our credit. So let us know, for the sake of our peace of mind, if you do have some concern in it, and do not be angry that we ask you about it – our brotherly duty required us to write to you about it. You always think highly of England's power, and the positive news which has been received here about the defeat of the Hessian troops could look bad for England. Therefore we must write to you about it.[84]

When Yehiel suggested to his brothers in 1778 that they sell in Holland some of the Government paper for which he had contracted, their response was far from enthusiastic. They replied that they had no experience in this field and that brokers were needed for such transactions and, above all, they doubted whether, in view of England's difficult position, it would be wise to undertake this sort of business.[85] Yehiel had evidently stressed in his letter that it was an honour to be granted a share in the loan and recalled earlier Jewish financiers of the City. His brother Jacob replied:

Concerning the new loan: Of course there was a big scramble for it and it was a honour in the time of Sampson Gideon and [Aaron] Franks. But dear Yehiel, to compare those times with the present! England did not owe one tenth of the amount and she was in a flourishing state. As now exactly the opposite is true – as it seems to us – it will be difficult to get money, and as long as England has not finished with America, we consider all its undertakings to be without substance.[86]

The Amsterdam brothers persisted in this opinion for several years. Jacob argued that they had no resources to spare for such business: if they had a few millions more than they needed, he would not have objected.[87] Repeatedly he warned his brother not to meddle in loan contracting. In the end he seems to have relented a little, perhaps because he realized that in any case Yehiel failed to obtain large amounts and that the risk was not excessive. When Yehiel was refused a share in the loan of 1783, Jacob consoled him in words which reflect the jealousy of the merchant towards the financier who makes 'easy' profits:[88] 'Of course this causes sorrow and heartgrief and is a bad thing . . . it seems that you and we cannot make easy profits and must exert ourselves so much in order to win an honest penny. God will provide something good by other means.'

As for the remittance of moneys, only the biggest financiers could undertake transactions in this field, remitting money for the British Crown to its allies or for the provision of the army abroad. Yehiel Prager probably never dreamt of playing an independent role in these affairs, but he did undertake small remittances as agent for the Jewish banker and court-agent Meyer Michael-David of Hanover.

The Pragers' connection with the house of Michael-David had apparently been formed by the Amsterdam branch. On the death in 1764 of Joseph Salomons, the well-known Ashkenazi merchant of London, Yehiel succeeded him as Michael-David's representative in London.[89] Yehiel at first did some transactions in bills of exchange on behalf of the Hanoverian house, but he showed little enthusiasm for it and the ties loosened after 1765.[90] In 1770 the correspondence became lively once more, but it now dealt mainly with remittances between England and Hanover – a flourishing business at a time when the two countries were bound together by a personal union. There were always a number of Hanoverians at the Court of St James, for whom Michael-David acted as banker. Yehiel Prager would pay out sums of money required by these persons and, in return, draw on Michael-David's branch in Hamburg.[91] Sometimes he served in a similar way Hanoverian merchants on visits to London. These banking transactions were rather small affairs and when Meyer Michael-David undertook in 1777 to transfer yearly £14,000 from Hanover to England on behalf of the crown, he did not entrust Prager with the handling of the business in London.[92] The biggest single transaction which Yehiel did for him was the remittance to Hanover of £10,000 – part of the dowry of the Queen of Denmark.[93] It is doubtful whether the Pragers of London derived any substantial profits from their connection with Michael-David. They probably maintained it chiefly because in time of need they could draw on the Hanoverian house and because the remittance business gave Yehiel access to a certain group of courtiers in London.[94]

Chapter 11
The firm in the Anglo–Dutch trade

As was customary in the international trade of that period, the Pragers did not specialize in a single category of goods, but dealt in many dozens of items. The house did not, however, have widespread international connections, of the kind maintained, for instance, by the Francos. It is true that it had, at one time or another, correspondents in Leghorn, Lisbon, Antwerp, Rotterdam, Hamburg, Berlin, Basle, Copenhagen, Petersburg, and Charleston, and we have already mentioned the firm's relations with the bankers Tourton and Baur and Michael-David of Paris and Hanover. Yehiel Prager sometimes sold small quantities of tobacco in Hamburg,[1] Spanish wool was ordered from Bilbao, and the Amsterdam house from time to time sold goods abroad – in Denmark,[2] Germany, and Switzerland. But these connections, and particularly those maintained by Yehiel Prager of London, were not very important. Yehiel, though he dealt in imported goods, was principally an exporter, not an importer. He purchased the goods in London and re-exported them mostly to his brothers in Amsterdam who, on their part, seem to have sold most of the merchandise in Holland itself, as was customary among the local merchants of the first hand.[3] Only in the 1780s did the Pragers decide to establish permanent connections overseas by sending several of their sons to the United States and to India. The Pragers were active mainly in Anglo-Dutch trade, and their connections outside this trade were usually mere ramifications of the main business. The goods in which the Pragers dealt were typical for the Anglo-Dutch trade in the eighteenth century – chiefly colonial goods of all kinds. Both London and Amsterdam were distribution centres for colonial goods and many of these passed both cities – they were usually disembarked in London or one of the out-ports and sent on to Amsterdam or Rotterdam. A considerable part of this merchandise was again re-exported from Holland, sometimes after receiving some treatment there, and sent to different parts of Europe, but especially to Germany and the Baltic area.

The house dealt in a great variety of products, imported from America, Asia and Africa: North American tobacco and rice,[4] West Indian sugar and coffee,[5] cocoa from the West Indies and Caracas,[6] indigo from South Carolina, the West Indies, and Guatemala,[7] Mexican cochineal,[8] cotton from the West Indies, Guiana, and the Levant,[9] South American hides, uncut diamonds from Brazil and India, Indian and Chinese 'drugs', Coromandel thread, and African gum. As the firm's account books from the period of its prosperity have not survived, we are unable to determine the relative importance of the various items in its business, but there can be no doubt that tobacco and drugs headed the list. This could be expected. North American tobacco was one of the staple products of the British plantations. By the second half of the eighteenth century England consumed most of the sugar which it received from its colonies,[10] but the greater part of the tobacco was re-exported to the Continent – between 50 and 100 million lbs were consigned yearly during the 1760s and 1770s.[11] Holland, which had an extensive tobacco industry, was during the whole of the century the biggest customer of English tobacco and itself re-exported a considerable part of it.[12] No wonder tobacco was a major item in the business of a firm mainly concerned with Anglo-Dutch trade, and the American War was consequently a serious blow to the Pragers. British shipping suffered heavy losses, Virginia and Maryland became battlefields, and the supply of tobacco decreased sharply. Early in 1775 the Pragers were still hoping that the troubles in America would continue, causing tobacco prices to rise. But after the struggle had gone on for months and years and tobacco had disappeared from the market, things looked somewhat different and the Pragers were now yearning for peace.[13] Certain quantities of American tobacco still reached Holland, mainly through France, but in 1779 Yehiel Prager stated that the whole of the tobacco which came through France was less in quantity than the tobacco which they alone used to sell in peace time.[14] This situation lasted for five years and caused serious harm to the firm. After the war, tobacco gradually regained its former importance in the Pragers' affairs, partly thanks to their new American house, but even more because, despite the radical change which had occurred in the relationship between England and North America, American tobacco soon found its way back to its old channel and again reached Europe mostly through England. By 1787 tobacco figured once more as the most important item in the firm's business: in February of that year it had 110,000 gulden invested in tobacco, out of a total invested capital amounting to 270,000 gulden.[15]

Another category of goods which was prominent in the Pragers' business were 'drugs' – a term which covered a variety of items. There were firstly the materials used in various industries: alum (needed for dyestuff production and the treatment of hides), barilla (also used by the dyestuff industry), tincal[16] (important in glass-making and also used in the melting and assaying of metals and for veneering ceramics), and 'dragon-blood' (for coating wood). This group also included several sorts of gum essential for the printing of cloth. It should be noted, however, that the most important gum – the gum senegal[17] – was usually not included at all in the category of 'drugs'. The group also included several kinds of varnish, especially Indian shellac, which became an important Indian export item as a result of the development of the art of varnishing in Europe during the seventeenth century.[18] Secondly there were the materials used by the pharmaceutic industry, like camphor and rhubarb, and, finally, a few spices were, for one reason or another, grouped under 'drugs'. In this category were cinnamon-like spices: cassia, cassia buds, chinese cinnamon, and cardamom.[19] By 1730 England had become, according to Defoe, the greatest European importer of drugs from overseas.[20] Holland, however, remained an important market, and it seems that in this branch it held on to its position as a European entrepôt more than in any other field of commerce, importing large quantities, both for its own consumption and industry and for re-export to other parts of the Continent.[21] But Holland's direct imports of drugs from overseas did not satisfy its requirements and it had to purchase large quantities from the English, notwithstanding the high protective tariff imposed by the Dutch Government in order to safeguard the interests of the Dutch East India Company. Drugs were less prominent in the business of the English East India Company than in the private trade of her ships' captains. During the 1770s Yehiel and Leib Prager formed widespread connections with this group of seafarers and acquired a strong position on the drug market of London. It is quite possible that the disappearance of tobacco from the market during the American war drove them to seek alternative business elsewhere, but even when the tobacco trade revived after the peace of 1783, drugs continued to play an important part in the firm's affairs and when Yehiel decided in the years 1786 and 1787 to embark on a series of speculations, he did so in two fields, tobacco and drugs.

Despite the large number of goods in which the firm dealt, one can discern clear fields of specialization in its commercial activity. On the one hand, the Pragers specialized in certain categories of goods and on the other they limited themselves, on the whole, to Anglo-Dutch commerce. On some occasions, seizing a favourable opportunity, they would step outside the familiar terrain – selling guns on commission[22] or consigning American ginseng to China –[23] but these were clearly exceptions to the rule. The Pragers dealt mainly in colonial goods. They did not export English products to Holland, nor did they trade in goods which England used to import from Holland, like flax and paper, except in as far as these were colonial goods, like cochineal or cotton. There was one exception to this rule, Spanish wool, which was of such high quality that even England imported it. But wool, being a raw material, resembled the sort of goods in which the Pragers were wont to deal. On the other hand, the firm did not usually handle the few finished products imported from the colonies like Indian cloth or Chinese porcelain, although both were prominent in the business of many Jewish merchants who were active in Anglo-Dutch trade. The tendency of the Pragers to confine themselves to Anglo-Dutch trade is strikingly reflected in the fact that they did not usually deal even in familiar goods if they did not fall into the framework of this trade. Despite their frequent transactions in North American tobacco and South American hides, they did not trade in local tobacco and hides. They bought and sold Indian and Chinese silk, American rice, and West Indian coffee – all products current in Anglo-Dutch trade – but not Italian silk, rice, or Javanese coffee, which were not.

The firm had to set these limits to its business because its resources of capital and credit were not inexhaustible and also because even the international merchant required some knowledge of the goods in which he dealt, though he used to rely heavily on brokers. In addition, it was not always easy to gain a foot-hold in new branches. An instructive example of this difficulty is the failure of the Pragers' attempt to break the tea monopoly of R. Voute, the Amsterdam agent of the English East India Company, although they enjoyed the support of a group of

Amsterdam tea merchants. Transactions in teas are mentioned in only three of the extant Prager letters antedating the attempt to break Voute's monopoly in 1785/6. In 1765 Richard Glover, a London merchant, mentions a consultation which he had with Yehiel Prager about tea, and expresses his readiness to buy up to £20,000 in partnership. In 1779 Voute himself offered to get Yehiel orders for the entire tea cargo taken from a French prize. In 1782, the Amsterdam Pragers received a consignment of tea in commission from Antwerp.[24] The East India Company had a monopoly on the importation of tea into England, but, as the quantities which it imported from the East were not always sufficient to answer the demand in England, it used to buy additional quantities on the Continent. In 1785 several Dutch tea merchants tried to make use of Yehiel Prager's connections in India House, in order to break the monopoly of Voute. But Yehiel was not able to dislodge Voute, who was apparently backed by the house of Hope and others.[25] When it became clear that their efforts were of no avail, Jacob Prager wrote to his brother in London: 'we cannot undertake big things in an article which is not familiar to us.'[26]

Despite the growing importance of the outports, especially Liverpool and Glasgow, the place of the big international merchant was still in London. The outports took an increasing share in the trade with North America, the West Indies, and West Africa, but the trade with India and the Far East remained a monopoly of London – the seat of the East India Company. Even the West India trade continued to be directed by a small group of London merchants. It must not be forgotten that London had become a money market of international standing, with close ties to the financial centre of Amsterdam and the credit facilities available in the City were incomparably better than in the outports. We have already discussed the remarkable degree of financial flexibility which the Anglo-Dutch merchant enjoyed, thanks to the bills trade between London and Amsterdam.

Owing to the disappearance of most of the account books and letter-books of the London house, our knowledge of its purchasing activity in England is somewhat fragmentary, especially in respect to the buying of West India goods. But certain conclusions can be reached. Most Western goods were undoubtedly bought in London – the letters which the firm received from the outports show that it did not maintain regular connections there. In 1767 Yehiel Prager twice ordered tobacco from Glasgow, but he did not keep up this connection.[27] In 1773 the house started a correspondence with several merchants in Liverpool, but it seems that this did not represent a new trend in the Pragers' business policy, but was brought about by the presence in Liverpool of Leib Bing, a young Jewish merchant from Germany, whom Yehiel Prager had taken under his wing. Though this correspondence lasted, with some interruptions, until 1775, it shows only one transaction which Yehiel actually did with a Liverpool house. Of greater significance were the ties which the London Pragers maintained with a number of southern ports and with Bristol. Although colonial goods did not regularly reach the southern ports, salvaged goods were occasionally sold there, and during war-time, many of the ships captured from the enemy were brought there and the prize-goods sold at public sales. In 1772–3 the Pragers had a correspondent at Seaford and they once bought indigo and coffee there.[28] After the French had intervened in the American war, the sale of prize-goods became a flourishing business, and Yehiel Prager started a correspondence with agents in Bristol, Portsmouth, Poole and Dartmouth, buying mainly hides there. These transactions were accomplished with the help of the Jewish broker Lara and were the special province of Leib Prager, who at that time became a sort of travelling agent for the firm in the South of England.[29]

A merchant like Yehiel Prager had to have the main seat of his business in London. It might be wondered why he did not endeavour to form closer and regular connections with the new western ports, which received a considerable part of the produce of the Western hemisphere. Such connections would obviously have given him greater flexibility and manoeuvring power in his commercial affairs. The letters which the firm received from the outports give a clue to a possible explanation. It emerges from them that the outports had no regular sea-connection with Amsterdam. Ships sailed regularly to several German ports – Hamburg, Bremen and Stettin – as well as to Rotterdam, but goods destined for Amsterdam had usually to be sent through Rotterdam.[30] This circuitous way involved serious disadvantages for a merchant whose main business was with Amsterdam. The consignment of goods by way of Rotterdam not only required the employment of a local factor there and thus increased expenses, but it was also impossible to evade the payment of customs there, as the Pragers were able to do in Amsterdam. In addition, the outports' connection with Rotterdam was interrupted by winter conditions for what seems an inordinately long period.[31] The problem of transport was aggravated in war-time, when merchants hesitated to consign their goods in English ships and preferred neutral ones. It was just then that Yehiel Prager started to make purchases in outports and was confronted by this problem in a most serious manner. In December 1779 his brother Jacob told him:

> That almost 21,000 hides are now being sold in an outport, about 200 miles distant from there [i.e. from London] (how is the place called?)[32] – if no ship can be had for it, too, it is, of course, an abominable thing. You must know this and, in our opinion, if people had not been deterred by it in Bristol, you would not have been able to buy those [hides] so cheaply.[33]

The trade of the British outports grew concurrently with that of Amsterdam's competitors on the Continent and from the start they adapted themselves to the new situation, tending to dispense with the services of Amsterdam as an intermediary market, but firms trading mainly with Amsterdam, or those which dealt in Indian and Chinese goods, had still to transact most of their business in London. The majority of Jewish merchants belonged to this category – a fact which helps to explain the absence of big Jewish houses from the outports.

Because the Pragers did most of their buying in London, information concerning it is meagre. Business in the City was mostly conducted by direct negotiation – on the Exchange, in coffee houses or in the firm's office – and the little correspondence we have is not very informative. There is, however, one aspect of the firm's business activity in London on which material at our disposal throws a fuller light – the purchase of merchandise from the East India Company. It has already been mentioned that the law required that all goods imported by the Company or by private persons, trading with the Company's permission, must be sold in London by public sale. We have seen how the law was evaded by the importers of diamonds and circumvented by the buyers of Indian cloth. The buyers of drugs, too, found a method which enabled them to frustrate the purpose of the law. While most Indian cloth was imported by the Company itself, and diamonds by private merchants acting under the Company licence, the importers of drugs were mostly ships' officers, especially captains of East Indiamen. The value of drugs was low, in relation to their weight, and consequently it did not pay the Company to import them. The ship-captains, on the other hand, who had to pay no freight for goods imported within their 'priviledge', could realize handsome profits on this kind of merchandise.[34] The concentration of drug imports in the hands of ship-captains opened the way to an evasion of the law prescribing public sale, through private agreements between the importers and the buyers. This was not done, as in the case of diamonds, with the active co-operation of the Company, but the latter was undoubtedly well aware of the methods employed and did nothing to protect the spirit of the law.[35] In a document dated 1790 a Jewish merchant by the name of Eleazar Levy Isaac described how transactions were concluded before the public sale was held:

> by the rules established by the East India Company for regulating the private trade of their officers, all the goods and merchandizes which such officers bring to England as their privilege or private trade are sent to the warehouses of the said Company, and such goods and merchandizes are sold for the benefit of such officers at the public sales of the said Company, and the money arising from such sales, after deducting the duties and expenses, is paid to or for the use of such officers whose goods are so sold ... and it is usual for the merchants who trade and deal in such East India goods, immediately on the arrival of the East India ships to contract with the officers of such ships for the purchase of their merchandize at a price certain, and then the merchant who so contracts is looked upon as the owner of the goods ... so contracted for, from the time of the contract; and when the same goods and merchandizes are afterwards sold at the sales of the East India Company, the contractor buys them in and pays for them to the original owners according to the price before contracted, without any regard being had to the price bid for the same at such public sale.[36]

Drugs were very often bought by this method and a merchant had to enjoy both a strong standing in India House and wide connections among the captains of East Indiamen in order to buy drugs on a large scale.

Yehiel Prager strove systematically to strengthen his position in both spheres. The common method of acquiring influence in India House was to buy a share in the Company, which entitled its owner to participate in the election of the Directors. It was, of course, a rather expensive method – the interested merchant had to withdraw many thousands of pounds from his business and to put them into stocks. For a house like that of the Pragers, which suffered from a perpetual shortage of capital, this was a heavy sacrifice, but Yehiel Prager apparently considered it worthwhile.[37] The purpose of holding a considerable number of Company shares was obviously not merely to exert influence on the Court of Directors, but to acquire the prestige connected with possession of influence in India House, which was useful for business in the City generally and for dealing in East India goods in particular.[38] There were other ways of acquiring a standing in Company circles, from the cultivation of personal friendships to outright bribery. Yehiel Prager employed all possible means for strengthening his position and his standing as one of the leading diamond merchants of London undoubtedly helped him in his endeavours.[39] In the 1780s Prager was obviously considered as a man possessing a great 'interest' in India House. This is clearly reflected in the letters of his Dutch brothers and of Leib Prager,[40] as well as in the appeals for help addressed to him by various people: a labourer who sought work in the Company's warehouses,[41] a Jewish merchant who applied for the position of a broker,[42] and another who was in financial trouble and relied on Prager's influence with the Directors of the East India Company to straighten things out.[43] On one occasion a group of Jewish-Dutch merchants asked Prager to effect the postponement of a sale of cloth by the Company which had been fixed for the eve of the feast of Tabernacles,[44] and the correspondence of 1785 includes several letters by persons seeking Prager's support in the elections for the Court of Directors. Prager had many friends in India House and this was well known in the City and in Amsterdam.

The Pragers also had good connections in the circle of ship-captains, pursers and the like. Here, apparently, an important part was played by Leib Prager whose pleasant personality helped him to establish the necessary connections. He had a number of personal friends among the officers of East Indiamen, one of whom – George Elliot – became familiar with the family and later married one of Yehiel Prager's daughters. Leib was on a

Committee, the members of which were apparently either City merchants or ship-captains; its main function was probably to exert the right kind of influence on India House.[45] The Pragers cultivated these connections as part of their effort to acquire a footing in the drug market, and in 1779 Yehiel was already informing drug merchants in Amsterdam that he had special opportunities for buying goods in fore-sales, thanks to his connections with ships' officers.[46] The fore-sale was concluded by means of a written contract between seller and buyer. One such contract, dated 3 March 1784, has been preserved among the Prager Papers. It is signed by Robert Wigram – probably a broker – and by Leib Prager, and it stipulated that Yehiel Prager would buy, at an agreed price, all the shellac brought by Captain Robert Scott in the ship *Neptune*, the seller undertaking to pay the customs and the fees due to the Crown. Payment was to be made in two instalments: the first on delivery of the power of attorney, the second after the settlement of accounts with the East India Company, that is after the public sale.[47] The goods thus sold were put up for public sale like all other goods imported by the Company with its permission, but, as we have seen, this was a purely fictitious sale: the seller was paid the pre-arranged price, without any regard to the price at which the goods were sold 'at the Company's candle'. The merchant who had made such a contract was, of course, always able to outbid all others, knowing that the price at which he took the goods was merely nominal. On many occasions, however, the buyer became the seller at the public sale, though he could not appear openly as such. If the bidding at the sale exceeded the price agreed upon in the contract, the buyer had the right to decide whether he should refrain from making the highest bid, and thus let some other merchant take the goods.[48] In such a case, the difference between the price fixed in the contract and the price actually paid at the public sale was divided equally between the two sides to the contract.[49] It goes without saying that goods imported by ships' officers were not always sold in this way. Under certain conditions the importer might decide that he was likely to get a better price at the public sale, or the potential buyers might hope for low prices at the sale and consequently refrain from buying directly. But the Prager letters show that fore-sales were very common.

What were the reasons which caused both importers and buyers to prefer a fore-sale to a public sale? For the ship-captain who imported goods from India, a direct sale offered a number of clear advantages. He received part of the price on the spot, without having to wait for the settlement of accounts by India House. He sold all his merchandise by a single transaction – it was usually one of the conditions of these contracts that the buyer must take the whole quantity imported by the seller – and he did not have to worry about the possibility that part of it might be left on his hands. This was of special importance for a person who was frequently absent from England for long periods of time. But the main consideration in favour of direct sale was, perhaps, the ships' officer's fear of combinations of buyers at the public sale. By selling his goods beforehand to a local merchant, he passed on to him this risk of low prices, while keeping the right to part of the profits in case the goods were sold at the public sale at a price higher than that which he had received for them.

The buyer's motives in agreeing to a fore-sale seem somewhat more complicated. To a large extent, the seller's advantages were the buyer's disadvantages. The City merchant who bought East India goods directly from the importer had to include in his calculations an interest on the first instalment – which he had to pay at once – for the period between the payment of the first instalment and the date on which the second instalment fell due. He received the goods no earlier than if he had bought them at public sale, and in the latter case he would have to pay the whole price only after the settlement of accounts by the East India Company. For the Pragers, with their ever-present problem of financing, this involved more than an additional outlay, because it increased considerably the period of time which elapsed between the date on which they had to pay part of the price for the merchandise and the receipt of the proceeds after they re-sold it. Another disadvantage which the buyer had to put up with lay in the obligation to take the entire consignment imported by the seller, which often was not all in his line. A document relating to the sale of goods by the captain and purser of the ship *Lascelles* to Yehiel Prager (1763?) shows that the latter had to take a quantity of cloth as well as fans and mats, in addition to the drugs in which he was really interested.[50] Unless he intended to take the goods himself, the buyer undertook all the risks involved in a public sale, including that of combinations by his competitors.[51]

The disadvantage of buying by fore-sale were succinctly

summed up by Jacob Prager. After telling Yehiel that the Amsterdam merchant de Wolff had approached them about the purchase of Chinese cinnamon in London, he went on:

> But to buy in fore-sale is inexpedient. In the first place – one has to pay immediately; furthermore – if prices at the public sale are high, one has to give the seller one half, and then it takes a long time till accounts are settled, and in addition one has to buy all goods from the ship concerned, which sometimes include items difficult to sell, so that what one loses on them may be more than the profit on the marketable goods.[52]

Why then did a merchant like Yehiel Prager often decide to buy in fore-sale? The basic consideration in favour of such a course was, of course, the hope that he would pay less than if he tried his luck at the public sale, or that he may be able to 'sell' at least part of the merchandise to other buyers at the sale and pocket half the difference. These prospects for easy and quick profits partly outweighed the disadvantage of having to pay half the price to the importer a considerable time before receiving the goods. But there was more to it than that and fore-sales would probably not have become so common had there been no other considerations in their favour. By buying through fore-sale all or a great part of a certain category of goods which were imported during the season from the East, a merchant could hope to dominate the market and to dictate prices to his competitors. Under favourable conditions, he could, by skilful bidding, 'chase prices up' – as the Pragers used to call it – at the public sale. He could do this without hesitation, fortified, as he was, by the assurance that in any case he would not have to pay more than had been agreed on beforehand with the importer. When market conditions were favourable his bidding would call forth high bids by other potential buyers and he had only to decide if, and at what price, it was expedient to let others take the merchandise. As a result he not only pocketed half the difference between the price he had paid and that at which he let the goods 'go' at the public sale, but also improved the market conditions for the goods which he retained or which had been in his possession before.[53] The fore-sale thus became a powerful instrument in the hands of merchants seeking to dominate the market, but it was not without its dangers. When Yehiel Prager embarked in 1786 on his great speculation in drugs, he tried to move the fore-sales completely out of his competitors' reach by transferring them overseas. Yet, despite his initial success, this policy in the end became a major cause of the firm's ruin after his death.

We have seen that in the eighteenth century a great part of Europe's imports from overseas was handled by the two central markets of London and Amsterdam. This system was made possible by the small distance between the two cities and the excellent shipping services which connected them. Most of the ships which plied between the two ports were small Dutch vessels, whose captains had great experience in navigating the Zuider Zee, which had to be crossed in order to reach Amsterdam. There were also several English ships sailing between England and Holland: some of their captains are described in an amusing manner in the Prager Papers. The Pragers had a soft spot for ship-captains. The following quotation from a letter of Jacob to Yehiel Prager will serve to illustrate the humorous vein which often appears in the normally matter-of-fact business letters. It describes Captain Smith, who had brought the Pragers a cargo of hides from England and had run aground in the Zuider Zee. It was written while Smith was at the Pragers' office:

here comes, this moment, the sailor from Elsfleth into our office – dead drunk, we cannot understand a word of what he is saying. We have never seen a man so drunk, and yet he is asking for a little drink!...to such people one is supposed to entrust one's property!...how shall we get rid of the drunken seaman? He is still standing here, virtually unable to talk, and nevertheless insists that we give him a glass of gin. God, what a comedy with this rascal! Here comes my son Meyer into the office – the sailor jumps up like mad and embraces Meyer – he has just arranged his hair – he dishevels his hair! Meyer throws him off and does not know what is going on. Finally says the drunkard Smith: 'My dear Sir, are you here? I'll return to Poole with you!' In short, he thinks Meyer is Leibkhe [Leib Prager], he does not want to let him go. He says something, that he has a jug which Meyer (he means Leibkhe) has asked him to bring us. He wants to go and fetch it and bring it this afternoon. What we say – that he is a brother of Leibkhe – is to no avail. He wants to go to the Exchange with my son Isaiah, so that for the time being we are rid of him.[54]

But the English ships did not sail as regularly as the Dutch and it seems that they usually preferred Rotterdam to Amsterdam. The Pragers had greater confidence in the Dutch captains, because they had a better knowledge of the Zuider Zee and because they knew how to handle the Dutch customs authorities. Jacob Prager wrote:

> We have since received yours of the 7th with the accounts of everything laden on Baker [i.e. on Captain Baker's ship]. This damned rascal of a seaman has sailed with his ship straight into the boom [harbour]. Now it is impossible to smuggle a single item of all the merchandize, everything must be declared correctly. This comes from [employing] foreign seamen. The devil take him. It will certainly make a difference of 200 [gulden] on his cargo. It cannot be changed.[55]

Holland was known for its policy of low tariffs and there were categories of goods on which custom duties were so low that there was no point in smuggling them in.[56] Nevertheless, duties on a number of items were far from negligible and the Prager letters show that both bribing of customs officials and smuggling were very common and practised by respectable merchants as a matter of routine.

The Pragers used to bribe customs officers who were willing, if properly paid, to give low estimates of the value of imported goods. But for some reason this was not possible in regard to drugs, on which there was a duty of 5 per cent, although a reduction of one-sixth seems to have been customary. The Pragers therefore used to smuggle the drugs which Yehiel sent them from London, with the help of the boatman who transferred the goods from the ship to the quay. Jacob Prager described their method, after 18 cases of cassia consigned to them had been seized by the authorities in December 1785:

> All other merchandize we can unload on application [for an estimate], and then it is weighed at the harbour and the value estimated – which is done very moderately by the officials if the boatman gives them something. But for drugs [the value] must be stated – one may conceal 1/6 of the merchandize – or one must smuggle. Suppose such a box of Cassia is worth f.400 – one could declare it to be worth f.300; that would make at 5%, f.16.10. If we smuggle it costs only about f.4.[57]

The Amsterdam Pragers seem to have regarded smuggling as an act to which no moral stigma attached. It is true that an undertone of self-justification can be discerned in a few words on the subject which Jacob Prager added some days later: 'Everyone smuggles, even the authorities themselves.'[58] But the possibility that their reputation may be damaged by their being caught in the act of smuggling does not seem to have occurred to the Pragers; they only regretted the financial loss involved.

Yehiel Prager apparently viewed these matters in a somewhat different light, although, in the absence of his letters to Amsterdam, it is difficult to say with certainty whether he was invariably opposed to smuggling. When the Pragers established a branch house at Ostend, Yehiel warned his nephews that they should not indulge in smuggling.[59] But smuggling flourished at Ostend, and Jacob Prager was prompted to suggest to his brother that he should find a way of smuggling goods into England, in order to enable them to compete with other merchants. It emerges from Jacob's answer to Yehiel's reply that the latter had refused categorically to do anything of the sort: 'That you know how Jews do business, and do not want to concern yourself with smuggling – God forbid, we also do not think [you should]. But as the children have very good opportunities, could not something be done in conjunction with a reliable house, like that of Simon Tanhum?'[60] The mention of Jews may possibly show that, unlike his brothers in Amsterdam, Yehiel feared not only a pecuniary loss in case of discovery, but also damage to his reputation.

The goods which the house in Amsterdam received from London were sold to all sorts of buyers. Schematically it can be said that the 'first hand' or 'sea merchant' sold to the 'second hand',[61] but in reality this order of business was often not strictly adhered to, and a link or two in the chain of middlemen was frequently passed over. Goods were sold to exporters, wholesale merchants, manufacturers, refiners, brokers and even shopkeepers. To some extent the category of buyers to which the importers used to sell was dictated by the character of the goods. For some kinds of merchandise the schematic order of middlemen was almost obligatory. Thus David Prager informed his brother about the accepted way of selling wax in Amsterdam: 'And you must know that the consignments which sea merchants receive are always sold to grease merchants, who resell them to candle-makers by the barrel with ½% or 1% profit.'[62] But merchandise like tobacco and drugs, needed both for domestic consumption and for re-export, could be sold to merchants of all kinds, as well as to manufacturers and refiners. The Pragers in Amsterdam endeavoured to establish direct relations with Dutch refiners of drugs – especially of tincal and camphor. The refiners, on their part, were eager to buy from merchants of the first hand and even to buy directly from London, thus bypassing retailers and reducing the price. It seems that it was due to the Pragers' close connections with refiners like Johannes Ploos and Nicholas Kiere that they were accepted as equals in the small circle of major drug merchants in London and Amsterdam only a few years after they had entered the drug trade as commission agents.[63] The importer did not usually deal directly with shopkeepers, but when small lots were offered at public sales the latter had an opportunity to compete with the big merchants, as he could then dispense with the additional profit which was normally taken by the wholesale merchant.[64] When there was a buyers' market, the importer would sometimes even deign to approach the shopkeepers directly,[65] although he could never hope to sell him large quantities at a time and had to grant a longer credit than was otherwise customary.[66]

Colonial goods were usually sold in Amsterdam on credit and no self-respecting merchant would demand cash payment from reputable houses. As Jacob Prager wrote on 23 August 1784: 'it is impossible to sell here for cash, and it is not consistent with our honour to demand such a thing from good houses.' It seems that, on the whole, payment had to be made three months after delivery of the goods, but for coffee the customary period was two months, while in the case of sugar, though the nominal period was three months, it was in reality often four to five months because the sugar refiners were traditionally not bound to receive the merchandise until only a month or two after the formal conclusion of the sale.[67] Furthermore, payment day was not always strictly adhered to, and under favourable market conditions the buyers were often able to insist on a longer period of credit than was customary.[68] These usages aggravated the difficulties which the Pragers had in financing their business. In London cash payment was more common, so that in many cases the house had to invest its money not merely for the time between the purchase and the re-sale of the goods, but had to wait for an additional period of several months, till payment became due in Amsterdam.

This meant that, even when the goods were re-sold immediately, about half a year elapsed before the money could be re-invested.[69]

Merchandise was normally sold in Amsterdam through brokers. The 'courtage' or brokerage was invariably included in calculations relating to sale in Amsterdam.[70] To judge by the Pragers' letters, the merchant's dependence on the broker was very great. The latter specialized in a limited range of goods and was therefore much more of an expert than the merchant, who dealt in a great variety of items. It is true that Jacob and David Prager considered themselves as great experts on cochineal and Spanish wool,[71] but it is quite clear that their knowledge was limited even in the case of goods with which they dealt constantly, like tobacco and hides.[72] One must also remember that the broker's superior proficiency and his greater familiarity with the market were not the only causes for the merchant's dependence on him. The market for a number of goods was entirely dominated by brokers and a merchant who did not have their goodwill was unable to do much business in these particular items. The broker Wils dominated the cotton market and represented combinations of thread merchants;[73] it was impossible to sell eastern silk in Amsterdam against the will of the broker Van Goor,[74] while the Jew 'Reb Mendele' was all-powerful in the chinaware business.[75] In the tobacco trade the brokers did not wield such absolute power, but the position of the major tobacco brokers was, nevertheless, very strong. In September 1784 the Amsterdam Pragers informed Yehiel that their tobacco broker had taken a companion into partnership 'and it will be a great help to us that we now have these two brokers'.[76] A few weeks later Jacob wrote about their tobacco business: 'Thank God we have the chief brokers, who are loyal to us and who have a thorough knowledge of everything that happens in this article in all 7 provinces and virtually all orders that arrive must fall into their hands'.[77] The merchant had to pay for this service and not merely in money. Once he had engaged a broker or brokers to act on his behalf, he was bound to them and could not make use of the services of their competitors. When, at one time, Yehiel suggested to David Prager that he should try to approach other brokers than those with whom he usually worked, he was told by his brother:

To engage other brokers could be a great disadvantage, in my opinion, because De Leff knows all tobacco merchants here and all are glad to buy through him ... so that if we engage other brokers, we shall in the first place, have him against us, and shall, by God, not realize such prices as we have up to now.[78]

The merchant had to decide in each case whether to sell his goods directly – 'from the hand' as the Pragers used to call it – or whether to try his luck in public sale. The Pragers, and undoubtedly other merchants too, generally preferred the direct sale. A public sale involved additional costs[79] and an unsuccessful sale was liable to bring about a fall in prices[80] and the seller ran the risk that he would be left with the goods of inferior quality on his hands.[81] But, under certain conditions, a public sale seemed preferable. It is difficult to say exactly what those conditions were. On the whole, a buyers' market encouraged public sales, although there was always a danger, in such a situation, that a public sale would only aggravate it and bring about a further fall in prices. There were, nevertheless, considerations in favour of a public sale: it enabled the seller to reach a wider circle of clients and to try to maintain prices by participating himself, as a buyer, in the sale.

Speculations were a common phenomenon in Anglo-Dutch commerce.[82] The reasons must, to a large extent, be sought in the nature of this trade and in the conditions under which it functioned: the great distances between the primary producers and the ultimate market, the large number of middlemen who separated the producers from the consumer, and the frequent lack of prior knowledge concerning the quantity and quality of the expected goods, all tended to encourage speculation. These causes became even more potent in war-time: certain sources of supply were blocked altogether, communications were disturbed and even if merchants received information about the latest tobacco crop or the quantity of camphor which was being consigned to Europe, there was no certainty that they could safely act on it, as one could in times of peace. Such conditions offered tempting opportunities for quick and large profits to merchants ready to take considerable risks and to trust their own prognosis of market trends. Large-scale speculation required considerable capital resources and, in this respect too, the circumstances under which Anglo-Dutch merchants operated were unusually favourable to this kind of business, thanks to the incomparable credit facilities available in both London and Amsterdam. There is a basic difference between casual speculations and the large-scale, planned speculation. The first sort has a rather passive character and the single merchant taking part in it does not play an independent role in market developments. He merely defers the sale of his goods, hoping that prices will rise or that potential buyers will finally consent to pay the price he is asking. Even a small merchant can take part in a speculation of this kind, on condition that his colleagues act in a like manner. The planned speculation, on the other hand, represented more than a mere attempt by a merchant or a group of merchants to exploit favourable market trends. It was usually characterized by endeavours, on the part of the speculator, to dominate the market and to force his conditions on the buyers. A speculation of this kind could be undertaken only by a merchant possessing considerable capital resources and wide connections. He could expect large profits in case of success, but failure might spell disaster.

The Pragers, and in particular the brothers in Amsterdam, were cautious merchants. During the whole period of which the internal correspondence has survived, the latter only once succumbed to temptation and started a major speculation. They soon repented of their daring and managed to extract themselves somehow, thanks to the help of their broker.[83] It goes without saying that they, like all other merchants, from time to time indulged in speculations of the casual sort. Thus at the start of the war in America they held on to their tobacco in the hope that the high price in London would soon affect the market in Amsterdam. Even this minor speculation illustrates the financial problem which speculators had to face:

> We still do not notice any effect of the rise in tobacco [prices in London]. All those who have bought before the rise, or when it started, have what they need and everyone prefers to wait before buying – people say that this situation may last 2 months. If they see then that the rise is founded, they will buy what they need. The sellers tell all the brokers, as we do, not to show anything for the time being. But, in our opinion, they are going about with an harpoon in the body, just like us, and would sell if they could do so to advantage.[84]

The Pragers were sometimes willing to risk a limited speculation, which did not involve any ambition to dominate the market.[85]

But, on the whole, caution was triumphant, and during the Anglo-Dutch war they never took risks based on uncertain political or military forecasts.[86] Their most daring venture during that period was the establishment of a house in Ostend – a 'speculation' which indeed proved successful. Jacob Prager on one occasion explicitly objected to their taking part in speculations. In a letter to his brother Yehiel he wrote: 'That you think much business is to be expected is good. But if you want to put money into things on which we cannot expect much profit and which must be held as a speculation, this does not serve us . . .'.[87]

Yehiel Prager was more audacious than his brothers in Amsterdam. It seems that he was by nature more inclined to take risks, but there were also strong non-personal factors which caused the London house to take a bolder line in business. The initiative usually lay with it, because most purchases were made in London, which was, besides, fast becoming the biggest commercial centre in the world, while Amsterdam was already on the decline. Thanks to his greater vitality, and helped by the better opportunities of London, Yehiel Prager – the youngest of the brothers – became the senior partner in the firm. In the 1770s he succeeded in gaining for himself a strong position in the diamond trade and on the drug market, and was soon considered as one of the leading merchants in both branches; within a period of 25 years the humble agent of a Dutch house had become a rich and respected City merchant. In the 1780s Yehiel Prager could, naturally, afford to take much greater risks than he had been able to do in the 1760s, and the boldness and volume of his purchases more than once frightened his more conservative Dutch brothers.[88] But even Yehiel did not undertake a really big speculation before 1786. In that year he embarked almost simultaneously on two enormous speculations – one in tobacco, the other in drugs.

Yehiel did not consult his brothers before he acted, preferring to confront them with a *fait accompli*, and it is clear that the big tobacco speculation came as a complete surprise to them. It is therefore impossible to say with certainty why he suddenly decided to tread this dangerous path. Perhaps he hoped that he would thus be able to overcome the stagnation which had marked the firm's business since the end of the American war; despite Yehiel's success in London, the state of the partnership was not very encouraging at that time. In April 1786 Jacob Prager wrote about the profits of the preceding year: 'if the situation does not improve, God forbid, this year may be even worse, because a quarter of the year has already gone and if, God forbid, tobacco does not rise, and the present transaction in drugs does not turn out well, we do not know from what we shall earn our subsistence.'[89] Yehiel's decision was also closely connected with Leib Prager's voyage to India in 1786. Yehiel had been planning this voyage for some years, hoping that it would enable his nephew to set himself up as an independent merchant and that, once in India, he could help him in his attempt to gain a dominant position in the diamond and drug trades.[90] Leib was to see to it that the greater part of these goods would be directed to his uncle in London and thus eliminate all effective competition there.

At first sight there seems to have been little connection between these developments and Yehiel's tobacco speculation. In fact, however, the second speculation was apparently a direct outcome of the first. During the summer of 1786 prices on the drug market showed a dangerous tendency to fall and the Pragers had to face the possibility that the speculation might not only end in failure, but would ruin the house. It is very likely that, perceiving the danger, Yehiel Prager decided to embark on another speculation as a measure of despair, hoping that, if it succeeded, it would at least partly compensate him for the great losses he was already expecting in his drug business. Although there is no explicit evidence to support this hypothesis, there can hardly be a different explanation for the fact that Yehiel embarked upon a second speculation at a moment when the house was facing the worst danger to its existence since the economic crisis of 1772. While the speculation in drugs and the plans relating to the diamond trade were born of self-assurance and strength, it seems that the tobacco affair reflected a fear of disaster. The tobacco speculation was of secondary importance only in the sense that it seems to have resulted from the unfavourable development of the earlier speculation and affected the future of the firm merely because it failed to offset the losses caused by the collapse of the drug market. The capital involved in the two speculations was approximately equal: about £40,000 invested in each. But, while in the drug business the Pragers acted alone, two other merchants took part in the tobacco speculation. The drug speculation was started about half a year before the tobacco speculation, but lasted much longer – it was in fact only wound up several years after Yehiel's death in 1788.

During the American war tobacco disappeared from the Pragers' business for several years. The trade revived after the peace of 1783, but under different conditions from those to which the Pragers had been accustomed before 1776. The American exporters were now under no legal obligation to consign their tobacco through England and could send it directly to Holland, France, Germany, and other countries in Europe, thus theoretically making the London–Amsterdam link to some extent superfluous. The Pragers foresaw this development and, when it became clear that peace was imminent, decided to send several of their children to the United States in order to establish a trading house there. But the young men encountered great difficulties and their early tobacco consignments brought only losses. The European tobacco market remained unstable and, though prices had fallen considerably on the restoration of peace, they were still high in comparison with pre-war prices.[91] American independence deprived the City of the dominant position in the tobacco trade which it had enjoyed before the war. The change may be illustrated by quoting from two letters of Jacob Prager, one written on the eve of the war and the other two years after the conclusion of peace. In 1775 he wrote about the tobacco trade: 'When people play the fiddle there [in London], we here must dance'.[92] Ten years later he wrote:

> Anyhow, we tell you people are not guided by prices in London as in former times. Everybody receives [tobacco], even Copenhagen receives directly; they choose from it the sorts they require and send those which are of no use to them here [to Amsterdam]. And the same places and all Germany, which formerly ordered [tobacco] from here, now get their own supply and do not need Holland. And it is strange that that which arrives here directly from America is immediately sold by [public] sales at any price, with great loss, and sales continue all the time.[93]

Complaints of this kind appear regularly in the Pragers' letters between 1783 and 1786; nonetheless American tobacco exports gradually returned to the old channel[94] and in the summer of 1786 Yehiel Prager came to the conclusion that conditions justified an attempt to monopolize Maryland tobacco in London and Amsterdam. He began to purchase Maryland tobacco in September or October 1786, in partnership with the Anglo-Dutch merchant Peter Stapel, and some time later they were joined by Van Notten, a leading member of the Dutch business community of London. The tobacco was apparently purchased through the Jewish tobacco broker Brandon and the whole speculation was conducted throughout by the Pragers of London and Amsterdam. The speculation started with a comparatively small purchase – 135 barrels, worth about £2,500 – but thereafter it developed rapidly, as Prager bought all the Maryland tobacco which arrived in London. The first result of this policy was a rise in prices, but he now had no alternative and was obliged to go on buying in order to maintain prices. Yehiel's brothers in Amsterdam were staggered by this unexpected change in their traditional policy of caution. Already in October, when Jacob learned that Yehiel was about to buy 300 barrels, in addition to the 135 he already held, he wrote: 'We must say – you are a courageous man'.[95] Whether it was courage or desperation which drove Yehiel he continued to buy, and in early December Jacob wrote again: 'We perceive that we must have patience and keep our courage as well as you do, but at the same time we tremble with palpitation when we think of the engagement we have entered.'[96] Before this letter was sent off, news came from Yehiel that he had purchased another 69 barrels. Jacob expressed anxiety: 'Dear Yehiel, we have courage enough, but when we see the amount of bills we have accepted, our hair stands on end.' David Prager wrote: 'Shema Israel, how many barrels more are there [i.e. in London]', but he agreed that they could not allow anyone else to buy the same sort of tobacco at a lower price than they had paid.[97] In fact, the Amsterdam brothers had yet no idea of the true proportions of the speculation. Jacob Prager was never to learn the truth; in December 1786 he was taken ill with what he described as 'fiebres catoralis' and in January he died. His passing away was a severe blow to the house, but the business had to be carried on and there was little time for mourning. David Prager, who now assumed command in Amsterdam, wrote in mid-January that apparently much more tobacco had arrived than had been expected by Yehiel and that they alone already held more than the total amount which, according to his earlier estimate, was to be placed on the London market. Yehiel had written that about £10,000 was already invested in tobacco: 'that means about 500 barrels', exclaimed the astounded David.[98] But even that was only a beginning; when the buying at last ceased they had some 2,000 barrels of Maryland tobacco on their hands.[99]

The speculation was, indeed, a dangerous one. An ideal speculation does not leave a real alternative to the buyers and so forces them either to buy or to go out of business. In order to create such a situation in the tobacco trade, Yehiel Prager and his partners would have had to buy up all Virginia tobacco, in addition to the Maryland tobacco which they held. As this was clearly beyond their power, they had to rely on a certain degree of rigidity in the market which prevented the prices of one sort of tobacco from affecting those of another. Maryland tobacco was considered superior to Virginian,[100] and it seems that within certain limits the prices of Virginia tobacco did not affect those of Maryland tobacco. In December 1786 Jacob Prager wrote that the Amsterdam tobacco merchants thought that the tobacco which they were then expecting was Maryland, but that they would speak differently when they learned that it was Virginia.[101] A few days later Yehiel reported that a large quantity of tobacco had reached London, but most of it was Virginia. At the end of January David Prager commented on the sale of Virginia tobacco in London: 'Presumably this has no effect on Maryland tobacco, but it still is a certain hindrance, because he [the broker Pieter de Wolff] thinks that it [i.e. the Virginia tobacco] will be sold cheaply at the public sale.'[102] It seems that it was impossible to rely too much on the rule that the price of one sort of tobacco had no influence on the prices of other sorts. This is confirmed by a passage in Jacob Prager's letter of November 1786: 'If tobacco goes high in peace-time people turn to all kinds of secondary sorts'.[103] Merchants were also prepared to buy new tobacco if it was cheap enough. As a rule, it was impossible to sell tobacco which was less than a year and a half old,[104] but the rule did not always apply: 'Of course, when the new crop arrives and is sold cheaper pro-rate than the old one, then people help themselves with the new crops and mix it with the old one which they still have.'[105] Anyhow, the assumption that the availability of one kind of tobacco did not affect the prices of other kinds seems to have held good within certain limits and it is perhaps thanks to this that the speculation did not end in disaster. On the other hand, it is clear that the Pragers' inability to control Virginia tobacco was a primary cause of its failure.

The tobacco which arrived in Amsterdam directly from America presented another major obstacle to the successful prosecution of the speculation. It was not so much a danger as a continuous nuisance, aggravated by the fact that the Dutch importers of tobacco were usually small merchants, who had to sell immediately and at any price. David Prager had to stop the sale of their tobacco whenever a consignment arrived from America and was able to resume it only after all American tobacco had been sold.[106] To all this was added an unforeseen calamity: the Dutch Civil War. The conflict between the Patriots and William V reached its climax just when David Prager had begun to sell the first barrels of tobacco. These troubles came at a very inopportune moment, from the point of view of the Pragers. For weeks on end trade was at a standstill and tobacco could not be sold. In early June 1787 David wrote: 'I am quite fed up with the Exchange and with the whole country. One is unable to earn anything and, on top of that, to live in such an upheaval!'[107] The failure of the speculation cannot, though, be ascribed to the Civil War; it could probably not have been brought to a successful conclusion in normal times. But the disturbances caused a serious delay in sales and this aggravated the financial problems confronting the firm and prolonged the exasperating process of liquidating the speculation.[108]

The sale of the tobacco in Amsterdam was delayed at the start by winter, which was then a dead season in Amsterdam's commerce. With the freezing of the Rhine the export route to Germany was closed and the Dutch tobacco exporters were in no hurry to renew their stock. Only in late February or early March could sales be re-started, and even then conditions were most unfavourable for the Pragers. They did not dominate the market and had to sell by small lots consisting of a few dozen barrels each. 'And you see, don't you, how we struggle and with difficulty sell small lots' wrote David Prager to his brother in May.[109] Profits amounted to no more than 5 to 10 per cent – which was considered disappointing in an ordinary transaction, not to speak of a speculation. By the constant sale of small quantities David managed to get rid of the greater part of the tobacco by the autumn of 1787, winding up the speculation without disaster and even retaining a small profit.[110] But it is doubtful whether the result justified the investment and it certainly was not worth the exertion and the nervous tension which the speculation had inflicted upon the Pragers. David himself summed up the situation in August, when the end was at last in sight: 'By heaven, we are lucky to get off like this. It could have been a big blow, Heaven forbid, and I wish we could sell the rest in like manner.'[111]

Several factors contributed to the failure of the speculation. The fact that England was unable to monopolize American tobacco, as it had done in former times, and the Dutch Civil War, were serious disadvantages. Yet the primary cause of failure must be sought in the firm's limited resources, which did not enable the Pragers, even with the help of their partners, to gain a dominant position in the Anglo-Dutch tobacco trade. When one bears in mind that Yehiel Prager had, at the same time, £40,000 invested in drugs, it is a sheer wonder that he could concurrently carry on another speculation, on a similar scale, and emerge unscathed. Moreover, the firm's capital was not sufficient for financing the speculation, and it is not clear how Yehiel Prager got the necessary means. At the beginning of December he reported that Van Notten would lend him the sum necessary to finance the Pragers' share in the speculation, at 5 per cent interest, but a few days later he wrote that he had not taken this money.[112] He could never have managed it, but for the high prestige and credit which the house enjoyed both in London and Amsterdam.

The big speculation in drugs began in 1786, but none of the three brothers lived to see its end – the last camphor was only sold in 1793, about a year after the death of David Prager, the last of the brothers. Drugs were a relatively recent addition to the firm's trade. During the 1770s the Pragers passed from commission business in drugs to independent undertakings, and when tobacco disappeared from the market as a result of the American war, Yehiel found a substitute in drugs. The quantities which he bought in London in the early 1780s frequently caused concern to his Amsterdam brothers, and their letters show that the European market was often over-supplied with eastern drugs.[113] This phenomenon was probably closely connected with the nature of the drug trade, which was mostly carried on by officers of East Indiamen, who had only a limited choice of goods which they were allowed to import, so that the adjustment of imports to the state of demand in Europe was more difficult than in the case of items imported by the East India Company itself. Be that as it may, it is quite possible that it was precisely this periodical flooding of the drug market which gave Yehiel Prager the idea that it might be worth while to make an all-out attempt to establish the firm as the arbiter of the drug trade. Yehiel achieved a standing of some importance on the drug market by systematically building up connections with ships' officers in the service of the Company. He now planned to strengthen his position further, making use of Leib Prager's voyage to India in order to get hold of the officers even before they arrived in England and while they were still out of reach of his competitors. Acting on his uncle's instructions, Leib signed contracts for the purchase of drugs with ships' officers whom he met at the Cape of Good Hope[114] and apparently with others whom he met in India on his arrival there.

The first stage of the speculation was thus carried out smoothly and according to plan – most of the camphor and cassia brought to England in 1786 by the East India ships' officers probably came into Yehiel's possession. But even before Leib had reached the Cape of Good Hope and signed the first contracts there, prices of drugs began to fall in Europe. The price of camphor on the Amsterdam exchange was 2.55 gulden per pound during the first three months of 1786. In April – one month after Leib Prager had left for India – the price fell to 2.35 gulden and it continued to fall throughout the summer, reaching 1.73 gulden in November. There was a temporary stabilization in 1787 (average price: 1.73 gulden per pound), but a further fall occurred in 1788/9, the average for 1788 being 1.59 gulden, and that for 1789 1.44 gulden per pound, only a little more than three-fifths of the average price for 1785.[115] In 1790 prices began to rise gradually, but it was not before 1795 that the average price of 1785 was reached again. The price of cassia fell too, though apparently less disastrously than that of camphor. Posthumus, in his work on the history of prices in Holland, does not give the prices of cassia on the Amsterdam exchange, but he has a table showing prices of cinnamon, for which cassia served as a substitute.[116] Cinnamon stood at 9 gulden the pound during the first four months of 1786 and at 8 gulden from May of that year to April 1787. The price fell again to 7.25 gulden in May 1787, then remained stable at that level until early 1788, when it again rose to 8.50 gulden. In the spring of 1789, however, there was another sharp decline to 6.80 gulden per pound, and this tendency persisted till 1791 when the average price of cinnamon was only 6.69 gulden.[117]

It is not clear what caused this sudden fall in the prices of drugs. Several years later Leib Prager ascribed it to the Dutch Civil War,[118] but this explanation is hardly tenable, in view of the fact that the Dutch Civil War did not assume the character of an armed conflict before the spring of 1787, and there is no indication that the conflict had an adverse effect on trade before that time. A purely economic explanation sounds more plausible: it would seem that the precarious balance between supply and demand was seriously disturbed as a consequence of increased imports of drugs by ships' officers, whose choice of items was severely limited by the East India Company's regulations, and later also by the Company itself.[119]

Already in April Jacob Prager was worrying about the outcome of the speculation: 'Dear brother, we are undertaking great things and we should be very sorry if, God forbid, we do not carry through this business with honour.' When the Amsterdam Pragers learned in June that 120,000 lbs of cassia had arrived in London, David wrote: 'Shema Israel, how can such consignments be consumed?'[120] Yehiel Prager's drug speculation demonstrates in a striking manner the handicaps confronting the overseas merchant in an age which lacked the means of quick communication. The first indications of a dangerous development in the drug trade could be discerned about a month after Leib Prager's departure for India and before he had opportunity to sign a single contract. But Yehiel had no way of altering his instructions before Leib reached India. In fact, the latter received his uncle's new orders only about half a year after his arrival and not before he had signed many contracts based on the prices prevalent at the time of his departure from England.[121] Despite this inauspicious beginning, Yehiel did not despair. In his first letters to Leib he did not cancel his instructions according to which Leib had to conclude contracts for the purchase of camphor and cassia, but only adjusted the prices in accordance with developments in Europe. Prices continued to decline, however, and during 1787 enormous quantities of drugs reached London which Yehiel was forced to buy in conformity with the contracts signed by his nephew. He attempted to cancel the contracts, but the ships' officers concerned had no reason to oblige him: on the contrary their agreement with Leib Prager enabled them to escape serious losses.[122]

The whole future of the firm was now in great danger. It was not only a matter of financial losses, but of the house's reputation as a respectable and cautious concern. At that moment the London branch suffered a blow from which it was never to recover: in February 1788 Yehiel died after a short illness. The direction of the English house passed into the hands of Jacob's son, Meyer, who was visiting London on his way from America when Yehiel died, and of Yehiel's son Mordecai (Mark), a youngster aged 22. It is doubtful whether these two would have been able to maintain the good name of the house in normal times; they were certainly not equal to the challenge which they now had to face. At the time of Yehiel's death, the firm held £37,000 worth of camphor and at least £5,000 was invested in cassia,[123] so that the amount invested in drugs was about equal to the total capital of the London house. Yehiel's successors had to face a problem which would have baffled a merchant of much greater experience. It is true that Yehiel had managed to dislodge his major competitors, like Blankenhagen and Grote, but in the meanwhile a typical buyers' market had developed in Europe. In one respect Leib Prager's activity in India aggravated the situation, because the East India Company tried to use his services in an attempt to dominate the drug trade, which had hitherto been in the hands of its ships' officers, and thus added to the large quantities which were reaching Europe. Two passages taken from letters of the East India Company to its Bengal Council attest to the hopes which the Company pinned on the purchase of drugs by Leib Prager on its behalf:

> We must observe that by putting Mr. Prager under the ultimate control of the Board of Trade ... it was by no means our intention to prevent the full exertion of Mr. Prager's judgement in this branch of our investment, respecting the quality and assortment of drugs to be in future purchased on the Company's account, since our sole motive in bestowing this appointment on Mr. Prager proceeded thru an opinion that thru his endeavours, this article, which has hitherto proved in general a losing one, would be productive, on the sales in England, of very considerable profit.

Two years later India House wrote to Bengal:

> We were in hopes from the competency of Mr. Prager's judgement in the article of drugs, as well as his knowledge of the state of the markets at home, that some advantage would have been derived from such of your late consignments as fall under this description. The issue has proved otherwise, as you will observe by inspecting the accompanying accounts of profit and loss.[124]

The Pragers were therefore unable to monopolize even the drug market of London, and London was not the sole importer of eastern drugs. Consignments also reached Amsterdam, Copenhagen, Ostend, Lorient and, last but not least, Lisbon.[125] In May 1789 David Prager reported about camphor: 'This is an article with no great consumption. Indeed, if nothing would arrive for 5 years, there would still be enough in Europe.'[126] In cassia, too, according to David, there was enough stock to last ten years.

Despite these adverse conditions, the Pragers managed to sell £17,000 worth of camphor during 1788, but thereafter sales came to a complete standstill which lasted several years. The remaining merchandise was mortgaged[127] in order to unfreeze the firm's capital, thus causing additional expenses on account of interest. The house stopped the sales after 1788 in an attempt to push prices up, or, at least, to prevent a further decline. Such an attempt would have been doomed to failure if the house had continued to sell, and between 1789 and 1791 the Pragers were even forced to buy further quantities of camphor, as part of their endeavours to break the combination of buyers which had been formed against them in London.[128] They hoped that this policy would enable them to force prices up and to create more favourable conditions for the eventual sale of the stock remaining on their hands.

The Pragers' most dangerous competitors were the English and Dutch East India Companies. In the autumn of 1788 the English Company was about to put large quantities of camphor on the market. The Pragers approached the Company's Committee of Private Trade and, pointing out that they and the Company were the sole holders of large quantities of camphor in London, they threatened to sell their stock at a low price if the Company would not agree to co-operate with them in their endeavours to stabilize the price.[129] These tactics were apparently successful,[130] but in the summer of 1789 Meyer Prager was nevertheless forced to participate himself in a public sale of camphor arranged by the Company, instructing his broker not to let the camphor go at less than £11 5s. 0d. per 50 lbs. This he managed to effect, but only at the price of buying £2,200 worth of camphor himself. It seems that the house of Muilman participated in this action, designed to prevent prices from falling in London, and that they helped the Pragers to finance the transaction. On the face of it, it was a remarkable achievement that Meyer managed to get the co-operation of this great house, with which he also undertook joint tobacco transactions. Earlier the Pragers had always regarded Muilman as a rival, and it is not impossible that Meyer's 'success' was in reality a sign of weakness: that Muilman consented to co-operate with him because they had ceased to regard him as a serious competitor.

At the same time the Dutch East India Company put about 50,000 lbs of camphor on the market. Here, too, a combination of buyers was formed, consisting of five camphor distillers. But the situation was more complicated than in London, because the Dutch Company sold its camphor in a series of sales, held at its various branches.[131]

David Prager now once more showed that dexterity which had always marked his own and his late brother's actions. With the help of the distiller Kiere, who had for long been closely connected with the house, he was able to make a breach in the combination of buyers. Kiere undertook to help Prager to maintain the price in the approaching sales and, in return, the latter promised to take over two-thirds of the camphor which Kiere would have to buy, to advance him the money for his own third, and to sell him camphor at a low price on request. Prager also agreed that the camphor still held by the London house would not be sold at less than £12 per 50 lbs. The whole plan was based on the assumption that no additional camphor would arrive from the East – as had been reported by Leib Prager from India.[132]

A meeting of the merchants, distillers and brokers, who made up the combination of buyers, was held four days before the first sale of the Dutch East India Company, which was to take place at its Zeeland branch. The purpose of the meeting was explained by David Prager in a letter to the London house: 'This always takes place before one has to give the orders for the sales, and from here letters are sent to the brokers in Zeeland who then buy all drugs, which are therefore divided by average and everyone receives his pro rata share.'[133]

At this meeting Kiere acted in accordance with the agreement which had been concluded between him and David Prager. The latter reported to London:

Now, when the subject of camphor was broached, everyone was asked up to what price he was prepared to give orders. Some said – L.24–25 [Flemish pounds].[134] Thereupon our broker said that these [bidders] would not be able to get anything, because he has orders to buy the whole lot at a higher price. Finally L.26 was reached and he again replied that he had higher orders. To those who wanted to take the lot at a price exceeding his highest limit, Kiere said at first that this is too high for him. At last he pretended to be induced to take a lot or two at this price, so that we shall get nothing from [the sale] in Zeeland, except that we must share in what Kiere has to take. Possibly he will get only one lot (each lot has lbs 1,000 to lbs 1,200), and we think this will be very advantageous for your stock, God willing.[135]

Kiere had played his cards skilfully. At the Zeeland sale the camphor went at 26¾ Flemish pounds, Kiere having to take about one-fifth of the total quantity sold. At the buyers' meeting which preceded the Amsterdam sale – in which the Company put on the market about half the quantity of camphor in its possession – Kiere again managed to manœuvre the participants in such a way that a decision to buy at the relatively high price of 27 Flemish pounds was taken. As for the sales at the remaining branches of the East India Company, Kiere agreed with the Pragers that they should not give any orders for the purchase of camphor, on the assumption that Kiere and the other distillers would buy at 26½ Flemish pounds. The Pragers promised to take half of the camphor purchased by Kiere. When the sales ended in the second half of November, David Prager could be well satisfied with his achievement. He had succeeded in maintaining the price of camphor and, although he had to buy another 6,000 lbs, this was only 1/8 of the total quantity sold[136] – which was by far less than what he had expected he would have to take in order to prevent a fall in prices.[137] About the same time the English East India Company sold another quantity of camphor. The Pragers again took part – as buyers – and succeeded in keeping the price at about the same level as had been achieved in Holland, having to take only a small quantity for themselves.[138] Following these sales, the prices of camphor at the Amsterdam exchange rose a little. In the autumn of 1790 David Prager again intervened successfully in the sale held at the Amsterdam branch of the Dutch Company[139] and the two houses even managed to sell certain quantities of camphor without causing a renewed fall in prices. In the following year David Prager once more undertook steps designed to maintain the price – by now political developments in France were helping to push up commodity prices, although the rise in camphor was still more nominal than real.[140]

The Pragers were thus able, thanks to the combined action of the Amsterdam and London houses, to prevent a further deterioration of the situation. But the damage which had been caused by the initial failure of the speculation was beyond repair. Although the price of camphor was substantially higher at the end of 1791 than it had been in 1789/90, it was still about 20 per cent lower than the price which the commodity had fetched in early 1786. In the spring of 1792, the London house still held £14,000 worth of camphor, or about a third of the quantity it had possessed at the start. The hopes that the supply of camphor from the East would stop did not materialize. Even before Prager and Kiere had time to put the plan into operation they learned that their calculations were wrong.[141] Three years later Leib Prager commented on the intention of a certain merchant to stop the import of camphor to Europe: 'It reminds me of the story of Joshua, who stopped the sun and the moon. He [i.e. the above-mentioned merchant] could as well have promised to do the same.'[142] The speculation was finally wound up in 1793.

Between 1790 and 1793 the London house suffered a series of new misfortunes: a considerable part of the firm's capital was squandered by young Mordecai, the widow Esther quarrelled with her brother Meyer and, on top of it all, David Prager died in 1792 and Leib Prager died in 1793. Within 6 years all the senior members of the firm had disappeared one after the other, and Esther Prager, having lost her husband, father, uncle and brother and been betrayed by her eldest son, was completely discouraged. In 1793 she sold the rest of the camphor at a low price[143] and proceeded to liquidate the house.

The story of Amsterdam's decline as a centre of international trade, after the great days of the seventeenth century, is well known. It was closely connected with London's rise to preeminence. It is true that London did not entirely replace Amsterdam as a distributor of colonial goods and during the greater part of the eighteenth century Amsterdam retained a considerable importance not only as a financial centre, but as a market for colonial goods: a considerable part of the goods imported by London from overseas was still being distributed through Holland.

But, despite the rapid growth of international trade during the century, Anglo-Dutch trade remained static: even in absolute figures it showed some tendency to decline,[144] while Holland's relative importance in England's trade decreased rapidly. In 1696/7 41½ per cent of England's exports were sent to Holland but in 1772/3 the figure was less than 13 per cent.[145]

Amsterdam's decline as a staple-market gained momentum during the last quarter of the century and this is clearly reflected in the letters of the Prager brothers who felt the consequences keenly. The decline of Anglo-Dutch trade had a direct effect on the prosperity of the firm. Until 1770, approximately, the Pragers seem to have been expanding their business continuously, advancing to a position of eminence in both London and Amsterdam. But after 1775 the letters contain frequent complaints about the state of business, and it would seem that these amount to more than the usual grumbles in which most merchants are apt to indulge from time to time. There is no information concerning the firm's profits before 1774, and for the period 1774–86 the profits of only six years are known,[146] but to judge from the figures we have, and from the Pragers' comments on them, it would seem that business was not as good as in the past. Among the years of which we know the profits 1777 was the best, with a profit of 46,324 gulden, or a little over £4,000. Jacob Prager's only comment on this was that he hoped the following year would bring better profits, but that this would be impossible without better business. We do not know the result of the firm's balance sheet for 1778, but we do have a preliminary estimate of profits, amounting to about 40,000 gulden, which prompted Jacob to write to his brother: 'We think that this year will yield about f 40/m. This is not too ample, considering your consumption and ours, and yet it is unexpectedly lucky . . .'.[147]

One has the definite impression that the Pragers had been used to better times, but during the following period none of the years of which the profits are known yielded even 40,000 gulden and only in 1782 and 1784 did profits exceed 30,000 gulden.[148] At best, Jacob Prager consoled himself with the thought that things could be still worse.[149] The difference in size between Yehiel Prager's estate and that of his brother Jacob has already been mentioned. Yehiel's greater wealth undoubtedly reflects the better business opportunities offered by London; he left his heirs a business worth £48,000, while Jacob's estate amounted to no more than £6,000 (65,000 gulden). It is true that Jacob had divided part of his possessions between his children during his lifetime,[150] but the difference between his and Yehiel's wealth was still considerable. The fact that within a few years of his settlement in London Yehiel became the senior partner is also revealing. We cannot say with certainty what sort of transactions contributed to the wealth which Yehiel acquired outside the partnership business, but there is good reason to suppose that these additional profits derived chiefly from his diamond trade.[151] This branch was, admittedly, not necessarily typical of the general state of commerce, but it would seem that it too reflected the eclipse of Amsterdam by London; although Holland remained the seat of the diamond industry, London was now the place to do business in stones.

Amsterdam's position was at first only partially impaired by the rise of London. Holland lost the near-monopoly it had formerly enjoyed in many branches of overseas trade and England disappeared from its list of customers for colonial goods.[152] But Holland, as we have seen, continued to play an important part in colonial trade: while London was now the major importer of colonial goods, Amsterdam was still the central market for the distribution of these goods throughout Europe. During the later part of the eighteenth century, however, Amsterdam's position deteriorated further. There was a marked shift in England's commercial relations from north-western Europe to the Baltic and the Mediterranean.[153] At the same time, other commercial centres in Northern Europe established direct connections with London and even with the producer-countries overseas, and developed a commercial and financial apparatus of their own, which enabled them to dispense with the services of Amsterdam.[154] The chief of these new rivals was Hamburg, followed by Bremen, Emden and Copenhagen, while in Holland itself the competition of Rotterdam was being increasingly felt by Amsterdam. The Prager letters are full of complaints about the rivalry of Hamburg and other ports, even before the Anglo-Dutch war, which caused grave harm to Amsterdam's position. To quote Jacob Prager, writing in the spring of 1779 about the state of the coffee trade:

With reference to our last letter, I report that coffee is approximately worth its purchase price. The reason for high prices there [in London] must be that all Germany buys there, and here all holders are left with it on their hands. And there are virtually no new commission orders – all the world buys there. This is why prices here are stagnant.[155]

Amsterdam suffered from two major drawbacks which helped the new distribution centres to steal her trade: difficulties of access and high charges. Amsterdam was not an ideal harbour – the modern canal connecting it with the North Sea did not yet exist – and to reach the port, ships had to cross the Zuider Zee, the navigation of which required much experience. Foreign ships usually preferred Rotterdam,[156] and we have already seen that the English outports, which were not served by Dutch ships, traded mainly with the latter port. During the winter months Amsterdam was entirely cut off from the sea and sometimes ships became stuck in the frozen Zuider Zee for weeks on end. With the melting of the ice, Amsterdam was flooded by goods, which introduced an element of instability into the market.[157] The rise of the new North European centres inevitably made trading through Amsterdam an unnecessary luxury. It entailed additional expenses – and charges in Amsterdam were uncommonly high. This has already been pointed out by van der Kooy[158] and is authenticated by the letters of the Pragers, who were fully aware of this cause of Amsterdam's weak position. In August 1774 Jacob answered a complaint of Yehiel that tobacco was fetching better prices in Hamburg than in Amsterdam:

I do not know that we have written anything to annoy you, God forbid. You write that Brandon has received a sales-account of tobacco and it brings 2 1/4 pennies there. In Hamburg one does not pay customs nor freight and less weighage and discount for waste than here [in Amsterdam]. This may make a difference of 1/4 penny. In Hamburg they also have no Rotterdam, as we have here.[159]

About the advantages of direct purchase in London Jacob wrote:

The hides which have been bought there, and of which you could buy nothing for the Gentile there – never mind. People who have to buy here [in Amsterdam] by order from abroad can [afford to] pay higher prices in London than here. Imagine Antwerp people buying here, where charges have already been added for freight and insurance on the voyage here and weighage and brokerage in London and import [customs] here. And then, again, freight, brokerage and export [customs] and commission here. So they can buy much more advantageously in London than here.[160]

As a result of these causes, Amsterdam's position was already precarious before 1775. The last quarter of the century saw its final decline, accelerated by three man-made calamities: the American war, which involved the Dutch in their fourth war against England, the Dutch Civil War, and, in the 1790s, the war against France.

The American war seriously dislocated Britain's commerce and, indirectly at first, also impaired Dutch trade. The situation was very different from that which had existed during the Seven Years' War, when, after a short period of stagnation, England's trade had flourished as never before. In April 1789 Jacob Prager wrote to Yehiel in London: 'Enclosed is your account current. It is not too ample. We hope the merciful God will make this year better. It is lamentable that, while we always had such fat years in wartime, now there is such a big war and so little happens in trade to our advantage ...'.[161]

The letters of this period are full of complaints about the confused political situation and the general instability which hamstrung business. Amsterdam, in particular, felt the effects of the depression in England's trade because its position was, in any case, less secure than it had been. To all this was added in 1780 the calamity of the Anglo-Dutch war. Those Dutch merchants who hoped to profit from England's distress made a costly miscalculation[162] and the first to be hit were, of course, the merchants who traded chiefly with England. Jacob Prager had no illusions about the meaning of an Anglo-Dutch conflict: 'And if this continues, all trade will flow away from here and everything will have to go through Ostend, Hamburg and Bremen. And in this way all trade may flow away from here, God forbid. What sudden troubles these are! Who would have thought of such a thing?'[163]

The declaration of war resulted in a complete commercial standstill, lasting several months.[164] The Dutch partially overcame this crisis: the postal services between London and Amsterdam were not cut off[165] and merchandise was consigned to Holland by way of Ostend and even directly, by ships ostensibly sailing to Emden.[166] But all this was a far cry from the regular shipping services which connected Holland with England in peacetime and the cost of cargoes sent through Ostend was about 6 per cent higher than that current in Anglo-Dutch trade – a considerable difference, considering the low average profits in this trade.[167] Dutch ships sailing under neutral flags resumed the maritime connections with the sources of supply in France, Spain and overseas,[168] but trade between London and Amsterdam continued at low ebb[169] and the tendency of consumer countries to dispense with the services of Amsterdam became more and more pronounced. Jacob Prager wrote in May 1785:

> The quantity of hides which is here is unbelievable. Once, before the war, everyone ordered [goods] from here, but since hides have been imported in wartime directly from Spain through Ostend, and from Ostend to Liège and Verviers etc. these [places] have retained this supply through Ostend, and are not obliged to [pay] import and export customs and other expenses, of weighage and brokerage, which have always been added here, when [goods were] ordered from here. This has virtually drawn the whole of this trade away from here, and therefore hides are very cheap now.[170]

The gravity of the situation towards the end of the war is reflected in the bitterness of Jacob Prager's reply to Yehiel's complaints about the sad state of their affairs in Amsterdam:

> Had that which has taken place here since [the beginning of] the war happened in another state, had their commerce been held in stranglehold, all navigation hindered, had they received such blows as the merchants here have, we should like to see if, with trade banished from there in like manner, they could yet stand up to it as [we have done] here.[171]

Peace did not restore former conditions. The dislocation caused by the war only accelerated a process which had started long before. Goods again reached Amsterdam regularly, but exports were slack[172] and in April 1783 Jacob Prager reported that there was no demand from the North Sea and Baltic areas, which had used to order goods from Amsterdam at this time of the year.[173] In the summer of the same year Jacob wrote:

> Let God, be He Blessed, guard [us] from bad times. In one moment one may lose [all] that one has acquired in 50 years.

This country has lost much of its commerce by this deplorable war and we fear that we shall not in our lifetime again do such flourishing business as in the past, because demand has virtually disappeared and all seafaring monarchies receive merchandize directly from East and West.[174]

Things did not get better during the following years. In the autumn of 1785 Jacob wrote that he could not remember such bad times in trade:[175] 'We work like slaves, but in vain'.[176] Early in 1786, three years after the end of hostilities, he pointed out that Holland had lost much trade since the war: 'No devil asks for cassia, for [cassia] buds, for shellac and of course not for cardamom'.[177] That was how matters stood when the struggle between William V and the Patriots reached its climax. Already in the autumn of 1786 the City showed growing reluctance to do business with Holland because of the political instability and a pessimistic attitude prevailed in regard to the country's future.[178] In the spring and summer of 1787 the Dutch became completely engrossed in their conflict which, under existing conditions, bordered on economic suicide. Business suffered from advancing paralysis and the Exchange was half empty. At the end of April David Prager reported:

And the party opposing His Excellency the Prince is every-where victorious, and depose authorities at their pleasure. If things continue like this, everything will be finished soon and order restored, God willing. In the meanwhile it greatly impedes all commerce. One sees and hears nothing on the Exchange but of this affair, and all the time many armed citizens are about.[179]

The expectation that a victory of the rebels would bring back normal conditions did not materialize. The struggle went on, business remained bad and credit became increasingly difficult to get.[180] 'Money is very scarce here, and Jews are running about with discount – they already give 4 1/4% to 4½%'. And in mid-June: 'by day and night one sees thousands of armed citizens, on foot and on horse, but no one thinks of business, only of deposing authorities and putting others in their place'.[181] The Dutch paid dearly for their domestic strife. Contrary to David Prager's expectations, it was the Stadtholder who finally gained the upper hand. Life returned to normal, but the damage which the upheaval had caused to the country's trade was permanent. The Prager letters of the period 1788–90 reflect a continuous economic depression. In 1788, a few months after order had been restored, David wrote:

> And for the time being we see no improvement here. And the recent discord here has certainly taken away much trade from here, and orders from everywhere are sent to other places and, of course, to there [London]. All drug merchants here complain vehemently that all orders from Germany etc. are sent there directly, and they here are left with their goods on their hands.[182]

Meyer Prager, who in the summer of 1788 visited Amsterdam for the first time since his departure for America five years earlier, wrote: 'I find Amsterdam much changed. Business is bad because the war has ruined much'.[183] Amsterdam's money market, which formerly had not been affected by the decline in the city's commerce, was now seriously disturbed. In February 1789 David Prager wrote: 'It is impossible to describe how scarce money is here and how [difficult] to get discount. People run about with [bills drawn on] good houses, offering 5%, but without avail. Should this last a long time, God forbid, everyone will be ruined.'[184] Meyer Prager had already some time before expressed concern about the situation of the Amsterdam house 'because I know how difficult it is to get money in Holland'.[185] But the foundations of the Dutch money market were not as shaken as those of its regular trade and it was capable of recuperation. By September 1790 the situation had changed again and David Prager wrote: 'Trade here is generally much depressed, everyone, except the bill merchants, is complaining bitterly.'[186] Any hopes which may still have been entertained for the recovery of Holland's trade were shattered by the events following the French Revolution – which goes a long way to explain the Pragers' hate of the revolutionaries.[187]

The decision of the London Pragers, in 1794, to break off the connection with the Amsterdam house is a striking manifestation of the final decline of Amsterdam's staple-market. In the autumn of that year Esther Prager instructed her cousins in Amsterdam to send her goods to Hamburg, as a cautionary measure. Wolf Prager wrote in reply: 'What times we are going through: merchandize is to be sent away from here because of fear! Could anyone have imagined such a thing?'[188] When the French invaded Holland in January 1795, communications with England were cut off. The last letter of the Amsterdam house to the Pragers of London is dated 9 January 1795. A year later the contract between the two houses expired and Esther Prager decided not to renew it. On hearing of her decision, her brother Isaiah, who was then in India, wrote to her: 'With the contract with Holland which terminated 1 Jan[uar]y 96 you have done right to give it up. It can now be of no use, and must that country go to the ground. I shall be very glad to see my final account with them upon paper.'[189]

The decline of Amsterdam's staple-market did not impair its position as a central money market, a source of cheap credit and a centre of discount and exchange transactions, in which Jews played a prominent role. Van der Kooy thought that the financial activity had a beneficial effect on Amsterdam's regular commerce and slowed down its decline: 'Capital still caused goods to flow through our ports'.[190] This may well have been so, but if we examine the influence of exchange business on Amsterdam's staple-market during the 1770s and 1780s in the light of the Prager letters, we soon discover that, at least at that time, the financial activity, far from acting as a brake on the process of commercial decline, actually accelerated it.

Both London and Amsterdam were centres of the precious metals trade. A considerable part of the silver and gold which reached London from Spain and Portugal was forwarded to the Continent by way of Amsterdam. Sometimes the flow of precious metals changed its direction because of temporary conditions prevailing on the market, but usually the direction was from London to Amsterdam. The flow of precious metals, as well as consignments of bills of exchange payable in other countries and accompanied by drawings from London on Amsterdam or remittances of bills from Amsterdam to London, brought about a rate of exchange between the two cities which was unfavourable to trade because it increased the prices of goods sent from England to Holland. The Prager letters abound with complaints about the high rate of exchange caused by the continuous consignments of gold and silver from London to Amsterdam, a trade carried on mainly by Jewish exchange merchants.[191] The following passage describes the effect of foreign bills of exchange, sent from London, on the rate of exchange:

It is a damned business with the bills. Jews who receive foreign bills from there [i.e. from London], and Gentiles too, must make remittances in return. They go to Hope's house and to Muilman's, before the Exchange, and take virtually all their bills. The latter then come to the Exchange with the little they have left and fix a high rate. Subsequently other people who have bills follow their lead, and [buyers] must pay [them], too, a high price, and Jews win much money by this. The most important are the Kampen family. Do not say that I am writing you this, but they are chiefly to blame. People who have to draw from there [London] at long time also make remittances here, on David Kampen, Stapel etc. and order them to be discounted here, and remittances at short and long time to be made in return, and the Kampens earn commission and brokerage on it. This keeps the rate-of-exchange high.[192]

Another passage describes the effects of consignments of precious metals on the rate of exchange. This particular case concerns smuggling of gold guineas by the brothers Cantor:

Bills on there [London] were today also lower, and if it wasn't for the people who are getting guineas by every post and who take all [bills], whereby the firms [dealing in bills] make good profits, the rate would be 4 gr[oats] cheaper. It is unbelievable: the Cantors receive £12[000] to £15,000 with every post, others too, even Gentiles receive. De Crone told us that last Wednesday he had received from his people in Zeeland guineas worth £5,000. Moses Gettingen buys every post for over 100,000 from the Cantors.[193]

Even a Jewish merchant like Yehiel Prager was liable to become incensed at the Jewish exchange merchants whom he blamed for the high rate of exchange which was impairing the regular trade between England and Holland. His brother Jacob answered him in a more detached vein: 'As to bills – we do not think that Jews are to blame. If they make profits, they are right. Meanwhile the rate of exchange is harming merchandize and deprives trade of its profits.'[194] In view of the smallness of the profits which could usually be expected in Anglo-Dutch trade, a high rate of exchange was liable to reduce the profitability of transactions to zero or even below and destroy all incentive to do business: 'It is impossible that the rate of exchange will remain as it is, because no one

here can order goods from there at such a rate of exchange –
neither manufactured goods nor other merchandize.'[195] In the
seventeenth century this would perhaps have constituted no more
than a minor nuisance: Amsterdam's position was then too strong
to be shaken by a certain rise in prices. But by the end of the
eighteenth century it had become extremely vulnerable and it
was quite impossible to enforce lower prices in London or to sell
dearer in Holland simply because the high rate of exchange
increased costs. The English exporter or the Dutch importer had
to bear the losses, which they could ill afford.

To sum up: Amsterdam's exchange trade prospered at the
expense of its staple-market. In a way, the history of the Pragers'
firm represents a hopeless struggle for the maintenance of a
tradition of a business concerned exclusively with goods. The
biggest houses in Anglo-Dutch trade – Hope and Muilman –
while still dealing in merchandise, appear in the Prager letters
mainly as leading exchange merchants. Apart from the diamond
trade, the exchange trade was undoubtedly the most important
field of Jewish business activity within the framework of Anglo-
Dutch commerce. The Pragers were often tempted by the opportunities for quick profits offered by the exchange trade,[196] but they
could not hope to gain a permanent foothold in it as long as they
clung to their conservative commercial policy. Their limitation to
trade in goods, while it contributed much to the firm's good name,
seriously reduced its chances of surviving under the new conditions and was a major cause of its elimination from Anglo-Dutch
trade after 1790. The following passages illustrate the conflict of
interests between the regular and the exchange merchants.

Jews snatch away at once what they can on the Exchange . . . it
is [to pay] for pieces of eight which they are ordering. People
say it gives a net profit of 1½% to 2%. It needs no brains and no
cleverness and we cannot compete with them. They must remit
from here because they cannot draw from there [i.e. from
London].

Or again,

You do not know how it pains us when we sustain losses because
of the rate of exchange and this takes much of the profits away.
Jews are making lots of money now, there never were such
times for Jews. They are earning enormous amounts on foreign

bills, gold and silver, and if Jews would not send gold and silver from here and would take bills [instead], the rate of exchange would be much higher still.[197]

The firms which were active in Anglo-Dutch trade had either to adapt themselves to the new situation or to turn to other fields of business. It was the latter course which the Pragers of Amsterdam adopted in the 1790s.

Chapter 12
The Jewish framework

The important part which the Jews of London played in the importation of uncut diamonds from overseas has already been studied. The relevant documentary sources supply very little information on the second stage of the diamond trade: the link between London, the commercial centre of the trade, and the industrial centres of Amsterdam and Antwerp. The Prager letters, however, constitute a rich and unique source of information on this section of the diamond trade, which was also, to a large extent, in Jewish hands. In the eighteenth century the Dutch imported only insignificant quantities of uncut diamonds from the East, and after 1730 the diamond industry was dependent on two main sources of supply: London and Lisbon. London had a near-monopoly on Indian diamonds,[1] while Brazilian diamonds reached Amsterdam both legally – directly from Lisbon – and illegally, through London. In Portugal the diamond trade constituted a crown-monopoly and was leased to a contractor, who was usually Dutch. During most of the period covered by the Prager letters – up to 1787 – the contract was held by a certain Gildemeester, who used to distribute the stones several times a year to a limited group of customers in Amsterdam.[2] In 1787 the contract passed into the hands of the Jewish merchant Benjamin Cohen (also known as Benjamin Amersfoort), an acquaintance of the Pragers, who held it for a few years.

Formally, the possessor of the Portuguese contract had the exclusive right to distribute Brazilian diamonds in Europe. But, as the Prager letters show, side by side with this legal trade there existed a flourishing contraband trade through London. The diamonds were smuggled in the same packet-boats which carried Portuguese gold from Lisbon to Cornwall. There is, naturally, no possibility of determining either the volume of this illegal trade or its importance compared with the legal trade. But the Prager letters do show that Brazilian stones regularly reached the London market and that the 'new sort' (Brazilian diamonds) could be had there with the same ease as the 'old sort' (Indian diamonds).[3]

Although the Pragers never received diamonds from Gildemeester, they often dealt in Brazilian diamonds which they received from Yehiel Prager in London.[4]

We have no statistical data concerning the Jewish share in the Anglo-Dutch diamond trade, but if the impression gained from the Prager letters is correct, it was not smaller than their share in diamond imports from India, and perhaps even exceeded it. The letters do not mention a single non-Jewish firm among the major wholesale diamond merchants of London, who bought the uncut diamonds brought from India and Brazil, or imported them themselves and consigned them to Amsterdam. The Prager letters seem to show that the trade was chiefly concentrated in the hands of a few Ashkenazi families: Gompertz, Norden, Ferde (Marcus),[5] Tutshke,[6] and the Goldsmids as brokers. Only in the second line came Portuguese houses like Mendes da Costa, Aguilar and Franco. These firms were still very prominent as importers of diamonds from India, and there are two possible explanations for their more humble place in the Prager correspondence. It is quite conceivable that they concentrated mainly on imports, and sold the diamonds they received from India to Ashkenazi merchants in London, but the possibility must also be borne in mind that the Prager letters do not reflect the real importance of the Sephardi houses in the Anglo-Dutch diamond trade, because the Pragers did, on the whole, do business mainly with Ashkenazim. *Prima facie*, however, the Prager letters point to an Ashkenazi predominance in the trade and they give reason to suppose that most buyers of diamonds in Amsterdam, merchants as well as cutters, were also Ashkenazim.[7] We have a description of the excitement caused by the arrival of diamonds in Amsterdam:

> The Nordens have received diamonds, Brazilian as well as Bengalese,[8] and Ferde have a share in them together with the Nordens. There was a concourse today – the whole congregation rushed there, but no one bought anything. There are many belonging to the Norden family who are merchants, brokers and artisans [i.e. diamond cutters], everyone wants to get priority. The devil knows what is going on there.[9]

It is true that several non-Jewish firms, like Hope, Abrahams and others,[10] also received diamonds from London, but it seems that they usually functioned as agents for Jewish houses in London. The Gompertzes, especially, appear to have preferred non-

Jewish agents, either because they lacked close family connections in Amsterdam or because they mistrusted Jewish agents, who normally had an interest of their own in the diamond trade.[11]

The Pragers were late-comers to the diamond trade. In the 1760s Yehiel Prager kept up relations with a number of precious-stone merchants of Amsterdam and the Hague, but he acted mainly as an agent for the sale of polished stones and jewellery. Yehiel tried to exploit his connections to one of those Dutch merchants – Barukh Cantor – in an attempt to gain a foothold in the trade in uncut diamonds, but without much success.[12] In the summer of 1766 Yehiel was told by his brother Jacob that Cantor preferred to buy uncut diamonds from the firm of Hanover in Amsterdam, rather than in London, and Jacob added: 'we do not understand this trade with Jews'.[13] Yehiel, however, persisted in his attempts, and about 1770 he began to do business in uncut diamonds on a considerable scale. Thereafter his progress was rapid. His success was probably due to the crisis then prevailing in the diamond trade, in the course of which a large proportion of diamond imports from India passed into the hands of non-Jews, remitting fortunes acquired in the East. Yehiel skilfully made use of the conditions thus created. He formed connections with people like Clive, Verelst, and Macartney, who were importing great quantities of diamonds from India: according to Verelst, Yehiel bought most of the stones imported by himself and by Clive.[14] By 1774 Yehiel was in a position to enter a temporary partnership with the firms of Norden and Gompertz[15] and it would seem that both the idea of a marriage between Leib Prager and a daughter of the Nordens,[16] which was entertained for a time, and the subsequent antagonism between the two houses, reflect Yehiel Prager's growing importance in the diamond trade. In 1777 Jacob Barnet described Yehiel as 'the most eminent diamond merchant in England'[17] and, though Barnet's desire to flatter may have caused him to exaggerate, it is revealing that such a statement could be made at all only 10 years after Yehiel's first unsuccessful attempt to do business in uncut diamonds. Even more significant is the suggestion, made in 1778 by Yehiel's agent in Lisbon, that he should join a partnership which was to be formed with the purpose of negotiating with the Portuguese Crown for the right to market Brazilian diamonds.[18]

In the later 1770s there was a fierce competition between the chief diamond merchants of London – the houses of Gompertz,

Norden and Prager. The Pragers of Amsterdam were frightened by Yehiel's daring and by his readiness to risk losses in order to defeat his rivals.[19] They, nevertheless, did all in their power to assist him and succeeded in forming a close connection with the Yerogam brothers, who in the 1780s were, according to David Prager, the most eminent diamond cutters of Amsterdam.[20] But Yehiel was apparently not satisfied with them and from 1779 onwards he sold most of his diamonds to Jewish merchants in the City[21] and also maintained business connections with Antwerp, which specialized in the working of small and cheap stones.[22] Diamonds almost disappeared from the joint affairs of the London and Amsterdam houses and the few consignments which Yehiel continued to send his brothers usually contained refuse. In July 1782 David wrote him:

> Not only do I not get any satisfaction out of such business, but I sat for 3 whole days with merchants to inspect the diamonds. You can imagine that each requires about 3 hours to inspect them properly. Gentiles run away immediately when they hear the prices. Jews too, but they add a remark: 'We do not understand – we buy from other people who buy from your brother, but that is good merchandize and the sellers are entirely satisfied with the prices which they receive. How does it happen that you get such inferior stuff and ask so much more than its value?' We do not know what to answer them. They also say: 'We know your brother had most of the diamonds which were in London'.[23]

By 1777 Yehiel felt that his position was strong enough to enable him to become an independent importer of Indian diamonds and in 1785 he sent his nephew Leib to India, in an attempt to gain a dominant position in the trade. He indeed became, and remained for a number of years, the biggest importer of Indian stones, but, as we have seen, this undertaking did not really justify itself, despite its apparent success. Like the other gambles on which Yehiel embarked during the last years of his life, this, too, ended in failure. Apart from the connections with the house of Michael-David of Hanover, Aaron Meyer of Berlin, and Abraham Salomons of Jamaica, the diamond trade was the only field of commercial activity in which the Pragers maintained close and permanent business connections with Jews. The three other branches of Anglo-Dutch trade in which Jews were prominent – the exchange trade, transactions in stocks, and the cloth trade – were none of them of great importance to the Pragers, despite the fact that their letters supply much interesting information on the exchange trade and the cloth trade. Although the Pragers' business was not a typically Jewish one, their correspondence sheds light on several aspects of Jewish commercial activity which were not confined to the diamond trade.

The business of the Prager brothers was anything but worldwide. The brothers confined themselves primarily to Anglo-Dutch trade, and their undertakings outside this field were really ramifications of their main business, to India in the case of their diamond trade and to North America in the framework of their tobacco business, and even these overseas extensions of their activity conformed to the firm's tradition of a family business. The house cannot therefore serve as an example for the widespread international connections which are commonly regarded as a typical attribute of Jewish commerce. Its papers are, however, a good illustration of the importance of Yiddish as an international language of Ashkenazi Jewry, greatly facilitating connections between merchants of different countries. Connections with Jewish houses outside England and Holland were of a casual nature and, apart from the diamond trade, relations with Jewish merchants in the firm's Anglo-Dutch affairs were of secondary importance. The firm maintained a more than transient correspondence with only three Jewish merchants abroad.[24] They were Michael-David of Hanover, Aaron Meyer of Berlin, and Abraham Salomons of Jamaica. Only the first was of real importance to the Pragers. The mere fact that Yehiel Prager became the London agent of Meyer Michael-David, succeeding the great Joseph Salomons only two years after he had permanently settled in London, was a striking achievement. It greatly enhanced Prager's standing in the City and for that cause would probably have been worthwhile even if it had brought him no immediate material benefits. The connection, however, was advantageous in other respects too. As we have seen, the exchange transactions between the two houses were not a success, but Michael-David became an important source of credit for the Pragers, nor should one underrate the importance of Yehiel Prager's connections with Hanoverian courtiers at St James, which he was able to form as agent of Michael-David.

The correspondence with Aaron Meyer of Berlin was potentially not without value, in view of Meyer's kinship with the Ephraims, the most prominent of Jewish mercantile houses in Berlin.[25] But notwithstanding the large number of Meyer's letters preserved among the Prager Papers, the actual business done by the two houses in common was rather insignificant. The Pragers were not acquainted with the goods in which Meyer specialized, like wood, potash, and salt, and Berlin had not yet attained the rank of major commercial centre.

The connection with Abraham Salomons was formed when he went (or returned) to Jamaica in 1777. From that time until Yehiel's death in 1788 they corresponded regularly. Prager acted as Salomons' London agent and sold sugar, pimento, ginger, cotton, mahogany, and other West Indian goods on his behalf. These transactions were of modest size and it is clear that Salomons' resources were limited. The goods which he consigned to London were of the kind which the Pragers used to handle, but, judging from the many complaints in Salomons' letters, Yehiel Prager does not seem to have been especially interested in this connection.[26] The correspondence, in fact, contains only one letter which is of more than minor interest: a request by Salomons for the assistance of the Ashkenazi community of London in the building of a synagogue in Kingston.[27]

The business connections which the Pragers maintained with Jews within the framework of Anglo-Dutch trade (excluding the diamond trade) were of two kinds; connections with Sephardim in the course of the firm's regular business, and connections with Ashkenazi cloth merchants – a branch which had a pronounced Jewish aspect, but was of secondary importance to the Pragers, whose business, with its emphasis on colonial goods, was indeed closer to the Sephardi than to the Ashkenazi commercial tradition. Yehiel Prager regularly employed three Sephardi brokers, Jacob and Gabriel Israel Brandon and Abraham Lara.[28] The latter used to purchase West Indian and South American goods like cotton, indigo, and hides on his behalf,[29] while the Brandons were tobacco specialists and were among the most prominent brokers on the Royal Exchange.[30] The relationship between them and the Pragers was a close one and in 1784 young Gabriel Israel Brandon requested Leib Prager to use his uncle's influence in order to obtain for him a broker's position.[31]

The Pragers also did business with a number of Sephardi

merchants, all of them members of well known families: Hananel Mendes da Costa, Hananel d'Aguilar, as well as Jacob and Francis Franco, are frequently mentioned in the letters. The old prestige which still attached to these names was no longer wholly justified. The most reputable among them was Hananel Mendes da Costa, who had taken over the extensive business of his father Jacob with East and West, and whose diligence earned the praise of the Prager brothers of Amsterdam,[32] who were usually very sceptical about the dependability of Sephardi firms. But even he had temporarily to stop payments in 1785.[33] Hananel d'Aguilar was a son of the well-known Diego (Moses) Lopes Pereira, Baron d'Aguilar. He asked Yehiel Prager to help him when he went bankrupt in 1781. Jacob and Francis Franco were the sons of Moses Franco and grandchildren of Jacob Franco, who, together with his brother Abraham, had established the great firm of Franco early in the eighteenth century. Jacob senior died in 1777, aged 90, and left each of his grandchildren £40,000, which they invested in a firm – the 'Franco and Lindo' of the Prager correspondence, so called because it was directed by Elias Lindo.[34] The Pragers from time to time undertook transactions in partnership with one or another of these houses, or acted as their factors. It was a measure of the high regard which the Pragers enjoyed that these Sephardim trusted them with goods – like diamonds, dye-stuffs, hides, drugs, tobacco, coffee, and cotton – in which the Pragers themselves dealt regularly.[35] Occasionally the house made transactions in common with the brokers Lara and Brandon, who were unable, because of their official standing, openly to carry on a business of their own,[36] and in the 1780s the Pragers became the Amsterdam agents of the Jewish brokers Israel and Lindo of London, who specialized in dye-stuffs.

Yehiel Prager made use of his connections with Ashkenazi houses to gain a foothold in branches in which Jews were prominent, though they were outside the Pragers' normal field of activity, such as the cloth and the porcelain trades. We have already discussed the role of Jews as buyers of damaged cloth from the East India Company. The Pragers did not take a direct share in this business and regarded it with a certain amount of suspicion,[37] but Yehiel Prager, nevertheless, occasionally invested in it. He was able to do so thanks to the good services of three merchants with whom he maintained friendly relations, two of whom – Levy Barent Cohen and Simon Tanhum (Daniels) – were the organizers of the cloth merchants' corner of 1778. The third was Jacob ben Moshe, whom the Pragers always mentioned by the diminutive Yakobkhe. He was an Amsterdam merchant who used to come over to London for the sales of the East India Company. With the help of these people Yehiel got a share in the cloth purchased from the Company, and it emerges that he participated in the buyers' combination of 1778.[38] Simon Tanhum used to employ the Amsterdam house of the Pragers as his agents, consigning to it goods purchased in London.[39] The readiness of the cloth merchants to let an outsider like Yehiel Prager share in their business was probably due to his 'influence' at India House, which made the same people turn to him when they wanted to induce the Company to postpone a cloth sale, because it coincided with a Jewish holiday. For services like this, he was paid by a small share in this business, in which he never played a direct or active role.

The Prager Papers show clearly that Jews, as a group, did not enjoy the same degree of trust which was normally accorded to the Christian merchant. The Pragers were extremely proud of the good name they had made for themselves, which, according to them, was equivalent to that of respectable gentile firms and much superior to that of most other Jews. In the winter of 1778 Jacob Prager wrote: 'We think that, with the help of God, we are doing very well with our credit, that we can maintain it in such a way. And, with the help of God, we have the best credit, the like of which no Jews ever had, and no less than eminent Gentile merchants.'[40]

In December 1781 Jacob wrote that one should be cautious in regard to exchange business and added: 'but our credit, thank God, is 100 times and 1000 times better than that of other Jews'.[41] Jacob regarded their standing with the Paris banking house of Tourton as unusual for a Jewish firm: 'We do not think that a single Jew has such credit with Tourton or with anyone in the world'.[42] The Pragers evidently valued their reputation highly, and after Yehiel's death his brother David emphasized the importance of maintaining it 'as we have established it to this day, for which there is little precedent among Jews'.[43] The mistrust in the reliability of Jewish firms was reflected most conspicuously in the discounting of bills: it was more difficult to discount bills drawn on Jews, especially when the economic situation in general was not stable. Jews were the first to feel the pinch when credit became scarce and even the Bank of England discriminated between Jewish and other discounters. At the time of the great economic crisis of 1772 Meyer Michael-David wrote that the Bank of England was rejecting Jewish bills,[44] and six years later it was being told in Amsterdam that the Bank of England was refusing to discount bills drawn on Jews.[45] Again, in March 1784 Yehiel reported that the Bank refused to discount bills bearing Jewish names.[46] The rate of discount was also higher in the case of Jews. Jacob Prager told Yehiel in February 1780:

> Enclosed is the third of the latest bills of exchange from Lisbon. We have not yet discounted the bill on Ferde. People give 2¼% or 2½% [for bills drawn] on Gentiles, and [for bills drawn] on Jews 3½% are demanded, except when people can have [bills drawn] on us, [in which case] they get the same as [for bills drawn] on good houses.[47]

Meyer Michael-David wrote on 9 Adar II 5632 (14 March 1772), concerning bills drawn on him by Yehiel Prager at an unfavourable rate of exchange: 'The worst is that one has to sell Jewish bills for at least 1/16 shilling less', though he added somewhat paradoxically: 'May be that in the present critical time Jewish bills will improve, God willing'.[48]

In June 1781 Jacob Prager wrote: 'You can imagine the discredit which has again set in here, and especially where Jews are concerned'.[49] The following passage also illustrates the difficulties encountered by Jews who wanted to discount bills in London:

> If we could have the full rate of exchange for bills drawn on there [London], and if we could draw to the order of Gentiles, then we should draw. But to [draw to order of] Jews – so that the latter would rush around seeking to discount them – that you do not want, do you? – as you write about Gettingen, that he is damaging your reputation.[50]

On the other hand, Isaac Prager denied in 1793 that bills drawn on Jews could not be discounted in Amsterdam, 'and Jews are maintaining themselves during these times better than others'.[51]

Business connections with Christians added to a Jew's prestige and were considered a great advantage. When Yehiel Prager expressed doubts about the advisability of marrying one of his nieces to the exchange merchant Moses Gettingen, her father

[Jacob] wrote to point out his merits, one of which was that 'he also has business connections with many Gentiles'.[52] Drawing bills on a non-Jewish merchant not only made discount easier and cheaper, but also enhanced the drawer's standing if he was a Jew. The bill-broker Eleazar Kampen (Salomons) once advised the widow Esther Prager to draw on a non-Jewish house because this would improve her credit.[53]

What were the causes of this attitude? A partial explanation must be sought in certain irrational factors. The Pragers themselves, who were observant and proud Jews, were not above accusing Jews, as a group, of sharp practices in business.[54] It is doubtful, however, whether these imputations of collective guilt were entirely justified: one must not forget the Jewish tendency to semi-humorous self-accusation. On the part of non-Jews, too, there was undoubtedly a measure of irrational anti-semitism or 'rishes', as Jews used to call it. The Pragers, as well as the Hanoverian banker Meyer Michael-David, thought that anti-Jewish sentiments underlay the Bank of England's discrimination against Jews in matters of discount.[55] One can also observe a tendency to draw unfavourable conclusions about Jews as a group from the collapse of a single Jewish firm. On hearing that Jewish merchants had suffered heavy losses in a ship disaster because their goods were not insured, Jacob Prager wrote: 'It discredits Jews and gives them a bad name that they take such risks'.[56] It appears that in this respect people made no distinction between Sephardim and Ashkenazim. When Yehiel reported from London that orders had been received from people in Amsterdam not to take bills from Jews, Jacob retorted: 'That orders are said to have been received from here not to take from Jews, must be because of the Portuguese [Jews] who have gone bankrupt'.[57] And when the grandson of the Jewish merchant Hertz Yoffe broke in 1789, David Prager, fearing that Jews in general might be discredited, remarked: 'It also does not contribute to the good name of Jews'.[58] It can hardly be doubted that an element of prejudice was not absent from the application of the principle 'All Israel are responsible for each other'. But to some extent it was justified, in view of the close business connections among Jews. And although the importance of Jewish and Gentile anti-semitism should not be discounted, the basic causes must be sought in the special character of Jewish commercial activities.

The prominence of exchange transactions in Jewish business

activities has already been mentioned. The exchange trade was characterized by opportunities for quick and large profits, on the one hand, and by the necessity of constantly taking considerable risks, on the other. Conditions were apt to change overnight and it was even more difficult to foresee developments than in other branches of commerce. Transactions in precious metals, often illegal, formed an integral part of this trade – a fact which contributed neither to its stability nor to its reputation. In 1784, for example, the Bank of England flatly refused to discount bills of Jews dealing in precious metals.[59] Of still greater weight was the dependence of the exchange merchant on the stability of the firms in the bills of which he dealt. Bankruptcies caused a chain reaction among exchange merchants, who were among the first victims of every economic crisis.[60] When two Jewish houses broke in the spring of 1783, David Prager wrote: 'These 2 houses are causing a big turmoil here, and Jewish exchange dealers are unfortunately losing considerably by it'.[61] And after the bankruptcy of the non-Jewish house of Boulanger, David wrote in a similar vein: 'Jews – virtually all exchange dealers – are involved in it'.[62] Jacob Prager personally experienced these dangers when his son-in-law Moses Gettingen, whom he described as a man both rich and cautious, faced disaster as a result of the bankruptcy of one of his clients in Hamburg. All ended well, but it was a narrow escape.[63]

The Pragers accordingly regarded the exchange trade with considerable suspicion. Others had similar misgivings, so that Jews, as a group, were considered to be less stable and dependable than Christians, in whose affairs exchange transactions did not play such a preponderant part. A firm like that of the Pragers, which did not regularly deal in bills of exchange and precious metals, was able, after having acquired a reputation for stability and integrity, to break through this wall of suspicion which confronted most Jewish merchants. But even the Pragers could not always escape the consequences of this attitude.[64] The exchange trade cast a shadow over the entire Jewish business community.

The second half of the eighteenth century witnessed the rise of several Ashkenazi families to a position of eminence equal to that of the foremost Sephardim, and by the close of the century it became evident that the days of Sephardi dominance within the

Jewish community were over. In the middle of the century no Ashkenazi could yet have hoped to equal great Sephardi merchants, like Joseph Salvador and Sampson Gideon, while 50 years later the Ashkenazi Goldsmids had become the foremost Jewish businessmen in the City. It is not surprising that this process of economic rise, on the one hand, and of decline, on the other, was a cause of constant friction between the two Jewish communities, and the strained relationship is clearly reflected in the Prager letters.[65] The attitude of the Amsterdam Pragers and of other Ashkenazim to their Sephardi correligionists sometimes amounted to outright hostility. In 1775 Jacob Prager wrote a gleeful letter to Leib Bing, who was then in London, telling him about the collapse of the plans of Aaron Capadoza – a prominent Sephardi – to celebrate his silver wedding with much pomp. According to Prager, Capadoza had invited Amsterdam's notables, as well as the chief merchants and many Portuguese Jews, 'but he declared that he wanted no Ashkenazim at the celebration'. Having undertaken preparations on a grand scale and incurred much expense, Capadoza was informed by the mayor that he could not permit the celebration 'and does not want any new ceremonies here', as Jacob Prager put it. The Ashkenazim were evidently overjoyed by this humiliation of the snobbish Sephardi: 'It is impossible to describe the lament of the Sephardim. Who knows if 1000 enemas have not been given? We are very sorry that you are not here and that you cannot smell the Portuguese's open wound . . .'.[66] Jacob closed this not very delicate description by suggesting that the story should be published in the English press. A few days later he returned to the subject in a letter to his brother adding: 'It is impossible to describe the hatred which now exists here between Sephardim and Ashkenazim. We keep aloof from it.'[67]

Though they may have kept aloof, the Pragers were certainly not impartial. Early in 1781 a quarrel broke out between the Ashkenazi and Sephardi exchange merchants of Amsterdam. The Ashkenazim maintained that the Sephardi exchange merchants were discriminating against them in favour of Christian merchants, and they decided to retaliate. Jacob Prager co-operated wholeheartedly and wrote to his brother: 'You must take nothing further [i.e. bills of exchange] on Leghorn, even if it is very advantageous. All [Ashkenazi] Jews have written this to London, because only Portuguese [Jews] take [these bills] here, and they give a high price to Gentiles and from Jews [i.e. Ashkenazim] they want to have them virtually for nothing. One must teach them a lesson.'[68] The fact that this ban was carried into effect and that Ashkenazim in London refused to take from Sephardim bills drawn on Italy and Spain testifies to the strength of communal solidarity.

That the Pragers refused, on the whole, to get involved in these animosities is understandable in view of their business ties with several Sephardi merchants. In consequence of the reduction in the number of merchants of the Portuguese community who dealt in goods, a well-established Ashkenazi firm had better chances than in earlier times to foster connections of this kind and to get commissions from members of the other community.[69] Between 1775 and 1780 Yehiel Prager was able to enter into a business relationship with three Sephardi houses. The attitude of the Amsterdam brothers to these connections was somewhat ambiguous. Although the heyday of the Sephardi merchants had passed, these firms still counted for something. The capital at their disposal put them in approximately the same category as the Pragers,[70] but they had much better international connections. Moreover, some of the old prestige still attached to their names. When the Pragers first received commissions from d'Aguilar and Franco of London, Jacob Prager wrote: 'Such a commission gives us a great reputation and also brings us customers through [the broker] de Bruyn'.[71] In the spring of 1781 Jacob recommended to Yehiel 'a Sephardi Portuguese – a neighbour of ours' by the name of Emanuel Cortissos, who was going to London in an attempt to recover goods lost in consequence of the British occupation of the Dutch island of St Eustatius.[72] Jacob asked his brother to help this man, pointing out that he would thus make a great name for himself in Amsterdam and get many new commissions.[73]

The Pragers were, however, very careful not to go out of their way to get orders from the Sephardim,[74] or to let them think they were bestowing favours. They were extremely contemptuous of the lavishness of many Sephardi families[75] and, what is more, were always sceptical about the stability of their commercial affairs. This is especially true in regard to exchange business: it would seem that the Pragers' dislike of this was especially pronounced when Sephardim were concerned in it. When a rumour spread, in 1775, that a Sephardi of Bordeaux by the name of Brandon had gone bankrupt, Jacob warned his brother: 'Be careful with Sephardim'. At the end of the letter he returned to the subject, expressing the hope that the rumour would turn out to have been unfounded, but repeating his warning: 'Nevertheless, you must in future avoid [making exchange deals with] Sephardim, come what may'.[76] In June 1781 Jacob expressed relief because they had stopped doing exchange business with d'Aguilar and Mendes da Costa,[77] and his suspicions were confirmed a few months later, when d'Aguilar went bankrupt. The Amsterdam brothers told Yehiel that they also refused to do exchange business with Lindo,[78] unless Yehiel could attest that he was 'of the best'. They did not want to be suspected of prejudice – 'We have no grudge against any Portuguese'[79] – but only three weeks later Jacob advised Yehiel to stop all dealings in exchange with Portuguese Jews. Informing him that a bill drawn on Vencie by Abraham Haim Franco of London had been protested, he concluded: 'In short, you must refrain from [dealings with] Portuguese as if they were under a ban'.[80] About a year later, in the summer of 1782, Jacob wrote in a similar vein, after receiving bills from Hananel Mendes da Costa of London: 'We do not want to have any dealings with him or with any other Portuguese, nor must you do anything with them, not even with Lindo'.[81] In view of what we know about the three Sephardi houses with whom the Pragers dealt, their misgivings were well founded. D'Aguilar went bankrupt in 1781; Hananel Mendes da Costa had to stop payments in 1785; and the brothers Franco, unlike their father and grandfathers, were gentlemen of leisure who preferred play to work and left the direction of the firm to their clerk Elias Lindo.[82]

The maintenance of a normal business relationship between Ashkenazim and Sephardim was also made difficult by constant suspicion that the other side was giving preference to members of its own community. When d'Aguilar came to Amsterdam in 1778, Jacob wrote that he would meet him and hoped that he would be useful to them, 'but we fear that we shall not be able to do business with him, because he is staying with Sephardim'.[83] On another occasion, when Jacob discovered that the Castros of Amsterdam had boxes similar to those in which they themselves had received cassia from the Francos of London, he concluded that the latter had also sent a consignment to Castro and wrote to Yehiel: 'In any case, you see that the Sephardim are perfidious, damn them all, Amen!'[84] In 1785 Jacob proposed that he send to England a Sephardi called Senator, in order to buy wool on their behalf. He reassured Yehiel that 'if he engaged to serve us, he

will certainly not bind himself to any Sephardi there'. He nevertheless suggested that Yehiel should keep him in his house and
not let him out before sale-day.[85] Even the tobacco broker
Brandon, who had been serving the London house from the time
of its establishment, was liable to come under suspicion, as is
shown by a passage from a letter of David Prager, written in
August 1789: 'We believe that he [Brandon] gives preference to
Sephardim – to Cortissos and the brothers Mendes. The Castros
are continuously receiving tobacco and are selling very cheaply.'[86]

In conclusion it should be said that, although there is no direct
evidence concerning Yehiel Prager's attitude to Sephardim, he
may well have been less suspicious and untrusting than his
brothers. The fact that he initiated most of the firm's connections
with Sephardim and that he employed Sephardi brokers like
Lara and Brandon over many years points to a more benevolent
attitude.

One of the most interesting aspects of Jewish business life in the
eighteenth century, as reflected in the Prager letters, is the weight
which the single merchant attached to Jewish public opinion.
This was true even in the case of the Pragers, although their
business was not characteristically Jewish and in many respects
was similar to a great number of non-Jewish firms in London and
Amsterdam. The Pragers – and we can speak mainly about Jacob
and David of Amsterdam – were observant Jews, but their
religious outlook was both liberal and tolerant. They observed
the main precepts of the Jewish religion, celebrated the Jewish
festivals in the traditional manner and attended synagogue regularly. It goes without saying that they ate only kosher food. In
general, they were proud Jews and despised people who strove to
conceal their religion and were ashamed of it.[87] David Prager
from time to time served as community leader (parnas) and, notwithstanding his brother Yehiel's cynical attitude, took his duties
very seriously. At the same time the Pragers took a positive view
of European culture and had a low opinion of Jewish religious
scholarship. In 1778 Amsterdam's Chief Rabbi, Saul Loewenstamm, published his book *Binyan Ariel*. He gave three copies to
Jacob Prager, who wrote to his brother:

The President of the [rabbinical] Court here has printed a book
and has distributed it. He gave us one for you and we paid him

for it. We report this to you because we know he sent a consignment to a person in London for distribution there. Possibly you
will be presented with one there too – if so, you must say that
we have written to you that we paid for you. Do you want all
three, mine and David's included? You can have all three. It is
the most unnecessary thing in the world and only meant for
making money.[88]

They gave their children an essentially modern education, at the
hand of private tutors who taught them mainly languages, arith-
metic, Jewish subjects and music. When Mordecai Prager was
sent in 1780 to spend a period of time with his Dutch uncles, his
father Yehiel expressed his dislike of the idea that Mordecai
might be taught too much Gemara (Talmud) while in Amsterdam,
to which David Prager replied: 'I have written enough about
your son Mordecai, may he live. You need not fear – he will not
learn too much Gemara. Nevertheless, it is no disgrace to be
conversant with it, besides other fields of knowledge and
languages.[89] David Prager, at least, did not despise learning and
was proud of the erudition of the youngsters in Amsterdam and
especially of his son Wolf.[90] They also supported the advanced
educational opinions propounded at that time by Naphtali Herz
Weisel. When he published his book *Divrei Shalom Ve-emet*
('Words of Peace and Truth'), in which he advocated a combination of secular and religious education for Jewish children, Jacob
Prager wrote: 'The little book of Reb Herz Weisel is causing
great agitation among the rabbis, and yet what he writes is the
pure truth.'[91] But they were very careful not to overstep the limits
set by Jewish public opinion and endeavoured to prevent their
children from going too far in imitating the ways of the Gentiles.
There was the ever-present fear that they might acquire a bad
reputation in consequence of their children's behaviour, which
would make it difficult to marry them advantageously.

A good illustration of this point of view can be found in a
passage taken from a letter of Jacob Prager, replying to Yehiel,
who had ridiculed their brother David's support of a resolution
condemning a certain Elias Hanover because he had shaved on
the Sabbath before attending synagogue. Jacob admitted that the
prohibition was superstitious, but maintained that it had to be
enforced in order to teach obedience to the individual. He went
on:

Now, we are Jews and have children whom we must establish among Jews. And we have already made ourselves such a name by our relations with Jacob Herzfeld[92] and wretched Leib [Bing] that people have on several occasions recoiled from establishing a relationship with us ... in short, one can be a good Jew and still behave properly, and this will not lessen our honour in the eyes of the Gentiles.[93]

Although the Pragers had little respect for rabbis, they appreciated the necessity of keeping up good relations with them. This was true even in the case of a deposed rabbi. The Amsterdam brothers were for some time concerned with Rabbi Zalman Meshulam Emden, who had been ousted in 1780 from his post as rabbi of the Hambro Synagogue in London, against Yehiel Prager's wish. In accordance with Yehiel's instructions, his brothers paid the rabbi the sum of £100 in the summer of that year, and Jacob Prager wrote in this connection: 'He is not worth more, but one must, of course, keep on good terms with such people for the sake of appearances.'[94]

The Pragers were frequently worried lest the younger generation, which identified itself with its Jewish surroundings to a much lesser degree than its parents, should go too far. The arguments used by the parents were always the same, namely that one must not acquire a bad reputation among Jews, never that such behaviour was culpable in itself. When Meyer Prager first came to Ostend and before he and his associates established a household of their own, he used to dine at the table of another Jew. His father Jacob explained that 'he must do this for the sake of Jews'.[95] When the young Pragers went to Philadelphia in 1783 they took along a supply of food for the whole journey, although they were usually rather lax in keeping the dietary laws. After their arrival in America they avoided Jewish society and when their uncle Yehiel heard about it he wrote to them: 'I am sorry to hear this. You know my opinions. Keep on good terms with people. You need certainly not keep company with low persons, but, for God's sake, don't avoid everyone. You must not do this.'[96]

When the plan of Leib Prager's voyage to India was first mooted, his father wrote him:

If you do go, you would have to go like a Jew. How can this be done in a manner which will seem proper to our people? If this is not arranged in such a way that Jews cannot raise objections, we shall acquire a dreadful reputation among Jews. Imagine that you had children and must marry them to Jews. Jews the world over would hold our family in utter contempt. How will you see to this?'[97]

Even if we take into account the fact that Jacob tried every argument in order to dissuade his son from going to India, it is obvious that the passage quoted reflects a sincere conviction. Leib Prager himself realized the weight of considerations of this kind. In 1792 he scolded his brother Meyer for giving a bad example to the young Pragers in London: 'I have the impression that in many respects you have shown a bad example to Mordecai and the younger children, particularly in religious matters. You know that I, too, am not superstitious, but I have always observed the main points and have given no offence to Jews . . .'.[98]

The cares of the family – both close and distant – imposed a heavy financial burden on the Pragers. They had to see to it that their adolescent children got an appropriate start in life and they had to support a considerable number of poor relations. Such problems were not, of course, peculiar to Jewish merchants, but they were probably more difficult in their case. There can certainly be no doubt that the placing of their sons was a far graver problem for Jews than for Gentiles. Many opportunities were open to the son of a Christian merchant. If he did not want to continue in his father's business, he could go into the army, the navy or the merchant marine, the civil service or the Church; he could become a lawyer or a physician. The son of a Jewish merchant, on the other hand, had almost no choice but to follow in his father's footsteps. Even the alternative course of scholarly and spiritual pursuits was closed to people like the Pragers, who had received an essentially non-religious education. Some young Jews studied law or medicine,[99] but in these callings, too, there were few opportunities for Jews, and a merchant like Jacob Prager held them in contempt.[100]

The three Prager brothers had between them about 15 sons and 10 daughters. It is obvious that there was no place in the business for all the sons, and many of them had to be provided for elsewhere, while the daughters had to be married in a manner appropriate to their parents' standing. All this cost a great amount of money and the Pragers were constantly worrying about the future of their children. On the occasion of the bar-mitzva[101] of his twin sons, David Prager told his brother: 'Dear Yehiel, We are getting, thank God, a whole regiment of big boys. Where does one find good employment for each?'[102] These worries naturally increased as the children grew to adolescence, and projects of sending them overseas were being considered. When Yehiel's eldest son, Mordecai, celebrated his bar-mitzva Jacob asked if one of the sons could be sent to India, pointing out that 'we have no employment for all'.[103] The establishment of the branch house in Ostend was, it is true, an emergency measure and not a step designed to provide employment for the family's youngsters, but it pointed to a possible solution of the problem. The successful manner in which three of the young men of Amsterdam conducted the Ostend house for a period of two years naturally encouraged the Pragers to let them continue on their own after the war, at some other place. The new political and commercial conditions made the United States the obvious choice. The Pragers' decision to establish a house in Philadelphia was mainly motivated by their desire to provide for their children's future. When Jacob first suggested the idea to Yehiel, he wrote: 'If peace does come, we really do not know how matters will stand with dear Ostend. What do you think, would it not be good, once peace has come, if we establish a house in America? Your children are also growing up. Where does one find good employment for all?'[104]

Yehiel's children were too young to take part in the establishment of the Philadelphia house, and so only Jacob's and David's sons went out to America. But Yehiel made it a condition of his support in establishing the house that some of his own sons would later be accepted as partners.[105] In March 1783 Jacob wrote to Yehiel:

> As you do everything for the well-being of your children and of ours, so we do the same, for the same reason. And this will be my care as long as I and my brother David live, and as long as God, be he blessed, gives us strength to work, certainly nothing will be left undone, God willing, and we shall certainly give you all the assistance we can.[106]

In the summer of the same year the young Pragers embarked for America. At about the same time Esther Prager gave birth to her third daughter. David congratulated his brother and his sister-

in-law (and niece), adding: 'Dear Yehiel and Esther, if it continues like this, America, too, will be too small!'[107] It is evident
that one of the reasons which impelled Yehiel Prager to send his
nephew Leib to India was, besides his ambitions in the diamond
and drug trades, to establish a foot-hold in India which would
one day enable him to send out one or more of his own children.
In fact, three of his sons were sent there after his death,[108] but by
then circumstances were not favourable and none of them was
able to establish the foundation of a commercial career in the
East.

The outlay on voyages overseas and on investments in the
business undertakings established there seriously taxed the firm's
resources, which, in any case, were never very ample.[109] Dowries
constituted an even heavier burden and they brought no immediate gain to the family's business affairs. The marrying-off of the
children was not merely a matter of parental concern, but had
the character of a business transaction. The aim was not just to
find suitable partners for the children, but to enlarge the firm's
connections and to increase its prestige. A good match would
benefit all members of the family. When Jacob Prager was
negotiating the marriage of his daughter Reiskhe to Moses
Gettingen, he told Yehiel that it would cost him £2,000 'which in
truth is beyond my capacity, but it would be good for all our
other children'.[110] When the marriage was finally agreed upon,
after two and a half years of bargaining, Jacob reported that the
dowry would amount to 18,000 gulden – 'It is very difficult for me
to pay such a sum, but what alternative have I? God will
help ...'.[111] How heavy the burden was is best shown by the fact
that, while the nominal value of Jacob's estate was approximately
100,000 gulden, only 65,000 gulden remained at the time of his
death. The rest had been paid out to his children during his lifetime.[112]

The support of poor relations was another burden which the
family and the firm had to carry. The Jewry of Western and
Central Europe had not yet attained that general prosperity which
it began to enjoy in the course of the nineteenth century. Well-to-
do merchants like the Pragers had close relations unable to maintain themselves and in need of constant help. Perhaps this was
also partly due to the fact that Jacob, David, and Yehiel Prager
were the first generation to attain the rank of major merchants and
naturally left their relations far behind. But it would seem that

the whole situation was not untypical for the Ashkenazi merchant class of that period. During a time of recurring economic crises and decreasing profits in Anglo-Dutch trade, these obligations were sharply felt. The Pragers did what they regarded as their duty, but they cannot be said to have been particularly enthusiastic about it. They often complained about their needy relatives and treated them with some roughness.

The Pragers had three or four married sisters, of whom two or three had to be supported.[113] Their brother-in-law in Offenbach went bankrupt during the economic crisis of 1763 and died at an unknown date. From that time the brothers in Amsterdam sent their sister every week 25 gulden, until she had married off her three daughters, after which they reduced the allowance to 20 gulden. In 1784 Jacob calculated that this sister had cost them 45,000 gulden (over £4,000) since 1763.[114] About a year earlier he had written to Yehiel on this subject:

> We do not understand which members of our family burden you there. All receive [assistance] from us, on your behalf too. The children of Schnitzler are entirely cared for and receive their subsistence from us, except one who is said to be there [in London] and to have taken a wife, as we hear. Moses Waag [a brother-in-law] gets ample subsistence from us. Sheinkhe in Offenbach gets f.20, German money, from us each week – equivalent to about f.21 [Dutch money] – she can amply subsist on it. Children of our sister in Berlin: there is only one Tuviah, to whom we send every New Year and Passover a gift for you and us. Perhaps you let beggars pester you. Why do it? And may be you received begging letters from those mentioned above? . . . We know they can write artful begging letters, but we have become obdurate in these matters. I do not want to dwell on this any longer and it is disgusting to think what we have to bear.[115]

Not only blood-relations required help and received it. After the death of his wife in 1785, Jacob told Yehiel that her brother had been receiving a fixed allowance from them every Purim and New Year, for the last 20 years: 'my late wife has had great burdens imposed on her by her family. The child is dead – the fatherhood is over . . . you are too good, and your charity attracts such clients. To do good is not a bad thing, but those who receive it [i.e. the charity] want to turn it into a debt.'[116]

Yehiel seems to have been more generous than his brother, who often scolded him for it. To the above-quoted letter Yehiel replied that charity should be given with good grace. Jacob agreed, but added: 'Nevertheless, one must not live like that. The better one is, the more one harms oneself'.[117] The different attitudes of the two brothers to questions of charity was not merely a matter of character and outlook. Yehiel was much richer than his brothers in Amsterdam and was better able to help the less fortunate members of the family. In 1778 Jacob Prager reckoned that out of a profit of 40,000 gulden which the firm had made during that year, about 3,000 gulden were spent on the support of poor relations[118] – an impressive proportion, especially in view of the fact that the firm's profits in that year were far above the average for that period.

All these obligations constituted a heavy burden, and there can be little doubt that many Jewish merchants laboured under similar disadvantages. They may well have contributed to their initial inability to make full use of the economic opportunities which England and Holland offered to the enterprising merchant and financier.

Abbreviations

B.M.	British Museum
CB	I.O.L., Records of the East India Company, Court Books, vols 32–88 (1680–1780)
CCM	*A Calendar of Court Minutes of the East India Company, 1635–1679*, ed. E. B. Sainsbury, with an introduction and notes by Sir William Foster and W. T. Ottewill (1907–38)
CCR	I.O.L., Records of the East India Company, Reports and Resolutions of the Correspondence Committee, vols 1–13 (1719–80)
CSP–EI	*Calendar of State Papers, Colonial Series, East Indies, China and Japan, 1513–1634*, ed. W. Noel Sainsbury (1860–92)
EcHR	*Economic History Review*
EFI	*The English Factories in India, 1618–1684*, ed. Sir William Foster and Sir Charles Fawcett (1906–55)
HAHR	*Hispano-American Historical Review*
I.O.L.	India Office Library
JHSE Misc.	*Jewish Historical Society of England, Miscellanies*
JHSE Trans.	*Jewish Historical Society of England, Transactions*
JQR	*Jewish Quarterly Review*
LRE	*Letters Received by the East India Company from its Servants in the East, 1602–1617*, ed. R. C. Danvers and W. Foster (1896–1902)
MLR	I.O.L., Records of the East India Company, Miscellaneous Letters Received, vols 1–77 (1701–85)
MMC	I.O.L., Records of the East India Company, Madras Mayor's Court – Proceedings, R.328, vols 67–109 (1732–70)
MPP	I.O.L., Records of the East India Company, Madras Public Proceedings (Consultations), R. 239, vols 86–90 (1712–29); R.240, vols 1–30 (1730–70)
PAJHS	*Publications of the American Jewish Historical Society*
P.R.O.	Public Record Office
SP/Portugal	P.R.O., State Papers – Portugal

Notes

Note Places of publication are given only for books published outside the United Kingdom.

INTRODUCTION

1. See Philo-patriae, *Further Considerations on the Act to Permit Persons Professing the Jewish Religion to be Naturalized by Parliament* (1753), 51. For the difficulties encountered by Jews who wanted to take a part in the Russian trade see *The Case of Mr Anthony da Costa with the Russian Company.*
2. Meyer Michael-David to David Prager, 12 Nissan 5533 – 5 Apr. 1773, P.R.O. C111/3.
3. *The Works of the Right Honourable Joseph Addison,* with notes by Richard Hurd (1854–6), IV, 13–14.

CHAPTER 1

1. See L. D. Barnett (ed.) *Bevis Marks Records,* II (1949).
2. See his petition of March 1728 in P.R.O. SP/Portugal 100/39.
3. See C. Roth, *A History of the Marranos* (Philadelphia, 1932), 275, 283–4. On the settlement of Spanish and Portuguese Jews in Latin America and their commercial activity there, see M. Kayserling: *Christoph Columbus und der Antheil der Juden an den spanischen und portugiesischen Entdeckungen* (Berlin, 1894), 114; C. H. Haring, *Trade and Navigation between Spain and the Indies in the Time of the Hapsburgs* (Cambridge, Mass., 1918), 105. Of special interest is A. Bab's book, *Die Juden in Amerika spanischer Zunge,* the first three chapters of which were published in *Jahrbücher für jüdische Geschichte und Literatur,* 1925–7. See also C. B. Liebman, 'The Jews of colonial Mexico', *HAHR,* XLIII (1963), 95–108. D. G. Smith has recently questioned the accepted view that Portugal's foreign trade in the seventeenth century was almost entirely in the hands of 'New Christians'. However, the subject still awaits systematic investigation. See D. G. Smith, 'Old Christian merchants and the foundation of the Brazil Company, 1649', *HAHR,* LIV (1974), 233–59.
4. See A. Wiznitzer, 'The Jews in the sugar industry of colonial Brazil', *Jewish Social Studies,* XVIII (1956), 189. See also P.R.O. C12/1002.4 for details of the activities of Moses Marcus Monforte and his London agent, Daniel de Flores.
5. V. M. Shillington and A. B. W. Chapman, *The Commercial Relations of England and Portugal* (1907), 227–8 and 248.
6. On the ascendency of the English in Portugal's trade and the importance of the Methuen Treaty see SP/Portugal 89/64, Report on Trade with Portugal, 1767; Shillington and Chapman, *op. cit.,* 224–5, 241, 248; A. Christelow, 'Great Britain and the trades from Cadiz and

Lisbon to Spanish America and Brazil 1759–1783', *HAHR*, xxvii (1947), 2ff.
7. On the changes in the character of England's commerce with Portugal and Brazil see A. K. Manchester, *British Pre-eminence in Brazil. Its Rise and Decline* (Chapel Hill, 1933).
8. C. R. Boxer, 'Brazilian gold and British traders in the first half of the eighteenth century', *HAHR*, xlix (1969), 470.
9. On the importance of the Brazilian consumers' market for Anglo-Portuguese trade, see Shillington and Chapman, *op. cit.*, 225. See also D. Defoe, *A Plan of the English Commerce* (1730 edn), App. pp. 11–12.
10. See unpublished work: 'An Essay on the Nature and Methods of Carrying on the Trade to the South Sea', B.M. Add.Mss.28140.
11. See G. de Ustaritz, *Théorie et pratique du commerce et de la marine* (Paris, 1753), 88–9.
12. The French had the biggest share in the Cadiz trade after the War of the Spanish Succession: see J. O. Maclachlan, *Trade and Peace with Old Spain, 1667–1750* (1940), 25.
13. See Defoe, *op. cit.*, 18ff. See also R. Davis, 'English foreign trade 1700–1714', *EcHR*, 2nd ser. xv (1962/3), 286–7.
14. Sailings between Spain and its colonies were less regular than those between Lisbon and Rio de Janeiro (see de Ustaritz, *op. cit.* p. 101). On the difficulties of trade through Cadiz see Maclachlan, *op. cit.*, 15–25, A. Christelow, 'Great Britain and the trades from Cadiz and Lisbon', *op. cit.*, 20.
15. See *ibid.*
16. Answers to a questionnaire, apparently by Joseph Salvador, B.M. Add.Mss.37383 fos. 130–1. The Dutch base of the contraband trade was at Curaçao.
17. See R. D. Hussey, 'Antecedents of the Spanish monopolistic overseas trading companies', *HAHR*, x (1929), 21.
18. D. Macpherson, *Annals of Commerce, Manufactures, Fisheries and Navigation* (1805), 398. On the contraband trade between Jamaica and the Spanish Main see Defoe, *A Plan of the English Commerce* (1st edn, 1728), 244. See also N. Magens, *The Universal Merchant* (1753), 68; Answers to a questionnaire, apparently by Joseph Salvador, B.M. Add.Mss.37383 fos. 130–1; L. J. Ragatz, *The Fall of the Planter Class in the British Caribbean 1763–1833* (1929), 113–14.
19. See L. S. Sutherland, *A London Merchant 1695–1774* (1933), 19–20.
20. See SP/Portugal, 89/37; P.R.O. C11/1523.21 (reply of Catherine da Costa Villa Real).
21. Magens, *op. cit.*, 67.
22. Joseph Salvador to Charles Jenkinson, M.P., 28 Jan. 1766: B.M. Add.Mss.38399 f.225.
23. D. Defoe, *The Complete English Tradesman* (4th edn, 1738), II, 134.
24. Charles Compton to the Duke of Newcastle, Lisbon: 19 May 1731, P.R.O. SP89/37.
25. The petition of Benjamin Mendes da Costa concerning this affair is in SP/Portugal 100/39, March 1727/8. On his connections with Portugal see p. 30 above.
26. For information on Joseph Villa Real and his escape from Portugal see P.R.O. C11/1523.21.

27. Lord Tyrawley to Newcastle, Lisbon, 18 May 1731 and 23 May 1732. SP/Portugal 89/37.
28. See P.R.O. C11/785.12 and C11/2293.5.
29. In his will (1743) his name is given as Miguel Vianna, or Abraham Dias, or Fernando Fernandes (see *Anglo-Jewish Notabilities, their Arms and Testamentary Dispositions*, 1949, 222). On the change of name see also Tyrawley to Newcastle, Lisbon, 21 Aug. 1732, SP/Portugal 89/37.
30. Petition of Miguel Vianna, n.d. (passed on to Tyrawley on 29 June 1732), in SP/Portugal 100/40, concerning his own and his family's persecution by the Inquisition (see also Tyrawley to Newcastle, Lisbon, 23 May 1732, SP/Portugal 89/37).
31. Tyrawley to Newcastle, Lisbon, 18 May 1731, SP/Portugal 89/37.
32. Compton to Newcastle, 12 Jan. 1732, SP/Portugal 89/37.
33. SP/Portugal 89/90, fos. 102 and 100/40.
34. Tyrawley to Newcastle, 23 May 1732, 27 June 1732, SP/Portugal 89/37.
35. The following table gives the names of several Lisbon agents of Jewish City merchants:

Merchant	Agents	Approximate period	Source (P.R.O.)
Andrew Lopes	Antonio Maria Porsile		
	Jacquaz da Costa	1705	C5/235.1
Simon Francia	Santeul	1710	C9/225.39
Isaac da Souza	Jeronimo Henriques		
Portello	de Castro	1715	C11/2726.23
Philip and John			
Mendes da Costa	Joseph Townshend	1715	C11/2364.51
Francis Salvador	John Wingfield		
	Roberts and Bristow	1720	C11/480.45
Benjamin Mendes			SP/Portugal
da Costa	Beroardi and Medici	1730	100/39
Elias de Paz	Burdett, Lockwood and		
	Hanway	1730	C12/1202.26
Gabriel Lopes			SP/Portugal
Pinheiro	Buller and Bear	1730	89/37
Duarte Rebello (Isaac)	William and John Mayne		C12/1279.2
de Mendoca	Benjamin Barons		C12/809.16
	Edward Burn	1750	C12/497.5

Five out of nine merchants had English agents. See also petition of Miguel Vianna (SP/Portugal 89/90, f. 102), stating that he consigned goods to English, Portuguese, Dutch and Hamburg houses at Lisbon.
36. P.R.O. C11/1523.21 (bill).
37. P.R.O. C12/1279.2 (reply); C12/809.16; C12/497.5.
38. Tyrawley to Newcastle, Lisbon, 26 Sept. 1732 and 23 May 1732, SP/Portugal 89/37. H. E. S. Fisher, to whom the author is indebted for several references concerning Jewish activity in Portuguese trade,

thinks that Tyrawley's description of the Jews' role was exaggerated. Lacking statistical data, it is difficult to judge whether it was and to what extent. See H. E. S. Fisher, *The Portugal Trade* (1971), 56.

39. See M. Woolf, 'Joseph Salvador, 1716–1786', *JHSE Trans.*, xxi (1962–7), 105–6.

40. See J[onas] H[anway], *Letters Admonitory and Argumentative from J.H—y, Merchant, to J.S—r, Merchant* (1753).

41. The Spaniards used to classify slaves according to slave 'units' called 'piezas de Indias', erroneously translated into English as 'pieces of Indies'. The unit represented a healthy slave, aged between 18 and 20, while women, children, older or disabled slaves were estimated as fractions of a full unit (see J. F. King, 'Evolution of the free slave trade principle in Spanish colonial administration', *HAHR*, xxii (1942), 36 n. 3). On the 1696 Assiento see G. A. Beltran, 'The slave trade in Mexico', *HAHR* xxiv (1944), 428.

42. On Lopes' commercial affairs see P.R.O. C9/467.2; C5/235.1; C5/594.182; W. S. Samuel, *Some Notes on 17th Century London Jews* (1937), 25.

43. See the contract, C9/449.39.

44. See Castres to Amyand, Lisbon, 26 June 1753, SP/Portugal 89/48.

45. Philo-patriae, *Considerations on the Bill to Permit Persons Professing the Jewish Religion to be Naturalized by Parliament* (1753), 58.

46. See MLR 28, f.135; CB 58, f.475.

47. P.R.O. C9/461.38; C9/467.2; C7/642.24; C11/2364.51.

48. See P.R.O. C11/2112.10; C11/2104.12; see also H. S. Q. Henriques, 'The Jews and the English law', *JQR*, xiv (1904), 339; Samuel, *op. cit.*, 25–6; P.R.O. C9/224.26.

49. See *JHSE Trans.*, ix (1918–20), 44–6.

50. See Philo-patriae, *Considerations*, 32.

51. There were three persons called Francis Salvador, although only two are generally known. Francis (Daniel) Salvador, mentioned here as 'junior', is normally known as Francis Salvador senior. His grandson, Francis Daniel the second, usually called 'junior', was killed in North America during the Revolution. The Francis mentioned here as 'senior' is Francis (Jacob) Salvador, apparently an uncle or a cousin of the first Francis Daniel. Francis Daniel the elder and his son Joseph were the most prominent figures in the English branch of the family.

52. Joseph Salvador of Amsterdam was father of Francis (Daniel) Salvador and grandfather of the English Joseph Salvador.

53. Francis Daniel Salvador married Rachel, the daughter of Moses Mendes da Costa.

54. Moses de Medina of London and Isaac and Solomon (Hisquiah) de Medina of Amsterdam were the sons of Joseph de Medina, also of Amsterdam. Moses de Medina married Deborah, daughter of his famous uncle, Sir Solomon de Medina.

55. P.R.O. C11/1425.28, C11/1792.60, C11/2731.159.

56. See P.R.O. C11/1701.1.2.3.

57. See 'An Account of Freight of Gold from Portugal', Cholmondeley Houghton Mss., Cambridge University Library P.89(17/2).

58. See pp. 114–16.

59. For the petition of 1732 see P.R.O., T1/278, f.228; see also pp. 114–15 above.

60. For the omission of Jewish names from petitions of Portugal merchants see a petition of 6 June 1711 in SP/Portugal 89/89 and one of 1756 in Sutherland, *op. cit.*, 136–40.
61. K. R. Maxwell, 'Pombal and the nationalization of the Luso-Brazilian economy', *HAHR*, xlviii (1968), 614.
62. P.R.O. C11/1658.11.
63. P.R.O. C12/72.23; C12/2387.21.
64. P.R.O. C12/56.51.
65. P.R.O. C11/2477.9.
66. P.R.O. C11/811.27.
67. P.R.O. C12/2206.40.
68. P.R.O. C11/1253.1. Alvaro (Jacob Israel) Lopes Suasso was the son of Francisco Lopes Suasso, Baron d'Avernas le Gras. The document includes copies of letters from the agents of Suasso in Spain, dated 1737 and 1738, with English translations.
69. P.R.O. C12/334.39.
70. P.R.O. C12/2028.24.
71. P.R.O. C12/2326.104.
72. William and John Turry were also the Cadiz agents of Moses de Medina (see P.R.O. C12/2206.40).
73. See also P.R.O. C12/1487.13.
74. Philo-patriae, *Further Considerations*, 46–7.
75. J. H[anway], *Letters Admonitory, op. cit.*, 41–2.
76. See A. Christelow, 'Contraband trade between Jamaica and the Spanish Main, and the Free Port Act of 1766', *HAHR*, xxii (1942), 309.
77. See also B.M. Add.Mss.37383, fos. 130–1.
78. P.R.O. C12/292.23.
79. For the balance of investments see P.R.O. C12/292.23 (schedule); see also App.A.
80. For the text of the petition see M. J. Kohler, 'A memorial of Jews to Parliament concerning Jewish participation in colonial trade, 1696', *PAJHS*, xviii (1909), 123.
81. See V. L. Brown, 'Contraband trade, a factor in the decline of Spain's Empire in America', *HAHR*, viii (1928), 178.
82. See E. Long, *The History of Jamaica* (1774), II, 295.
83. F. Armytage, *The Free Port System in the British West Indies* (1953), 7, and F. W. Pitman, *The Development of the British West Indies 1700–1763* (New Haven, 1917), 28–9.
84. P.R.O. CO137/9, f.79.
85. See Chancery cases, Benjamin da Costa *et al. v.* William Whitehead *et al*; see also P.R.O. C11/2526.26.
86. For the text of the petition see J. A. P. M. Andrade, *A Record of the Jews in Jamaica, from the English Conquest to the Present Time* (Kingston, 1941), 16. The names, as given by Andrade, are in many cases misspelled.
87. For some names it is impossible to say with certainty whether they are Jewish.
88. See pp. 47, 60–4 above.

CHAPTER 2

1. See Appendices D and E.
2. On Sir Solomon de Medina, see O. K. Rabinowicz, *Sir Solomon de Medina* (Jewish Historical Society of England, 1974). On the Dutch firm of Josef de Medina en Zoonen see J. G. van Dillen, 'De economische positie en betekenis der Joden in de Republiek en in de Nederlandsche koloniale wereld', *Geschiedenis der Joden in Nederland*, ed. O. Brugmans and A. Franks (Amsterdam, 1940), 585. Josef was brother to Sir Solomon and father of Moses de Medina.
3. For a detailed table showing the share of the firms of Medina and Salvador in the trade see Appendix F.
4. See pp. 145, 153
5. There are two series of account books of the East India Company: General Ledgers and General Cash Journals. The second series gives more detailed information on the sellers of silver and most of the data are taken from it.
6. CB 56, f.572 (4 Feb. 1736).
7. CB 62, f.333 (1 July 1747); I.O.L. General Cash Journals, July 1747.
8. CB 62, f.66 (2 June 1746); CB 63, f.66 (6 July 1748).
9. On Gideon's financial activities see L. S. Sutherland, 'Sampson Gideon: eighteenth century Jewish financier', *JHSE Trans.*, xvii (1951–2), 79.
10. CB 61, fos. 248, 263 (27/29 March 1745).
11. See CB 63, f.632, for a copy of Gideon's letter and of the contract which was signed by Bristow (on behalf of himself and Salvador) and by David Pratviel and Sampson Gideon (as witness).
12. I.O.L., General Cash Journals, August 1749–February 1750.
13. On the Mocatta family see L. Wolf, *Essays in Jewish History* (1934), 219 *seq.*
14. On Mocatta and Keyser's business of precious metals see P.R.O. E112/1621.1527; on Alexander Isaac Keyser see E112/1582.382.
15. CB 70, f.294; CB 71, fos. 21, 245, 275, 293; CB 72, fos. 205, 210; CB 73, fos. 158, 165, 177, 183, 194, 207, 222, 235, 244, 254, 263, 275, 288, 320, 330, 335, 340, 344, 353, 375, 421; CB 74, f.35.
16. See J. H. Clapham, *The Bank of England* (1944), 136.
17. J. Addison, *The Works of the Right Honourable Joseph Addison* (1854–6), iv, 13–14.
18. See N. Magens, *The Universal Merchant* (1753), 42.
19. See Philo-patriae, *Further Considerations on the Act to Permit Persons Professing the Jewish Religion to be Naturalized by Parliament* (1753), 50–1.
20. See Jacob Prager to Yehiel Prager, Amsterdam, 16 Dec. 1783, 18 May 1784.
21. See Philo-patriae, *Further Considerations*, 48.
22. *Ibid.*, 49.
23. For further information on some of these activities see P.R.O. C11/669.4, E112/1660.2690 and the Prager letters.
24. See L. D. Barnett (ed.), *Bevis Marks Records* i (1940), 21–2.
25. On the supply of bills drawn on Madrid by Joseph Pereira and his Ashkenazi partner Benjamin Levy see P.R.O. C9/174.39. On their connections with Amsterdam see C9/193.9. On Francis de Caseris'

activity as exchange broker on the Royal Exchange see C9/224.31. On the activities of Moses de Medina see C12/2206.40.

26. See pp. 265–6 above.
27. Meyer Michael-David to Yehiel Prager, Hamburg, 6 Tamuz 5526 (13 June 1766), P.R.O. C111/10.
28. See pp. 249–52 above.
29. See, for example, letters to Yehiel Prager from Jacob and David Prager of 7 Sept. 1781, 16 Oct. 1781, 16 Apr. 1782, and 1 Aug. 1783.
30. See p. 195 above. For a detailed investigation of the business activities of the house of Hope, see M. G. Buist *At Spes Non Fracta: Hope & Co. 1770–1815* (The Hague, 1974).

CHAPTER 3

1. The point of view of the plantation owners was put in a memorandum of the Council for Foreign Plantations, submitted to the Crown in July 1661, after a request by three Jews for permission to settle and trade in Barbados had been referred to the Council: P.R.O. C.O. 1, 15, No. 75.
2. Sir William Davidson, the English agent at Amsterdam, reported in 1668 that there was an English ship at Amsterdam 'fully laden for the account of the Jews of Amsterdam for the Barbados': P.R.O. C.O. 1, 23, No. 99.
3. See C. Roth, *A History of the Marranos* (Philadelphia, 1932), 288–9; M. Kayserling, 'The Jews in Jamaica and Daniel Israel Lopez Laguna', *JQR*, xii (1900), 712.
4. See pp. 45–9 above.
5. For the text of the petition see M. J. Kohler, 'A memorial of Jews to Parliament concerning Jewish participation in colonial trade, 1696', *PAJHS*, xviii (1909), 123.
6. For the text of the petition see H. S. Q. Henriques, 'Proposals for special taxation of the Jews after the Revolution', *JHSE Trans.*, ix (1918–20), 44–6.
7. For the text of the petition see J. A. P. M. Andrade, *A Record of the Jews in Jamaica, from the English Conquest to the Present Time* (Kingston, 1941), 16.
8. See Philo-patriae, *Further Considerations on the Act to Permit Persons Professing the Jewish Religion to be Naturalized by Parliament* (1753), 49–50.
9. For England's trade with the West Indies, see R. Pares, *A West-India Fortune* (1950); *idem*, *War and Trade in the West Indies 1739–1763* (1936); F. W. Pitman, *The Development of the British West Indies, 1700–1763*; L. J. Ragatz, *The Fall of the Planter Class in the British Caribbean 1763–1833* (New York, 1929).
10. See Ragatz, *op. cit.*, 101.
11. See Pitman, *op. cit.*, 28–9. On London's supremacy in the sugar trade, see E. Merritt, 'The triangular trade', *Business History*, iii (1960), 1–7.
12. See N. D. Davis, 'Notes on the History of the Jews in Barbados', *Publications of the American Jewish Historical Society*, xviii, 129.
13. In a personal letter to Sir Lewis Namier (11 Nov. 1957), Professor Pares

wrote: 'I have racked my brains to discover what I know about Jewish merchants trading with the West Indies. I believe it amounts to uncommonly little.'

14. The P.R.O. has the private papers of Nathan Samson for the period 1700–20. Samson was a Jewish merchant of New York who had connections in England, and later settled in London. Most letters are written in Yiddish (C104/13–14). See also:

C11/2002.1, concerning the business of Moses Alvares of London, who was closely connected as agent and partner with Isaac and William Kops of Amsterdam. They traded mainly with Jamaica and also had business connections in New York. Their agent there was Isaac Gomes.

C11/462.35, concerning the business of Joseph Lopes of London. In 1717 Lopes sent a shipload of goods to Boston, where his agent, Isaac Lopes, supplied the ship with a cargo of fish and staves for Spain. This journey was typical for an important branch of Anglo-Spanish trade.

C11/1770.27 contains information on Isaac Miranda's three-cornered trade between London, New York and the West Indies (1718–21).

C11/2238.41 shows Abraham Dias Fernandes' connections with New York. His agents there were Lewis and Mordecai Gomes.

E112/1213.2521 contains information on the partnership between Isaac Levy of London and Nathan Levy and David Franks of Philadelphia.

E112/1613.1247 is about Mordecai and Levy Sheftall of Savannah, Georgia. In 1766 they sought connections in London. On the Sheftalls see D. T. Morgan, 'The Sheftalls of Savanah', *Jewish Historical Quarterly*, LXII (1972/3), 348–61.

C12/1519.16 (1772) concerns the partnership of Aaron and Uriah Hendricks. 'Uriel Hendricks – living or residing for many years before the death of his said late father, Aaron Hendricks, at New York in America, and his late father being concerned in a very extensive way in trade in England, had frequent occasion to correspond with his said son in that way, and in the course of such correspondence the said Aaron Hendricks sent and consigned . . . to his said son various goods, wares and merchandizes to a very considerable amount, in consequence of orders given by him for that purpose, and the said Aaron Hendricks likewise sent . . . to his said son various other goods . . . to be disposed by him abroad as factor or as agent.'

E112/1708.3919 concerns Chaim Levy of London and his connections with Rhode Island, where his father Benjamin and his uncle were established as merchants.

15. See D. Macpherson, *Annals of Commerce, Manufactures, Fisheries, and Navigation* (1805), 581; E. R. Johnson *et al.* (eds), *History of the Domestic and Foreign Commerce of the United States* (Washington, 1815), 74, 120–1. See there table of exports by the Thirteen Colonies, showing the prominence of the tobacco colonies, Virginia and Maryland.

16. See K. Sullivan, Maryland and France, 1774–1789 (Philadelphia, 1936), 2–3; T. J. Wertenbaker, *The Planters of Colonial Virginia* (Princeton, 1922), 122; L. Hühner, 'The Jews of Virginia from the earliest times to the close of the eighteenth century', *PAJHS*, XX (1911), 85.

17. See Hühner, *op. cit.*, 85. J. R. Marcus, who has recently published the

results of his very extensive research into the economic activities of American Jews in that period, reached identical conclusions: see J. R. Marcus, *The Colonial American Jew 1492–1776* (Detroit, 1970), II, 641.

18. On the Franks family see C. Roth, *The Great Synagogue, 1690–1940* (1950), 61–3; *idem, The Rise of Provincial Jewry* (1950), 16; E. N. Adler, *London* (Philadelphia, 1930), 119. See also P.R.O. C11/1755.28 and *Letters of the Franks Family, 1733–1748,* ed. L. Hershkowitz and I. S. Meyer (Studies in American Jewish History, No. 5, American Jewish Historical Society, 1968). Aaron Franks was also the foremost Jewish ship-owner of his time: see M. Woolf, 'Eighteenth-century London Jewish shipowners', *JHSE Misc.*, ix (1974), 199.
19. P.R.O. C11/2716.8. This document gives in full the sailing instructions issued by Sampson Levy.
20. P.R.O. E112/1592.636, C12/33.30. Moses Franks and his partners obtained loans to finance their business, on the security of Government paper, with the help of the broker David Salomons, Moses Franks' cousin.
21. P.R.O. C12/597.20.

CHAPTER 4

1. CB 34, f.18 (27 Aug. 1684).
2. CB 36, f.277 (17 Jan. 1695).
3. Francis Chamberlayne to Robert Nightingale, London, 10 Apr. 1707; P.R.O. C108/203.
4. CB 45, f.281 (16 Jan. 1713). The contention that England had been a centre of the diamond trade for 70 years is not accurate. In this respect the petition of 1695 came nearer the truth by stating that the private diamond trade had been legalized 40 years earlier, and that since then it had become an English trade. The greater historical accuracy of this petition can perhaps be explained by the fact that some of the pioneers of the English diamond trade were still living when it was submitted.
5. P.R.O. T1/278, f.228.
6. CB 46, f.380 (22 June 1715).
7. 6 George II, C.7.
8. We have seen that already in the 1670s Dutch diamond merchants imported Indian stones through London. Another example of this practice dates from 1700; in February of that year Francisco Pereira of London presented to the East India Company a certificate signed by Redrigo Alvares Pinto and five other (unnamed) merchants of Amsterdam, empowering him to receive from the Company diamonds which had arrived for them from India (CB 38, f.113, 27 Feb. 1700).

Although Holland continued to import diamonds directly from India throughout the eighteenth century, there can be no doubt that the great majority of Indian stones cut in Holland were imported through London. This is clearly shown for the last quarter of the century by the Prager Papers. Figures relating to diamond sales by the Dutch East India Company between 1775 and 1779 show that at that time the Company's diamond trade was of no significance: only in one of these years were more than 1,000 carats sold, and in 1779 the total amounted to 41 carats only: *Encyclopedie Méthodique* – Commerce (Paris–Liège, 1783–9), 'Holland' vol. 2, 594; K. Glamann, *Dutch–Asiatic Trade, 1620–1740* (Copenhagen, 1958), 18.

    The discovery of diamonds in Brazil to some extent made Amsterdam independent of the English source, but London also became an important distribution centre for Brazilian stones.

9. See H. Heertje, *De diamantbewerkers van Amsterdam* (Amsterdam, 1936), 24–5; J. G. van Dillen, 'De economische positie en betekenis der Joden in de Republiek en in de Nederlandsche koloniale wereld', in O. Brugmans and A. Franks, *Geschiedenis der Joden in Nederland* (Amsterdam, 1940), 574–5; H. I. Bloom, *The Economic Activities of the Jews of Amsterdam* (Williamsport, 1937), 40 *seq*. The Prager Papers, too, demonstrate the importance of the Jews in the Amsterdam diamond industry.

10. D. Jeffries, *Treatise on Diamonds and Pearls* (2nd edn, 1751), 152. Although '¾' should not be accepted literally, there can be no doubt about London's importance as a market for polished diamonds. This is clearly seen in Yehiel Prager's correspondence with Jewish jewellery merchants in London during the 1760s.

    In 1746 the diamond merchants Levy and Ruben Salomons testified: 'That Salomon Norden and Company, merchants at Amsterdam, have frequently employed these defendants as their agents in London to sell and dispose of diamonds and other jewels for them.' P.R.O. C11/2713.2 (1746).

11. CB 34, f.19 (27 Aug. 1684).
CB 35, f.34 (7 Sept. 1684).
CB 45, f.285 (21 Jan. 1713).

12. Letters of G. Ongarety to Sir Stephen Evance, P.R.O. C111/50; Thomas Pitt to Robert de Beauvoir, Fort St George, 23 Jan. 1703, B.M. Add.Mss.22847, f.12. See also Jeffries, *op. cit.*, 70.

13. CB 34, f.74 (10 Dec. 1684).

14. Public Dispatches from England, vol. 5 – 2.7.1684, quoted in H. D. Love, *Vestiges of Old Madras, 1640–1800* (1913), I, 485–6.

15. *Ibid., ibid.* These interlopers most probably were connected with the smuggling trade carried on by Jews when the diamond trade was monopolized by the Company (see pp. 69–70 above).

16. On the first Jewish merchants in Madras see pp. 154–6 above.

17. H. S. Q. Henriques, 'Proposals for special taxation of the Jews after the Revolution', *JHSE Trans.*, IX (1918–20), 45.

18. The Dutch-Jewish diamond merchant Isaac Abendana did business at Masulipatam under the protection of the New East India Company: see pp. 155–6 above.

19. Thomas Wooley to Thomas Pitt, London, 10 Mar. 1702. B.M. Add.Mss.22852, f.155.

20. MLR 48, f.183.

21. See P.R.O. C12/259.9, C12/1454.106, C11/1481.18. In C12/259.9 there is a copy of a bond given by Rowland Aynsworth, of the *Sussex*, to Sampson Gideon, for a bottomry loan of £2,000 which he received in 1736. C12/1454.106 gives the contents of a similar bond received by Aaron Franks in 1745.

22. The statement frequently made that Joseph Salvador was a Director is

wrong. On Salvador's activity as one of the leaders of the Clive
Faction see L. S. Sutherland, *The East India Company in Eighteenth
Century Politics* (1952), 118.

23. See K. Glamann, *Dutch-Asiatic Trade, 1620–1740* (Copenhagen, 1958), 132 *seq.*
24. See *ibid.*, 212 *seq.*; A. Aspinall, *Cornwallis in Bengal* (1931), 183.
25. *CCM, 1677–9* (26 Sept. 1679).
26. CB 83, f.44 (May 1774) and CB 87, f.580 (17 Mar. 1779).
27. See, for instance, MLR 24, f.85 (5 Sept. 1733).
28. Jacob Prager to Yehiel Prager, Amsterdam, 20 Aug. 1776.
29. I.O.L., Home Miscellaneous, vol. 14, Sale List 1721/22.
30. Jacob Prager to Yehiel Prager, Amsterdam, 14 May 1779.
31. Jacob Prager to Yehiel Prager, Amsterdam, 27 Jan. 1784.
32. Jacob Prager to Yehiel Prager, Amsterdam, 10 Feb. 1784.
33. Jacob Prager to Yehiel Prager, Amsterdam, 13 Feb. 1784.
34. Jacob Prager to Yehiel Prager, Amsterdam, 4 Jan. 1785.
35. Isaac Prager to Esther Prager, Amsterdam, 10 Dec. 1793.
36. P.R.O. C12/589.1; C12/579.19.
37. P.R.O. C12/579.19; C12/589.1.
38. *Ibid.*
39. The following are the names of the Jewish buyers who attended the secondary sale which took place on 25 June 1778 at Mile End, and the value of goods bought by each:

> Simon Daniels, £10,825
> Levy Barent Cohen, £3,455
> H. A. Cohen, £886
> Cosman, £578
> J. Moses, £539
> L. Salomons, £463
> J. M. Moses, £443
> A. Hart, £363
> Barnet, £213
> Spier, £212
> Emanuel, £159
> N. Moses, £122
>
> Total purchases by Jewish buyers, £18,258
> Total purchases by non-Jewish buyers, £5,827
> Total value of goods sold, £24,085

40. Jacob Prager to Yehiel Prager, Amsterdam, 23 June 1778.
41. Jacob Prager to Yehiel Prager, Amsterdam, 5 Mar. 1784.
42. David Prager to Yehiel Prager, Amsterdam, 3 Oct. 1787.
43. Jacob Prager to Yehiel Prager, Amsterdam, 1 Jan. 1782.
44. Jacob Prager to Yehiel Prager, Amsterdam, 5 Feb. 1782.
45. Jacob Prager to Yehiel Prager, Amsterdam, 4 June 1782.
46. Jacob Prager to Yehiel Prager, Amsterdam, 25 Oct. 1782.
47. Jacob Prager to Yehiel Prager, Amsterdam, 25 Mar. 1783.
48. That is, if he could not sell the goods before payment was due to the East India Company.
49. Jacob Prager to Yehiel Prager, Amsterdam, 27 Apr. 1784.
50. MLR 29, f.32.
51. MLR 64, f.133.

CHAPTER 5

1. According to MacCarthy, the mining of diamonds in India started between 600 A.D. and 800 A.D.: J. R. MacCarthy, *Fire in the Earth* (New York and London, 1942), 21.
2. M. H. Bauer, *Edelsteinkunde* (Leipzig, 1896), 179. For a description of Indian diamond production and trade see G. Lenzen, *The History of Diamond Production and the Diamond Trade* (1970), 31–41.
3. Lenzen, *op. cit.*, 102–10; H. Heertje, *De diamantbewerkers van Amsterdam* (Amsterdam, 1936), 13.
4. *Ibid.*, 17.
5. J. B. Tavernier, *Travels in India* (2nd edn, 1925), II, 95.
6. *CSP – EI, 1513–1616*, 370.
7. *EFI, 1622–23*, 221. See also T. I. Poonen, 'Early history of the Dutch factories of Masulipatam and Petapoli, 1605–1636', *Journal of Indian History*, xxvii (1949), 271–2, and K. Glamann, *Dutch-Asiatic Trade 1620–1740* (Copenhagen, 1958), 18.
8. Glamann, *op. cit.*, 12, 25.
9. *First Letter Book of the East India Company 1600–1619*, 299.
10. *CCM, 1651–54*, 59.
11. *EFI, 1655–60*, 362. (Ambergris was used for the making of perfumes, and cuff was apparently a sort of uncut diamond.)
12. The resolution of the Court of Directors of 1664, *CCM, 1664–67*, 18.
13. In a report written in 1674 it was stated that permission had been granted to all persons to trade to India in precious stones etc.: 'The Company not finding it convenient for itself to trade in diamonds, bezoar stones, amber greece, musk, pearl and other fine goods.' *CCM, 1674–76*, 134.
14. Cf. A. Scott and L. Atkinson, *A Short History of Diamond Cutting* (1888), 11.
15. *CCM, 1660–63*, 223.
16. *Ibid.*, 225.
17. See C. Roth, 'The Resettlement of the Jews in England', in *Three Centuries of Anglo-Jewish History*, ed. V. D. Lipman (Jewish Historical Society of England, 1961), 7, 8; E. R. Samuel, 'The first fifty years', *ibid.*, 31–2, 35; *Letters of Denization and Acts of Naturalization for Aliens in England and Ireland*, I (1661) (Publications of the Huguenot Society of London, XVIII, XXVII, XXV).
18. Fernando Mendes and Alvaro da Costa to Sir George Oxenden, 25 Mar. 1668: B.M. Add.Mss.40701, f.92.
19. Heertje (*op. cit.*) pointed out that in Spain and Portugal Jews had frequently dealt in precious stones, and that they maintained their connections with their relatives in India after settling in Holland (p. 17). Fischel found evidence for the existence of a sizeable Jewish community in Goa from the second half of the sixteenth century, quoting Mandelslo (1639): 'having their temples and synagogues and for the most part speak the Spanish tongue.' – W. J. Fischel, 'Leading Jews in the service of Portuguese India', *J.Q.R.*, N.S. XLVII.
20. The names of the merchants were: Alvaro da Costa, Fernandes Mendes, George and Domingo Rodrigues Francia, Manuel Martinez Dormido, Francis de Lis, Duarte and Francisco da Silva, Manuel and Gabriel da

Fonseca, Jacob Abas, Gomes Ruiz, Salvador Andrade. – B.M. Add.Mss.40699, f.49.

21. L. Wolf, 'The Jewry of the Restoration, 1660–1664', *JHSE Trans.*, v (1902–5), 19.

22. Samuel da Vega, who had accounts at Backwell's, died in the Great Plague of 1665. I could not establish the date of death of Isaac d'Azevedo who is also listed by Wolf, but was not a correspondent of Oxenden.

23. Barnardiston was a Director from 1661 and Deputy Chairman from 1668 to 1670.

24. Barnardiston to Oxenden, London, 6 Mar. 1666. B.M. Add.Mss.40700, f.102.

25. *CCM, 1664–67*, 301.

26. *CCM, 1671–73*, 59.

27. 'Signor Alvaro da Costa pruduces an attested copy of an Act of Parliament for his Naturalisation, and is admitted to the freedom of the Company by redemption.' (From the Court Minutes 5 Aug. 1668, *CCM, 1668–70*, p. 82.) At that time new members still had to take a special oath: see CB 32, f.18. Naturalization by Act of Parliament was later no longer possible for Jews.

28. *CCM, 1674–76*, 244, 251; *CCM, 1677–79*, 31, 202–4.

29. *CCM, 1674–76*, 140.

30. *EFI (Western Presidency), 1670–77*, 111.

31. L. Wolf: *Essays in Jewish History* (1934), 112–13.

32. *CCM, 1671–73*, 246.

33. Reeves 113. The will is mentioned by Wolf. I have not seen the original, but a copy given to me by Mr Edgar Samuel.

34. Marques asked that the sum be remitted to Machado in Spanish coins through Surat.

35. *CCM, 1677–79*, 17.

36. *Ibid.*, 282, 287.

37. CB 33, f.225 (22 Feb. 1684).

38. See pp. 141–2 above on the English diamond industry. It is improbable that the English industry was ever able to cut and polish more than a fraction of the uncut stones arriving from India. By the middle of the seventeenth century Amsterdam was the chief centre of the industry (see Heertje, *op. cit.*).

39. Tapan Raychaudhuri, *Jan Company in Coromandel* (The Hague, 1962), 173.

40. Barnardiston to Oxenden, London, 6 Mar. 1666. B.M. Add.Mss.40700, f.102.

41. *CCM, 1677–79*, 210.

42. Resolution of the Court of Directors, 26 Oct. 1677, *CCM, 1677–79*, 101.

43. *Ibid.*, 220. The Committee of Private Trade was asked to compare the figures of exports and imports. It is not clear whether regular checks of this kind were instituted in this period, though later they became a matter of routine.

44. M. Lowenthal, *The Memoirs of Glückel of Hameln* (New York, 1932), 33–4.

45. *CCM, 1677–79*, 300.

46. *CCM, 1677–79*, 234.

47. CB 32, f.13 (30 June 1680).
48. CB 32, fos. 61–2 (22 Oct. 1680).
49. CB 32, f.16 (9 July 1680).
50. CB 32, f.32 (15 Sept. 1680).
51. *EFI (Coast and Bay), 1678–84* – Dispatch of 5 Jan. 1681.
52. Sir Josiah Child, *A New Discourse of Trade* (1698), 5.
53. On Child and Barnardiston see T. B. Macaulay, *History of England*, ed. C. H. Firth (1913–15), V, 2099–100. Child's chief opponents were the Whigs Barnardiston and Thomas Papillon.
54. Quoted by W. J. Fischel in 'The Jewish merchant colony in Madras', *Journal of the Economic and Social History of the Orient*, III (1960), 91.
55. *EFI (Bombay, Surat and Malabar), 1678–84*, 273 (letter of 15 March 1681).
56. CB 32, f.219 (29 Mar. 1682).
57. The name of the ship is omitted in the minutes.
58. CB 33, f.29 (30 Aug. 1682).

CHAPTER 6

1. CB 33, f.29 (30 Aug. 1682).
2. *Ibid.*
3. CB 33, f.37 (13 June 1682).
4. CB 33, f.208 (12 Dec. 1683).
5. CB 34, fos. 18–19 (27 Aug. 1684).
6. CB 35, f.34 (17 Sept. 1687).
7. See chiefly CB 35, f.34 (7 Sept. 1687).
8. See T. B. Macaulay, *History of England*, ed. C. H. Firth (1913–15), V. 3277–8.
9. On Herne see 'Sir Francis Child' in *Dictionary of National Biography*, and R. D. Richards, *Early History of Banking in England* (1929), 130, 178.
10. About this group see pp. 99–101 above. Besides Herne it included Sir Stephen Evance, Sir Francis Child, and Sir Richard Hoare.
11. CB 36, f.277 (17 Jan. 1695).
12. CB 37, f.141 (5 Jan. 1697).
13. CB 37, fos. 224, 253 (10 Dec. 1697, 25 May 1698). CB 38, f.268 (1 Apr. 1698).
14. The Directors expressed their gratitude to the Committee which had conducted the negotiations relating to the diamond trade and secured the permission for renewal of the private trade 'for their great pains and trouble in this affair': CB 38, f.268 (1 Apr. 1698).
15. Goa, 15 Nov. 1701, P.R.O. C111/50 (original translation from Portuguese).
16. 9 and 10 William III, C. 44.
17. CB 43, f.779 (11 Nov. 1709).
18. CB 45, fos. 281–2 (16 Jan. 1713).
19. Thomas Pitt to Sir Thomas Cooke, Fort St George, 18 Oct. 1701: B.M. Add.Mss.22844, f.22.
20. Thomas Pitt to Alvaro da Fonseca, Fort St George, 17 Oct. 1701: B.M. Add.Mss.22844, f.13.

21. Thomas Pitt to Sir Stephen Evance, Fort St George, 19 Oct. 1701: B.M. Add.Mss.22844, f.9.
22. Sir Stephen Evance to Thomas Pitt, London, 12 Jan. 1704, P.R.O. C110/28.
23. CB 42, f.80 (7 Dec. 1705).
24. The figures here given were calculated from Customs accounts by Bal Krishna. The account books of the Company do not give reliable data before 1713. However, the accuracy of the figures given by Bal Krishna is also somewhat doubtful, as they do not tally with the data extracted from the Company's books for the period following 1713: Bal Krishna, *Commercial Relations between India and England, 1601–1757* (1924), 312.
25. It is of course impossible to make conjectures about the volume of illegal trade. We have, however, reason to believe that it was particularly extensive during the first decade of the eighteenth century.
26. CB 43, f.766 (4 Nov. 1709). I have not been able to trace the text of the proposal. It is mentioned in the Court minutes, according to which it was signed 'by Sir Stephen Evance, Mr. Bradyll and four others'.
27. CB 43, fos. 779–80 (11 Nov. 1709). It is not clear whether the original proposal suggested the lifting of all limitations on the private coral trade; presumably it did.
28. CB 47, fos. 300–1 (8 Mar. 1717).
29. The petition was signed by John Mendes da Costa, Francis Salvador, Aaron Pacheco, Jeosuah Gomez Serra, Henry Merttins, James Lewis Borchere, Alvaro da Fonseca, Roger Bradyll, Anthony da Costa Jr, Samuel Lock and Jacob Fernandes Nunes: CB 45, fos. 281–2 (16 Jan. 1713).
30. The duties at that time were as follows:
    Exports: For rough coral and amber, 4 per cent; for coral beads, pearls, emeralds and other precious stones, 2 per cent.
    Imports: Diamonds, 7 per cent (this apparently included the 1 per cent customs duty). See CB 41, f.101 (24 Feb. 1703), CB 43, fos. 779–780 (11 Nov. 1709), CB 45, fos. 281–3 (16 Jan. 1713). (In addition the chief of the factory, where the diamonds were bought, had a right to 2½ per cent of their value in his capacity as compulsory agent. The other (and usually real) agent received another 2½ per cent. These payments, however, were in the nature of agents' commission and not duties: 5 per cent was the commission rate paid on diamond transactions in India.)
31. CB 45, f.266 (2 Jan. 1713).
32. CB 45, f.279 (16 Jan. 1713).
33. CB 45, f.281 (16 Jan. 1713).
34. This was either Anthony or John Mendes da Costa.
35. The important regulations were: a) consignments sent for the purchase of diamonds must be addressed to the Governor at Fort St George and to a second person to be chosen by the exporter. The Governor has a right to half the commission. b) Ship captains to receive ¼ per cent of the value of diamonds imported and of silver exported in their ships. c) Ship owners to receive ¼ per cent of the value of diamonds imported in their ships. d) The importers to pay custom duties and, in addition, a 5 per cent duty to the Company. e) The duties on coral exports etc.,

as fixed in 1705, to remain in force. f) The duty on silver exports to be abolished. – CB 45, f.285 (21 Jan. 1713), CB 45, f.292 (28 Jan. 1713).
36. CB 45, f.314 (18 Feb. 1713).
37. CB 46, fos. 380–1 (22 June 1715).
38. Marcus Moses and Isaac Franks.
39. Another regulation passed at the time made it obligatory to include in all consignments for the purchase of diamonds 10 per cent in English products (CB 47, f.244, 9 Jan. 1717). This rule was never consistently enforced, perhaps because it was feared that a strict enforcement would harm the Company's own exports. In 1717 Alvaro da Fonseca was allowed to export glass in fulfilment of this obligation, but a similar request by Roger Bradyll and Joseph da Silva in the following year was rejected, as was Isaac Franks' application for licence to export £300 worth of tin to India with Haim Moses and Nathan Goldschmid, 'having obliged me to send out ye said 10% in the product of England'. (The original application has been preserved.)
   In 1721 the Court of Directors empowered the Treasury Committee to relax the enforcement of the 10 per cent rule as it saw fit, but a year later it instructed the Shipping Committee to insist on adherence to it. It seems that thereafter the rule fell into abeyance. See CB 47, fos. 244, 284; CB 48, fos. 177, 217; CB 49, f.52; CB 50, f.181; MLR 10/51.
40. See P. Masson, *Les compagnies du corail* (Paris, Marseille, 1908); *idem*, *Histoire des éstablissements et du commerce français dans l'Afrique Barbaresque 1560–1793* (Paris, 1903), 504–22; and E. W. Streeter, *Precious Stones and Gems, their History and Distinguishing Characteristics* (1877), 255–6.
41. William Biddulph to the East India Company, Surat, 28 Oct. 1613, *LRE*, I, 301.
42. Leib Prager to Yehiel Prager, Calcutta, 3 Dec. 1788, P.R.O. C111/6.
43. Streeter, *op. cit.*, 256.
44. *EFI, 1618–21*, 259; *ibid., 1661–64*, 390.
45. John Brown to the East India Company, 10 Feb. 1618. *EFI, 1618–21*, 10.
46. A report sent from Goa in December 1644 said: 'Had your Corall come with this shipping, it had produced good proffitt; nor can it faile whensoever it arrives in these parts. So great a quantity cannot be produced in Europe yearly as would vend here.' *EFI, 1642–45*, 226–7.
47. See also *CSP-EI, 1617–21*, 471, where Marseilles is mentioned as the chief coral market. But Leghorn's importance was growing, and in 1626 the Court of Directors debated whether the coral of Marseilles or that of Leghorn was of better quality.
48. De Castro was also buying coral from Neapolitan sellers: P.R.O. C12/2150.1 (1781), reply; *ibid.*, schedule, Abraham de Castro to Mark Gregory, Leghorn, 22 Oct. 1779.
49. The Company's agent John Brown wrote in 1621 from Patna, concerning the sale of amber: 'Yt ys not a commodity which yields ready money . . . a commodity that will not sell on any great quantity, but in small parcells . . . so a small quantity will furnish a great many of these merchants.' *EFI, 1618–21*, 259.
50. *LRE*, I, 33, 307.
51. Between 1620 and 1640 the East India Company used to order its

coral from a Florentine firm, but in 1640 the commission was transferred to Job Throgmorton at Leghorn, and until the end of the century the Company bought the coral from English agents at that town. See *CCM, 1640–43*, 55.

52. *CSP–EI, 1621–24*, 539; *CSP–EI, 1630–34*, 283, 562; *CCM, 1635–39*, 101. In his youth Thomas Mun lived for many years in Italy and was active in business there.
53. *CCM, 1640–43*, 72, 83, 110, 140.
54. *EFI, 1642–45*, 178; *ibid., 1651–54*, 84.
55. *EFI, 1642–45*, 230–1; *ibid., 1646–50*, 36, 84, 186, 196; *ibid., 1651–54*, 41–2, 57.
56. *EFI, 1618–21*, 13, 32, 326; *ibid., 1624–29*, 55; *ibid., 1646–50*, 36.
57. *EFI, 1618–21*, 13, 249; *ibid., 1622–23*, 307.
58. *CCM, 1655–59*, 49; *EFI, 1661–64*, 33.
59. *EFI, 1634–36*, 24, 227.
60. *EFI, 1661–64*, 33.
61. i.e. between £15,000 and £20,000.
62. *EFI, 1661–64*, 387.
    CSP–EI, 1621–24, 531.
    EFI, 1642–45, 67, 193; *ibid., 1646–50*, 163–4; *ibid., 1651–54*, 220.
63. *CCM, 1660–63*, 214, 235, 319–20, 342, 350–4; *ibid., 1664–67*, 2, 165; *ibid., 1668–70*, 61, 66, 126, 347; *ibid., 1674–76*, 308–9.
64. *EFI, 1661–64*, 193.
65. *EFI, 1668–69*, 276.
66. *CCM, 1668–70*, 34, 162.
67. *CCM, 1671–73*, 14, 112, 198.
68. *CCM, 1674–76*, 157. Licence and transportation fees were 1 per cent of the value for stockholders, 2 per cent for others.
69. When the private trade in diamonds and some other specified goods was permitted again in 1682, coral beads were not included.
70. CB 34, f.79 (21 Jan. 1685).
71. *Ibid.*
72. CB 34, f.171 (23 Nov. 1688).
73. CB 43, fos. 779–80 (11 Nov. 1709). Borneo remained a secondary source for diamonds throughout the eighteenth century. 'Bezoar-stone' was found in the stomach of a number of animals, especially wild goats. It was believed to possess antitoxic qualities. These 'goods' had no real importance in the trade.
74. I.O.L. General Cash Journals.

CHAPTER 7

1. The Borneo diamonds did not have a tangible effect on the European market in the eighteenth century, so that India had a virtual monopoly in the branch till 1730.
2. J. Mawe, *A Treatise on Diamonds and Precious Stones* (2nd edn, 1823), 3; see also J. P. Calogeras, *A History of Brazil*, trans. and ed. P. A. Martin (Chapel Hill, 1939), 38.
3. 1728 is usually given as the first year of Brazilian diamond exports. It seems, however, that the first large consignment did not reach

Portugal before 1729. In the business correspondence which I have
seen Brazilian diamonds are mentioned for the first time in January
1730. In November 1730 Sir James Tobin wrote that a *second*
consignment of diamonds had arrived from Brazil (Sir James Tobin to
John Roach, 27 Nov. 1730, P.R.O. C108/95).
4. D. Jeffries, *Treatise on Diamonds and Pearls* (2nd edn, 1751), 66.
5. Sir James Tobin to John Roach, London, 28 Jan. 1730, 10 Feb. 1730,
27 Nov. 1730, 3 Dec. 1731, 4 Feb. 1732: P.R.O. C108/95.
6. Compton had no way of correctly estimating the value of diamonds
imported from Brazil, and he himself tells of rumours that they
exceeded £1 million. Probably even Compton's estimate was
exaggerated, but mere belief in such figures had a disastrous effect on
the trade.
7. Compton to Newcastle, Lisbon, 18 Apr. 1733, SP/Portugal, 89/37.
8. John Roach to Sir James Tobin, Fort St George, 11 Dec. 1730,
P.R.O. C108/95.
9. John Roach to Sir James Tobin, Fort St George, 29 Aug. 1732,
P.R.O. C108/95. John Roach to Aaron Franks, Fort St George,
29 Aug. 1732, P.R.O. C108/95.
10. Jeffries, *op. cit.*, 78.
11. MMC R.328/67, f.148.
12. See General Cash Journals 1730–40.
13. Tyrawley to Newcastle, Lisbon, 2 May 1732, SP/Portugal, 89/37.
For Pombal's estimate that the major part of capital produced by the
Brazilian gold and diamond mines passed to Great Britain see
K. R. Maxwell, 'Pombal and the nationalization of the Luso–
Brazilian economy', *HAHR*, xlviii (1968), 610.
14. It is not certain whether figures of diamond imports from India were
published regularly. If so, this would have tended to worsen the
unstable market condition caused by the Brazilian discovery.
15. T 1/278, f.228.
16. Tyrawley to Newcastle, Lisbon, SP/Portugal, 89/37.
17. Both Tyrawley and Compton stressed the importance of the English
diamond industry which, according to Jeffries, writing 20 years later,
had almost ceased to exist.
18. Compton to Newcastle, Lisbon, 12 Jan. 1732, SP/Portugal, 89/37.
19. CSP/*Calendar of Treasury Books and Papers 1731–34*, 233, 284.
20. 6 George II, C.7.
21. See registration of licences in Court Books.
22. CB 54, f.201 (31 Dec. 1730); f.209 (13 Jan. 1731); f.412 (29 Sept. 1731);
f.462 (24 Nov. 1731); CCR 2 (12 Jan. 1731).
23. CB 57, f.555.
24. MPP R.240/2 (13 Dec. 1736); CB 57, f.519 *seq.* (23 Nov. 1737,
9 Dec. 1737, 16 Dec. 1737).
25. CB 55, fos. 477, 481 (24/26 Oct. 1733).
26. CB 56, f.174; MPP R.240/2, f.159 (July 1735); CB 57, f.162
(13 Oct. 1736); MLR 27, f.129.
27. MLR 26, f.15 (September 1735).
28. CCR 2 (8 Sept. 1735).
29. 9 and 10 William III, C.44.
30. CCR 2 (2 Dec. 1735); CB 56, fos. 423, 438, 510, 541.
31. CCR 2 (2 Dec. 1735).

32. R. Southey, *History of Brazil* (1810–19), III, 281–2; Mawe, *op. cit.*, 52. See also p. 323 n.3 concerning the quality of Brazil diamonds.
33. Southey, *op. cit.*, III, 278.
34. *Ibid.*, 278–80.
35. *Ibid.*, 637; Calogeras, *op. cit.*, 38.
36. Southey quotes Almeyda who alleged that there was a conspiracy by 'foreigners and Jews' to dominate the diamond trade, 'for who in Portugal would purchase diamonds? Not the Portuguese, it was well known', *op. cit.*, III, 279.
37. Matthew Carrett to Yehiel Prager (4 Apr. 1778, P.R.O. C111/2). See also David Prager to Yehiel Prager, 22 Feb. 1778, P.R.O. C111/8, and Southey, *op. cit.*, III, 824, n.1.
38. M. G. Buist, *At Spes non Fracta – Hope & Co. 1770–1815* (The Hague, 1974), 385.
39. The Prager papers show that between 1775 and 1790 Brazil diamonds were regularly consigned from Lisbon to London.
40. Compton to Newcastle, Lisbon, 12 Jan. 1732, SP/Portugal, 89/37; J. Mawe, *Travels in the Interior of Brazil* (1812), III, 355; Southey, *op. cit.*, III, 626; Calogeras, *op. cit.*, 41.
41. For the volume of sales of Brazilian diamonds between 1753 and 1760 see H. E. S. Fisher, *The Portugal Trade* (1971), 24.
42. Data concerning sales of Brazilian stones are given in W. L. Eschwege, *Brasilien, die neue Welt* (Braunschweig, 1830), I, 112. G. Lenzen, *The History of Diamond Production and the Diamond Trade* (1970), 121, estimated that the discovery of diamonds in Brazil caused an approximately eight-fold increase in the supply to Europe of rough diamonds. The estimate is based on somewhat doubtful assumptions and in view of the above-quoted figures seem grossly exaggerated.

CHAPTER 8

1. CB 66, fos. 258, 261–2; CB 69, fos. 210, 225, 233.
2. CB 59, f.244 (13 Mar. 1741).
3. See, for example, E. Harrison to Thomas Pitt, Fort St George, 17 Sept. 1715, P.R.O. C110/28: 'Corall does not now yield prime cost and silver clears 25%'.
4. CB (1748–51). The value of consignments between 1748/9 and 1750/1 were as follows:

	Silver	Coral	Unspecified (silver and coral)
	£	£	£
1748/9	107,000	53,000	32,000
1749/50	182,000	68,000	32,000
1750/1	82,000	44,000	48,000

5. Between 1752 and 1780 silver exports for the purchase of diamonds only rarely had any significance (notable exceptions were 1764/5 with £64,000; 1765/6 with £30,000; and 1773/4 with £22,000).
6. P.R.O. C12/1291.18 and C12/1291.17.
7. This was a customary clause in bottomry bills, it being uncertain

whether ships would arrive at their originally named port of destination.

8. See for example MMC R.328/102, fos. 175 *seq.*

9. MMC R.328/87 f.71; CB 67, fos. 198, 262, 583; CB 68, f.467.

10. CB 61, fos. 427, 455; CB 62, fos. 167, 472. CB 63, fos. 141, 146, 158, 171, 178, 181, 274, 419; 433, 492, 524, 545, 578, 585, 645.

11. MMC R. 328/102, f.222; CB 68, fos. 497, 574.

12. P.R.O. C12/557.25 (1774); MMC R.328/97, f.620.

13. It seems that Bombay had a good market for precious stones. Ashkenazi merchants like Levi and Ruben Salomons, Joseph Salomons, Isaac Levy, Samuel Moses and Meyer Heyman sent stones and pearls to Bombay. At Surat there resided in the 1740s and 1750s two Jewish merchants of London, the Ashkenazi Abraham Elias (1741–54) and the Sephardi Solomon Franco (1743–8). When Franco in 1742 applied to the East India Company for permission to proceed to Bombay, he explained that he intended 'to engage in the diamond trade in these parts' (MLR 31, f.89). In fact, during the time these two resided at Surat, silver was sent there and to Bombay for the purchase of diamonds by David Levy, Judith Levy, Asher-Isaac Levy, Joseph and Nathan Salomons. After the fall of Madras in 1746, several merchants ordered their consignments to be delivered to Elias and Franco at Surat, but a permanent market for diamonds did not develop there. In 1787 Leib Prager, then at Benares, tried to buy diamonds at Surat through his friend Wilkinson, who replied, however, that only few stones were to be had there. Prager remarked on this: 'It is no wonder, because there were no buyers.' (Leib Prager to Yehiel Prager, Benares, 26 Apr. 1787, P.R.O. C111/6.)

14. Despite the proximity of some of the important diamond mines to Bengal, there was no important diamond market in this part of India before 1770. In 1728 the brothers Franco and Jacob da Costa applied for permission to export coral to Bengal, but 'as often diamonds are not to be had at Bengal' they asked to be allowed to send the proceeds to Madras or remit them home, by Company bills (CCR 2, 25 Oct. 1728). Coral exports to Bengal, however, did not reach serious proportions before the second half of the century. When the Company tried in 1766 to enforce the clause obliging the coral exporters to return the proceeds in diamonds, Joseph Salvador wrote to the Directors: 'Such order is impossible to be executed in the Bengal, Malabar Coast and China trade to all which at present the exportation extends with great appearance of improvement.' (MLR 48, f.183).

    The growth of coral exports to Bengal is also reflected in the permission which the Company gave in 1762 to the Governor of Bengal to levy the same personal duty on silver and coral imports as was due to the Governors of Madras and Bombay (I.O.L., Despatches to Bengal, 2, 413, 19 Dec. 1762).

15. At the beginning of the eighteenth century, China served as a sort of intermediary in the diamond trade. Silver was sent from London to China, where it was worth more than in India, and was used there to purchase gold which was sent to India for the purchase of diamonds for Europe. We have details concerning a complicated transaction by Alvaro da Fonseca. Da Fonseca's agent bought for him gold in China and sold it at Madras. The proceeds were lent by Thomas Pitt, who

served as da Fonseca's agent at Madras, at respondentia on a voyage from Madras to China and back. When the debt was returned, plus premium and interest totalling 25 per cent, Pitt invested the money in diamonds, which he sent to da Fonseca in London (see da Fonseca's account with Thomas Pitt, January 1709, P.R.O. C110/28). See also John Fellows to Thomas Pitt, London, 25 Nov. 1700, B.M. Add.Mss. 22851, f.83; Sir Stephen Evance to Thomas Pitt, London, 6 Feb. 1702, B.M. Add. Mss. 22851, f.12: E. Harrison to Thomas Pitt, Fort St George, 30 June 1715, P.R.O. C110/28.

In the 1760s coral exports to Canton were also started. Several London merchants, among them the Jewish firms of Franco and Ephraim d'Aguilar, sent consignments. In China there was of course no possibility of investing the proceeds in diamonds, and they were remitted home by bills of exchange. See MMC R.328/102, f.108 (1761); CB 75, f.298 (1766); MLR 48, fos. 262, 268 (1766); CB 76, fos. 374, 398, 403 (1767); CB 77, f.234 (1768).

16. It is often impossible to say to which port a consignment was sent. The Court Books frequently give no details beyond 'to India' or 'to the East Indies'.

17. In 1785 Governor Macartney stated that his income from coral imports amounted to 1,000 pagodas per annum out of a yearly total of 43,000 pagodas. See H. D. Love, *Vestiges of Old Madras, 1640–1800* (1913), III, 228.

18. See, for example, MMC 328/91, f.220 *seq.*

19. See, for example, Ephraim Isaac to Henry and Peter Muilman and Joseph Salomons, 9 Sept. 1750, P.R.O. C12/2034.10; also Joseph Fowke and Ephraim Isaac to Joseph Salomons, 17 Aug. 1750, *ibid.*

20. See MMC R.328/68, f.7 *seq*; R.328/69, fos. 16–17; R.328/73, fos. 77–8.

21. MMC R.328/73, fos. 49–50.

22. MPP R.239/90, f.83. For complaints concerning the flooding of the Indian market and low prices as a result see Sir Stephen Evance to Thomas Pitt, London, 11 Jan. 1703, P.R.O. C110/28; 12 Jan. 1704, C110/28; J. Roach to Sir James Tobin, Fort St George, 11 Dec. 1730, C108/95; Robert Orme to Thomas Godfrey, Fort St George, 24 June 1757, I.O.L. Orme Mss. O.V. 222; John Debonaire to Michael Salomons, Fort St George, 18 June 1761, MMC R.328/102, f.177. The last mentioned letter implies that the flooding of the market was not a rare event: 'Coral abounds and is in less demand, the quantity come and coming out being very considerable will much lower the price, and whenever this is the case you had better avoid sending any.'

23. V. Ball, *The Diamonds, Coal and Gold of India* (1881), 4; J. R. MacCarthy, *Fire in the Earth – The Story of the Diamond* (New York and London, 1942), 22; M. Bauer, *Edelsteinkunde* (Leipzig, 1896), 171 *seq.*

24. I.O.L. Orme Mss. O.V. 150, f.29 *seq.*

25. See Thomas Pitt to Sir Stephen Evance and Thomas Coulson, Fort St George, 31 Jan. 1701, P.R.O. C110/28; John Debonaire to Michael Salomons, Fort St George (no date, 1761 or 1762), MMC R.328/102, f.181.

26. MPP R.239/87, fos. 108, 147.

27. 'diamonds must be bought with ready money, and not on trust, and sometimes I have lodg'd money 7 or 8000 pagodas in the countrey, which has layn their [sic] 8 or 10 months.' (Thomas Pitt to John Fellows, Fort St George, 1 Oct. 1702, B.M. Add.Mss.22845, f.47). John Debonaire stated that 'diamonds are seldom or never purchased on credit'. MMC R.328/97, f.628.

28. MPP R.240/29, fos. 106–7 (14 Feb. 1770).

29. Jacob di Natal Levi Sonsino and Co. to Solomon and Moses Salomons and to Levy and Samuel Moses, London, 10 Dec. 1753, MMC R.328/82, fos. 108–9.

30. Evidence for a coral-diamond barter trade is to be found in a statement by Domingos da Cruz, Solomon Salomons' clerk in Madras (P.R.O. C12/1270.8). In 1788 Leib Prager wrote home: 'I hear that Pelling at Madras are exchanging diamonds for coral beads with diamond merchants, which is very advantageous for them.' (Leib Prager to Yehiel Prager, Calcutta, 12 Dec. 1788, P.R.O. C111/6).

31. MPP R.240/29, fos. 106–7.

32. See p. 175 above. The only earlier combination which I was able to discover was one between Governor Harrison of Madras and two other persons, which, however, concerned only big stones: 'In order to prevent the black rogues from imposing upon us, Benyon L'Apostre and myself have agreed together to buy all great stones joyntly' (E. Harrison to Thomas Pitt, Fort St George, 7 Jan. 1713, P.R.O. C110/28). It is perhaps not without significance that this combination was formed during the short period in which there was no Jewish diamond agent at Madras.

33. 'They [the Indian diamond merchants] first find out what sorts are wanted, and then shew such goods and put their price. If they are sold, they have their demand, for they suppose themselves to be the only judges of their value, and it does not appear that anyone has disputed the truth of it . . . It seems as if our traders thought the India people were masters of some rule for that purpose, by placing such confidence in them' (D. Jeffries, *A Treatise on Diamonds and Pearls* (2nd edn, 1751), 80, 82). Jeffries' statement cannot be regarded as completely reliable, having been written in order to prove the importance of his method for valuing diamonds. It must also be borne in mind that Jeffries was a jeweller and not an importer of diamonds. On the other hand, he undoubtedly had some knowledge of the diamond trade and there must have been some truth in his statement.

34. Jacob di Natal Levi Sonsino and Co., giving instructions to Solomon and Moses Salomons and Levy and Samuel Moses about the investment of the proceeds of their coral, wrote: 'and for the net produce you'll invest it in diamonds, of the best sort and assortments, as we don't doubt you are well acquainted with what is more proper for this market.' (London, 10 Dec. 1753, MMC R.328/82, fos. 108–9.) A few years later Aaron Franks wrote to his agents at Madras: 'I won't fix on any assortment, but leave it to you to purchase what you think most to my advantage, if any rough stones shall offer, at a reasonable price, that will make round brilliants will answer, square brilliants or brilliant drops will not, unless bought cheap.' (MMC R.328/97, f.631, 18 Jan. 1759).

35. Thomas Godfrey to Thomas Saunders and Solomon Salomons, London,

30 Nov. 1753, P.R.O. C12/1720.8. See also Sir James Tobin to John Roach, London, 1 Dec. 1727, P.R.O. C108/95.

36. 9 and 10 William III, C.44.

37. CB 42, f.104 (11 Jan. 1706); CB 43, f.325 (10 Nov. 1708); CB 51, f.379 (6 Aug. 1725); CB 56, f.119 (23 Aug. 1734); CB 62, f.434 (9 Dec. 1747).

38. CB 44, f.10 (26 Apr. 1710); CB 64, f.154 (12 Sept. 1750); CB 69, f.186 (1 Oct. 1760).

39. CB 63, fos. 169, 172 (2/7 Dec. 1748); CB 70, f.232 (16 Dec. 1761); CB 74, f.274 (4 Dec. 1765); I.O.L., Despatches to Bengal, Vol. 2, f.1048 (16 Mar. 1768).

40. 43 George III, C.68.

41. Around 1800 pearls became a more important import item from India than diamonds. In 1802 £12,531 worth of pearls were imported, compared with £7,385 of diamonds (Mocatta and Goldsmid Copy Book No. 13). The law to which these letters refer concerned only pearls, and that is surely the reason why only pearls are mentioned. The East India Company had always regarded diamonds and pearls as belonging to the same category.

42. Mocatta and Goldsmid Letter Book, Letters No. 15, 16 (15 Aug. 1803, October 1803). The letter explains why public sales are not possible in a trade which is wholly based on confidential deals. It proceeds: 'From considerations of this nature, the East India Company, in levying their duties . . . submitted always to take them on invoice price, a public sale of pearls being made only pro forma, where the proprietor was the purchaser of course.' The memorandum states: 'The sales at the India House, having been heretofore merely nominal, and the value ascertained by the register sent to the India Company from India; which valuation they were constantly put up at, and bought in by the agent of the Company for account of the proprietors'.

43. CB 48, f.335 (25 July 1719); CB 51, fos. 22, 33, 361 (29 Apr., 6 May 1724, 14 July 1725); CB 53, f.276 (13 Aug. 1729).

44. In 1781 insurance premiums jumped from 7–8 per cent to 20–25 per cent (Israel Levin Salomons [Yehiel Prager] to de Castro, Pelling and de Fries, London, 31 May 1781). Jacob Barnet wrote to Yehiel Prager in the same year: 'I tremble at the enormous price of insurance, which swallows up all my profits, this is one evil among many which war creates, for my part I must devoutly pray for peace.' (Benares, 9 June 1782.) See also Pelling and de Fries to Israel Levin Salomons, Fort St George, 25 Oct. 1782, P.R.O. C111/8.

45. Leib Prager to Yehiel Prager, Calcutta, 19 Feb. 1787, P.R.O. C111/6.

46. See letter by Leib Prager where he says, on the authority of an ex-Director of the Royal Exchange Insurance Company, that the insurance companies were prepared to cancel a policy, retaining a mere ½ per cent of the insured value, and that they were particularly flexible where pearls and diamonds were concerned, because they did not involve a risk of partial damage (e.g. by sea water) and because in case of disaster there was sometimes a chance of saving them. (Leib Prager to Yehiel Prager, Calcutta, 9 Jan. 1787, P.R.O. C111/6.)

47. See form of obligation by Joseph Salvador (1756) in *Industrial Diamond Review*, xix, 58.

48. CB 53, fos. 323, 401 (15 Oct. 1729, 14 Jan. 1730).

49. John Roach to James Tobin, Fort St George, 30 Jan. 1732, 12 Jan. 1733, 28 Sept. 1733.
50. I.O.L. Despatches to Madras, 2, f.389 (27 Jan. 1762); *ibid.*, 6, fos. 443–4 (25 Nov. 1775); *ibid.*, 12, fos. 479–80 (12 Apr. 1786).
51. Aaron Franks wrote to John Debonaire and Peter Mariette: 'If any man of war should come home, you may make me returns in them unregistered'. London, 18 Jan. 1759, MMC R.328/97, f.631. Michael Salomons to John Debonaire: 'You'll observe to give underhand what you possibly can, in order to prevent registering.' 1 Jan. 1761, MCC R.328/102, f.248.
52. CB 74, fos. 254, 262–3, 266, 274–5.
53. Jacob Prager to Yehiel Prager, Amsterdam, 26 Sept. 1774, P.R.O. C111/13.
54. MPP R.239/89, f.249 (1724).
55. John Mawe, *A Treatise on Diamonds and Precious Stones* (2nd edn, 1823), 3.
56. P.R.O. C12/1275.5.
57. 24 Sept. 1793, London, P.R.O. C111/160.
58. P.R.O. C12/1922.29 (1756) reply.
59. Mocatta and Goldsmid to Messrs. Law, Bruce and Co., 24 Nov. 1802 (Mocatta and Goldsmid, Letter Book).
60. David Prager to Esther, Meyer and Mordecai (Mark) Prager, Amsterdam, 5 Aug. 1788, P.R.O. C111/8.
61. See the declaration of the diamond broker Abraham de Paiba (MCC R.328/102, fos. 188–9). De Paiba declared that he sold a diamond parcel belonging to Michael Salomons, to Gompertz and Heyman of London. When the latter found that they had been cheated, de Paiba could no longer sell closed bulses belonging to Salomons, but had to open them and sell them at a loss.
62. See P.R.O. C12/1339.25. Isaac Siprut de Gabay remarked that he sometimes lost on bulses sold unopened, but that on the whole it was worth his while to sell by this method. (C12.1275.5 reply [1757–59]). It seems that as far as weight and numbers of diamonds in the bulses were concerned, the invoices made out in India were generally reliable. Thus the experienced Amsterdam diamond merchant Barukh Cantor wrote about closed bulses: 'It has never happened that anything has been found missing.' (Barukh Cantor to Yeheil Prager, Amsterdam, 22 Tamuz 5526 [29 June 1766] P.R.O. C111/1.)
63. Jacob Prager to Yehiel Prager, Amsterdam, 13 Aug. 1784, P.R.O. C111/5.
64. 'I hear diamonds sell best at public outcry' (Thomas Pitt to Sir Stephen Evance, John Dolben and Robert Pitt, Fort St George, 27 Sept. 1706, P.R.O. C110/28). Evance replied that it was impossible to sell the diamonds by public sale because they had been sent unregistered (11 Feb. 1707).
65. 'I am afraid that at a public sale I should suffer by the combination which generally takes place at those times among the buyers, who are principally Jews.' (The Widow Salomons to Messrs Muilman, London, 5 Nov. 1793, P.R.O. C111/148, f.76.) Goldsmid and Mocatta, explaining the disadvantages of a public sale, wrote: 'a chance of a combination among the purchasers, which can only be guarded against by our putting a value on each parcel and buying some again.' (See Mocatta

and Goldsmid to Mr Pearson, 31 Dec. 1801, Mocatta and Goldsmid
Letter Book;) 'long experience in the diamond trade has prejudiced me
against public sales.' (The Widow Salomons to Messrs Muilman,
6 Dec. 1793, P.R.O. C111/148.)

66. Leib Prager wrote to Esther Prager, concerning diamonds he was
sending her from India: 'It would be best if the merchants came to
you to see the diamonds, because if they are entrusted open [i.e. not in
closed bulses] through brokers they may be interchanged, so be careful
and take the hint.' (Calcutta, 11 Nov. 1791, P.R.O. C111/6.) In another
letter Prager wrote: 'I agree with you that it sometimes is advantageous to sell through brokers, but this involves a large measure of
trust – if the broker wants to do so, he can substitute bad diamonds
for good ones, and when refuge [diamonds] are concerned it cannot be
detected, even by the greatest experts.' (Benares, 20 June 1792,
P.R.O. C111/6.) See also Barukh Cantor to Yehiel Prager, Amsterdam,
22 Tamuz 5526 (29 June 1766), P.R.O. C111/1; Joseph ben Mordecai
to Yehiel Prager, Amsterdam, Ellul 5526 (1766), P.R.O. C111/1;
Jacob Barnet to Yehiel Prager, Amsterdam, 2 June 1780 (includes a
warning against relying on Asher Goldsmid as diamond broker); the
Widow I. L. Salomons to Messrs Muilman, London, 8 Oct. 1793,
P.R.O. C111/148, f.72.

67. See Mocatta and Goldsmid. Letter Book.

68. Jeffries, *op. cit.*, 43–4.

69. David Prager to Esther, Meyer and Mordecai Prager, Amsterdam,
5 Aug. 1788, P.R.O. C111/8.

70. I.O.L. Auditor's References, Vol. 1, Answer of Abraham and Jacob
Franco and Aaron Franks, 17 Jan. 1752.

71. See Jeffries, *op. cit.*, 115. David Prager to Esther, Meyer and Mordecai
Prager, 21 Apr. 1788, 2 May 1788, P.R.O. C111/8; Mocatta and
Goldsmid to Thomas Coults & Co., 5 Mar. 1800 (Mocatta and
Goldsmid Letter Book).

72. See Jacob Prager to Yehiel Prager, 25 Oct. 1774, 9 May 1775, P.R.O.
C111/13; 12 May 1778, C111/3; 1 Apr. 1783, C111/9; David Prager
to Esther, Meyer and Mordecai Prager, 24 Sept. 1788, C111/8.

73. Jeffries pointed out the influence of fashion on the prices of diamonds
(*op. cit.*, 5).

74. John Dolben to Thomas Pitt, London, no date, P.R.O. C110/28.
Dolben gave this information on the authority of the Jewish merchant
Abraham Nathan. See also Francis Chamberlayne to Robert Nightingale
(London, 10 Apr. 1707) concerning the harm done to the German
diamond market by Charles XII's raid into Saxony (P.R.O. C108/203).

75. Jacob Prager to Yehiel Prager, Amsterdam, 6 Feb. 1784. See also
Sutherland and Co. to Yehiel Prager, Petersburg, 17 June 1774,
P.R.O. C111/4.

76. Philip Masson to Sir Richard Hoare, Paris, 8 Apr. 1716 (Hoare's Bank,
Correspondence with P. Masson as to diamonds, 1713–16). For the
effect of the war on the diamond market see also: John Dolben to
Thomas Pitt, London, 18 Jan. 1709, P.R.O. C110/28; Robert Orme to
John Sarjent, 9 Nov. 1757 (I.O.L. Orme Mss. O.V. 222, f.24).

77. D. and J. de Neufville to Sir Richard Hoare, Frankfort, 16 Dec. 1713
(Hoare's Bank, Correspondence between Sir R. Hoare and Daniel and
James de Neufville of Frankfort, 1713–16). After George III's recovery,

Leib Prager wrote from India: 'I hope that now that the King is better, diamonds will be again in demand.' (Benares, 16 July 1789, P.R.O. C111/6.)

78. In November 1792 Esther Prager wrote to her brother Leib in Benares: 'Indigo . . . bids fair to be a better trade than diamonds if the French Nation is transformed into a republic.' (London, 26 Nov. 1792, P.R.O. C111/147, f.296.)

79. Thomas Pitt and G. Addison to Thomas Marshall, Fort St George, 22 Jan. 1709: 'Sure there is a mystery in itt and the jewellers have combin'd together to depreciate all diamonds and employ some of their tribe to buy 'em up and share the gain among them, or there could never be such a horrid complaint as we are advised from all hands.' (B.M. Add.Mss.22850, f.115.) It is impossible to say whether this supposition had any truth in it.

80. P.R.O. C110/28.

81. P.R.O. C11/777.1 (1733/4); C12/1195.64 (1763).

82. P.R.O. C12/2400.20 (1766–8).

83. SP/Portugal 89/37 2 May 1732, 12 Jan. 1732.

84. 6 George II C.7.

85. Philo-patriae, *Considerations on the Bill to Permit Persons Professing the Jewish Religion to be Naturalized by Parliament* (1753).

86. Jeffries, *op. cit.*, 101.

87. Accounts of sale of diamonds: per *ffame*, P.R.O. C110/28; per *Dutchess* and other ships (1705), per *Tankerfield* (1708–9), P.R.O. C110/81.

88. E. Harrison to Robert Adams, Whitehall, 31 Jan. 1721, P.R.O. C110/145.

89. The fact that these are *declared* values imposes a certain caution, although the temptation to declare lower values in order to pay less duty must have been largely counterbalanced by the fact that the invoices which went with the diamonds also served as a basis for fixing their price in London (see pp. 138–9 above).

90. P.R.O. C12/292.23, 1st schedule to reply of Rebecca Mendes da Costa.

91. P.R.O. C11/1971.12 (1713), schedule to replies.

92. The brothers Muilman were Dutch-born and their firm was among the biggest in Anglo-Dutch trade during the eighteenth century. It seems that there were ties of personal friendship between Joseph Salomons and the Muilmans, whom he appointed executors of his will (CB 72, f.29).

93. P.R.O. C110/28. The Jewish buyers were: Isaac Henriques Sr, Joseph Ferdinando, Pacheco, Gomes-Serra, Salvador, David Nunes, Solomon de Medina, Nathan, de Castro, Alvaro Nunes, Philip Martines, Ephraim Abarbanel, Robles, Barrow, Aboab, Alvares, Franco.

94. P.R.O. C12.1971.12. John Pitt, Thomas Pitt's cousin, was the chief of the New Company's factory at Masulipatam.

95. Nine out of ten merchants were Jews: Josua Gomes Serra, Abraham Nathan, Joseph Robles, Joseph Ferdinando, Joseph Mussaphia, Moses Nunes, Philip Martines, Isaac de Castro, Aaron Pacheco, Matthias Alvares, Peter Henriques.

96. P.R.O. C110/81. The Jewish buyers were Pacheco, Martines, Faros, M. Moses, Nathan, Salvador.

97. Jacob Prager to Yehiel Prager, Amsterdam, 28 Oct. 1785.

98. H. Verelst to Sir Robert Barker, Wadworth, 2 Nov. 1781, P.R.O. C111/10.

99. P.R.O. C11/462.1 (reply).
100. Thomas Marshall to Thomas Pitt, London, 29 Jan. 1709, P.R.O. C110/28. See also G. Dolben to Thomas Pitt, London, 18 Jan. 1709, *ibid.*
101. G. Dolben to Thomas Pitt, no date (about 1707 or 1708), P.R.O. C110/28.
102. H. Schnee, *Die Hoffinanz und der moderne Staat* (Berlin, 1953–5), II, 14 *seq.*
103. P.R.O. C11/462.1; C11/2696.29.
104. Jeffries, *op. cit.*, 143.
105. Selma Stern, *The Court Jew*, for information on the activity of German court-Jews as agents for precious stones.
106. Thomas Pitt to Sir Stephen Evance, Alvaro da Fonseca and Robert Pitt, Fort St George, 7 Oct. 1702, P.R.O. C110/28.
107. Alvaro da Fonseca to Thomas Pitt, London, 8 Nov. 1708; Thomas Pitt to Sir Stephen Evance and Robert Pitt, Fort St George, 24 Sept. 1705; G. Dolben and Sir Stephen Evance to Thomas Pitt, London, 20 Apr. 1708 (P.R.O. C110/28).
108. P.R.O. C11/1716.11. For Hope's connections among Jewish diamond merchants in London see Buist, *op. cit.*, 385.
109. CB 46, fos. 227–8 (17 Dec. 1714).
110. CB 46, f.297 (16 Mar. 1715).
111. CB 46, fos. 380–1 (17 June 1715). There can be no doubt that this is an allusion to French attempts to gain a foothold in the Indian diamond trade with which Marcus Moses was connected.
112. Francis Salvador to the East India Company, February 1752, I.O.L. Auditors' References, Vol. I. Jacob Salvador was very young at that time, and it would seem that most of the consignments sent under his name really belonged to his father, Francis Daniel. The people who traded under the cover of his name were described as 'his relations and friends'.
113. MMC R.328/82, f.370 *seq.*; Account of estate of Solomon Salomons by his trustees, MMC R.328/84 (pages in the book are not numbered).
114. Philo-patriae, *Further Considerations on the Act to Permit Persons Professing the Jewish Religion to be Naturalized by Parliament* (1753), 44. It should be noted that Philo-patriae does not say explicitly that the Jews in London acted as agents of Leghorn Jews, but only that the coral was sent to India 'by means' of the London Jews.
115. Mocatta and Goldsmid to Richard Clark, London, 7 Mar. 1800 (Mocatta and Goldsmid, Letter Book).
116. C. Roth, *The Great Synagogue, London, 1690–1940* (1950), 49.
117. MMC R.328/103, f.975 *seq.*, London, 10 Dec. 1765.
118. For the partnership between the Francos and Aaron Franks in coral exports see Auditor's References, Vol. I (Abraham and Jacob Franco's reply to a questionnaire of 17 Jan. 1752). For the partnership between Thomas Godfrey and Aaron Franks see P.R.O. C12/1270.8.
119. P.R.O. C9/105.47.
120. On the activity of B. Rodrigues, de Porto and Alvaro da Fonesca between 1685 and 1700 see W. J. Fischel, 'The Jewish merchant colony in Madras (Fort St George) during the 17th and 18th centuries', *Journal of the Economic and Social History of the Orient*, III (1960), 93.
121. On Rodrigues Salvadore's activities during the 1680s see *ibid.*, 83–9.

He was the brother of the London diamond merchant Francis Salvadore.

122. Love, *op. cit.*, II, 7; Alvaro da Fonseca to Thomas Pitt, London, 14 Jan. 1707, P.R.O. C110/28; Francis Chamberlayne to Robert Nightingale, London, 10 Apr. 1707; Robert Nightingale to Francis Chamberlayne, Fort William, 14 Dec. 1707; Robert Nightingale to Francis Chamberlayne, Fort William, 5 Nov. 1708; Robert Nightingale to Francis Chamberlayne, Amsterdam, 16 Aug. 1709, all P.R.O. C108/203.

123. A. M. Hyamson, *David Salomons*, 2–4; CB 51, f.483 (7 Jan. 1726); John Roach to Aaron Franks, Fort St George, 24 Aug. 1731, P.R.O. C108/95; P.R.O. C12/1878.10 (1758); C12/33.30 (1764–5).

124. Records of Hoare's Bank:
    1. 'Money lent on bond and other securities 1696–1716', fos. 85, 96 113.
    2. Sir Richard Hoare to Marcus Moses, 1 Mar. 1706, Letterbook 1701–6 ('Letters to Customers').
    3. Marcus Moses to Sir Richard Hoare [Paris?], 29 Dec. 1712; Philip Masson to Sir Richard Hoare, Paris, 30 Jan. 1715, 30 Mar. 1715, 13 July 1715, 8 Apr. 1716, 25 May 1716, 25 July 1716 ('Correspondence with P. Masson of Paris as to diamonds, 1713–1717').
    MPP R. 239/87, f.97 *seq.*; P.R.O. C11/1755.28 (1716); MLR 5, f.124; CB 45, fos. 281–2; CB 46, fos. 123, 380–1.

125. M. J. Cohen, *Jacob Emden – a Man of Controversy* (Philadelphia, 1937), 46; Roth, *op. cit.*, 114 *seq.*; P.R.O. C11/1486.23 (1730).

126. P.R.O. C12/2033.28 (1757–9); C12/1835.12 (1754–7); MPP R.240/8, f.2 *seq.*

127. P.R.O. C12/2033.28 (1757–9).

128 In 1710 de Castro married Rachel, daughter of Abraham Bravo. He was Secretary of the Portuguese Community in London from 1732 till his death in 1740. See A. M. Hyamson. *The Sephardim of England* (1951), 194.

129. Isaac de Castro – a son of Solomon de Castro – settled in Leghorn. It is probable that Abraham Isaac de Castro, who exported coral to India in 1780, was his son. (For the information concerning Isaac de Castro I am indebted to Mr Alfred Rubens of London, who has studied the history of the family. For Abraham Isaac de Castro see P.R.O. C12/2150.1.)

130. The East India Company apparently did not stick to formalities and permitted the return of the diamonds under the name of the real owner, although the coral sent out for the purchase of the diamonds had been exported under another person's name.

131. CB 63, f.203 (4 Jan. 1749).

132. Fort St David Records.

133. Joseph Dias Fernandes was allowed to proceed to India in October 1763, and in November security was given on his behalf by Benjamin Mendes da Costa and Moses Dias Fernandes.

134. MMC R.328/103, fos. 977–8.

135. *Ibid.*, fos. 979–80.

136. *Ibid.*, fos. 929–32.

137. CCR, II (6 Nov. 1729).

138. In 1744 the Committee of Correspondence recommended that permission be given to Samuel de Castro and David Lopes Fernandes 'to reside in India as free merchants in the diamond and coral way', but there is no other evidence that such a category of merchants was ever formally recognized or that Jewish merchants in India were restricted to diamond and coral business. CCR, III (3 Jan. 1749).
139. *Ibid.*, X, f.191 (10 Dec. 1772).
140. MMC R.328/87, f.68.
141. P.R.O. C12/1270.8.
142. H. Furber, *John Company at Work* (Cambridge, Mass., 1948).
143. Fischel, *op. cit.*, 103–7.
144. MMC R.328/70, fos. 99–100; MMC R.328/72, f.187 *seq.*; MMC R.328/83, f.191 *seq.*, f.199 *seq.*
145. MMC R.328/83, fos. 370–3.
146. P.R.O. C12/526.15 (1757), bill.
147. Auditor's References, Vol. I, 4 May 1752.
148. P.R.O. C12/2033.28 (Answer of Samuel Moses).
149. P.R.O. 12.1270.8 (reply).
150. MMC R.328/84 (Account of Estate of Solomon Salomons).
151. MMC R.328/96, f.13 *seq.*
152. MMC R.328/81, f.188 *seq.*
153. George Jones to Levy Moses, Tranquebar, 20 Oct. 1748, P.R.O. C12/2033.28.
154. P.R.O. C12/526.15 (1757), bill.
155. De Castro, Pelling and de Fries.

CHAPTER 9

1. In the five-year period of 1752–6 the average yearly value of diamond imports was £128,000; in the period 1757–61 it was £56,000. One has, however, to bear in mind the possibility that in the first years of the war there was an increase in illegal imports.
2. I.O.L., Despatches to Madras, I, fos. 1028–9 (23 Jan. 1759).
3. *Ibid.*, III, fos. 463–5 (21 Nov. 1766). On the involvement of the Dutch East India Company in remittances by Englishmen from India see O. Feldbaek, *India Trade under the Danish Flag* (1969).
4. CCR, VI (16 Oct. 1766).
5. CB 75, f.228 (17 Oct. 1766).
6. MLR 48, f.185.
7. *Ibid.*, f.183. For Salvador's position in the Clive Faction see L. S. Sutherland, *The East India Company in Eighteenth Century Politics* (1952), 118.
8. CB 75, f.261 (7 Nov. 1766).
9. MPP, R.240/28, f.329 *seq.* In November 1766 the Directors put a limit to the amounts which the Presidencies were permitted to draw on the Company. The rate of exchange was also reduced from 8 shillings the pagoda to 7 shillings 8 pence for the Company's people and 7 shillings 4 pence for others. In March 1780 it was ordered that Fort St George may not draw more than £30,000 a year, and the rate of 7 shillings 4 pence was made general. I.O.L., Despatches to Madras, 3, fos. 463–4 (21 Nov. 1766); *ibid.*, 4, fos. 49–52 (11 Mar. 1768).

10. Dame Lucy Sutherland pointed out that the fall of Madras marks the end of the period in which the Company was able to conduct its affairs in India on a purely commercial basis. Thereafter it became involved in Indian politics. See Sutherland, *op. cit.*, 46.

11. MLR, 59, f.79.

12. The *Asiatic Annual Register*, 1799; Misc. Transactions 50; See also J. Fowke [to W. Hastings?], 13 Aug. 1781, B.M. Add.Mss.29150, fos. 74–5.

13. H. Verelst to Sir Robert Barker, 2 Nov. 1781, P.R.O. C111/10.

14. W. Hastings to Robert Palk, Fort St George, 2 Apr. 1770 – *HMC Report on the Palk Manuscripts*, 124. W. Hastings to J. Wood-man, 2 Jan. 1774, B.M. Add.Mss.29134, f.233. See also P. J. Marshall, 'The personal fortune of Warren Hastings', *EcHR*, 2nd ser., xvii (1964/5), 284–300.

15. See Appendix IX.

16. The text of this petition has been published by L. Wolf in *JHSE Misc.*, i, 39.

17. See, for example, Joseph Salvador's letter to Clive of 26 Nov. 1766, published by M. Woolf in *JHSE Trans.*, xxi (1962–7), 122.

18. Circular of Jacob Barnet, enclosed with his letter to Yehiel Prager of 15 June 1779, P.R.O. C111/4.

19. De Castro, Pelling and de Fries wrote to Yehiel Prager: 'Mr. Barnet appears to us to be an honest, well meaning man, but extremely weak and inexperienced.' (Fort St George, 20 Mar. 1780, P.R.O. C111/5.) A similar impression is gained from Barnet's own letters.

20. The problem of the high insurance premiums is mentioned in Jacob Barnet's letter to Yehiel Prager, Benares, 9 June 1782, P.R.O. C111/7. Barnet himself was under arrest during the disturbances. (Jacob Barnet to Yehiel Prager, Benares, 9 June 1782, P.R.O. C111/7.)

21. Jacob Barnet to Yehiel Prager, Benares, 20 Aug. 1783, 22 Mar. 1784 (P.R.O. C111/8); 4 Nov. 1784, 14 Nov. 1784 (C111/6).

22. Jacob Barnet to Yehiel Prager, Benares, 25 Jan. 1783, P.R.O. C111/8.

23. Joseph Fowke to Francis Fowke, Calcutta, 21 Sept. 1784, I.O.L. Fowke Mss., Mss. Bur., E.6, Letter No. 29.

24. Pelling and de Fries to Yehiel Prager, Fort St George, 6 June 1785, P.R.O. C111/6. Already in February, Pelling and de Fries wrote: 'Rough diamonds continue very scarce with us, the tide of the trade is turned entirely towards Bengal, where they being purchased mostly by persons returning home, can afford to pay more than merchants that purchase them as trade.' (Fort St George, 5 Feb. 1785, P.R.O. C111/10.)

25. Pelling and de Fries to Yehiel Prager, Fort St George, 12 Jan. 1786, P.R.O. C111/10.

26. Israel Levin Salomons to the Court of Directors of the East India Company, London, August 1785, MLR, 77, No. 63.

27. Jacob Prager to Yehiel Prager, Amsterdam, 20 Jan. 1786. Holden Furber, who obviously had no knowledge of the Prager letters in the P.R.O., maintained that the big diamond merchants persuaded the Company to let Leib Prager go out to India in order to regulate the diamond trade. The Prager Papers do not supply any evidence which would tend to confirm this view. (See Furber, *op. cit.* 230–1.)

28. I.O.L., Despatches to Bengal, 14, fos. 430 *seq.* (8 Mar. 1786). At the

same time the Directors wrote to the Council at Bengal: 'As we conceive it of very great importance to the Company to restore the said diamond trade, in order to render it an advantageous mode of remittance of private property, and to secure a regular and fair payment of the duty due to the Company in respect to such trade, we direct . . . that you afford Mr. Salomons and his agents every protection and assistance in your power in carrying on the said trade to the best advantage'.

29. *Ibid.*, 15, fos. 303 *seq.* (12 Apr. 1786).
30. Leib Prager to Yehiel Prager, Benares, 24 Dec. 1786.
31. Leib Prager to Yehiel Prager, Calcutta, 21 Feb. 1787.
32. I.O.L., General Cash Journals 1787–93.

Year	Total value of diamond imports £	Value of diamonds imported by Yehiel Prager (Israel Levin Salomons) £
1787	83,100	26,500
1788	117,500	44,200
1789	112,000	41,100
1790	78,800	26,200
1791	57,100	20,300
1792	85,200	40,600
1793	78,400	29,200

33. Leib Prager to Yehiel Prager, Calcutta, 4 Nov. 1789, P.R.O. C111/6.
34. Leib Prager to Yehiel Prager, Benares, 22 Aug. 1787, 6 July 1788, P.R.O. C111/6.
35. Leib Prager to Yehiel Prager, Benares, 31 July 1788, P.R.O. C111/6.
36. Leib Prager to Yehiel Prager, Calcutta, 4 Mar. 1787; Benares, 24 June 1787; Calcutta, 21 Aug. 1787; P.R.O. C111/6.
37. Leib Prager to Yehiel Prager, Benares, 6 July 1788, P.R.O. C111/6. Prager had to pay for the diamonds which he bought at Benares with bills drawn on Calcutta. These bills were paid in gold coins.
38. Leib Prager to Yehiel Prager, Benares, 6 July 1788, P.R.O. C111/6.
39. Leib Prager to Yehiel Prager, Calcutta, 4 Nov. 1789, P.R.O. C111/6.
40. Leib Prager to Yehiel Prager, Calcutta, 17 Nov. 1791, P.R.O. C111/6.

CHAPTER 10

1. *Elliot* v. *Willis* (Chancery Cases).
2. 19 Apr. 1780, 5 Oct. 1784, as well as a letter dated on the eve of Succoth (Tabernacles) of the Hebrew Year 5548 (26 Sept. 1787), in which David Prager wrote that if new developments would occur in the negotiations then being conducted between Prince William V and the rebels, he would inform Yehiel 'by an uncircumcised one'.
3. After Isaac Prager took over the direction of the Dutch house, the Hebrew date was dropped from the Amsterdam letters.
4. 23 Aug. 1787, 24 Aug. 1787, 9 Oct. 1787. The forgery of the dates was done rather carelessly, and thanks to the fact that there are usually three dates on the letters (the general date in the letter, the date in the postmark, and the Hebrew date) it has been possible to determine

the true dates of all the letters bearing forged dates. Their (original) dates are: 3 Mar. 1786, 25 Apr. 1786, 5 May 1786, 19 Sept. 1786, 20 Oct. 1786, 3 Nov. 1786, 1 Dec. 1786, 12 Dec. 1786, 30 Dec. 1786.

5. Jacob Prager visited his London relations in 1780 and again in 1786. On the latter occasion he heard George III speak in Parliament and witnessed an attempt to raise a balloon (14 July 1786, 21 July 1786). It seems that Yehiel never visited Amsterdam after he had permanently settled in London in 1762.

6. The letters of April 1792 to March 1793 are in an advanced state of decay and are illegible.

7. Meyer Prager headed the Ostend branch from 1781 to 1783 and the Philadelphia house from 1784 till his return to Europe late in 1787. Thereafter the American house was managed by his brother Yehiel Jr ('Yehielke') and his cousin Meyer Jr ('Meyerke').

8. The letters throw little light on the early history of the firm – they include no childhood memories or the like. The passage mentioning the small beginning of the house appears in a letter of Jacob Prager, dated 23 Sept. 1783, dealing with their losses and lost debts: 'And it is a great miracle that since we have gone into trade – and what did we amount to? – and despite all the fatal times which we have gone through we have emerged with unbroken heads.' The contract of 1762 states that 'the firm under the name of Widow Levi Salomons and Sons has been in existence for many years' (P.R.O. C111/15).

9. The first contract between the Prager brothers was signed in 1752 (see contract of 1762, P.R.O. C111/15), but no papers of the period prior to 1762 have survived. Preaching moderation to his nephews in Philadelphia, Yehiel Prager wrote: 'I was in London for 10 years prior to my marriage, satisfied with lodgings' (2 June 1784, P.R.O. C111/157). Prager was endenized in May 1765 under the name of Israel Levin Salomons. See 'A list of Jewish persons endenized and naturalized 1609–1799', *JHSE Trans.*, xxii (1968–9), 132.

10. P.R.O. C111/15.

11. The second contract is not extant. For references to the new arrangement see 9 May 1775 and 6 May 1783.

12. The Pragers' prestige as a dependable firm was greatly enhanced by the fact that they safely came through these crises. This is clearly reflected in the letters of Meyer Michael-David.

13. 2 Feb. 1787.

14. About the difficulties which Jews had in getting permission to settle in Ostend in 1781 see S. Ullman, *Histoire des Juifs de Belgique jusqu'au 19e siècle, 1700–1830* (Le Haye, 1934), 34–5. The famous house of Boason in the Hague helped the Pragers to get a recommendation from the Imperial envoy in the Hague to the aldermen of Antwerp, requesting them to induce the municipality of Ostend to grant Meyer Prager and his associates the right to reside in the town (29 Jan. 1781).

15. 16 Apr. 1782; 17 Dec. 1783; 12 June 1783.

16. 27 June 1783.

17. See F. L. Nussbaum, 'The American tobacco trade and French politics', in the *Political Science Quarterly*, xl (1925).

18. Esther Prager to David Prager, London, 13 Mar. 1792, P.R.O. C111/160.

19. Esther Prager to Leib Prager, London, 1 May 1792, P.R.O. C111/147.

20. *Ibid.*
21. From 1788 the firm was called 'Widow Israel Levin Salomons and Prager', and was a partnership of Esther and her son Mordecai. The firm was wound up in 1793, but revived in 1794.
22. 4 Feb. 1794, P.R.O. C111/148.
23. Esther Prager to Isaiah (George) Prager, London, 21 Jan. 1796, 20 Sept. 1796, P.R.O. C111/148).
24. Jessy, the eldest daughter of Yehiel and Esther Prager, married Benjamin Goldsmid in 1787. Benjamin's father, Aaron, had for many years been closely acquainted with the Pragers. See L. Alexander's gossipy book, *Memoirs of the Life and Commercial Connections . . . of the Late Benjamin Goldsmid* (1808), 41–2. A drawing of Jessy Prager-Goldsmid is reproduced in this book. At the time of her marriage to Benjamin Goldsmid, he and his brother Abraham had not yet attained the fame and fortune which they later acquired, although the family already belonged to the upper stratum of the Ashkenazi community. The Goldsmids' meteoric rise began after the outbreak of the war with revolutionary France, when they became loan contractors to the Government.
25. For a description by Esther Prager of the firm's decline after her husband's death see P.R.O. C12/659.35 and C12/653.4.
26. 14 Apr. 1778.
27. M. Warburg to Leib Prager, 8 Sept. 1768, P.R.O. C111/4. J. Fridrickson to Leib Prager, 26 Oct. 1782, P.R.O. C111/5.
28. 17 Feb. 1778.
29. 20 Feb. 1778.
30. 13 Aug. 1781.
31. 31 Mar. 1778.
32. 23 Apr. 1778.
33. In 1787 Jacob had a nominal capital of £10,000 invested in the business. From the method of dividing the profits it emerges that David's capital investment was the same as Jacob's, while Yehiel's was about 50 per cent larger, so that the firm's total capital amounted to about £35,000.
34. 7 Mar. 1788.
35. The prevalence of this kind of credit has been pointed out by van der Kooy (see his *Hollands stapelmarkt en haar verval*, Amsterdam, 1931, 51). He says that Amsterdam financed most of her foreign trade by discount credit.
36. 16 Oct. 1772.
37. 1 Mar. 1785, 21 Apr. 1788.
38. 10 Apr. 1775, 2 June 1779, 17 Dec. 1789, 16 Mar. 1784, 5 Sept. 1784.
39. 17 Apr. 1778, 9 June 1778, 22 Oct. 1784, 20 Feb. 1789.
40. 24 Mar. 1778, 12 May 1778, 23 Mar. 1784. The last-mentioned letter speaks about the Bank of England's refusal to discount bills drawn on Jews.
41. A firm pawning large quantities of goods also endangered its good name (see 5 Feb. 1782). Nevertheless, pawning seems to have been resorted to fairly often in order to get money (2 Apr. 1783).
42. 5 Mar. 1782, 18 May 1784.
43. 20 May 1785. See also 21 June 1785.
44. The firm was at first known by the name 'Tourton et Baur', later as

'Tourton et Ravel': see 28 Mar. 1775, where Jacob calls Tourton 'this treasure'. In 1781 Tourton made a considerable credit available to the new house of the Pragers in Ostend, and in 1784 to the Philadelphia house, thereby giving the Pragers invaluable help in the establishment of the two houses (12 Nov. 1781, 12 Mar. 1784). About transactions with Tourton see 10 Jan. 1775, 14 May 1779, 7 Sept 1784, 16 Mar. 1790. For an example of how the connection with Tourton was utilized to finance a big purchase of diamonds, see 16 Sept. 1774. Jacob informed Yehiel that for this purpose he could draw up to 100,000 Kronen (about £12,500) on Tourton, at two and a half to three months. When payment became due, they would ask Tourton to draw on the Amsterdam house, 'So we should have a lot of time to pay out of [the proceeds of] the diamonds'.

45. 24 Apr. 1778.
46. 11 Nov. 1793.
47. C. H. Wilson, *Anglo-Dutch Commerce and Finance in the Eighteenth Century* (1957), 41.
48. On this problem see R. B. Westerfield, *Middlemen in English Business, Particularly between 1660 and 1760* (New Haven, 1915), 357.
49. The correspondence between Yehiel Prager and Aaron Meyer covers a period of 13 years – from 1765 till 1778 – though there were several interruptions and though there were no regular business connections between them after 1768. On the whole, it would seem that Yehiel Prager was not very eager to do business with Meyer, and that both he and his brothers did not trust him entirely. Meyer's letters to Yehiel Prager, written between 1765 and 1778, are in P.R.O. C111/3, 4, 10.
50. Leib Prager visited Amsterdam in 1781 and talked to about one hundred merchants there, in an endeavour to get orders for the London house. Jacob told Yehiel that he himself should have come to Amsterdam years earlier in order to form such connections (31 Aug. 1781).
51. 15 May 1787.
52. 14 Nov. 1780, 28 Nov. 1780.
53. 19 Nov. 1782, 9 Feb. 1781.
54. 24 Feb. 1775, 26 Dec. 1777. See also 9 Sept. 1774, 21 Jan. 1775, 31 Jan. 1775.
55. 12 Oct. 1778, 23 Oct. 1778, 14 Nov. 1778, 14 Aug. 1781, 19 Dec. 1782.
56. 27 Mar. 1778, 30 June 1778, 13 Nov. 1787.
57. 27 Mar. 1778, 30 June 1778.
58. 9 Feb. 1779.
59. 23 July 1779.
60. 30 Nov. 1781.
61. 11 July 1786.
62. Westerfield, *op. cit.*, 357.
63. As to data concerning Anglo-Dutch trade in the eighteenth century see: H. C. Diferee, *De geschiedenis van den Nederlandschen handel tot den val der Republiek* (Amsterdam, 1908), 455–6.
64. See C. Whitworth, *State of the Trade of Great Britain* (1776), xxvi; van der Kooy, *op. cit.*, 51.
65. 14 Apr. 1781.
66. 14 Apr. 1780.

67. 11 May 1784.
68. 1 Sept. 1786.
69. Yehiel Prager to the house of Prager in Philadelphia, 27 Feb. 1784, P.R.O. C111/157.
70. 18 Feb. 1780. About deliberations concerning the question whether it was worthwhile to undertake exchange business in order to get other transactions see also 28 Aug. 1778, 1 June 1779.
71. 9 July 1782.
72. 3 May 1793.
73. During the American war the Pragers made special efforts to get orders for stocks; big loans contracted by the British Government at the time inflated the stock market, while the firm's profits from its regular trade shrank because of the war.
74. *Confusion de Confusiones* – the name of Joseph de la Vega's book about the Amsterdam Exchange (1688).
75. 11 Aug. 1787.
76. 19 Sept. 1781.
77. 25 May 1782.
78. 17 Jan. 1783.
79. Leib Prager to Meyer Prager, Calcutta, 1 Sept. 1792, P.R.O. C111/6.
80. On the importance of Government loans in the London money market see L. B. Namier, *The Structure of Politics at the Accession of George III* (1929), 46.
81. *Ibid.*, 58.
82. We have an indication that already in 1775 Yehiel Prager received a share in the loans, together with Anthony Bacon (Anthony Bacon to Yehiel Prager, n.d., P.R.O. C111/3). There is also a note from Lord North to Prager and a number of other merchants, dated 14 Jan. 1774 (C111/4), informing them that he would be glad to see them at Downing Street on Saturday, 22 January. This note was sent to Prager's address, but there is no evidence in the Prager Papers to show that he in fact received a share in the loan in that year.
   In C111/3 there is a communication from the Secretary of the Treasury, John Robinson, to Prager, informing him that he had been allotted £10,000 (April 1776), and in March 1778 he was informed by Robinson that he would receive a £20,000 share in the loan (C111/2). There is also a letter of James Bourdieu, dated 18 Apr. 1783, informing Prager that they had been jointly allotted £30,000 (C111/9), but it emerges from a letter of Jacob Prager that nothing came of this in the end (29 Apr. 1783). The amounts allotted to Prager were, in fact, insignificant. A list of major loan contractors for the year 1759, published by Namier, shows allotments amounting to between £250,000 and £500,000 each (*op. cit.*, 55).
83. Yehiel Prager Jr to Yehiel Prager, Ostend, 6 Mar. 1782.
84. 16 Aug. 1776.
85. 6 Feb. 1778, 10 Feb. 1778.
86. 3 Feb. 1778.
87. 2 Mar. 1779.
88. 29 Apr. 1783.
89. Shortly after Joseph Salomons' death, the Amsterdam merchant Jacob Herzfeld (Wolff) wrote to his friend Yehiel Prager that he had recommended him as an agent to the brothers Michael-David, who

had replied that if Joseph Salomons' son, Michael, would not satisfy them, they would approach Prager (Jacob Herzfeld to Yehiel Prager, Amsterdam, 15 Mar. 1763, P.R.O. C111/10). The correspondence between Michael-David and Yehiel Prager started in the spring of 1764. The Hanover house of Michael-David was directed by David Michael-David, and the Hamburg branch by his brother Meyer. David died in 1766, whereupon Meyer moved to Hanover and managed the whole business from there. The Michael-David letters which have been preserved among the Prager Papers touch upon several matters of general interest. About the Michael-David family see S. Gronemann, *Genealogische Studien über die alten jüdischen Familien Hanovers* (1913), 91 *seq.*

90. Already in the summer of 1764 Meyer Michael-David complained that Yehiel Prager was not sending him bills, while others were receiving 'bundles' (10 Tamuz 5524 – 10 July 1764). It seems that a few months later Michael-David despaired of regular bill business with the Pragers, and in the late summer they wrote that the bill trade with London was not profitable. This was obviously a pretext for breaking off the business connections with the Pragers. See letter of 21 Elul 5524 (18 Sept. 1764), P.R.O. C111/3.

91. Hanoverians who made use of Yehiel Prager's services were Alvensleben, Best and Hinuber. It is possible that Prager's connection with General Wallmoden, later British Ambassador in Vienna, was also formed with the help of Michael-David. Among the Prager Papers there are many letters of Wallmoden, mainly concerning the latter's stock affairs. Later Yehiel tried to make use of his acquaintance with Wallmoden in order to attain rights of residence in Ostend for his nephews, and apparently also in order to gain permission for Leib Prager to settle in India (Wallmoden to Yehiel Prager, Vienna, 17 Nov. 1781, P.R.O. C111/8). On Wallmoden's recommendation, Yehiel also became Baron Hans von Hardenberg's agent.

92. Michael-David offered to give Prager a share in this transaction, but nothing came of it, apparently because Yehiel refused to guarantee the bills which he was to send Michael-David (Meyer Michael-David to Yehiel Prager, Hanover, 13 Elul 5537 – 15 Sept. 1777, P.R.O. C111/3).

93. The transaction concerned the transfer of money on behalf of Caroline-Mathilda, George III's sister and ex-queen of Denmark. Caroline-Mathilda was arrested and banished after being accused of an illicit relationship with the Danish statesman Struensee. She settled in Celle, in the kingdom of Hanover. It does not clearly emerge from Michael-David's letters what sums were to be transferred on her account from England. They apparently included her pension of £5,000 and probably the return of her dowry. Meyer Michael-David asked Yehiel Prager in the spring of 1773 to approach Hinuber and persuade him to entrust the remittance of the moneys to him. When these negotiations were successfully concluded, Michael-David gave Prager only a quarter share in the transaction. Prager was greatly incensed by this, maintaining that he had obtained the contract for the remittance for Michael-David, which the latter denied. (See Meyer Michael-David's letters of 2 Nissan 5533 – 26 Mar. 1773 *et seq.*, P.R.O. C111/3).

94. To judge from his brothers' letters to him, Yehiel Prager used to brag about his influence with the ruling circles of London. When Meyer Michael-David denied that Yehiel had got him the remittance of the moneys for the ex-queen of Denmark (see preceding note), he nevertheless added: 'I am very pleased that you have such influence in the Court of His Majesty the King; they are really benevolent rulers.' (25 Sivan 5533 – 16 June 1773), P.R.O. C111/3.

CHAPTER 11

1. In the 1760s Yehiel Prager undertook joint tobacco transactions with Jan Abraham Willink of Hamburg. In 1770 he switched to the Jewish firm of Joseph da Fonseca David and Son; he sent them several consignments of tobacco, but refused to do any partnership business with them. The connection with da Fonseca lasted only until 1772. Prager thereupon tried to interest Meyer Michael-David in tobacco business, but without success. It seems that Prager did not again try to trade directly with Hamburg in tobacco – perhaps his close ties with Amsterdam prevented him from gaining a permanent foothold in the rival market.

2. In the 1760s Yehiel Prager maintained a correspondence with his relative Simon Hecksher of Copenhagen, and in 1778 he undertook a transaction in common with Asher Anschelhausen of that city. But these Danish connections were of no real significance.

3. About the 'merchants of the first hand' and 'merchants of the second hand' see T. P. van der Kooy, *Hollands stapelmarkt en haar verval* (Amsterdam, 1931), 21.

4. Rice had been South Carolina's most important product since the beginning of the century and largely supplanted Italian rice in the European market. The greater part of the rice which England imported from Charleston was re-exported to the Continent, chiefly to Holland and to Germany.

5. In the seventeenth century coffee was brought to Europe mainly from South-Western Arabia, but after 1720 Java and the West Indies became the chief suppliers. The French West Indies at first produced greater quantities of coffee than the British islands, much of which was consigned to Bordeaux. After the Seven Years' War, however, Jamaican coffee plantations were considerably extended in order to meet growing European demand, and London became an important market for coffee.

6. Venezuela was an important producer of cocoa, but despite the Spanish monopoly, Amsterdam remained the central market for Venezuela cocoa. About 1770 the cocoa plantations of Jamaica, as well as those of Grenada and St Vincent – which had passed from French into British possession as a result of the Seven Years' War – were considerably extended.

7. The development of the West Indian production of indigo went hand in hand with a rapid increase in European demand for this product and the growing fashion of wearing blue clothes. England's dependence on foreign indigo ceased as a result of the meteoric rise in South Carolina's indigo exports, which increased eightfold between 1747

and 1775. Towards the end of the century, however, Indian indigo largely supplanted the South Carolina product.

8. It seems that Mexico remained the chief supplier of cochineal to Europe throughout the eighteenth century. Consequently, London did not become a distributor of the product but imported Spanish cochineal for domestic consumption. The Prager letters usually refer to the consignment of cochineal from Amsterdam to London, but cochineal imported from Holland had a bad reputation in England.

9. The United States became the prime supplier of cotton only in the early nineteenth century. In the eighteenth century cotton was imported mainly from the Dutch colonies on the Guiana Coast (Surinam and the areas of Berbice and Esequibo), the West Indies and Turkey. The cotton of Guiana was considered superior to others and was about 50 per cent dearer than Turkish cotton. As a result of the growth of Britain's textile industry, the demand for cotton increased steadily, and it was one of the few items in the Pragers' business which was usually sent from Amsterdam to London.

10. The popularity of the new beverages, which required sweetening, caused a corresponding increase in the consumption of sugar. England consumed 15 times more sugar in 1800 than in 1700.

11. D. Macpherson, *Annals of Commerce, Manufactures, Fisheries and Navigation* (1805), 583.

12. L. A. Harper, *The English Navigation Laws* (New York, 1939), 255.

13. 21 Mar. 1775, 17 Feb. 1778.

14. 11 May 1779.

15. These figures are taken from the only surviving account of investments, included in David Prager's letter of 20 Feb. 1787. About £8,000 were invested in tobacco and 25,000 gulden in transport and customs on tobacco.

16. Borax is refined tincal.

17. Till the Seven Years' War, the trade in gum senegal was almost entirely in the hands of the French. During the war the British seized the French ports in the Senegal area, and at the conclusion of peace they retained the ports at Senegal and Gambia. Consequently part of the gum senegal trade passed into their hands.

18. C. J. Singer *et al.* (eds), A *History of Technology* (1954–8), 696.

19. A distinction should be made between *cassia ligea*, a spice resembling cinnamon, and *cassia fistula*, which had pharmaceutical uses. The Pragers traded only in the first-named product. Chinese canel is even more similar in taste to cinnamon than cassia.

20. D. Defoe, A *Plan of the English Commerce* (2nd edn, 1730), 165–6.

21. Most of the camphor imported into Europe was worked in Holland.

22. In 1784 the Amsterdam Pragers received eight cannons in commission from London, for sale in Amsterdam: 'A rare thing', remarked Jacob Prager (23 Nov. 1784). They managed to sell the guns only several months later. In March 1785 Jacob wrote to Yehiel: 'A strange question you ask, whether by f.43 or f.44 for the cannons we mean per pound or per 100 pounds. We mean per carat.'

23. Ginseng, a spice, was grown chiefly in North America. Its main market was China.

24. R. Glover to Yehiel Prager, Weybridge, 12 Oct. 1765, P.R.O. C111/1; Jacob Prager to Yehiel Prager, 19 Jan. 1779, 29 Mar. 1785, 4 Nov.

1785, 15 Nov. 1785, 18 Nov. 1785, 22 Nov. 1785, 13 Jan. 1786, 25 Jan. 1786, 7 July 1786; David Prager to Yehiel Prager, 29 Dec. 1786; Yehiel Prager to Meyer Prager & Co., London, 11 June 1785, P.R.O. C111/6.

25. Macpherson, *op. cit.*, IV, 51, and R. Voute's book about the tea trade, *Korte beschouwing van den daadlyken toestand van den theehandel* (Amsterdam, 1792). About Voute's connection with the East India Company see also Hoh-Cheung and L. H. Mui, 'The Commutation Act and the tea trade in Britain, 1784–1793', *EcHR*, 2nd ser., xvi (1963–4), 238–9.

26. 31 Mar. 1787.

27. For a time Yehiel Prager corresponded with G. Oswald and Co. of Glasgow. He ordered tobacco from them in September and again in December 1767, but it is not clear whether his orders were, in fact, carried out. This connection did not last – there is one later letter from Oswald, written in 1769, in which he says that he had not heard from Prager for a long time. Oswald's letters are in P.R.O. C111/1.

28. See John Bean's letters in P.R.O. C111/3–4.

29. When Jacob Prager was informed, in July 1781, that his son Leib had returned from his journey without having achieved much, although he had covered his expenses, he commented: 'For his trouble he has again seen a part of England.' (9 July 1781.)

30. John Kennion to Yehiel Prager, Liverpool, 6 May 1773, P.R.O. C111/4; Arnold Meyer to Yehiel Prager, Liverpool, 4 May 1773, C111/4; Thomas Mears to Yehiel Prager, Liverpool, 21 May 1773, C111/4; Meyer and Wilckens to Yehiel Prager, Liverpool, 28 Feb. 1774, C111/4; Daltera and Roche to Yehiel Prager, Bristol, 25 Nov. 1778, C111/2.

31. S. Sandys to Yehiel Prager, Liverpool, 28 Jan. 1775, P.R.O. C111/4. About the role of Rotterdam as a port of transit see pp. 214–15 above.

32. This refers to Dartmouth. The fact that an experienced merchant like Jacob Prager did not remember the name of the place demonstrates how recently the southern ports had begun to play a role in international trade.

33. 17 Dec. 1779.

34. See I.O.L., Despatches to Bengal, 20, f.811 *seq.*

35. When the Pragers were still novices in the drug trade – around 1775 – Jacob Prager feared that buying in 'fore-sales' might injure their reputation and warned Yehiel not to buy in this manner, because people in Amsterdam might stop giving him orders if it became known there. A few years later Jacob had grown accustomed to 'fore-sales' and regarded them as a normal way of doing business, of which one need not be ashamed. If he now had hesitations, they were based solely on practical considerations (3 Feb. 1775, 14 Feb. 1775, 21 Feb. 1775, 25 Apr. 1775, 16 Mar. 1779).

36. P.R.O. E112/1731 4458 (1790). Eleazar Levy Isaac states there that he dealt mainly in the purchase of Indian goods in London.

37. According to Meyer Prager, the firm had £10,000 invested in East India Company paper in 1789, in order to maintain 'influence' in India House (Meyer Prager to Amsterdam Pragers, London, 24 July 1789, P.R.O. C111/160). In 1791 Leib Prager complained bitterly about the neglect of their 'interest' in India House after

Yehiel's death: 'But I believe you have neglected your interest in the City. Yehiel, may he rest in peace, as well as I, have always endeavoured to have influence and interest with the Directors [of the East India Company], but it seems that all respect is gone' (Leib Prager to Esther and Meyer Prager, Benares, 20 Sept. 1791, P.R.O. C111/6).

38. This may explain the prevalent description of Yehiel Prager as 'a wealthy East India merchant', which has its origin in L. Alexander's book about Benjamin Goldsmid.

39. Yehiel Prager's connections with Clive and Verelst have already been mentioned. According to the latter, Yehiel had purchased most of the diamonds which they had brought from India. It seems that a real friendship grew up between Prager and Verelst. In a letter (St James Square, 11 July 1781, P.R.O. C111/9), Verelst sent his regards to Yehiel and Esther and inquired whether he could visit them the following Sunday and spend the night at their house. He also apologized for his wife's failure to visit them when she was in London.

   Yehiel was also acquainted with Warren Hastings and Lord Macartney, whom he described as his good friends. It is very probable that these connections, too, were formed in the course of diamond transactions (17 Jan. 1786).

40. Jacob Prager wrote on 18 Nov. 1785, in connection with their endeavours to get a commission for tea from the East India Company: 'So, do your best to make the Directors give a reply. You have such good friends among them, do you not?' In 1787 Leib Prager, who was then in India, asked his uncle to use his influence in order to get him an appointment in the Company's service: 'If you could get me into the service through your interest [i.e. influence], I would be very pleased. I think you have many friends and I too' (Leib Prager to Yehiel Prager, Calcutta, 5 Dec. 1787, P.R.O. C111/6).

   In the preceding year Leib had commented on the outcome of the elections to the Company's Court of Directors: 'I am glad that Michie is in the chair, as he is a very good friend of ours' (13 Sept. 1786, P.R.O. C111/6).

41. Edward Bartlett to Yehiel Prager, Hackney, 6 May 1786, P.R.O. C111/8).

42. Gabriel Israel Brandon to Leib Prager, 24 Sept. 1784, 1 Oct. 1784, P.R.O. C111/4. In the second letter Brandon wrote: 'I am confident that very few people have more interest than Mr. Salomons [Yehiel Prager].' In the same letter Brandon stated that the Chairman of the Court of Directors was under an obligation to Yehiel Prager and that he was his 'particular friend'.

43. This refers to Hananel d'Aguilar, who belonged to one of the most eminent Sephardi families in London. He and his brother went bankrupt in 1781 and it seems that Yehiel Prager intervened on his behalf at India House. In 1783 d'Aguilar wrote to Prager: 'I trust the alarm my hopes and expectation had on the first news of our friends' resignation, will be entirely eased and removed by the great influence and weight you will no doubt continue to have in the appointment of the said directors' (Hananel d'Aguilar to Yehiel Prager, Enfield, 2 Dec. 1783, P.R.O. C111/10).

44. This request was forwarded to Yehiel by his brother David, who

explained that they had approached him 'because they all know that you can attain at the Company whatever you want, and particularly as this can be to the Company's advantage' (12 Sept. 1787).

45. See the somewhat belated Christmas and New Year greetings, sent by a certain Smith, apparently a captain of an East Indiaman, to Leib Prager: 'My good friend – a merry Christmas and a happy New Year to the honble committee and in particular to you, my good friend. I now begin to look forward again with great pleasure in the hope of meeting our honble society by the middle of September next. I assure you that they are not forgot on board the *Dublin*. One toast is always the Committee.' (Smith to Leib Prager, Calcutta, 31 Dec. 1785, P.R.O. C111/8.) A few months later Leib, on his way to India, wrote in his Journal: 'Dear Mark, when you see any of the honourable members of the Committee, tell them that I have great concern to be absent from them.' (C111/6.)

46. N. Kiere to Yehiel Prager, Amsterdam, 7 July 1779, P.R.O. C111/2.

47. It is not clear what sort of power of attorney is meant. Perhaps the buyer had to authorize the seller to act on his behalf at the public sale, because the latter was formally regarded as the owner of the goods till after the sale. The contract is in P.R.O. C111/1.

48. 12 June 1778, 16 Mar. 1779.

49. This condition is not included in the contract of March 1784, but it is clear from Jacob Prager's letters that it was customary.

50. P.R.O. C111/1.

51. 24 Mar. 1780.

52. 22 Feb. 1782.

53. For considerations underlying the decision whether to buy by 'fore-sale' or at public sale see 16 Mar. 1779, 5 May 1780.

54. 18 Apr. 1780. For other descriptions of English ship-captains see 21 Dec. 1784 and 31 Mar. 1787.

55. 14 Sept. 1779. See also 8 Nov. 1785.

56. See 25 Sept. 1785, where Jacob writes about cochineal consigned to them by the Francos: 'We shall not smuggle it. It pays only a trifle.'

57. 6 Dec. 1785.

58. 20 Dec. 1785.

59. Meyer Prager to Yehiel Prager, Ostend, 1 Sept. 1781, P.R.O. C111/11.

60. 25 Dec. 1781.

61. van der Kooy, *op. cit.* 21.

62. 11 Aug. 1786.

63. Of special interest, in this connection, is Ploos' letter to Yehiel Prager of 17 Dec. 1773, P.R.O. C111/4.

64. A case of retailers taking part in a public sale is mentioned in the letter of 13 Dec. 1785.

65. 10 Feb. 1786.

66. 24 Mar. 1775.

67. See Jacob Prager's letter of 5 Mar. 1779: 'Our 13 barrels are not yet delivered. Such is this article – one cannot command the sugar-bakers when they must accept [the sugar]. Sometimes they accept immediately and sometimes they let it lie a month or more and pay 3 months after receipt [of the sugar].' See also 8 May 1781.

68. 18 Aug. 1786.

69. About the London custom of paying cash see 23 July 1784.

70. The Pragers included brokerage in all calculations of expenses on goods purchased in London. The customary rate was apparently 1 per cent of the value. See 10 Sept. 1779, 15 Nov. 1781, 24 Feb. 1783, 23 Nov. 1783 as well as Dirk de Veer to Yehiel Prager, Amsterdam, n.d. [1776], P.R.O. C111/3.
71. 17 Dec. 1779, 20 Feb. 1787. Although the international merchant could not hope to rival the broker's expertise, he, too, needed a wide knowledge in various kinds of goods. After returning from the inspection of damaged goods in Bruges, Meyer Prager Jr wrote: 'Now one can see clearly how useful it is to have a general knowledge of all goods and how this may help a person.' (Meyer Prager Jr to Yehiel Prager, Ostend, 25 May 1782, P.R.O. C111/11).
72. For a case of Yehiel Prager mistaking one kind of tobacco for another see 26 July 1784.
    In September 1782 Jacob informed Yehiel that the hides sent by the latter were not Buenos Aires hides, as he had thought: 'You are an expert in this as in elephant's tusks. Buenos Aires hides have no heads, no feet, and no tails.' (17 Sept. 1782.) Jacob himself revealed an astonishing ignorance in the matter of hides. In 1786 he admitted that he had not known till then that hides of many colours were always worth more than hides of uniform colour. (See 6 May 1786, which has explanatory drawings by Jacob in the margin.)
73. About the domination of the Amsterdam cotton market by Wils see 17 July 1778, 24 July 1778.
74. In a letter dated 10 Aug. 1775, Jacob warned Yehiel not to erase the numbers from the silk he had bought for the broker van Goor: 'Dear Yehiel, it is not advisable to erase the numbers and other marks, God forbid. We must act honestly. Except this van Goor there is no broker in this sort of silk, although [there are others] in Italian [silk]. And should we offer it to another broker or to merchants, and van Goor hears about it, as he certainly would immediately, he would obstruct us so that we should not be able to sell for half the value.'
75. 'Reb Mendele', the china-broker, is described as 'virtually the only broker for it [china], for Jews and Christians' (15 Oct. 1784).
76. 10 Sept. 1784.
77. 15 Oct. 1784.
78. 12 June 1784.
79. See 30 May 1780, where Jacob Prager compares the advantages of private as against those of public sale. He stresses the additional expenses which have to be incurred in the case of public sale. See also 2 June 1780 and 9 Mar. 1787.
80. 1 Nov. 1782, 25 July 1786, 16 Mar. 1790.
81. 9 Mar. 1787.
82. See C. H. Wilson, *Anglo-Dutch Commerce and Finance in the Eighteenth Century* (1941), 41.
83. About the gum transaction in which the Pragers became involved in 1774/5 see 30 Aug. 1774 and following letters. These letters reflect the speculative aspects of the business done on the Amsterdam exchange.
84. 26 Mar. 1775.
85. See 4 July 1783 which mentions a possibility of a speculation in cotton, and 20 Oct. 1787 for a speculation in cochineal.
86. For instances of the Pragers' reluctance to undertake risks during the

Anglo-Dutch War see 13 Feb. 1781, 20 Feb. 1781, 6 July 1781.
The firm's cautious policy was apparently typical for the attitude of
Amsterdam business at that time.

87. 3 Nov. 1778.

88. The differences of opinion between Yehiel and his brothers in
Amsterdam concerned mainly what the latter considered Yehiel's
excessive daring in diamond transactions during the 1770s and the
magnitude of his drug purchases in the 1780s.

89. 12 Apr. 1786. About the firm's condition at that time see p. 242 above.

90. There is no explicit evidence concerning the reasons which underlay
Yehiel Prager's decision to send Leib to India. It is probable that
Yehiel's letters to his brothers would not be more revealing, because,
as emerges from their replies, he did not explain his motives to them.
But the fact that Yehiel endeavoured to get Leib a monopoly of the
diamond trade in Benares and also the scale of the contracts for the
purchase of drugs, signed by Leib in pursuance of Yehiel's instructions,
point clearly to his intentions.

91. About the prices of tobacco during and after the American War see
N. W. Posthumus, *Inquiry into the History of Prices in Holland*
(Leiden, 1946), 203. Only in the early 1790s did tobacco prices return
to the level of the early 1770s. They began to climb once more in 1794,
as a result of the war with France. See also 22 Feb. 1785.

92. 10 Mar. 1775.

93. 14 Oct. 1785.

94. F. L. Nussbaum, 'The American tobacco trade and French politics',
Political Science Quarterly, XL (1925).

95. 31 Oct. 1786.

96. 8 Dec. 1786.

97. 19 Dec. 1786.

98. 16 Jan. 1787.

99. By the middle of June the Pragers had sold at least 250 barrels and
still had 1,800 on their hands (12 June 1787). Although this was a
staggering quantity for a firm like the Pragers, it represented less than
10 per cent of the quantity of tobacco re-exported in 1787
(26½ million lbs). It is interesting to note that in the following year
only a little over 7 million lbs were re-exported. See E. B. Schumpeter,
English Overseas Trade Statistics, 1697–1808 (1960), 62.

100. I. Schimmelpenninck to Yehiel Prager, Deventer, 5 May 1772,
P.R.O. C111/3.

101. 15 Dec. 1786.

102. 30 Jan. 1787.

103. 14 Nov. 1786.

104. 1 Feb. 1785.

105. 2 May 1785.

106. 14 Nov. 1786, 8 Dec. 1786, 6 Mar. 1787, 14 Apr. 1787, 4 May 1787,
21 Aug. 1787. On the difference between merchants who imported
tobacco from London and those who received directly from America
see 29 Mar. 1785, 8 Dec. 1786.

107. 5 June 1785.

108. Another obstructing factor may have been the competition of the
Western ports, though this does not explicitly emerge from the Prager
letters. From the late 1750s, Glasgow surpassed London as the fore-

most tobacco-importing port. See D. A. Farnie, 'The commercial empire of the Atlantic 1607–1783', *EcHR*, 2nd ser., xv (1962–3), 208.
109. 4 May 1787.
110. On 1 Jan. 1788 David Prager wrote that the profits of the preceding year were made mainly on tobacco and dyestuffs.
111. 17 Aug. 1787.
112. 5 Dec. 1786, 8 Dec. 1786.
113. 20 Aug. 1782, 16 Dec. 1782, 27 July 1784, 11 Jan. 1785, 1 Feb. 1785, 17 May 1785, 5 July 1785.
114. Leib Prager's journal, 10 June 1786, P.R.O. C111/6.
115. See Posthumus, *op. cit.*, 482–3.
116. Cassia was a cheap substitute for cinnamon, but the distinction between cassia and 'Chinese cinnamon', which is a true cinnamon, is not always clear, and it is not certain whether what Yehiel Prager held was *cassia lignea* or real cinnamon; the letters usually mention 'cassia', but on one occasion David Prager expressed his astonishment at the quantity of cassia and cinnamon still held by the London house (14 Apr. 1789).
117. Posthumus, *op. cit.*, 149.
118. Leib Prager to an unidentified correspondent, Calcutta, 17 Nov. 1791, P.R.O. C111/6.
119. Thus, there was an enormous increase in the imports of cassia and cassia buds from China by commanders and officers of the East India Company. The value of imports in 1785/6 was about 23 times greater than in 1775/6. See E. F. Pritchard, 'Private trade between England and China in the eighteenth century (1680–1833)', *Journal of the Economic and Social History of the Orient*, i (1958), 223.
120. 7 Apr. 1786, 13 June 1786.
121. Leib Prager to Yehiel Prager, Calcutta, 16 Feb. 1787, P.R.O. C111/6.
122. 31 Oct. 1786.
123. 21 Apr. 1789, P.R.O. C111/160.
124. I.O.L., Despatches to Bengal, 18, fos. 266 *seq.*; *ibid.*, 20, fos. 811 *seq.*
125. About the sale of Eastern drugs in various Continental ports see: 21 July 1780, 7 Jan. 1783, 27 July 1783, 11 May 1784, 6 July 1784, 27 July 1784, 13 Sept. 1785, 18 Oct. 1785, 5 May 1786.
126. 26 May 1789.
127. 24 July 1789.
128. 8 Oct. 1788, P.R.O. C111/147.
129. *Ibid.*
130. 11 Nov. 1788, P.R.O. C111/160.
131. During that summer drugs were sold at the Company branches in Zeeland, Delft, Rotterdam, Amsterdam, Horn and Enkhuizen (23 Oct. 1789).
132. 8 Sept. 1789, 11 Sept. 1789.
133. 16 Oct. 1789.
134. A Flemish pound was worth six gulden or a little more than half a pound sterling.
135. 16 Oct. 1789. Kiere's behaviour constituted an act of betrayal towards the combination, and David Prager warned the London house that if it became known, the plan would be doomed to failure 'and Kiere would be regarded as a scoundrel by his colleagues here' (23 Oct. 1789).

136. Kiere was obliged to take 12,000 lbs out of a total of 49,000 lbs sold; of this quantity, the Pragers had to take one-half (24 Nov. 1789).
137. 11 Sept. 1789.
138. 3 Nov. 1789.
139. 16 Nov. 1790. The camphor was sold for 28¾–29 Flemish pounds per lb.
140. Widow Salomons and Co. to Thomas Redhead, London, 8 Dec. 1791, P.R.O. C111/147.
141. 18 Aug. 1789.
142. Leib Prager to Esther Prager, Benares, 20 June 1792, P.R.O. C111/6.
143. The camphor was sold for £11. Esther's cousin Isaac, the new head of the Amsterdam house, resented this sale, maintaining that it had spoiled the market. (21 Sept. 1793, 10 Aug. 1793.)
144. During the first 40 years of the eighteenth century the average value of English exports to Holland amounted to £2,000,000 and in the following 40 years to £1,885,000. H. C. Diferee, *De geschiedenis van den Nederlandschen handel tot den val der Republiek* (Amsterdam, 1908), 455–6.
145. van der Kooy, *op. cit.*, 36.
146. For the years 1779 and 1780 there are only preliminary estimates.
147. 19 Jan. 1779.
148. The profits during the period 1774–86 were as follows:

1774	27,020 gulden
1775	?
1776	?
1777	46,324 gulden
1778	approximately 40,000 gulden (preliminary estimate)
1779	a small loss (preliminary estimate)
1780	?
1781	?
1782	35,751 gulden (not including the profits of the Ostend house)
1783	17,580 gulden
1784	33,325 gulden
1785	24,406 gulden
1786	14,178 gulden

    The profits of 1774 must not be taken as representing the normal net income of the firm in the period preceding the American War, because in that year the house suffered heavily from the fall in the prices of coffee (28 Apr. 1775). See also Posthumus, *op. cit.*, 78.
149. 19 Jan. 1779.
150. According to the available information, Jacob had three married daughters at the time of his death, who had, of course, received their respective dowries. In addition, the young Pragers who went to Philadelphia in 1783 received £500 from the Amsterdam house. Yehiel had only one married daughter (Jessy) at the time of his death; she had received a dowry of £2,000 when she married Benjamin Goldsmid.
151. It is clear from the letters of the Prager brothers that Yehiel undertook many diamond transactions on his own. The Amsterdam brothers knew this, but raised no objections. When Jacob visited London in 1786, he persuaded Yehiel to send them a consignment, but shortly after Yehiel was again selling the diamonds in London. In a letter dated 9 May

1775 Jacob mentioned diamonds and stocks as a potential private income of Yehiel. See also 4 July 1786, 25 May 1787.

152. C. Wilson, *Profit and Power – A Study of England and the Dutch Wars* (1957), 102.

153. R. Davis, 'English foreign trade 1700–1774', *EcHR*, 2nd ser., xv (1962–3), 288.

154. van der Kooy, *op. cit.*, 36–44.

155. 16 Mar. 1779. See also 25 Oct. 1774, 10 Jan. 1775, 5 June 1778, 12 Jan. 1779.

156. 5 Jan. 1779, 31 Oct. 1786, 7 Nov. 1786.

157. About the periodical dislocation of trade as a result of the freezing of the Zuider Zee see 19 Jan. 1779, 26 Jan. 1779, 14 Dec. 1780, 10 Dec. 1782, 17 Dec. 1784; G. Oswald to Yehiel Prager, Glasgow, 14 Dec. 1767, P.R.O. C111/1.

158. van der Kooy, *op. cit.*

159. 20 Aug. 1774.

160. 7 Apr. 1780.

161. 6 Apr. 1779.

162. As to the demand of commercial circles in Amsterdam for a tough line towards England see 11 Sept. 1778, 29 Sept. 1778, 30 Oct. 1778, 20 Nov. 1778, 5 Mar. 1779. Jan de Neufville, an acquaintance of the Pragers, was among the prominent exponents of this policy.

163. 27 Oct. 1780.

164. About the commercial standstill during the first months of the war see 16 Feb. 1781, 23 Mar. 1781, 9 Apr. 1781.

165. During the entire war a regular postal service was kept up between Hellevoetsluis and Harwich, but to be on the safe side the Pragers used for a time to send copies of their letters through Ostend, hence the double letters of this period.

166. On 6 July 1781 Jacob reported that ships were continuously arriving from London which had falsely given Emden as their destination. Among the Prager Papers is a bill of lading for 36 barrels of tobacco, consigned by Yehiel Prager to the Amsterdam house, marked 'per Embden' (enclosure in letter of 5 Nov. 1782). As to the trade between Liverpool and Ostend carried on by neutral ships see Gilbert and Co. to Yehiel Prager, Liverpool, 16 May 1781, P.R.O. C111/9.

167. As to the difference of 6 per cent in expenses, see 17 May 1781. In Anglo-Dutch trade a profit of 10 per cent was regarded as good and a profit of 20 per cent or more as exceptional (8 Jan. 1779, 5 Feb. 1779, 9 Jan. 1781, 22 Mar. 1782). In overseas trade much higher profits were necessary if commerce was to prosper. It is true that Jacob once remarked about a profit of 15 per cent made on tobacco consigned to them by the Philadelphia house: 'it is a very good business for the children' (19 Nov. 1784), but he was probably influenced by the fact that this was the youngsters' first successful transaction in America. Their uncle Yehiel had written to them at the beginning of the same year: 'You are mistaken if you consider 20 per cent a good profit on goods. In Europe you would be right, but take into account the length of time which elapses before people get their money back!' (Yehiel Prager to the House of Prager in Philadelphia, London, 4 Feb. 1784, P.R.O. C111/157).

168. 12 Apr. 1782, 16 Apr. 1782, 10 Sept. 1782.
169. 16 Apr. 1782.
170. 10 May 1785. The Pragers had certainly not foreseen this situation when, during the war, they shared in the efforts to concentrate the hides' trade in Ostend (15 Nov. 1781).
171. 27 Aug. 1782.
172. 19 Sept. 1783.
173. 8 Apr. 1783.
174. 7 Apr. 1783.
175. 4 Oct. 1785.
176. 14 Oct. 1785.
177. 7 Feb. 1786.
178. 31 Oct. 1786, 3 Nov. 1786. Edward Coxe to Yehiel Prager, London, n.d. [1786], P.R.O. C111/8.
179. 27 Apr. 1787.
180. 29 May 1787.
181. 15 June 1787.
182. 8 Jan. 1788.
183. 19 Jan. 1788.
184. 20 Feb. 1789.
185. 30 Dec. 1788, P.R.O. C111/160.
186. 28 Sept. 1790.
187. About the Pragers' negative attitude towards the French Revolution see 20 Oct. 1789, 3 Sept. 1790, 7 Jan. 1794, as well as the following letters from London to the Amsterdam house, in P.R.O. C111/161: 26 June 1792, 18 Sept. 1792, 22 Nov. 1793.
188. 14 Oct. 1794.
189. Isaiah Prager to Esther Prager, Calcutta, 30 Sept. 1796, P.R.O. C111/151 (a contemporary English translation of the original Yiddish letter, which has not been preserved).
190. van der Kooy, *op. cit.*, 41.
191. About the effect of gold and silver consignments by London Jews on the rate of exchange see 9 May 1775, 7 Sept. 1779, 19 Sept. 1783, 16 Dec. 1783, 18 May 1784, 20 Jan. 1786, 2 May 1786, 18 July 1786, 17 Oct. 1786. See also 8 June 1790 in P.R.O. C111/160.
192. 28 Dec. 1784.
193. 1 Aug. 1783.
194. 23 Nov. 1784.
195. 29 July 1788. See also 5 Jan. 1779, 21 Mar. 1780, where Jacob Prager explains how a small profit can be entirely wiped out by a slight rise in the rate of exchange, 27 Apr. 1784, 7/10 Sept. 1784, 7 Dec. 1784, 5 Oct. 1790 (P.R.O. C111/160).
196. 9 May 1775, 3 Apr. 1778, 23 Jan. 1781, 31 Aug. 1781, 10 Sept. 1781, 11 May 1784, 17 Oct. 1786.
197. 5 Dec. 1783, 29 Mar. 1785.

CHAPTER 12

1. The Prager letters mention only a single case of Indian diamonds not imported through London: in July 1783 Jacob Prager reported that the

merchants Jonah Kahn and Jacob Joffe had gone to Lorient in order to buy diamonds seized by the French on English ships (22 July 1783).

2. Gildemeester held the Portuguese contract for a period of about 30 years. He got it in 1757 or 1758 and kept it until 1787, when it was transferred to Benjamin Cohen. Gildemeester's clients were obliged to accept diamonds at each distribution, on penalty of being taken off the list if they refused. It seems that Gildemeester used to distribute every year 60,000 carats (25 Sept. 1778, 29 Sept. 1778), which made him a key figure on the diamond market of Amsterdam. See also Matthew Carrett to Yehiel Prager, 4 Apr. 1778, P.R.O. C111/2, and the following letters: 1 Nov. 1774, 6 Jan. 1775, 21 Mar. 1775, 15 May 1778, 21 July 1778, 25 Aug. 1778, 15 Dec. 1778, 20 Apr. 1779, 21 Dec. 1779, 18 Feb. 1780, 16 Mar. 1787, 31 Mar. 1787.

3. The Prager letters confirm the assumption that Indian diamonds were more highly valued than Brazilian stones, mainly because they lost less in cutting. In the 1780s we also find complaints about the deterioration in the quality of Brazilian diamonds. Nevertheless, when the prices of Indian stones were uncommonly high, buyers sometimes preferred the Brazilian sort which, unlike Indian diamonds, was sold open and could be inspected before the sale. It appears that about 1790 the quality of Indian stones also deteriorated, probably as a result of the exhaustion of the Indian mines, which was also reflected in a rapid reduction in the supply. This development partially explains Leib Prager's failure in India. About the relative qualities of Indian and Brazilian stones see 15 Nov. 1774, 22 Nov. 1774, 1 Aug. 1779, 26 Nov. 1779, 10 July 1783.

4. It seems that the Pragers never received diamonds on their own account directly from Lisbon, though in 1778 they received a consignment or two in commission from their Lisbon agent, M. Carrett. But Yehiel Prager made use of his Lisbon connections in another way: by purchasing stones from Carrett's brother in London. This trade was, of course, regarded as illegal by the Portuguese. See 17 Nov. 1778, 5 Jan. 1779, 22 Jan. 1779, 9 Feb. 1779, 16 Apr. 1779, 29 May 1781, 31 July 1781.

5. Samson Ferde is the same person as Samson Marcus. See 21 Mar. 1783, 25 Mar. 1783.

6. Leib Tutshke and his son Samuel are possibly the same as L. and Samuel Cohen. Leib Tutshke is mentioned in a letter written in 1780 by Rabbi T. Schiff – the chief Ashkenazi rabbi of London – to his brother in Frankfort. He writes that in the preceding year he had officiated at the marriage of the daughter of Leib Tutshke, whom he describes as a close friend of his and 'a very learned man, of high standing and very rich' (*JQR*, N.S., XI, 27).

7. In a letter dated 27 Apr. 1788 David Prager lists the names of the major diamond merchants of Amsterdam: Ferde, Cantor, Jerogam, Joseph Rosh – all Ashkenazim.

8. Indian stones are usually called 'Bengalese diamonds' in the Prager letters – reflecting the great change which had occurred in the Indian diamond market after 1765.

9. 29 July 1774. See also 9 May 1783.

10. In a letter, the first part of which is missing (apparently 13 Sept. 1774), Jacob Prager writes: 'As we hear, Hope has a big supply of diamonds

and cannot sell anything at his prices . . . and Gompertz will flourish as he did last year'. See also 3 Feb. 1775, 4 June 1779, 8 Feb. 1780, 3 Mar. 1780, 16 Apr. 1783, 17 Feb. 1784, 4 Sept. 1786, 11 Sept. 1787, 9 Nov. 1790. These letters show that for 15 years, at least, Hope served as Gompertz's Amsterdam diamond agent. All non-Jewish houses in Amsterdam acting as diamond agents employed the Jewish broker Ruben Keyser – the brother of the London Keyser (22 Nov. 1785).

11. On two occasions the letters mention Jewish agents of the Gompertzes – Eli Nijmegen and Benjamin Cohen (Amersfoort), who was Solomon Barent Gompertz's father-in-law (11 Sept. 1789). But the Gompertzes' chief agent was undoubtedly Hope. The Gompertzes' preference for non-Jewish agents is understandable in view of the excellent information service maintained by the Jewish diamond merchants, which ruled out any secrecy in the trade.

12. Barukh Cantor to Yehiel Prager, 3 Tamuz 5526 (10 June 1766), 22 Tamuz 5526 (29 June 1766), 9 Av 5527 (4 Aug. 1767), 22 Kislev 5530 (21 Dec. 1769), P.R.O. C111/1.

13. Jacob Prager's P.S. to Barukh Cantor's letter of 24 Elul 5527 (18 Sept. 1767), P.R.O. C111/1.

14. H. Verelst to Sir Robert Barker, Wadworth, 2 Nov. 1781, P.R.O. C111/10.

15. 16 Sept. 1774.

16. 14 Apr. 1780.

17. Jacob Barnet to Yehiel Prager, Cape of Good Hope, 6 May 1777, P.R.O. C111/2.

18. Matthew Carrett to Yehiel Prager, 4 Apr. 1778, P.R.O. C111/5.

19. The sharp competition which marked the London diamond market at that time is clearly reflected in the Prager letters. It seems that the main battle was waged by the Pragers on the one hand and the Gompertzes and Nordens on the other. See 19 Aug. 1774, 23 Aug. 1774, 15 Nov. 1774 ('De Wolfkhe told us that people had told him that you and Gompertz were ruining trade there, and are driving [prices] up and similar rumours').

20. The firm of Jerogam was under an obligation to the Pragers for having supported them when their diamond cutting business was still in its beginning. Jacob and David Prager had complete confidence in the Jerogam brothers and regarded the association with them as an important asset in view of their own inexperience in the diamond trade.

21. In 1787 Yehiel Prager explained on two occasions to his brother David why he was unable to send diamonds to Amsterdam. Of the reasons given by Yehiel only one is known (from David's reply), namely that the stones had to be sold on credit in Amsterdam, while cash had to be paid for them in London. David regarded this as the most weighty argument advanced by Yehiel (25 May 1787).

   In 1793 Esther Prager maintained that, as an importer, she could not send diamonds to Amsterdam if she did not want to incur the anger of those merchants who regarded this as their own particular sphere (24 May 1793, P.R.O. C111/160). It is, of course, possible that one of Yehiel's most important considerations against sending diamonds to Amsterdam was his unwillingness to share the profits with his brothers.

22. There was a lively trade in small, cheap, uncut diamonds between Amsterdam and Antwerp. Merchants from the latter city often visited Amsterdam in order to buy stones and they also kept up a direct connection with London. Thus, Yehiel Prager reported on 25 May 1779 that De Clerck of Antwerp was buying all the 'turn out' diamonds from Gompertz and other Jewish diamond merchants in London.

23. 9 July 1782.

24. The papers of the Amsterdam house not having survived, we cannot say with certainty what connections the Dutch Pragers maintained over the years, but it seems unlikely that they could have maintained important connections which would not have come to light through their letters to London, at least from 1775 onwards.

25. Aaron Meyer's father-in-law was the well-known court-Jew Veitel Heine Ephraim, who was also the head of the Jewish community of Berlin. Meyer is mentioned in Moses Mendelssohn's letters.

26. Yehiel Prager's chief consideration when he decided to establish commercial relations with Salomons in 1777 was perhaps that he might be able to get tobacco through him, at a time when tobacco was becoming scarce. But if that had been his expectation, he was soon disillusioned – in April 1778 Salomons wrote to him that little tobacco was reaching Kingston (28 Apr. 1778, P.R.O. C111/2). It seems that there was a general mistrust of West Indians in the City. In March 1779 Salomons wrote to Yehiel Prager: 'tho' whatever ideas you may harbour of the West Indians, you may rest assured I mean nothing but honour and honesty' (20 Mar. 1779, P.R.O. C111/2).

27. The letter, undated, is among Abraham Salomons' letters of 1787 (P.R.O. C111/6).

28. Abraham Lara and the two Brandons were all sworn brokers.

29. Robert Glover to Yehiel Prager, 25 Sept. 1766, P.R.O. C111/1; Tierney and Lilly to Yehiel Prager, 16 Mar. 1779, C111/3. See also Daltera & Roche to Yehiel Prager, Bristol, 7 Dec. 1779, C111/2. In this letter they inform Prager that a seller of hides in Bristol did not agree to Prager's conditions 'because of Mr. Lara's conduct on the day of the sale'.

30. According to Lucien Wolf, Gabriel Israel Brandon held the exclusive right to act as tobacco broker in London (L. Wolf, *Essays in Jewish History*, 1934, 217). The Brandons were tobacco brokers to the London house of the Pragers throughout its existence.

31. Gabriel Israel Brandon to Leib Prager, London, 24 Sept. 1784, 1 Oct. 1784, P.R.O. C111/4.

32. When Jacob Prager learned that Hananel Mendes da Costa had asked for a price-list, he commented: 'We expect much from him, he has daring and courage'. About Hananel Mendes da Costa's activity as managing partner in a ship trading with the Mediterranean, Spain and the West Indies, see P.R.O. C12/1696, 3572 (1783) and C12/596.1 (1785).

33. In the summer of 1778 d'Aguilar visited the Amsterdam Pragers and proposed to them joint enterprises to Gibraltar and Venice (28 Aug. 1778). Jacob Prager wrote about him: 'He talks nothing but trade and is heart and soul in it' (18 Sept. 1778).

34. About the firm of Francis and Jacob Franco see P.R.O. C12/1089.11

(1789) and C12/634.20 (1791). They approached the Pragers shortly
after the establishment of the firm (19 Jan. 1779).

35.

Partnerships of the Pragers and Sephardi firms 1778–84

(This and the following list have been compiled from the Prager letters and
are probably not complete)

Date	Name of Partner	Merchandise
1778	Hananel and David d'Aguilar	Coffee
1779	Hananel Mendes da Costa	Hides
1779	Hananel and David d'Aguilar	?
	d'Aguilar and Franco	Cochineal
	d'Aguilar and Franco	Hides
	d'Aguilar and Franco	Cocoa
	Lara	Indigo
	Hananel Mendes da Costa	Coffee
	Hananel Mendes da Costa	Hides
1782	Franco	Cassia
1782	Brandon	Coffee
1784	Franco	Tobacco

Commission business of the Pragers on behalf of Sephardi firms 1775–87

Date	Principal	Merchandise
1775	Hananel Mendes da Costa	Tobacco
1776	Hananel Mendes da Costa	Diamonds
1779	Hananel Mendes da Costa	Cocoa
1780	d'Aguilar	Diamonds
1781	d'Aguilar	Diamonds
1784	Franco	Cochineal
1785	Franco	Hides
1785	Franco	Cassia
1785	Franco	Indigo
1786	Franco	Indigo
1786	Lindo and Israel	Indigo and cochineal
1787	Lindo and Israel	Indigo and cochineal
1787	Hananel Mendes da Costa	Tobacco

36. See above. On 19 Sept. 1788, for instance, Meyer Prager wrote from
Amsterdam that if Brandon was their partner in tobacco, their
competitors would not be able to harm them.

37 The Amsterdam Pragers often had misgivings about the advisability
of undertaking joint transactions with Jewish textile merchants
(23 June 1778, 27 Dec. 1780, 25 June 1784), and they mistrusted both
Simon Tanhum and Levy Cohen. About the latter Jacob Prager wrote

on 11 Nov. 1782, after informing Yehiel that Cohen had sent benjamin to Amsterdam: 'We report this only in order that you beware of this Levy. Whenever he sees that you buy something, he buys [it] too. We have often observed it.'

38. 3 July 1778.
39. 7 Dec. 1781, 31 Jan. 1782, 25 June 1784.
40. 22 Feb. 1780.
41. 25 Dec. 1781.
42. 23 Nov. 1782.
43. 22 Feb. 1788.
44. 10 Nissan 5532 (13 Apr. 1772), P.R.O. C111/13.
45. 12 May 1778.
46. 23 Mar. 1784.
47. 18 Feb. 1780.
48. P.R.O. C111/3.
49. 22 June 1781.
50. 22 June 1784.
51. 16 Apr. 1793.
52. 13 Apr. 1781.
53. Esther Prager to Isaac Prager, London, 18 May 1792, P.R.O. C111/160.
54. There are many passages reflecting a critical attitude of the Pragers towards the conduct of Jews in business. It must be remembered, however, that the brothers' own conduct was not always above reproach, and it is quite possible that their remarks were not always meant to be taken quite seriously. They are not, however, without significance. See, for example, 28 Jan. 1779, 5 Oct. 1779, 24 May 1785, 8 May 1787.
55. When Meyer Michael-David learned in 1772 of the Bank of England's refusal to discount Jewish bills of exchange, he remarked: 'In fact you have more Jews' hatred there than we have here' (10 Nissan 5532 – 13 Apr. 1772, P.R.O. C111/3). Jacob Prager wrote in 1778: 'Is it true that there is a written announcement in the Bank there, saying that they do not want to discount [bills drawn] on Jews? There are letters here from Jews reporting this. Letters have also been sent by merchants here [in Amsterdam] to merchants there [in London], instructing them, in view of this, on no account to take anything [i.e. bills] from Jews, drawn on Jews in London. If this is true, it would constitute a great act of wickedness towards Jews on the part of the Bank there.' (12 May 1778).
56. 23 Apr. 1779.
57. 20 Nov. 1781.
58. 15 Sept. 1789.
59. 2 Apr. 1784.
60. The *Nieuwe Nederlandsche Jaarboeken* report a high percentage of Jewish bankruptcies in the crises of 1763 and 1772. See J. G. van Dillen, 'De economische positie en betekenis der Joden in de Republiek en in de Nederlandsche koloniale wereld', in *Geschiedenis der Joden in Nederland*, ed. G. Brugmans and A. Franks (Amsterdam, 1940), 581. Van Dillen, too, ascribes the extreme sensitivity of Jews to economic depressions to their intensive activity in the exchange trade. In a passage already quoted, Meyer Michael-David speaks of the many

Jews who were in trouble during the economic crisis of 1772 (Meyer Michael-David to Yehiel Prager, 20 Teveth 5533 – 15 Jan. 1773, P.R.O. C111/3).

61. 25 Mar. 1783.
62. 27 Mar. 1786.
63. 27 Mar. 1781, 21 June 1781, 22 June 1781, 22 June 1784.
64. Meyer Michael-David to Yehiel Prager, 19 Elul 5532 (17 Sept. 1772): 'That gentleman, Reb Yehiel Prager, in case you know the good man, has, I am sure, realized that the rates of exchange are rising, and has therefore drawn entirely on his house [in Amsterdam]. For us, however, there is a double loss: first – the rate of exchange, second – Jewish bills inevitably lose on being discounted in Ams[terdam].' (P.R.O. C111/3.)
65. About the strained relations between Sephardim and Ashkenazim in Amsterdam at that time see H. J. Zimmels, *Ashkenazim and Sephardim* (1958).
66. Jacob Prager to Leib Bing, Amsterdam letter of 10 Mar. 1775.
67. 21 Mar. 1775.
68. 29 Jan. 1781, 13 Feb. 1781. 'Jews' is here used in the sense of 'Ashkenazim'.
69. On 7 Sept. 1779 Jacob Prager wrote: 'Old Castro died today. He was over 80 years old. We do not know whether the business will go on. One son is capable but wild. It is possible that the Sephardim will now come to us.'
70. The house of Francis and Jacob Franco had an initial capital of £51,000 (P.R.O. C12/1089.11). Yehiel Prager's estate amounted to £48,000.
71. 5 Mar. 1789. De Bruyn was one of the firm's brokers in Amsterdam.
72. The Dutch island of St Eustatius became an important commercial centre during the American War. It was captured by the British shortly after Holland joined in the war and it seems that, as a result, Dutch Jews of the Portuguese community sustained heavy losses: see 8 May 1781.
73. 24 Apr. 1781.
74. When d'Aguilar (apparently David d'Aguilar) and one of the brothers Franco were visiting Amsterdam in the summer of 1779, Jacob Prager wrote: 'I have not yet seen Aguilar and Franco. They do not come to us, and if they do not come to us, they can dream of us coming to visit them.' (18 June 1779.)
75. A similar process of decline, on the one hand, and rapid economic expansion, on the other, was discernible among Hamburg Jews. Kellenbenz pointed out that one of the main causes may well have been the propensity of the Sephardim to maintain a refined way of life, while the Ashkenazim, on the whole, were economically more ambitious and prepared to accept a much lower standard of living in order to be able to devote as much as possible of their resources and energies to business. See H. Kellenbenz, *Sephardim an der unteren Elbe* (Wiesbaden, 1958), 469.
76. 24 Mar. 1775.
77. 21 June 1781.
78. This probably refers to the firm of Franco, managed by Elias Lindo.
79. 9 Oct. 1781.

80. 29 Oct. 1781.
81. 9 July 1782.
82. P.R.O. C12/1089.11.
83. 25 Aug. 1778.
84. 30 July 1789.
85. 11 Mar. 1785.
86. 4 Aug. 1789.
87. In January 1788 Jacob Prager told Yehiel that an unnamed Polish count of Grodno was looking for a Jew to serve him in a certain capacity. Jacob suggested that one Jost Hess of London may be suitable for the job, but that 'he must conduct himself as a Jew and not deride our religion.' (20 Jan. 1778.) See also 21 June 1785, 18 Sept. 1785, reflecting a critical attitude towards Benjamin Cohen (Amersfoort) because of his un-Jewish way of life.
88. 3 Apr. 1778.
89. 22 Aug. 1780.
90. 11 Aug. 1780.
91. 12 July 1782.
92. Jacob Herzfeld (Wolff), a friend of the German Jewish philosopher Moses Mendelssohn. He was on good terms with the Pragers and for several years corresponded with Yehiel Prager (P.R.O. C111/1).
93. 13 Nov. 1778.
94. 6 June 1780.
95. 27 July 1781.
96. Yehiel Prager to the house of Prager in Philadelphia, 4 May 1785, P.R.O. C111/157. Yehiel furnished his nephews with a letter of recommendation from his friend Solomon Henry in London to the famous house of Gratz in Philadelphia. Subsequently one of the Gratz brothers reported to Yehiel on the conduct of the young Pragers in Philadelphia. (About the Gratz brothers and their relations with Solomon Henry see E. Wolf and M. Whiteman, *The History of the Jews of Philadelphia from Colonial Times to the Age of Jackson*, Philadelphia, 1957, 36–65.)
97. 6 June 1785. See also 5 Dec. 1785 about the proposed marriage of Yehiel Prager's daughter Jessy.
98. Leib Prager to Meyer Prager, Calcutta, 1 Feb. 1792, P.R.O. C111/6.
99. See 9 May 1780 about Jacob Herzfeld's son, who was a physician, and 23 May 1786 about the lawyer Moses Shohet.
100. In the above-mentioned letter, dated 9 May 1780, Jacob Prager asked Yehiel to help Herzfeld's son, who had completed his medical studies in Goettingen and wanted to settle in England. Jacob added that 'it is indeed a miserable calling, but one can never know'.
101. The celebration of the Jewish boy's attainment of maturity at the age of 13, according to religious law and tradition.
102. 23 Dec. 1774.
103. 2 Feb. 1779.
104. 17 Dec. 1782. In an earlier letter Jacob Prager had already expressed the hope that they would be able to make satisfactory arrangements for all their children 'which will require some trouble' (4 June 1782 – there are two copies of the letter of this date, which are, however, identical only in part. The above quoted passage appears only in one copy).

105. 1 Aug. 1783. The Pragers who went to Philadelphia undertook to give a share of 12½ per cent to each of Yehiel Prager's children who would join their American house.
106. 11 Mar. 1783.
107. 27 June 1783.
108. In the 1790s Mordecai (Mark), Simeon and Leib Jr (Lionel) Prager went to India. Simeon died there in December 1793, while Mordecai and Lionel returned after a short sojourn in the East.
109. In February 1789 the firm had 50,000 gulden invested in the Philadelphia house, out of a total invested capital of 275,000 gulden (20 Feb. 1787).
110. 15 Sept. 1778.
111. Although business considerations played a paramount part in all matchmaking, personal factors were not without importance. When Gompertz of London put out feelers concerning the possibility of a match between Leib Prager and one of the daughters of the rich Benjamin Cohen, David Prager commented: 'We do not know all the daughters, but as we hear, they are ladies of easy virtue' (13 Aug. 1781). When Leib Prager, who was in India at the time, heard that a certain Dr Meyers of London was courting his sister Teibe, he wrote: 'You wrote me that Dr Meyers is courting her. If he is sure he loves her, it would be a good match, in my opinion. But it is much better to remain single than to repent later on and live unhappily' (20 Oct. 1789, P.R.O. C111/6). David Prager had gone even further when he had written some years earlier: 'Money really does not make one happy, to live cheerfully is everything' (22 Feb. 1780).
112. 2 Feb. 1787.
113. It seems that the only sister who did not need the assistance of the Pragers was 'Goldkhe', who was married to an Amsterdam merchant by the name of Levy (apparently his personal name). One sister lived in Offenbach and another in Berlin. It is not certain whether the latter is the same as 'Matta' who was married to Moses Waag.
114. 17 Feb. 1784.
115. 8 Apr. 1783.
116. 10 May 1785.
117. 20 May 1785.
118. 19 Jan. 1779.

Appendices

APPENDIX A. INVESTMENTS OF MOSES MENDES DA COSTA
(1756)
(from P.R.O. C12/292.23 – schedule)

	Total £	Investments in trade to Spain and her colonies	Investments in East India trade
Investments in goods	25,321	20,791	4,530 (All in coral)
Investments in bottomry loans	6,531	4,847	1,684
	31,852	25,638	6,214

Investments in goods   79.5%
Investments in bottomry loans   21.5%

Investments in trade to Spain and her colonies   80.5%
Investments in East India trade   19.5%

Destination of investments in goods to Spain and her colonies
(in £)

To Spain	Cadiz	7,893
	Seville	742
To colonies	Veracruz	8,067
	Cartagena	2,567
	Buenos Aires	990
	South Sea	532
	Total	20,791

APPENDIX B. THE HOUSE OF JOSEPH AND MENASSEH MENDES

Consignments from Barbados to London and from London to Barbados 1681–1709
(from P.R.O. C5/356/75)

a. Consignments from London to Barbados
Value of goods sent to Barbados (purchase prices in £)

Period	Value of goods	Annual average
12 Nov. 1681–20 Oct. 1682	3,016	2,585
1 Jan. 1683–1 Sept. 1685	5,103	1,914
1 Sept. 1685–2 June 1687	5,396	2,934
12 July 1687–20 Feb. 1689	4,755	2,195
8 Sept. 1689–10 Jan. 1692	7,922	3,278
2 Feb. 1692–1 Mar. 1694	6,099	2,361
20 Aug. 1694–20 Jan. 1697	9,634	3,400
29 June 1697–8 Sept. 1698	5,984	4,224
18 Nov. 1698–15 Feb. 1700	7,329	4,886
9 June 1700–26 July 1703	11,327	2,957
10 Apr. 1704–4 Mar. 1706	2,877	1,259
30 Aug. 1706–10 Aug. 1708	2,737	1,059

b. Consignments from Barbados to London

Period	Value of goods sent from Barbados to London (sale prices) £	Value of bills of exchange sent from Barbados to London
1681–1682	2,052	–
5 May 1683–12 Sept. 1685	3,790	1,400
23 Nov. 1685–25 Apr. 1687	2,882	2,614
15 July 1687–13 Mar. 1689	3,593	2,339
13 Mar. 1689–1 Oct. 1691	2,516	3,333
11 Oct. 1691–25 Feb. 1694	4,899	8,468
25 July 1694–29 Dec. 1697	2,109	9,554
24 Dec. 1697–5 Aug. 1698	3,826	3,145
25 Aug. 1698–31 Aug. 1700	3,876	14,898
15 Nov. 1700–25 June 1703	3,687	4,002
3 Nov. 1703–1 Sept. 1706	1,963	13,011
4 Sept. 1706–23 Dec. 1707	4,589	1,827
2 Jan. 1708–10 Nov. 1709	4,378	839
Total	44,160	65,430

APPENDIX C. SHARE OF JEWS IN GOLD SALES TO BANK OF ENGLAND 1710–30

(from Bank of England ledgers)

Period	Total sales £	Sales by Jews	Proportional share of Jewish sellers %
22 Feb. 1710–30 May 1711	81,501	9,564	11.7
12 July 1711–3 Dec. 1711	211,262	42,941	20.3
8 Dec. 1712–17 Dec. 1713	229,288	105,087	46.0
12 Sept. 1713–21 Jan. 1715	1,250,078	62,727	5.0
22 Jan. 1715–11 Jan. 1716	1,648,390	72,264	4.4
12 Jan. 1716–8 Jan. 1717	891,904	83,847	9.4
9 Jan. 1717–9 Dec. 1717	573,483	44,990	7.8
9 Oct. 1718–17 Dec. 1718	104,189	4,513	4.3
23 Dec. 1718–7 Jan. 1720	687,964	45,842	6.7
7 Jan. 1720–26 Nov. 1720	630,734	12,535	2.0
1 Dec. 1720–4 Oct. 1721	208,296	8,655	4.1
5 Oct. 1721–5 Jan. 1723	590,061	19,380	3.3
8 Jan. 1723–15 May 1724	680,606	9,438	1.4
24 Apr. 1724–31 Dec. 1724	135,449	–	0.0
9 Jan. 1725–Aug. 1730	1,824,910	263	0.0014

APPENDIX D. SHARE OF JEWS IN LOANS GIVEN BY BANK OF ENGLAND ON SECURITY OF GOLD DEPOSITS, 1713–22

(from Bank of England ledgers)

Period	Total of loans £	Loans to Jews	Proportional share of Jews in loans %
16 Feb. 1713–17 Dec. 1713	132,269	5,880	4.4
2 Jan. 1714–29 Jan. 1715	218,725	61,070	27.9
19 Feb. 1715–29 Dec. 1715	151,415	47,270	31.9
3 Jan. 1716–22 Dec. 1716	75,120	24,570	32.7
24 Dec. 1716–6 Feb. 1718	108,451	44,300	40.8
10 Mar. 1718–4 May 1719	44,013	29,215	66.4
22 May 1719–18 Jan. 1720	37,550	11,120	29.6
18 Jan. 1720–19 Oct. 1720	122,268	680	0.6
19 Dec. 1720–15 Nov. 1721	18,425	1,400	7.6
28 Feb. 1722–20 Dec. 1722	21,550	–	–
Total	929,786	225,505	24.3

APPENDIX E. SHARE OF JEWS IN LOANS GIVEN BY BANK OF ENGLAND ON SECURITY OF SILVER DEPOSITS, 1713–25

(from Bank of England ledgers)

Period	Total of loans £	Loans to Jews	Proportional share of Jews in loans %
18 Sept. 1713–26 Jan. 1714	45,513	11,125	24.4
14 Jan. 1715–2 June 1715	6,075	4,725	77.8
30 June 1716–16 Dec. 1717	653,071*	528,471	80.9
Oct. 1720	4,893	4,893	100.0
17 July 1721–9 Nov. 1721	54,730	43,500	79.7
14 Dec. 1721–10 Jan. 1723	136,646	84,385	61.9
21 Jan. 1723–20 Aug. 1723	39,829	14,279	35.8
18 Sept. 1723–22 Dec. 1724	71,436	27,515	38.5
20 Jan. 1725–29 July 1725	35,300	–	–
Total	1,047,493	718,893	68.7

* The main 'non-Jewish' depositor during this period was the East India Company

APPENDIX F. SHARE OF HOUSES OF MEDINA AND SALVADOR IN JEWISH GOLD SALES TO BANK OF ENGLAND, 1710–24

Period	Value of gold sold by Jews £	Value of gold sold by Medina	Value of gold sold by Salvador	Share of Medina %	Share of Salvador	Combined share of Medina and Salvador
2 Feb. 1710– 30 May 1711	9,564	4,339	2,700	45.4	28.2	73.6
12 July 1711– 3 Dec. 1711	42,941	17,073	6,831	39.8	15.9	55.7
8 Dec. 1712– 17 Dec. 1713	105,096	49,757	7,133	47.3	6.8	54.1
19 Dec. 1713– 21 Jan. 1715	62,726	43,823	2,978	69.9	4.7	74.6
22 Jan. 1715– 11 Jan. 1716	72,264	66,312	3,473	91.8	4.8	96.6
12 Jan. 1716– 8 Jan. 1717	83,847	57,334	15,876	68.4	18.9	87.3
9 Jan. 1717– 9 Dec. 1717	44,990	18,241	10,887	40.5	24.2	64.7
9 Oct. 1718– 17 Dec. 1718	4,513	4,513	–	100.0	–	100.0
23 Dec. 1718– 7 Jan. 1720	45,842	33,324	12,143	72.7	26.5	99.2
7 Jan. 1720– 26 Nov. 1720	12,535	4,226	1,110	33.7	8.9	42.6
1 Dec. 1720– 4 Oct. 1721	8,655	4,288	2,787	49.5	32.2	81.7
5 Oct. 1721– 5 Jan. 1723	19,380	–	12,904	–	66.6	66.6
8 Jan. 1723– 15 May 1724	9,438	–	9,345	–	99.0	99.0
Total	521,791	303,230	88,167	58.1	16.9	75.0

APPENDIX G. SHARE OF THE HOUSES OF MEDINA AND SALVADOR IN LOANS GIVEN BY BANK OF ENGLAND ON SECURITY OF GOLD, 1714–20

Period	Value of loans to Jews £	Value of loans to Medina	Value of loans to Salvador	Share of Medina %	Share of Salvador	Combined share of Medina and Salvador
2 Jan. 1714– 29 Jan. 1715	61,070	43,154	1,300	70.7	2.1	72.8
29 Jan. 1715– 29 Dec. 1715	47,279	35,980	4,700	76.1	9.9	86.0
3 Jan. 1716– 22 Dec. 1716	24,570	16,280	3,340	66.2	13.5	79.7
24 Dec. 1716– 6 Feb. 1718	44,300	17,510	14,650	39.5	33.1	72.6
10 Mar. 1718– 4 May 1718	29,215	22,800	6,415	78.0	22.0	100.0
22 May 1719– 18 Jan. 1720	11,120	5,270	5,850	47.4	52.6	100.0
Total	217,554	140,994	36,255	64.8	16.7	81.5

APPENDIX H. SHARE OF JEWS IN SILVER SALES TO EAST INDIA COMPANY, 1744–56

(from East India Company General Cash Journals)

Year	Total* £	From Jews	Proportional share of Jewish sellers %	Proportional share of Jewish sellers relative to total of private sellers
1744	132,896	32,201	24.2	–
1745	45,237	8,479	18.7	–
1746	–	–	–	–
1747	140,241	45,278	32.4	–
1748	853,849	22,997	2.7	16 (approx.)
1749–50	654,180	654,180	100.0	–
1751	1,041,793	170,088	16.3	36
1752	773,234	89,053	11.5	15.11
1753	628,885	154,152	24.5	–
1754	394,908	79,960	20.2	–
1755	238,894	10,728	4.5	17 (approx.)
1756	397,731	50,617	12.7	94

* The totals are not entirely reliable as payments to the Bank of England frequently appear under the Bank's name instead of under 'silver'

APPENDIX I. IMPORTS OF DIAMONDS FROM INDIA TO ENGLAND 1711–96

(according to the General Cash Journals of the East India Company)

Year	Total of imports £	Jews	Partner-ships	Non-Jews	Jews %	Partner-ships	Non-Jews
1711	13,100	2,600	–	10,500	19.8	–	80.2
1712	36,500	14,700	6,300	15,500	40.3	17.3	42.4
1713	40,300	20,400	–	19,900	50.6	–	49.4
1714	37,900	12,600	5,400	19,900	33.3	14.2	52.5
1715	37,100	13,000	3,400	20,700	35.0	9.2	55.8
1716	97,000	31,700	8,800	56,500	32.7	9.1	58.2
1717	101,800	57,500	20,800	23,500	56.4	20.4	23.2
1718	19,800	6,200	10,900	2,700	31.3	55.0	13.7
1719	21,500	7,700	7,500	6,300	35.8	34.9	29.3
1720	1,700	300	–	1,400	17.6	–	82.4
1721	51,300	38,900	4,600	7,800	75.8	9.0	15.2
1722	3,900	2,200	1,000	700	56.4	25.6	18.0
1723	59,400	47,800	3,700	7,900	80.5	6.2	13.3
1724	97,500	71,400	–	26,100	73.2	–	26.8
1725	110,900	86,200	4,300	20,400	77.7	3.9	18.4
1726	104,800	63,400	–	41,400	60.4	–	39.6
1727	100,300	48,800	11,900	39,600	48.6	11.9	39.5
1728	87,200	35,500	2,200	49,500	40.7	2.5	56.8
1729	84,400	48,700	1,300	34,400	57.7	1.5	40.8
1730	108,900	73,800	4,900	30,200	67.7	4.5	27.8
1731	57,700	26,100	9,800	21,800	45.2	16.9	37.9
1732	2,900	1,800	–	1,100	62.1	–	37.9
1733	4,200	4,000	–	200	95.2	–	4.8
1734	800	100	–	700	12.5	–	87.5
1735	17,400	13,900	–	3,500	79.9	–	20.1
1736	3,400	3,400	–	–	100.0	–	–
1737	2,700	2,600	–	100	96.3	–	3.7
1738	5,500	4,600	–	900	83.6	–	16.4
1739	13,200	10,500	–	2,700	79.5	–	20.5
1740	12,400	10,100	–	2,300	81.4	–	18.6
1741	56,400	47,700	300	8,400	84.6	0.5	14.9
1742	59,500	52,300	–	7,200	87.9	–	12.1
1743	95,800	85,100	–	10,700	88.8	–	11.2
1744	95,400	63,100	7,700	24,600	66.1	8.1	25.8
1745	5,600	2,300	–	3,300	41.1	–	58.9
1746	161,900	94,200	–	67,700	58.2	–	41.8
1747	1,500	800	–	700	53.3	–	46.7
1748	54,700	46,500	–	8,200	85.0	–	15.0
1749	185,900	134,800	2,700	48,400	72.6	1.5	25.9
1750	69,100	59,200	7,500	2,400	85.7	10.9	3.4

continued

Year	Total of imports £	Jews	Partner-ships	Non-Jews	Jews %	Partner-ships	Non-Jews
1751	189,400	137,100	600	51,700	72.4	0.3	27.3
1752	190,400	128,100	–	62,300	67.4	–	32.6
1753	111,400	87,300	–	24,100	78.6	–	21.4
1754	98,400	66,300	–	32,100	67.4	–	32.6
1755	119,900	97,400	–	22,500	81.2	–	18.8
1756	121,600	100,700	3,200	17,700	82.8	2.6	14.6
1757	39,800	30,800	–	9,000	77.4	–	22.6
1758	43,700	37,500	200	6,000	85.8	0.5	13.7
1759	66,500	32,300	4,900	29,300	48.6	7.4	44.0
1760	97,000	49,500	6,100	41,400	51.0	6.3	42.7
1761	32,400	14,900	8,500	9,000	46.0	26.2	27.8
1762	78,400	59,400	3,300	15,700	75.8	4.2	20.0
1763	110,200	71,800	10,900	27,500	65.3	9.9	24.8
1764	63,200	29,900	11,600	21,700	47.3	18.4	34.3
1765	116,000	68,300	3,300	44,400	58.9	2.8	38.3
1766	59,900	33,500	–	26,400	55.9	–	44.1
1767	307,600	132,400	6,400	168,800	42.9	2.1	55.0
1768	213,500	60,000	300	153,200	28.2	0.1	71.7
1769	201,500	79,700	3,400	118,400	39.7	1.7	58.6
1770	247,200	113,400	5,200	128,600	45.7	2.1	52.2
1771	185,300	81,700	4,800	98,800	44.2	2.6	53.2
1772	186,200	66,200	–	120,000	35.6	–	64.4
1773	138,400	42,800	–	95,600	31.0	–	69.0
1774	169,000	66,600	–	102,400	39.4	–	60.6
1775	157,600	53,800	–	103,800	34.0	–	66.0
1776	279,400	27,000	16,200	236,200	9.7	5.8	84.5
1777	209,400	51,200	31,800	126,400	24.5	15.2	60.3
1778	188,100	46,800	23,800	117,500	24.9	12.7	62.4
1779	84,800	23,900	7,500	53,400	28.2	8.8	63.0
1780	107,000	21,700	6,500	78,800	20.3	6.1	73.6
1781	88,900	22,900	900	65,100	25.7	1.0	73.3
1782	41,400	2,900	–	38,500	7.0	–	93.0
1783	72,000	6,800	1,700	63,500	9.4	2.4	88.2
1784	132,200	17,600	3,700	110,900	13.3	2.8	83.9
1785	119,600	38,700	–	80,900	32.2	–	67.8
1786	68,600	39,000	4,600	25,000	56.9	6.7	36.4
1787	83,100	35,900	25,700	21,500	43.2	30.9	25.9
1788	117,500	57,600	14,600	45,300	49.2	12.5	38.3
1789	111,700	59,500	12,700	39,500	53.1	11.3	35.6
1790	78,800	58,900	4,200	15,700	74.7	5.5	19.8
1791	57,100	39,100	10,800	7,200	68.5	18.9	12.6
1792	85,200	41,800	26,200	17,200	49.1	30.8	20.1
1793	78,400	41,400	11,200	25,800	52.8	14.3	32.9
1794	13,900	8,700	–	5,200	62.6	–	37.4
1795	9,700	4,800	–	4,900	49.5	–	50.5
1796	22,000	22,000	–	–	100.0	–	–

APPENDIX J. THE JEWISH SHARE IN CORAL EXPORTS TO
INDIA 1750-75 *

(according to the Court Books of the East India Company)

Year	Total value of licences issued £	Value of licences issued to Jews	Jewish share in licences issued %
1750/1	44,400	35,300	79.5
1751/2	69,100	48,900	70.8
1752/3	41,400	28,100	67.9
1753/4	92,100	61,100	66.3
1754/5	87,300	56,900	65.2
1755/6	67,000	46,000	68.7
1756/7	45,300	32,000	70.6
1757/8	28,800	19,000	66.0
1758/9	30,100	25,900	86.0
1759/60	40,700	29,800	73.2
1760/1	87,500	74,200	84.8
1761/2	84,200	79,200	94.1
1762/3	76,600	67,000	87.7
1763/4	94,100	78,400	83.3
1764/5	71,900	56,800	79.0
1765/6	109,200	88,300	81.0
1766/7	84,000	57,800	68.8
1767/8	64,400	46,400	72.0
1768/9	51,100	32,400	63.5
1769/70	43,100	32,300	74.9
1770/1	68,700	53,000	77.1
1771/2	49,700	37,700	75.9
1772/3	44,400	40,700	91.7
1773/4	59,000	39,200	66.4
1774/5	62,000	41,700	67.2
	1,596,100	1,208,100	75.7

* Consignments belonging to partnerships between Jews and non-Jews were here
regarded as the property of both partners in equal shares

APPENDIX K. PROFITS IN THE DIAMOND TRADE

Consignments of diamonds sent by George Jones and Levy Moses (Madras) to John Goddard and Henry Moses (London) 1744–9
(compiled from data taken from P.R.O. C12/2033.28 – schedule)

Year	Ship	Declared value in India £	Price received in London	Profit	Profit %
1744	Salisbury	2,407	3,390	983	41.0
	Montfort	1,153	1,626	473	41.0
	Heathcoate	2,104	2,924	820	39.0
1746–7	Benjamin	1,118	1,608	490	44.0
	Lincoln	2,412	4,166	1,754	73.0
	Dolphin	2,477	3,190	713	29.0
	Beaufort and Dorrington	498	676	178	36.0
1748–9	Severn	268	601	333	124.0
	Warwick	541	805	264	49.0
	Lapwing	526	736	210	40.0
	Total	13,504	19,722	6,218	46.0

Bibliography

Note Places of publication are given only for books published outside the United Kingdom.

A. MANUSCRIPT SOURCES

INDIA OFFICE LIBRARY
Records of the East India Company:
    Court Books, vols 32–88 (1680–1780)
    Reports and Resolutions of the Correspondence Committee,
        vols 1–13 (1719–80)
    Miscellaneous Letters Received, vols 1–77 (1701–85)
    Auditor's References, vols 1–3 (1740–82)
    Despatches to Madras, vols 1–12 (1754–86)
    Despatches to Bengal, vols 1–4, 17 (1762–9, 1786)
    Madras Mayor's Court – Proceedings, R.328, vols 67–109 (1732–70)
    Madras Public Proceedings (Consultations)
        R. 239, vols 86–90 (1712–29)
        R.240, vols 1–30 (1730–70)
    General Cash Journals 1730–1805
    European Inhabitants – Madras
Fowke Mss.
Orme Mss.

BRITISH MUSEUM
Papers of Thomas Pitt, Add.Mss.22,842–52
Papers of Sir George Oxenden, Add.Mss.40,496–700

PUBLIC RECORD OFFICE
Chancery bills and answers, 1680–1790, C5–C12
Exchequer bills and answers, 1730–80, E112
Chancery Master's Exhibits:
    Papers of Thomas Pitt, C110/28, C110/81
    Papers of Major John Roach, C108/95
    Papers of Sir Stephen Evance, C111/50
    Papers of Francis Chamberlayne, C108/203
    Papers of Israel Levin Salomons (Yehiel Prager)
        (see detailed list on p. 342), C111/1–18, 148–60
    Board of Trade Papers (T1)
    State Papers – Portugal (SP)

BANK OF ENGLAND
Ledgers 1697–1760

HOARE'S BANK, LONDON
Correspondence concerning diamonds

MOCATTA AND GOLDSMID, LONDON
Letter Book, 1800–17

PAPERS OF THE FIRM OF ISRAEL LEVIN SALOMONS (YEHIEL
PRAGER) – THE INTERNAL CORRESPONDENCE
(PUBLIC RECORD OFFICE: CHANCERY MASTER'S EXHIBITS)
    [A microfilm copy of the internal correspondence is available at the
    Central Archives for the History of the Jewish People, Jerusalem]
Letters of the Amsterdam house to the London house,
    1774–5, C111/13
    1776–7, C111/13
    1778, C111/3
    1779, C111/7
    1780, C111/7
    1781, C111/7
    1782, C111/9
    1783, C111/9
    1784, C111/5
    1785, C111/3
    1786, C111/8
    1787, C111/5
    1788, C111/8
    1789, C111/11
    1790–1, C111/11
    1793, C111/12
    1794–5, C111/9
Letter-book of the London house (letters to the Amsterdam house),
    1788–94, C111/160
Letters of the Ostend house to the London house,
    1781, C111/11
    1782–3, C111/10
Letters of the Philadelphia house to the London house,
    1783–92, C111/6, C111/7
Letter-book of the London house (letters to the Philadelphia house),
    1784–93, C111/157
Journal of Leib (Lyon) Prager,
    1786, C111/6
Letters of Leib Prager to the London house,
    1786–93, C111/6
Letter-book of the London house (letters of Esther Prager to
Leib Prager in India),
    1792, C111/155

B. PUBLISHED SOURCES

*The First Letter Book of the East India Company 1600–1619 – The Register
of Letters etc. of the Governour and Company of Merchants of London
Trading into the East Indies, 1600–1619*, ed. Sir George Birdwood,
assisted by William Foster (1893, reprinted 1965)

Letters Received by the East India Company from its Servants in the East, 1602–1617, ed. F. C. Danvers and W. Foster (1896–1902)

The English Factories in India, 1618–1684, ed. Sir William Foster [1618–69] and Sir Charles Fawcett [new series, 1670–84] (1906–55)

Calendar of State Papers, Colonial Series, East Indies, China and Japan, 1513–1634, ed. W. Noel Sainsbury (1860–92)

A Calendar of Court Minutes of the East India Company, 1635–1679, by E. B. Sainsbury, with an introduction and notes by [vols 1–8] Sir William Foster and [vols 9–11] W. T. Ottewill (1907–38)

Calendar of Treasury Books and Papers, 1729–1745, prepared by W. M. Shaw (1897–1903)

Historical Manuscripts Commission – Report on the Palk Manuscripts (1922)

Historical Manuscripts Commission, 13th Report, Appendix part 3. The Manuscripts of J. B. Fortescue preserved at Dropmore [Papers of Thomas Pitt]

C. BOOKS AND ARTICLES

Addison, Joseph, *The Works of the Right Honourable Joseph Addison*, with notes by Richard Hurd (1854–6)

Adler, Elkan N., *London* (Philadelphia, 1930)

Alexander, Levy, *Memoirs of the Life and Commercial Connections Private and Public of the Late Benjamin Goldsmid* (1808)

Andrade, Jacob A. P. M., *A Record of the Jews in Jamaica, from the English Conquest to the Present Time* (Kingston, 1941)

Anglo-Jewish Notabilities, their Arms and Testamentary Dispositions (Jewish Historical Society of England, 1949)

Armytage, Frances, *The Free Port System in the British West Indies – a Study in Commercial Policy 1766–1822* (1953)

Aspinall, Arthur, *Cornwallis in Bengal – the Administrative and Juridicial Reforms of Lord Cornwallis in Bengal, together with the Accounts of the Commercial Expansion of the East India Company 1786–1793, and the Foundation of Penang 1786–1793* (1931)

Bab, A., 'Die Juden in Amerika spanischer Zunge', *Jahrbücher für jüdische Geschichte und Literatur*, 1925–7

Bal Krishna, *Commercial Relations between India and England, 1601–1757* (1924)

Ball, Valentine, *The Diamonds, Coal and Gold of India, their Mode of Occurrence and Distribution* (1881)

Barnett, Lionel D. (ed.), *Bevis Marks Records* (1940, 1949)

Bauer, Max, *Edelsteinkunde* (Leipzig, 1896)

Beltran, Gonzalo A., 'The slave trade in Mexico', *HAHR*, xxiv (1944)

Bloom, Herbert I., *The Economic Activities of the Jews of Amsterdam in the Seventeenth and Eighteenth Century* (Williamsport, 1937)

Boxer, C. R., 'Brazilian gold and British traders in the first half of the eighteenth century', *HAHR*, xlix (1969)

Brown, Vera L., 'Contraband trade, a factor in the decline of Spain's Empire in America', *HAHR*, VIII (1928)

Brugmans, Hendrik and Frank A. (eds), *Geschiedenis der Joden in Nederland* (Amsterdam, 1940)

Buist, Marten G., *At Spes non Fracta – Hope & Co. 1770–1815* (The Hague, 1974)

Calogeras, Joao Pandia, *A History of Brazil*, translated and edited by P. A. Martin (Chapel Hill, 1939)

Child, Josiah, *A New Discourse of Trade* (1698)

Christelow, Allan, 'Contraband trade between Jamaica and the Spanish Main, and the Free Port Act of 1766', *HAHR*, XXII (1942)

Christelow, Allan, 'Great Britain and the trades from Cadiz and Lisbon to Spanish America and Brazil 1759–1783', *HAHR*, XXVII (1947)

Clapham, John H., *The Bank of England* (1944)

Cohen, Mortimer J., *Jacob Emden – a Man of Controversy* (Philadelphia, 1937)

Davis, N. Darnell, 'Notes on the history of the Jews in Barbados', *PAJHS*, XVIII (1909)

Davis, Ralph, 'English foreign trade 1700–1774', *EcHR*, 2nd ser., XV (1962–3)

Defoe, Daniel, *The Complete English Tradesman* (4th edn, 1738)

Defoe, Daniel, *A Plan of the English Commerce* (1st edn, 1728; 2nd edn, 1730)

Diferee, Hendrik C., *De geschiedenis van den Nederlandschen handel tot den val der Republiek* (Amsterdam, 1908)

Dillen, J. G. van, 'De economische positie en betekenis der Joden in de Republiek en in de Nederlandsche koloniale wereld', in *Geschiedenis der Joden in Nederland*, ed. O. Brugmans and A. Franks (Amsterdam, 1940)

Durga, Parshad I., *Some Aspects of Indian Foreign Trade 1757–1893* (1932)

Encyclopédie Méthodique – Commerce (Paris–Liège, 1783–9)

Eschwege, Wilhelm L. von, *Brasilien, die neue Welt* (Braunschweig, 1830)

Farnie, D. A., 'The commercial empire of the Atlantic, 1607–1783', *EcHR*, 2nd ser., XV (1962–3)

Feldbaek, Ole, *India Trade under the Danish Flag – European Enterprise and Anglo-Indian Remittance and Trade* (Scandinavian Institute of Asian Studies, Monograph Series No. 2, 1969)

Fischel, Walter J., 'The Jewish merchant colony in Madras (Fort St George) during the 17th and 18th centuries – a contribution to the economic and social history of the Jews in India', *Journal of the Economic and Social History of the Orient*, III (1960)

Fischel, Walter J., 'Leading Jews in the service of Portuguese India', *JQR*, N.S. XLVII (1956–7)

Fisher, Harold E. S., *The Portugal Trade – A Study of Anglo-Portuguese Commerce, 1700–1770* (1971)

Furber, Holden, *John Company at Work – A Study of European Expansion in India in the Late Eighteenth Century* (Cambridge, Mass., 1948)

Glamann, Kristof, *Dutch-Asiatic Trade 1620–1740* (Copenhagen, 1958)

Gronemann, Selig, *Genealogische Studien über die alten jüdischen Familien Hanovers* (Berlin, 1913)

Gutstein, Morris A., *Aaron Lopez and Judah Touro* (New York, 1939)

H[anway], J[onas], *Letters Admonitory and Argumentative from J.H—y, Merchant, to J. S—r, Merchant* (1753)

Haring, Clarence H., *Trade and Navigation between Spain and the Indies in the Time of the Hapsburgs* (Cambridge, Mass., 1918)

Harper, Lawrence A., *The English Navigation Laws – A Seventeenth-Century Experiment in Social Engineering* (New York, 1939)

Hedges, William, *The Diary of W. Hedges*, with notes by R. Barlow (1887–9)

Heertje, Henri, *De diamantbewerkers van Amsterdam* (Amsterdam, 1936)

Henriques, H. S. Q., 'The Jews and the English law', *JQR*, xvi (1904)

Henriques, H. S. Q., 'Proposals for special taxation of the Jews after the Revolution', *JHSE Trans.*, ix (1918–20)

Hershkowitz, Leo, and Meyer, Isidore S., *Letters of the Franks Family, 1733–1748* (Studies in American Jewish History No. 5, American Jewish Historical Society, 1968)

Hoh-Cheung and Lorna H. Mui, 'The Commutation Act and the tea trade in Britain, 1784–1793', *EcHR*, 2nd ser., xvi (1963–4)

Hühner, Leon, 'The Jews of Virginia from the earliest times to the close of the eighteenth century', *PAJHS*, xx (1911)

Hussey, Roland D., 'Antecedents of the Spanish monopolistic overseas trading companies', *HAHR*, ix (1929)

Hyamson, Albert M., *David Salomons* (1939)

Hyamson, Albert M., *The Sephardim of England – A History of the Spanish and Portuguese Jewish Community, 1492–1951* (1951)

Jeffries, David, *Treatise on Diamonds and Pearls* (1750; 2nd edn, 1751)

Johnson, Emory R. and others, *History of the Domestic and Foreign Commerce of the United States* (Washington, 1915)

Kayserling, Meyer, *Christoph Columbus und der Antheil der Juden an den spanischen und portugiesischen Entdeckungen* (Berlin, 1894)

Kayserling, Meyer, 'The Jews in Jamaica and Daniel Israel Lopez Laguna', *JQR*, xii (1900)

Kellenbenz, Hermann, *Sephardim an der unteren Elbe – ihre wirtschaftliche und politische Bedeutung vom Ende des 16. bis zum Beginn des 18. Jahrhunderts* (Vierteljahrsschrift für Sozial- und Wirtschaftsgeschichte, Beihefte Nr. 40, Wiesbaden, 1958)

King, James F., 'Evolution of the free slave trade principle in Spanish colonial administration', *HAHR*, xxii (1942)

Kohler, Max J., 'A memorial of Jews to Parliament concerning Jewish participation in colonial trade, 1696', *PAJHS*, xviii (1909)

Kooy, Tjalling P. van der, *Hollands stapelmarkt en haar verval* (Amsterdam, 1931)

Lenzen, Godehard, *The History of Diamond Production and the Diamond Trade* (1970)

Letters of Denization and Acts of Naturalization for Aliens in England and Ireland (Publications of the Huguenot Society of London, vols. xviii, xxvii and xxxv)

Liebman, Seymour S., 'The Jews of colonial Mexico', *HAHR*, xliii (1963)

Lipman, V. D. (ed.), *Three Centuries of Anglo-Jewish History – A Volume of Essays* (Jewish Historical Society of England, 1961)

Long, Edward, *The History of Jamaica* (1774)

Love, Henry D., *Vestiges of Old Madras, 1640–1800* (1913)

Lowenthal, Marvin (ed.), *The Memoirs of Glückel of Hameln* (New York, 1932)

Macaulay, Thomas B., *The History of England, from the Accession of James II*, ed. C. H. Firth (1913–15)

MacCarthy, James R., *Fire in the Earth – The Story of the Diamond* (New York and London, 1942)

Maclachlan, Jean O., *Trade and Peace with Old Spain 1667–1750 – A Study of the Influence of Commerce on Anglo-Spanish Diplomacy in the First Half of the Eighteenth Century* (1940)

Macpherson, David, *Annals of Commerce, Manufactures, Fisheries and Navigation* (1805)

Magens, Nicolas, *The Universal Merchant* (1753)

Manchester, Alan K., *British Pre-eminence in Brazil. Its Rise and Decline* (Chapel Hill, 1933)

Marcus, Jacob R., *The Colonial American Jew, 1492–1776* (Detroit, 1970)

Marshall, P. J., 'The personal fortune of Warren Hastings', *EcHR*, 2nd ser., XVII (1964–5)

Masson, Paul, *Les compagnies du corail – étude historique sur le commerce de Marseille aux XVI siècle et les origines de la colonisation française en Algérie–Tunisie* (Paris, Marseille, 1908)

Masson, Paul, *Histoire des établissements et du commerce français dans l'Afrique Barbaresque 1560–1793* (Paris, 1903)

Mawe, John, *Travels in the Interior of Brazil* (1812)

Mawe, John, *A Treatise on Diamonds and Precious Stones* (2nd edn, 1823)

Maxwell, Kenneth R., 'Pombal and the nationalization of the Luso-Brazilian economy', *HAHR*, XLVIII (1968)

Merritt, J. E., 'The triangular trade', *Business History*, III (1960)

Morgan, David T., 'The Sheftalls of Savannah', *American Jewish Historical Quarterly*, LXII (1972/3)

Namier, Lewis B., *The Structure of Politics at the Accession of George III* (1929)

Nussbaum, F. L., 'The American tobacco trade and French politics', *Political Science Quarterly*, XL (1925)

Pares, Richard, *War and Trade in the West Indies 1739–1763* (1936)

Pares, Richard, *A West-India Fortune* (1950)

Perry, Thomas W., *Public Opinion, Propaganda and Politics in Eighteenth Century England – A Study of the Jew Bill of 1753* (Cambridge, Mass., 1962)

Philo-patriae, *Considerations on the Bill to Permit Persons Professing the Jewish Religion to be Naturalized by Parliament* (1753)

Philo-patriae, *Further Considerations on the Act to Permit Persons Professing the Jewish Religion to be Naturalized by Parliament* (1753)

Pitman, Frank W., *The Development of the British West Indies 1700–1763* (New Haven, 1917)

Poonen, T. I., 'Early history of the Dutch factories of Masulipatam and Petapoli, 1605–1636', *Journal of Indian History*, XXVII (1949)

Posthumus, Nicolaas W., *Inquiry into the History of Prices in Holland* (Leiden, 1946)

Pritchard, Earl E., 'Private trade between England and China in the eighteenth century (1680–1833)', *Journal of the Economic and Social History of the Orient*, I (1958)

Rabinowicz, Oskar K., *Sir Solomon de Medina* (Jewish Historical Society of England, 1974)

Ragatz, Lowell J., *The Fall of the Planter Class in the British Caribbean 1763–1833 – A Study in Social and Economic History* (New York and London, 1929)

Raychaudhuri, Tapan, *Jan Company in Coromandel – A Study in the Interrelations of European Commerce and Traditional Economics* (The Hague, 1962)

Richards, Richard D., *The Early History of Banking in England* (1929)

Roth, Cecil, *The Great Synagogue, London, 1690–1940* (1950)

Roth, Cecil, *A History of the Marranos* (Philadelphia, 1932)

Roth, Cecil, 'The Resettlement of the Jews in England', in *Three Centuries of Anglo-Jewish History*, ed. V. D. Lipman (Jewish Historical Society of England, 1961)

Roth, Cecil, *The Rise of Provincial Jewry – The Early History of the Jewish Communities in the English Countryside 1740–1840* (1950)

Samuel, Edgar R., 'The first fifty years', in *Three Centuries of Anglo-Jewish History*, ed. V. D. Lipman (Jewish Historical Society of England, 1961)

Samuel, Wilfred S., 'Review of the Jewish colonists in Barbados 1680', *JHSE Trans.*, xiii (1932–5)

Samuel, Wilfred S., *Some Notes on 17th Century London Jews* (1937)

Schnee, Heinrich, *Die Hoffinanz und der moderne Staat. Geschichte und System der Hoffaktoren an deutschen Fürstenhöfen im Zeitalter des Absolutismus* (Berlin, 1953–5)

Schumpeter, Elizabeth B., *English Overseas Trade Statistics, 1697–1808* (1960)

Scott, Arthur, and Atkinson, Lewis, *A Short History of Diamond Cutting* (1888)

Shillington, V. M., and Chapman, Annie B. W., *The Commercial Relations of England and Portugal* (1907)

Singer, Charles J., and others (eds), *A History of Technology* (1954–8)

Smith, David Grant, 'Old Christian merchants and the foundation of the Brazil Company, 1649', *HAHR*, liv (1974)

Southey, Robert, *History of Brazil* (1810–19)

Stern, Selma, *The Court Jew – A Contribution to the History of the Period of Absolutism in Central Europe* (Philadelphia, 1950)

Streeter, Edwin W., *Precious Stones and Gems, their History and Distinguishing Characteristics* (1877)

Sullivan, Kathryn, *Maryland and France 1774–1789* (Philadelphia, 1936)

Sutherland, Lucy S., *The East India Company in Eighteenth Century Politics* (1952)

Sutherland, Lucy S., *A London Merchant 1695–1774* (1933)

Sutherland, Lucy S., 'Sampson Gideon: eighteenth century Jewish financier', *JHSE Trans.*, xvii (1951–2)

Tavernier, Jean B., *Travels in India* (2nd edn, 1925; original French edn, Paris, 1676)

Ullmann, Salomon, *Histoire des Juifs de Belgique jusqu'au 19e siècle; notes et documents 1700–1830* (La Haye, 1934)

Ustaritz, Geronimo de, *Théorie et pratique du commerce et de la marine* (Paris, 1753)

Vega, José de la, *Confusion de Confusiones* (Amsterdam, 1688)

Voute, Robert, *Korte beschouwing van den daadlyken toestand van den theehandel, zo in Europa in het algemeen, als in deze Republiek in het byzonder* (Amsterdam, 1792)

Wertenbaker, Thomas J., *The Planters of Colonial Virginia* (Princeton, 1922)

Westerfield, Ray B., *Middlemen in English Business, Particularly between 1660 and 1760* (New Haven, 1915)

Whitworth, Charles, *State of the Trade of Great Britain in its Imports and Exports Progressively from the Year 1697* (1776)

Wilson, Charles H., *Anglo-Dutch Commerce and Finance in the Eighteenth Century* (1941)

Wilson, Charles H., *Profit and Power – A Study of England and the Dutch Wars* (1957)

Wiznitzer, Arnold, 'The Jews in the sugar industry of colonial Brazil', *Jewish Social Studies*, xviii (1956)

Wolf, Edwin, and Whiteman, Maxwell, *The History of the Jews of Philadelphia from Colonial Times to the Age of Jackson* (Philadelphia, 1957)

Wolf, Lucien, *Essays in Jewish History* (1934)

Wolf, Lucien, 'The Jewry of the Restoration, 1660–1664', *JHSE Trans.*, v (1902–5)

Woolf, Maurice, 'Foreign trade of London Jews in the seventeenth century', *JHSE Trans.*, xxiv (1970–3)

Woolf, Maurice, 'Joseph Salvador, 1716–1786', *JHSE Trans.*, xxi (1962–7)

Zimmels, Hirsch J., *Ashkenazim and Sephardim – their Relations, Differences and Problems as Reflected in the Rabbinical Responsa* (1958)

Index

The index is comprehensive for persons and subjects. References to places and organizations (e.g., East India Company) are given only when the subject discussed is not otherwise covered by the index.

Portuguese and Spanish double surnames, with a few exceptions, are listed under the last name, e.g., David Lopes Fernandes under Fernandes, David Lopes. When such names are entered under the first surname the reader is referred from the second to the first name.

Abarbanel, Ephraim, 301
Abas, Jacob, 288
Abendana, Isaac, 130, 148, 150, 155–156, 285
Abendanon, Moses, 109
Aboab (merchant), 301
Abrahams, Francis, 196–7, 254
Achanda, Antonio and Simon Mendes de (business firm), 87
Addison, Joseph, 21, 55
Aguilar (Lopes Pereira) [business firm], 16, 144, 204, 254, 265–6
Aguilar (Lopes Pereira), de, David, 171, 328; Diego, Baron (Lopes Pereira, Moses), 31, 39–40, 45; Ephraim, 45, 126, 171, 296; Hananel, 259, 315, 325; Sarah (née Mendes da Costa), 45
Alexandria, 103
Alicante, 43
Almeyda, Juan de, 121
alum, 211
Alvarenga, Isaac da Costa, 36
Alvares, Isaac, 87, 109; Isaac Jessurun, 171; Lewis, 87; Matthias, 301; Moses, 283, 301
Alvensleben, 311
amber, 104, 291
ambergris, 82, 109, 285
American War, The, effect on trade, 230, 245, 310, 318
Amersfoort, Benjamin, see Cohen (Amersfoort), Benjamin
Amsterdam, decline as commercial entrepôt, 230, 241–52; diamond market, 89, 323–4; distribution centre of colonial goods, 72, 209, 243; importance as financial centre, 201, 248–52; Jewish self-defence, 186; North European rivals, 243–5, 248; sale of colonial

goods, 224–6; see also under brokers, diamond industry, precious metals, Rotterdam
Andrews, Matthew, 83
Anglo-Dutch War (Fourth), effect on trade and commercial relations during, 245–6, 321; see also under Ostend
Anglo-Russian trade, 17, 276
Anschelhausen, Asher, 312
Anson, Admiral, 52
Anthony, Edward, see Mendoca, Duarte Isaac Rebello de
anti-semitism and discrimination against Jews, 41, 48, 96, 262, 276, 280; see also under Bank of England, Jewish disabilities
Antwerp, diamond trade, 325; see also under diamond industry
Aranda, de (business firm), 50
army provisioning, 33, 37, 65
Arnold, George, 148
Asher (merchant), 193, 206
Ashkenazim, in Anglo-Dutch trade, 197; attitude to Sephardim, 246–247; in coral trade, 125; in diamond trade and industry, 125–127, 136, 138, 152–4, 254, 323
Assiento, 36
Avernas le Gras (Lopes Suasso), Baron Francisco de, 280
Azevedo, Isaac de, 288
Azulai, Moses, see Blaw (Azulai), Moses

Bacon, Anthony, 206, 310
Baker, Captain, 222
banking, 59
Bank of Amsterdam, 56–7
Bank of England, 56; discrimination against Jews, 261–3; loans on

Bank of England (*cont.*)
security of gold and silver, 51, 54, 333–4, 336; purchases of gold and silver, 50, 54–5, 333, 335; stock, 98
Barbados, balances of Jewish firm, 63; decline of Jews, 63–4; trade with, 60–1, 282, 332
barilla, 211
barley, 42
Barnardiston, Sir Samuel, 85, 88, 91, 289
Barnet (merchant), 286; Jacob, 174–175, 177–8, 255, 298, 305
Barons, Benjamin, 278
Barrow (merchant), 301; Moses (Lousada, Barukh), 144
Batavia, 82, 166
Behrens, Leffman (Cohen, Lipman), 149
Benares, coral trade, 103; diamond trade, 174–5, 178–9, 318
Bengal, 71, 164, 166, 172; coral trade, 171, 295; diamond trade, 295, 305, 323
ben Moshe, Jacob, *see* Moses, Jacob
Berakhel, Jacob, *see* Lis, Francis de
Berlin, Pragers' correspondent in, *see* Meyer (Yoresh), Aaron
Bernal (business firm), 144
Beroardi and Medici (business firm), 278
Best, 311
bezoar, 109, 287, 292
Bianchi, Francis, 152
Biddulph, William, 103
Bing, Leib, 214, 264, 269
Blankenhagen, C., and Co., 237
Blaw (business firm), 73
Blaw (Azulai), Moses, 109
Boason (business firm), 307
Bombay, 126–7, 129, 295; coral trade, 171
Borneo, coral trade, 108, 292; diamond trade, 81
bottomry loans, 46, 71, 285, 331
Boulanger (business firm), 263
Bourchier, Charles, 127; Richard, 126
Bowen, Evan, 142
Bradley, Daniel, 148, 171
Bradyll, Roger, 100–1, 148, 167, 290–1
Brandaos, Aaron, 39; Moses, 39
Brandon (business firm), 144
Brandon, Jacob and Gabriel Israel (sworn brokers), 197, 200, 231, 244, 258–9, 267, 325

Bravo, Abraham, 303
Brazil, gold trade, 28; Jewish immigration to, 26; Jews escape from, 60; trade with, 31
Brazilian diamonds, 28, 32, 123, 180; Anglo-Portuguese trade in, 41, 114–16, 253–4, 294, 323; contractors of, 121–2, 253, 255, 323; discovery and effect on coral-diamond trade, 1–2, 110ff., 141, 153, 158, 169, 285, 292–4; quality relative to Indian stones, 323; regulation of trade, 120–1, 253; sales by Portuguese Government, 123, 294; *see also under* Portugal
Bristow, John, 52, 121, 281
Britto, Abraham Lopes de, *see* Lopes, Andrew
Brochere, James Lewis, 290
brokers, in Amsterdam market, 225–6; brokerage, 225, 317; *see also under* precious metals
Bruyn, Jan Jacob de, 197, 265, 328
Buller, Messrs, 30–1
Buller and Bear (business firm), 278
Burdett, Lockwood and Hanway (business firm), 278
Burn, Edward, 278
Burnett, John, 47
Bury (diamond contractor), 121

Cadiz, 45, 125; English merchants in, 43–4
Calcutta, 129, 178–9; coral trade, 103; diamond trade, 175
camphor, 211, 224, 226, 235–41, 313, 320
Canton, coral trade, 296
Cantor, Barukh, 255, 299
Cantor brothers (business firm), 59, 250, 323
Capadose, Aaron, 43
Capadoza, Aaron, 264
Cardamom, 211, 247
Caroline-Mathilda (ex-Queen of Denmark), 208, 311–12
Carrett, Matthew, 121–2, 323
Cartagena, 43, 45, 47; Jews, 26
Caseris, Francis de, 281
cassia, 211, 222, 235–8, 247, 266, 313, 319; buds, 211, 247, 319
Castro, de (business firm of Amsterdam), 266–7, 328
Castro, de (family and business firm), 144, 156, 159–63, 168
Castro, de, Abraham, 104; Abraham

de Isaac, 303; Daniel, 127, 154, 160–3, 168; David, 136, 160; Isaac, 301, 303; Jeronimo Henriques, 278; Judith (*née* Mendes da Costa), 163; Moses, 70, 154, 159–63, 168; Rachel (*née* Bravo), 303; Samuel, 154, 159–62, 165, 168, 171, 304; Solomon, 159, 303

Catholics, in Spanish trade, 45

Chaim of Hameln, 89

Chamberlayne, Francis, 155

Chancery and Exchequer cases, 11, 37, 42

Charlestown (Nevis), 64

Child, Sir Francis, 149, 155; Sir Josiah, 91–2, 99–100

China, coral market, 129, 171; and diamond trade, 295

china ware, *see* porcelain

Cholmley, Nathaniel, 90

cinnamon, 211, 235, 313, 319

Clerck, de (merchant), 325

Clive, Robert, 149, 172, 177, 255, 315

cloth (damaged), Jews at sales of, 73–7, 259–60, 286

cochineal, 198, 210, 212, 225, 313, 316–17

cocoa, 210, 312

coffee, 210, 212, 214, 224, 243, 259, 312, 320

Cohen (Amersfoort), Benjamin, 122, 253, 323–4, 329–30; H. A., 286; Levy Barent, 75–6, 197, 259, 286; Lipman, *see* Behrens, Leffman

Compton, Charles (British Consul in Lisbon), 111, 115, 142, 293

conservatism of Jewish merchants, 19–20

Cook, John, 148

Cope, Joseph, 150

Copenhagen, Pragers' correspondents in, 312

coral industry, 103–4; coral trade, 46, 102ff.; connection with diamond trade, 107–9, 130; duties, 108–9, 118, 130, 290, 292, 295; private trade permitted, 100, 107–108; profits, 108, 130; prominence of Jews, 147–8, 339; return of proceeds by bills of exchange, 116–19, 125, 132, 169–71; sale in India, 131, 144, 296–7; share of Francos, 145–6; smuggling, 107, 137; sources of coral, 103; *see also under* Ashkenazim, Benares, Bengal, Bombay, Borneo, Brazilian

diamonds, Calcutta, Canton, China, Coromandel Coast, East India Company (English), Flanders, Florence, Genoa, Goa, India, Leghorn, London, Madras, Marseilles, Mecca, Naples, Surat

Corea, Isaac, 62

corn, 34, 37, 42

Coromandel Coast, coral trade, 103

Cortissos, Emanuel, 265

Cosman (merchant), 286

Costa (Mendes da), *see* Mendes da Costa

Costa, da (merchant), 101; Abraham, 39; Alvaro, 85–6, 107, 287; Anthony, 40, 43, 118, 290; Fernandes, 39; Jacob, 39–40, 130; Jacquaz, 278; Moses, 12

cotton, 61, 63, 210, 212, 225, 258–259, 313, 317

court-Jews, 149, 302

Crone, de (merchant), 250

cuff, 82, 287

Daniels (Tanhum), Simon, 73–6, 197, 223, 259–60, 286

Dawson (customs official), 85

Debonaire, John, 128, 297, 299

Defoe, Daniel, 27, 29, 211

Delmonte, Isaac Cohen, 168

diamond industry, in Amsterdam, 68, 81, 86, 88, 137, 141–2, 285; in Antwerp, 81, 137, 141, 256; in Holland, 243; in Italy, 81; in London, 141–2, 293; in Portugal, 81; *see also under* Ashkenazim

diamond mines, *see under* India

diamond trade, 12, 61, 67ff.; allowed to private merchants, 88; categories of merchants, 137–8; crisis after 1765, 147, 169ff.; Dutch competition, 81–2, 115; duties, 68, 83, 85, 88, 95, 114–15, 118–20, 129, 133–4, 290–1; French competition, 102, 152, 157–8, 302; insurance, 134–5, 140, 298; lack of flexibility, 112; mode of sale in London, 133–4, 138–9, 298–301; partnerships between Jews and non-Jews, 148; profits, 109, 143–4, 179–80, 298, 340; prominence of big merchants, 145; prominence of the Francos, 145; prominence of Franks, 153; sensitivity to market fluctuations, 110, 140, 300–1; share of Jews, 85, 88–9, 147, 173, 253–4, 337–8; smuggling, 86, 91–3, 101, 107,

diamond trade (*cont.*)
122–3, 127, 135–7, 253, 290, 304;
use of respondentia loans, 126–9,
136, 154, 304; *see also under*
Amsterdam, Antwerp,
Ashkenazim, Benares, Borneo,
Brazilian diamonds, Calcutta,
China, coral trade, diamond mines,
diamonds, East India Company
(Dutch), East India Company
(English), East India Company
(New), Flanders, Fort St David,
France, Germany, Goa, gold,
Hamburg, India, Leghorn,
London, Madras, Masulipatam,
Portugal, Prager (Levin Salomons)
[business firm], precious metals,
Sephardim, silver, South African
diamonds, Spain, Surat, Venice,
Vienna
diamonds, classification of, 140
Dias, Abraham, *see* Vianna, Miguel;
Abraham Fernandes, 283;
Abraham Lopes, 31; Emanuel
Vas, 87; Isaac Lopes, 43; Jacob
Lopes, 43; Melchior, 87
D'Israeli, Benjamin, 174
Dormido, Manuel Martinez, 84, 287
dragon blood, 211
drugs, 177, 196, 198–9, 210, 215–16,
218–19, 222, 224, 237, 248, 259,
314, 319; explanation of term,
211; Pragers' speculation in, 189–
190, 212, 220, 228–9, 234–41,
318–20; *see also under* East India
Company (Dutch), East India
Company (English), Zeeland
Dulivier, Pierre, 157
Dutch Civil War, effect on trade,
233–6, 245–7
Dutch East India Company, *see*
East India Company (Dutch)
dyestuffs, 198, 259, 319

East India Company (Dutch), 72;
Company's diamond trade, 88,
284–5; and drug trade, 211, 238–
240
East India Company (English),
archives, 12, 50; combination of
buyers at public sales, 74–6;
Company's coral trade, 104–9,
291–2; Company's diamond trade,
69–70, 81–2, 89–91, 94; control
of diamond trade, 135–6; and
diamond trade, 67ff., 81ff., 113,
125, 158, 305–6; diamond trade
of Company's servants and ships'

officers, 82, 87, 112, 147, 287; and
drug trade, 177, 237–8, 240;
Jewish stockholders, 85; and Jews,
71–2; Jews at public sales, 72–7,
217; monopoly of diamond trade,
69–70; monopoly of English
Eastern trade, 71–2; permission
of private diamond trade, 83–8;
94–5, 97, 292; privileges and
trade of ships' officers, 71, 172,
216, 218–19, 234–6; prohibition
of private diamond trade, 96–7;
purchases of silver, 51–3, 55, 336;
restrictions on diamond trade,
124; rules governing diamond
trade, 94–6, 290–1; *see also under*
coral trade, diamond trade, fore-
sales, Prager (Levin Salomons)
[business firm], silver
East India Company (New), 70, 96,
150; and diamond trade, 97–9,
285
economic basis of Jewish business, 18
Eleazar, Henry, 72–3
Elias (business firm), 145
Elias, Abraham, 163–4, 295
Elliot, George, 190–1, 217; Louisa
(*née* Prager), 217
Emanuel (merchant), 286
Emden, Rabbi Zalman Meshulam,
269
England, Jewish immigration, 25
Ephraim (business firm), 258
Ephraim, Veitel Heine, 325
Ergas, Emanuel, 152; Raphael, 152
Eschwege, Wilhelm L. von, 123
Espinoza (business firm) 144
Espinoza, Jacob, 40
Evance, Sir Stephen, 69, 97, 99–
101, 150, 289–90
Exchange business, 21; exchange
transactions and discount credit
in Anglo-Dutch trade, 53–5, 57,
193–6; effect on Anglo-Dutch
trade, 248–52; prominence of
Jews, 194–5, 249–52; *see also*
under Prager (Levin Salomons)
[business firm]

Falmouth, 37, 41, 115
Faros (merchant), 301
Ferde (Marcus) [business firm], 254,
261, 323
Ferdinando, Joseph, 301
Fernandes, David Lopes, 160, 165,
168, 304; Fernando, *see* Vianna,
Miguel; Joseph Dias, 160–1, 303;
Moses Dias, 303

Fischel, Walter J., 165
Flanders, diamond export to, 68
flax, 212
Florence, coral trade, 104
Flores, Daniel de, 276
Fonseca, Alvaro da, 43, 70, 99, 101, 148–50, 155–6, 167, 290–1, 295–296, 302; Gabriel, 287–8; Manuel, 287–8
Fonseca, da, Joseph David, and Son (business firm), 312
fore-sales, of East India goods, 213–214, 218–21, 314, 316
Fort St David, diamond trade, 165
Fort St George, *see* Madras
Forte, Pedro, *see* Pinheiro, Gabriel Lopes
Fowey, 39
Fowke, Francis, 175; Joseph, 165, 175
France, diamond exports to, 67–8, 87, 152
Francia, Domingo Rodrigues, 287; George Rodrigues, 287; Simon, 37, 278
Franco (business firm), 16, 43, 144, 197, 209, 254, 259, 265, 296, 316
Franco, Abraham and Jacob (business firm), 39–40, 42, 48, 51, 55, 61, 112–13, 118–19, 125, 139, 145–6, 148, 154, 159, 165, 168, 302
Franco, Francis and Jacob (business firm), *see* Franco and Lindo
Franco, Jacob, Moses and Raphael (business firm), 42, 170–4
Franco (merchant), 73, 301; Abraham, 49, 109, 114, 259; Abraham Haim, 266; Francis, 259, 266; Jacob, 109, 114, 259; Jacob Jr, 259, 266; Moses, 259; Raphael, 171; Solomon, 165, 295
Franco and Lindo (business firm), 259, 325, 328
Franklin, Benjamin, 193
Franks (family and business firm), 65, 145, 152–4, 156–7, 284
Franks, Aaron, 65, 71–2, 112–13, 119, 129, 136, 152–4, 156–7, 165, 167, 207, 284–5, 297, 299, 302; Abraham, 65, 152–4, 156; David, 283; Isaac, 51, 65, 113–14, 153, 156–8, 167, 291; Jacob, 65–6, 153; Moses Jr, 153, 174; Moses Sr, 65–6, 153–4, 284; Naphtali, 65, 153

'free merchants', *see under* India
French Revolution and revolutionary war, effect on trade, 241, 245, 248–9, 301, 318
fruit, 34

Gabay, Isaac Siprut de, 138, 299
Genoa, coral fishing, 103–4
Germany, diamond exports to, 67–8, 140, 149, 152
Gettingen, Moses, 250, 261, 263, 272;Reiskhe (*née* Prager), 272
Gideon, Sampson, 51–3, 71, 144, 207, 264, 281, 285
Gildemeester (diamond contractor), 122, 253–4, 323
ginger, 258
ginseng, 212, 313
Glasgow, Pragers' correspondent in, *see* Oswald, G. and Co.
Glover, Richard, 213
Glueckel of Hameln, 89, 131, 157
Goa, 37, 86; coral trade, 103, 106–7, 291; diamond trade, 69, 81, 87–8; Jews, 287
Godall, John, 39
Goddard, John, 143, 340
Godfrey, Thomas, 114, 132, 154, 302
Golconda, diamond mines, 130, 154
gold, 28, 38, 42; export for purchase of diamonds, 88, 94, 295; imports from Portugal, 38–42, 111; smuggling to Holland, 59; *see also under* Bank of England, Brazil, precious metals
Goldschmid, Nathan, 291
Goldsmid (business firm), 145, 154, 197, 254, 264, 308
Goldsmid, Aaron, 154, 308; Abraham, 191, 308; Asher, 53, 59, 300; Benjamin, 191, 308, 320; Jessy (*née* Prager), 308, 320, 329
Gomes, Lewis and Mordecai (business firm), 283
Gomes, Isaac, 283; Joseph, 144
Gomes de Mesquita, Abraham, 162
Gomes Serra, Josua, 109, 290, 301
Gompertz (business firm), 145, 154, 254–5
Gompertz (merchant), 73; Joseph, 136; Solomon Barent, 174, 324–325, 330
Gompertz and Heyman (business firm), 136, 154, 171, 299
Gonzales, Jacob, 49
Gordon, Lord, 186
Gratz brothers (business firm), 329

Grote (business firm), 197, 237
gum, 210, 317; gum senegal, 211, 313

Hales, Sir Joseph, 100–1
Hamburg, Pragers' correspondents in, 312; precious stones and diamond trade, 89; rivals Amsterdam, 243–5
Hancock (Englishman in India), 172
Hanover, Jewish charity in, 186; Pragers' correspondent in, *see* Michael-David
Hanover (family name), *see also under* Michael-David
Hanover, Elias, 268
Hanway, Jonas, 35, 44–5
Hardenberg, Baron Hans von, 311
hardware and pottery, 64
Harrison, Edward, 297
Hart, A., 286; Eleazar, 142; Moses, 153
Hastings, Warren, 172, 315
Hayter and Strong (business firm), 200
Hecksher, Simon, 312
Hendricks, Aaron and Uriah (business firm), 283
Hendricks, Herman, 136
Henriques, Alessandro, 152; Isaac Sr, 301; Joseph, 62; Peter, 301
Henry, Solomon, 329
Herne, Sir Joseph, 96–7, 289
Herzfeld (Wolff), Jacob B., 269, 310, 329
Hess, Jost, 329
Heyman (business firm), 145
Heyman, Meyer, 295; Moses Berend, 165
hides, 210, 212, 215, 225, 244, 246, 258–9, 317, 322, 325
Hindman, Thomas, 126–7
Hinuber, Charles, 311
Hoare, Sir Richard, 152, 157, 289
Hope (business firm), 59, 122, 194–195, 206, 213, 250–1, 254, 282, 302, 323–4
Howe, Sir William, 192

India, coral exports to, 70–1, 88, 125, 127–8, 160, 169–71, 294, 331, 339; decline of its diamond trade, 123, 323; diamond market, 112–13, 130–2, 169, 171, 173–6, 178, 180, 297, 305, 323; diamond mines, 130, 154, 172, 174–5, 180, 287, 295, 323; diamonds imported from, 51, 123, 304–5, 337–8; 'free merchants', 163–4, 304; transfer of private fortunes from, 91, 128, 137, 147, 169–70, 172–5, 177–9, 255; *see also under* coral trade
indigo, 198, 201, 210, 214, 258, 301, 312
Inquisition, The, in Lima and Mexico, 26; in Portugal, 25–6, 30–4, 278
Ironside, Lieutenant General, 172
Isaac, Eleazer Levy, 216, 314; Henry, 148, 154
Isaacs (business firm), 145, 154
Isaacs, Ephraim, 156, 165
Israel and Lindo (brokers' firm), 259

Jacobs, Abraham, 168
Jamaica, contraband trade with Spanish colonies, 28, 45–9, 61–3; Jews, 47–8; Pragers' correspondent in, *see* Salomons, Abraham; taxation of Jews, 49; *see also under* precious metals
Jeffries, David, 110, 112, 132, 142, 293, 297
Jerogam brothers (business firm), 256, 323–4
Jew bill dispute (1753), 33, 35, 37, 44
Jewish disabilities, in England, 18–19, 71–2, 85–6, 206
Jewish economic history, study of, 11
Jewish merchants, financial stability and reputation of, 195, 197, 223, 260–3
Joffe, Jacob, 323
Jones, George, 143, 158, 166, 168, 340
Joseph, Solomon, 142

Kahn, Jonah, 323
Kampen (Salomons), David, 250; Eleazar, 262
Kerridge, Thomas, 105
Keyser, Alexander Isaac, 51, 53; Ruben, 323
Kiere, Nicholas, 224, 239–41, 319–20
Kingston, Synagogue, 258
Kooy, Tjalling P. van der, 244, 249
Kops, Isaac and William (business firm), 283

Lamego (business firm), 55
Lamego, Isaac, 51; Moses, 40, 51, 71
L'Apostre, Benyon, 297

Lara, Abraham, 197, 214, 258–9, 267, 325
Leff, de (Amsterdam broker), 225
Leghorn, 87, 109; coral industry and trade, 103–4, 106, 108–9, 124, 160, 291; migration of Jews to England, 125; share of its Jewish merchants in English diamond trade, 151–2, 302
Levi, Aaron, 136; Abraham Heyman, 136
Levin Salomons (business firm), *see* Prager (Levin Salomons)
Levy (business firm), 154
Levy (merchant), 73; (relation of Prager brothers), 73, 330; Asher-Isaac, 295; Benjamin (of London), 281; Benjamin (of Rhode Island), 283; Chaim, 283; David, 164, 295; Isaac, 283, 295; Judith, 295; Nathan, 283; Sampson, 65, 284
Lima, 43; Jews, 26
Lima, Gabriel de, *see* Pereira, Jacob Alvares
Lindo (business firm), 16, 144, 191, 204–5, 266
Lindo (family), 53
Lindo, David, 191; Elias, 259, 266, 328; Elias (broker), 51; Isaac, 40, 51; Mark Prager, 191; Mathilda (*née* Prager), 191
linen, 64
Lis, Francis de (Berakhel, Jacob), 86–7, 287
Lisbon, English merchants, 26, 29–31, 33, 41, 278; Marranos, 29–30
Liverpool, rise of, 64
Lock, Samuel, 290
Loewenstamm, Rabbi Saul, 267
London, centre of diamond trade, 12, 67, 69, 86, 102, 109–10, 113–14, 141, 243, 253, 284–5; diamond market, 137–41, 324; money market, 28–9; *see also under* diamond industry, diamond trade, precious metals
Londonderry, Lord, 151
Long, Edward, 47
Lopes, Andrew (*alias* Britto, Abraham Lopes de, *alias* Noguera, Andreas Alvares), 35–7, 278–9; Isaac, 283; Joseph, 283
Lousada, Barukh, *see* Barrow, Moses

Macartney, Lord, 176, 255, 296, 315
Machado, John, 87, 288; Moses, 51, 53
Machoro, Moses, 139

Macpherson, David, 28
Madeira, 36, 38
Madras (Fort St George), 99, 165; capture by French (1745), 165–6, 168, 295, 305; coral trade, 106–8, 117–18, 130; diamond trade, 69–70, 90, 96, 98, 111, 113, 120, 125, 129–32, 136, 174–5, 295–7; Jewish merchants, 69–70, 154–69; Jewish servants, 167–8
Magens, Nicolas, 29
mahogany, 258
Malabar Coast, 71
Manila, 166
Marcus, *see* Ferde (Marcus)
Mariette, Peter, 128, 299
Marques, Abraham Hesquiah, *see* Rodrigues, Diego; Francis, 70
Marseilles, coral industry and trade, 103–4, 291
Marshall, Thomas, 149
Martines, Philip, 301
Masson, Philip, 140
Masulipatam, 70, 150; diamond trade, 81–2, 99, 155, 289
Mattos, de (business firm), 144
Mawe, John, 120, 122–3
Mayne, John, 34, 278; William, 34, 278
Mayne and Burn (business firm), 34
Mears, Charles, 126–7
Mecca, coral trade through, 105
Medina (business firm), 50, 54–5, 335–6
Medina, de, Deborah, 279; Gabriel, 87; Isaac, 39, 151; Joseph, 39, 279, 281; Moses, 39, 43, 109, 279–82; Sir Solomon, 39, 109, 279, 281, 301; Solomon Hisquia, 279
Mendele (personal name?) [broker of Amsterdam], 225, 317
Mendelssohn, Moses, 329
Mendes (business firm), 50, 267
Mendes, Joseph and Menasseh (business firm), 63, 332
Mendes, Abraham Lopes, 109; Alvaro, 109; Anthony, 39; Diego, 41; Lewis, 40; Moses, 41
Mendes da Costa (business firm), 16, 50, 55, 144, 160, 204, 254, 266
Mendes da Costa, Benjamin, 25, 30, 32, 40, 48–9, 51, 61, 71, 77, 114, 160, 278, 303; Fernando, 107; Hananel, 160–2, 170, 197, 259, 266, 325; Isaac, 170; Jacob Jr, 114; Jacob Sr, 39, 45, 109, 114, 259; John (of Amsterdam), 39;

Mendes da Costa (*cont.*)
John Jr (of London), 39, 41, 109, 278, 290; Joseph Jr, 39; Lewis, 39; Moses, 45–6, 51, 71, 144, 279, 331; Philip, 278; Rebecca (*née* Salvador), 45
Mendoca, Duarte (Isaac) Rebello de (*alias* Anthony, Edward), 33–4, 278
Merttins, Henry, 290
Mesquita (Gomes de), *see* Gomes de Mesquita
Methuen Treaty, 26
Mexico, Jews, 26
Meyer (Yoresh), Aaron, 185, 256–8, 309, 325
Michael-David (business firm), 204, 256, 310–11
Michael-David (Hanover), David, 311; Meyer, 19, 59, 185, 208–9, 257, 261–2, 311–12
Michie, John, 315
Minas Geraes, 110
Miranda, Isaac, 283
Mocatta (family and business firm), 51, 53, 144
Mocatta and Goldsmid (business firm), 53, 133, 139
Mocatta and Keyser (business firm), 53, 281
Mocatta, Abraham, 50–3; Abraham Lumbroso de Mattos, 53; Moses, 87
Modigliani, Nathan and Hananias (business firm), 77, 145, 148, 171, 174
Monforte, Moses Marcus, 26, 276
Montefiore (business firm), 145
Montefiore, Moses, 124, 171
Morais, Lewis de, 87
Morales, Bentura and Lopes de (business firm), 151
Morse, Nicholas, 136, 165
Moses (family and business firm), 145, 156–9
Moses (merchant), 73; Eleazar, 159; Haim, 163, 291; Henry, 136, 143, 166, 340; J., 286; (ben Moshe), Jacob, 73, 76–7, 260, 286; Joseph, 159; Joy (Freudchen) [daughter of Glueckel of Hameln], 158; Levy Jr, 159, 164; Levy Sr, 143, 158–9, 163, 165–8, 297, 340; M., 301; Marcus, 112, 130–1, 150–2, 156–8, 167, 291, 302; Moses, 158, 163; N., 286; Samuel, 136, 159, 166, 295, 297
Moses, Son and Co., 39

Motte, Thomas, 172
Muilman (business firm), 59, 148, 195, 238–9, 250–1, 301
Mun, Thomas, 104
musk, 109
Mussaphia, Joseph, 301

Naples, coral fishing, 103
Nathan, Abraham, 131, 149–50, 152, 156, 300–1
Neufville, Jan de, 321
Nevis, decline of Jews, 64
Newcastle, Lord, 31–2
New East India Company, *see* East India Company (New)
Nightingale, Robert, 155
Nijmegen, Eli, 324
Noguera, Andreas Alvares, *see* Lopes, Andrew
Norden (Salomons), *see also under* Salomons (Norden)
Norden (Salomons) [business firm], 254–6, 285
Norden (Salomons), Aaron and Solomon (business firm), 154, 162, 171, 174, 324
Norsa, Moses and Joseph (business firm, 174
North, Lord, 206, 310
North America, Jews in, 64; trade with, 65–6, 283–4
Nunes (business firm), 50
Nunes, Alvaro, 301; David, 301; Jacob Fernandes, 109, 114, 118, 290; Moses, 301

Ongarety, George, 97
Oporto, 38
Ostend, role during Fourth Anglo-Dutch War, 245–6, 322; *see also* Prager (Levin Salomons) [business firm], Ostend house
Oswald, G. and Co. (business firm), 314
outports, 192, 209, 213–15, 244, 314, 318; *see also under* shipping services
Oxenden, Sir George, 84, 86, 106–7

Pacheco, Aaron, 109, 290, 301
Paiba, de, Abraham, 139, 299; Moses, 37
Paiva, James de, 69–70, 154–5
Palk, Robert, 136, 172
Panna, 130
paper, 212
Papillon, Thomas, 289
Pares, Richard, 64, 282

Paris, Pragers' correspondent in, *see* Tourton and Baur

Patna, 174

pawning, as means of financing business, 196, 308

Paz, de, Elias, 278; Lewis, 148

pearls, sale of, 133–4, 298

Pelling and de Fries (business firm), 175

Pereira and Lima (business firm), 31, 39–41, 55

Pereira (Lopes), *see* Aguilar

Pereira, Francisco, 284; Isaac, 62; Jacob Alvares (*alias* Lima, Gabriel), 39–40; Joseph, 58, 109, 281

Persia, 166

Philadelphia, 65; *see also* Prager (Levin Salomons) [business firm], Philadelphia house

Philo-patriae (author of pamphlets in Jew-bill dispute), 16, 37, 45–6, 56–8, 61–2, 65, 142; *see also* Salvador, Joseph

piezas de Indias ('pieces of Indies'), 279

Pilkington, Raphael and Daniel (business firm), 43

pimento, 258

Pinheiro, Gabriel Lopes (*alias* Forte, Pedro, *alias* Vianna, Joseph or Daniel), 30–2, 37, 40, 278

Pinto, Redrigo Alvares, 284

Pitt, John, 148, 301; Robert, 150; Thomas, 70, 98–100, 148–51, 155, 157, 167, 295–6

Pitt diamond, 150, 155, 157

Ploos, Johannes, 224

Plymer (merchant of Madras), 99

Pombal, Sebastião José de Carvalho e Melo, Marquis de, 37, 121–2, 293

Pondicherry, 152, 157–8

porcelain, 212, 225, 259

Porsile, Antonio Maria, 278

Portello, Isaac da Souza, 109, 278

Porto, de, Domingo, 70, 155; Isaac, 70, 302

Porto Bello, 47

Porto Rico, 43

Portsmouth, 37

Portugal, diamond trade, 41, 87; disadvantages of Jews in trade, 29–30; export of diamonds, to, 68; official institutions represented by Jews, 35–7; trade with, 25, 27, 29–34, 54, 278–9; use of false names, 30–2, 34; *see also under*

Brazilian diamonds, diamond industry, gold, Inquisition, precious metals

Portuguese Jews, commerce of, 16

Portuguese Royal Guinea Company, 36

Posthumus, Nicolaas, 235

potash, 258

Prager (Levin Salomons) [business firm], 16, 154; account of investments, 313; business ethics, 199–201, 317; commission business, 197–9; conduct of business affairs, 191–2; contracting of government loans, 205–8, 310; diamond trade, 176–80, 186, 189–90, 198, 229, 243, 254–6, 306, 318, 320–1, 323–4; exchange business, 193–6, 202–4, 263, 310–11; financial basis, 187, 193ff., 308; financial business, 202–8; foreign correspondents, 209, 312; history and papers of, 12–13, 183–91, 248–9, 306–8; inability to trade in precious metals, 204; 'interest' in East India Company, 177, 217, 260, 314–16; Jewish connections, 256–60; Ostend house, 185, 188, 223, 228, 269, 271, 307, 309; partnerships, 196–7; Philadelphia house, 185, 188–9, 191, 203, 230, 269, 271, 307, 309, 320, 329–30; profits, 228–9, 242–3, 308, 310, 319–20; remittance of money, 208; smuggling, 222–3, 316; specialization, 212–13; speculations, 226–8, 317, *and see also under* drugs, tobacco; stock transactions, 204–5; *see also under* Berlin, Copenhagen, Glasgow, Hamburg, Hanover, Jamaica, Paris, Sephardim

Prager, Bela, 184, 273; David, 19, 73, 76, 122, 168, 183–4, 186–7, 193–4, 201, 203, 205, 223, 225, 231–4, 236, 238–41, 247–8, 260, 262–3, 267–8, 271–2, 308, 315, 319, 324, 330; Esther, 138, 176, 184, 186, 189–92, 204, 241, 248–249, 262, 271–2, 300, 308, 315, 320, 324; Henry, 191; Isaac, 74, 183, 189, 197, 204, 261, 306, 320; Isaiah (George), 189, 191, 221, 249; Jacob, 73–4, 76–7, 136, 140, 177, 183–4, 194–2, 199–200, 202–207, 213, 215, 220–6, 228, 230–232, 236, 242–7, 250, 255, 260–274, 308–9, 314, 317, 320, 324;

Prager (*cont.*)
  Jessy, *see* Goldsmid, Jessy; Joseph,
    191; Leib (Lyon), 103, 142, 147,
    164, 176–80, 185–6, 189–92, 198,
    205, 211, 214, 217–18, 221, 229,
    235–7, 239, 241, 255–6, 258, 269–
    270, 272, 295, 300, 305–6, 309,
    314–16, 318, 330; Leib Jr (Lionel),
    191, 330; Meyer, 184–5, 188–90,
    205, 221, 237–9, 241, 248, 269–
    270, 307; Meyer ('Meyerke'), 188,
    307; Mordecai (Mark), 176, 189–
    191, 237, 241, 270–1, 308, 316,
    330; Simeon, 191, 330; Teibe,
    330; Wolf, 189, 248, 268; Yehiel,
    59, 73, 76, 121–2, 149, 164,
    172, 174–5, 177–9, 183–7, 189–
    196, 198–201, 203–15, 217–23,
    225, 228–32, 234–7, 242–6, 250,
    254–6, 264–9, 271–4, 306, 309–
    310, 312, 315, 318, 320–1, 323–5,
    329–30; Yehiel Jr ('Yehielke',
    Michael), 188, 191, 307, 317;
    Yehuda Leib Sr, 186
Prager brothers, family obligations,
    270–4, 329–30; respect for Jewish
    public opinion, 267–70; views on
    international affairs, 192–3, 248,
    322; views on religion and
    education, 267–70, 329
Pratviel, David, 52, 281
precious metals, 37, 45, 61, 64, 204;
    Amsterdam market, 53; English
    exports, 53; exports for purchase
    of diamonds, 126–7, 154; imports
    from South America, 47; imports
    through Jamaica, 48–9, 57;
    imports through Lisbon and
    Cadiz, 57; Jewish brokers in
    London, 51–3; London market,
    50; trade between London and
    Amsterdam, 38–9, 57, 249–52;
    see also under gold, Prager (Levin
    Salomons) [business firm], silver
prize goods, 214
profits in international trade, 321;
    see also under coral trade, silver,
    Prager (Levin Salomons) [business
    firm]

Rabello, A. da Fonseca, 37
Recanati, Salvadore L., 152
Reesen (business firm), 197
respondentia loans, 71; *see also
    under* diamond trade
rhubarb, 211
rice, 34, 210, 212, 312
Rio de Janeiro, 110–11

Roach, John, 111–12, 156–7
Roberts and Bristow (business firm),
    278
Robles, Joseph, 301
Rodrigues (business firm), 50
Rodrigues, Alfonso (Sequeira, Isaac
    Israel de), 88, 107; Bartolomeo,
    70, 155, 302; Diego (Marques,
    Abraham Hesquiah), 87, 288;
    Gomes (Sequeira, Abraham Israel
    de), 87–8; Isaac, 36
Rosh, Joseph, 323
Rotterdam, 214–15; rivals Amster-
    dam, 244

St Eustatius, 328
Salomons (families and business
    firms), 145, 154, 156–7
Salomons (Norden) [business firm],
    154
Salomons (Norden), Levy and Ruben
    (business firm), 58–9, 136, 154,
    285, 295
Salomons (merchant), 73; Abigail
    (*née* Franks), 156; Abraham, 156–
    159, 167; Abraham (of Jamaica),
    256–8, 325; Benedictus, 156;
    David, 156–7, 284; (Kampen),
    David, *see* Kampen (Salomons),
    David; (Kampen), Eleazar, *see*
    Kampen (Salomons), Eleazar;
    Henry, 156–7, 166; Joseph, 51, 53,
    58–9, 126, 128–9, 148, 154, 208,
    257, 295, 301, 310–11; L., 286;
    (Norden), Levy, 129; Michael,
    128–9, 136, 170, 174, 299, 311;
    Moses, 156–7, 297; Nathan, 295;
    Philip, 136; Solomon, 132, 152,
    156–7, 165–7, 297
salt, 258
Salvador (business firm), 50–1, 54–5,
    144, 159, 301, 335–6
Salvador, Andrade, 288; Francis
    Daniel, 37, 39–40, 43–4, 49, 51–2,
    71, 109, 114, 119, 278–9, 290,
    302; Isaac, 39, 109, 119, Jacob,
    151, 279, 302; Joseph (of Amster-
    dam), 39, 279; Joseph (of London),
    29, 35, 37, 44–6, 49, 62, 70, 72,
    142, 171, 174, 264, 279, 285, 295,
    304, *and see also* Philo-patriae;
    Rachel (*née* Mendes da Costa),
    279
Salvadore, Francis, 303; Rodrigues,
    130, 155, 302–3
Samson, Nathan, 283
Santeul (business firm), 278
Saunders, Thomas, 132

Says, Edward, 92
Scott, Robert, 218
securities, 98
Sephardim, business associates of
  Pragers, 258–9, 326, 328; decline
  of Sephardi firms, 259, 263–7; in
  diamond trade, 138, 254; *see also*
  under Ashkenazim
Sequeira, Abraham Israel de, *see*
  Rodrigues, Gomes; Isaac Israel de,
  see Rodrigues, Alfonso
Serra (business firm), 145
Serra (Gomes), *see* Gomes Serra
Serra, Phineas, 170–1, 174
Seville, 46
Sheftall, Mordecai and Levy
  (business firm), 283
shellac, 211, 218, 247
Shiff, Rabbi David Tevele, 323
shipping services, between England
  and Holland, 221–2; between
  outports and Continent, 214–15,
  244
Shohet, Moses, 329
silk, 63, 148, 212, 225, 317
Silva, da, Duarte, 287; Francisco,
  287; Jacob Rodrigues, 109; Joseph
  Jr, 41, 291; Raphael Vas, 49
silver, 38, 42, 55; export for
  purchase of diamonds, 68, 88, 94,
  101–2, 125–9, 144, 154, 294, and
  East India Company restrictions
  on, 97–100, 101–2, 108, 157;
  duties, 292, 295; imports through
  Jamaica, 47; *see also under* Bank
  of England, East India Company
  (English), precious metals
silver lace, 43
Simons, Lazarus, 167–8
slave trade, 36, 43
Sluyter, Jan F. (business firm), 206
Smith, Captain, 221
Smyrna, 17
Sonsino, Jacob di Natal Levi & Co.
  (business firm), 145, 297
Soto, Abraham de, 87
South African diamonds, 123
Southey, Robert, 120–2
South Sea Company, 44, 47
Spain, diamond exports to, 68;
  disadvantages of Jews in trade,
  29–30; trade with, 25, 27, 42–9,
  331
Spanish colonies, trade with, 26–8,
  36, 42–9, 53, 61–3, 331
Spanish Flota system, English
  cargoes, 42–3
specialization in Jewish business,

15–21; *see also under* Prager
  (Levin Salomons) [business firm]
Speightstown, 63
spices, 211
Spier (merchant), 286
Stapel, Peter, 197, 231, 250
stock market, 20–1; *see also under*
  Prager (Levin Salomons) [business
  firm]
Streeter, Edwin W., 103
Sturt, Arthur, 33
Suasso, Alvaro (Jacob Israel) Lopes,
  43, 114, 280; Anthony Lopes, 71;
  Francisco Lopes, *see* Avernas le
  Gras, Baron de
sugar, 61, 63, 210, 224, 258, 313,
  316
Supino (business firm), 145
Supino (merchant), 73; Judah, 109,
  118–19, 170, 174
Surat, 69, 86–7, 92, 166; coral trade,
  103, 105–6, 108; diamond trade,
  83, 96, 129, 295

Tanhum, Simon, *see* Daniels
  (Tanhum), Simon
Tavernier, Jean B., 81
taxation of Jews, 38, 61
tea, 212–13, 315
thread, 210, 225
Throgmorton, Job, 292
tincal, 211, 224
tobacco, 65, 188–9, 209–10, 223,
  225–6, 230, 239, 244, 258–9, 267,
  312–13, 317–19, 325; Pragers'
  speculation in, 196, 211–12, 228–
  234
Tobin, Sir James, 111–12
Tourton and Baur (*later* Tourton and
  Ravel) [business firm], 196, 209,
  260, 308–9
Townshend, Joseph, 278
Turry, William and John (business
  firm), 43, 280
Tutshke (business firm), 254
Tutshke, Leib, 323; Samuel, 323
Tyrawley, Lord (British Ambassador
  in Lisbon), 31–4, 115, 142, 279,
  293

Utrecht, Treaty of, 28, 44, 155

Vanderton (diamond contractor),
  122
Van Goor (Amsterdam broker), 225,
  317
Van Notten, Peter and Charles
  (business firm), 197, 231, 234

Vansittart, N., 133
varnish, 211
Vega, Samuel da, 288
Venice, diamond exports to, 87
Vera Cruz, 42, 46
Verelst, Harry, 149, 172, 255, 315
Verge Vora, 105–6
Vianna, Joseph and Daniel (business firm), 39–40, 114
Vianna, Daniel, *see* Pinheiro, Gabriel Lopes; Joseph, *see* Pinheiro, Gabriel Lopes; Miguel (*alias* Dias, Abraham, *alias* Fernandes, Fernando), 31–2, 39–41, 278
Vienna, diamonds consigned to, 31
Villa Real, Emmanuel da Costa, 30; Joseph da Costa, 30, 33, 277
Voute, Robert, 212–13

Waag, Moses, 273, 330
Wallmoden, General, 311
Washington, George, 192
wax, 34, 223
Weisel, Naphtali Herz, 268
Westerfield, Ray B., 201
West Indies, Jewish settlement controversy, 60; Jews in trade of, 47, 60–4; trade with, 60–4, 213, 258; *see also under* Barbados, Jamaica, Nevis, St Eustatius
Wigram, Robert, 218
Willink, Abraham, 312
Wils (Amsterdam broker), 225, 317
wine, 37–8
Wingfield, John 278
Wolff, Jacob B., *see* Herzfeld (Wolff), Jacob B.; Pieter de, 196–197, 199–200, 220, 232, 324
wood, 258
Woodman, John, 172
Woodward (business firm), 31
wool, 199–200, 209, 212, 225, 266
woollens, 34–5, 37–8, 61

Ximenes, David and Isaac (business firm), 43
Ximenes, Samuel, 39

Yeruham, *see* Jerogam brothers
Yiddish, importance of, 257
Yoffe, Hertz, 262
Yoresh, Aaron, *see* Meyer (Yoresh), Aaron

Zeeland, sale of drugs in, 239–40
Zuider Zee, navigation of, 244, 321